WORD
BIBLICAL
COMMENTARY

WORD
BIBLICAL
COMMENTARY

VOLUME 43

Philippians

GERALD F. HAWTHORNE

WORD BOOKS, PUBLISHER • WACO, TEXAS

Word Biblical Commentary:
PHILIPPIANS
Copyright © 1983 by Word, Incorporated

Library of Congress Cataloging in Publication Data
Main entry under title:

Word biblical commentary.

   Includes bibliographies.
   1. Bible—Commentaries—Collected works.
BS491.2.W67   220.7'7   81–71769
ISBN 0–8499–0242–8 (v. 43) AACR2

Printed in the United States of America

5 6 7 8 9 9 AGF 1 9 8 7 6 5 4 3 2

To
Jane, Stephen, Lynn, James

Contents

Editorial Preface

The launching of the *Word Biblical Commentary* brings to fulfillment an enterprise of several years' planning. The publishers and the members of the editorial board met in 1977 to explore the possibility of a new commentary on the books of the Bible that would incorporate several distinctive features. Prospective readers of these volumes are entitled to know what such features were intended to be; whether the aims of the commentary have been fully achieved time alone will tell.

First, we have tried to cast a wide net to include as contributors a number of scholars from around the world who not only share our aims, but are in the main engaged in the ministry of teaching in university, college and seminary. They represent a rich diversity of denominational allegiance. The broad stance of our contributors can rightly be called evangelical, and this term is to be understood in its positive, historic sense of a commitment to scripture as divine revelation, and to the truth and power of the Christian gospel.

Then, the commentaries in our series are all commissioned and written for the purpose of inclusion in the *Word Biblical Commentary.* Unlike several of our distinguished counterparts in the field of commentary writing, there are no translated works, originally written in a non-English language. Also, our commentators were asked to prepare their own rendering of the original biblical text and to use those languages as the basis of their own comments and exegesis. What may be claimed as distinctive with this series is that it is based on the biblical languages, yet it seeks to make the technical and scholarly approach to a theological understanding of scripture understandable by—and useful to—the fledgling student, the working minister as well as to colleagues in the guild of professional scholars and teachers.

Finally, a word must be said about the format of the series. The layout in clearly defined sections has been consciously devised to assist readers at different levels. Those wishing to learn about the textual witnesses on which the translation is offered are invited to consult the section headed "Notes." If the readers' concern is with the state of modern scholarship on any given portion of scripture, then they should turn to the sections on "Bibliography" and "Form/Structure/Setting." For a clear exposition of the passage's meaning and its relevance to the ongoing biblical revelation, the "Comment" and concluding "Explanation" are designed expressly to meet that need. There is therefore something for everyone who may pick up and use these volumes.

If these aims come anywhere near realization, the intention of the editors will have been met, and the labor of our team of contributors rewarded.

General Editors: *David A. Hubbard*
Glenn W. Barker †
Old Testament: *John D. W. Watts*
New Testament: *Ralph P. Martin*

Author's Preface

Four years with Philippians seems like a long time. And it is! Yet it is not time enough to grasp completely all of the richness locked away in this beautiful letter that Paul wrote to his friends at Philippi, nor to master adequately the mass of literature that scholars, ancient and modern, have produced in an attempt to express what Paul meant by what he wrote. The Christ-Hymn itself (2:5–11), so majestic, so profound, could easily have absorbed the entire time allotted. And the literature on this single poem, so vast, so learned, could boggle far greater minds than mine. Thus to write this commentary has been an exercise in extreme pain and extreme pleasure. Ancient letters, by their very nature—a conversation halved—are not at all easy to piece together and understand. This fact coupled with the great Apostle's depth of thinking and depth of feeling expressed often in ambiguous and difficult Greek make the interpreter's task most arduous. But when the clouds part and the brilliance of Paul's ideas about God's saving activity in Christ break through, when one at last begins to feel the intensity of Paul's devotion to Christ and the sheer force of his appeal propelling him to follow the Savior—when all this happens as a result of painful mental toil, it constitutes rewards of incalculable delight, and the pleasure outweighs the pain.

I am debtor to so many that like Paul I should mention no names (cf. 4:21–23) lest inadvertently I should fail to mention even a single person to whom I owe a great deal. But unlike Paul I will take the risk. First, I am grateful to Professor Ralph P. Martin for inviting me to take part in this venture, and for his own superb literary contributions to the overall understanding of Philippians.

Then, too, I am greatly in debt to all those others who have gone before me, those many scholars of the first rank who long ago and more recently still have wrestled hard with the text of Philippians to interpret correctly and to express clearly its meaning. And if in places this commentary has but followed the thinking of others I make no apologies, since old thoughts are new to the new and quickly passing generations. To republish a thought, then, is to give it new life; it is a kind of resurrection of the dead. As someone quipped, "Why should a good observation or rule be lost because it is imprisoned in some monstrous folio? It is good to repeat worthy thoughts in new books, because the old works in which they stand are not read." Whenever I have borrowed another's idea, I have done my best to indicate this and to give credit to whom credit is due. If by chance I have failed in this endeavor at any point, I apologize, and hereby own my indebtedness to everyone whose writings I have read.

I am grateful, too, to my many students who tolerated me as I tested on them new ideas about Philippians. They were always patient and cheerful, but very ready to let me know the weakness of my arguments. I am certain I have been saved from many errors by their collected wisdom. Two former students in particular I wish to identify by name, John R. "Jack" Levison and Mark A. Rilling, both of whom have graduated with honors from Cambridge University, England, upon leaving Wheaton College. These young men allowed me to use them as sounding boards. They continuously supported me in my efforts, constructively criticizing, suggesting bibliography—books and articles I had overlooked—prodding to greater clarity and precision by their probing questions.

I am also grateful to my College—Wheaton College, and to its administrative officers, especially Dr. Ward Kriegbaum, Vice President for Academic Affairs, and Dr. William Henning, Dean of Arts and Sciences for their continued interest in and their determination to free two summers for me so that I might turn from teaching to writing.

Finally, I owe a very great debt of gratitude for the generous financial assistance that has come to me through the G. W. Aldeen Research Fund.

Wheaton, Illinois   GERALD F. HAWTHORNE
November, 1982

Abbreviations

A. General Abbreviations

A	Codex Alexandrinus	n.	note
Akkad.	Akkadian	n.d.	no date
א	Codex Sinaiticus	Nestle	Nestle (ed.) *Novum Testamentum Graece*
Ap. Lit.	Apocalyptic Literature		
Apoc.	Apocrypha	no.	number
Aq.	Aquila's Greek Translation of the Old Testament	NS	New Series
		NT	New Testament
Arab.	Arabic	obs.	obsolete
Aram.	Aramaic	OL	Old Latin
B	Codex Vaticanus	OS	Old Syriac
C	Codex Ephraemi Syri	OT	Old Testament
c.	*circa*, about	p., pp.	page, pages
cf.	*confer*, compare	par.	paragraph
chap., chaps.	chapter, chapters	Pers.	Persian
cod., codd.	codex, codices	Pesh.	Peshitta
contra	in contrast to	Phoen.	Phoenician
D	Codex Bezae	pl.	plural
DSS	Dead Sea Scrolls (see **F.**)	Pseudep.	Pseudepigrapha
ed., edd.	edited, edition, editor; editions	Q	Quelle ("Sayings" source in the Gospels)
e.g.	*exempli gratia*, for example	qt.	quoted by
Egyp.	Egyptian	q.v.	*quod vide*, which see
et al.	*et alii*, and others	rev.	revised, reviser, revision
EV	English Versions of the Bible	Rom.	Roman
		RVm	Revised Version margin
f., ff.	following (verse or verses, pages, etc.)	Samar.	Samaritan recension
		Sem.	Semitic
fem.	feminine	sing.	singular
ft.	foot, feet	Sumer.	Sumerian
gen.	genitive	s.v.	*sub verbo*, under the word
Gr.	Greek	Syr.	Syriac
Heb.	Hebrew	Symm.	Symmachus
Hitt.	Hittite	Targ.	Targum
ibid.	*ibidem*, in the same place	Theod.	Theodotion
id.	*idem*, the same	TR	Textus Receptus
i.e.	*id est*, that is	tr, trs.	translation, translator, translated
impf.	imperfect		
infra.	below	UBS	The United Bible Societies' Greek Text
in loc.	*in loco*, in the place cited		
Lat.	Latin	Ugar.	Ugaritic
LL.	Late Latin	u.s.	*ut supra*, as above
LXX	Septuagint	viz.	*videlicet*, namely
M	Mishna	vol.	volume
masc.	masculine	v, vv	verse, verses
mg.	margin	vs.	versus
MS(S)	Manuscript(s)	Vul.	Vulgate
MT	Masoretic text	WH	Westcott and Hort, *The New Testament in Greek*

B. Abbreviations for Modern Translations and Paraphrases

AmT   Smith and Goodspeed, *The Complete Bible, An American Translation*

ASV   American Standard Version, American Revised Version (1901)

Beck   Beck, *The New Testament in the Language of Today*

BV   Berkeley Version (The Modern Language Bible)

GNB   *Good News Bible*

JB   The Jerusalem Bible

JPS   *Jewish Publication Society Version of the Old Testament*

KJV   King James Version

Knox   R. A. Knox, *The Holy Bible: A Translation from the Latin Vulgate in the Light of the Hebrew and Greek Original*

LB   The Living Bible

Mof   J. Moffatt, *A New Translation of the Bible*

NAB   The New American Bible

NASB   New American Standard Bible

NEB   The New English Bible

NIV   The New International Version

Ph   J. B. Phillips, *The New Testament in Modern English*

RSV   Revised Standard Version

RV   Revised Version—1881–1885

TEV   Today's English Version

Wey   R. F. Weymouth, *The New Testament in Modern Speech*

Wms   C. B. Williams, *The New Testament: A Translation in the Language of the People*

C. Abbreviations of Commonly Used Periodicals, Reference Works, and Serials

AAS   *Acta apostolicae sedis*

AASOR   Annual of the American Schools of Oriental Research

AB   Anchor Bible

AbrN   *Abr-Nahrain*

AcOr   *Acta orientalia*

ACW   Ancient Christian Writers

ADAJ   Annual of the Department of Antiquities of Jordan

AER   *American Ecclesiastical Review*

AfO   *Archiv für Orientforschung*

AGJU   Arbeiten zur Geschichte des antiken Judentums und des Urchristentums

AH   F. Rosenthal, *An Aramaic Handbook*

AHR   *American Historical Review*

AHW   W. von Soden, *Akkadisches Handwörterbuch*

AION   *Annali dell'istituto orientali di Napoli*

AJA   *American Journal of Archaeology*

AJAS   *American Journal of Arabic Studies*

AJBA   *Australian Journal of Biblical Archaeology*

AJSL   *American Journal of Semitic Languages and Literature*

AJT   *American Journal of Theology*

ALBO   Analecta lovaniensia biblica et orientalia

ALGHJ   Arbeiten zur Literatur und Geschichte des hellenistischen Judentums

ALUOS   Annual of Leeds University Oriental Society

AnBib   Analecta biblica

AnBoll   Analecta Bollandiana

ANEP   J. B. Pritchard (ed.), *Ancient Near East in Pictures*

ANESTP   J. B. Pritchard (ed.), *Ancient Near East Supplementary Texts and Pictures*

ANET   J. B. Pritchard (ed.), *Ancient Near Eastern Texts*

ANF   The Ante-Nicene Fathers

Ang   *Angelicum*

AnOr   Analecta orientalia

ANQ   *Andover Newton Quarterly*

Anton   *Antonianum*

AOAT   Alter Orient und Altes Testament

AOS   American Oriental Series

AP   J. Marouzeau (ed.), *L'année philologique*

APOT   R. H. Charles (ed.), *Apocrypha and Pseudepigrapha of the Old Testament*

ARG   *Archiv für Reformationsgeschichte*

ARM   Archives royales de Mari

ArOr   *Archiv orientální*

ARW	Archiv für Religionswissenschaft	BHK	R. Kittel, Biblia hebraica
ASNU	Acta seminarii neotestamentici upsaliensis	BHS	Biblia hebraica stuttgartensia
		BHT	Beiträge zur historischen Theologie (BHTh)
ASS	Acta sanctae sedis	Bib	Biblica
AsSeign	Assemblées du Seigneur	BibB	Biblische Beiträge
ASSR	Archives des sciences sociales des religions	BibLeb	Bibel und Leben
		BibOr	Biblica et orientalia
ASTI	Annual of the Swedish Theological Institute	BibS(F)	Biblische Studien (Freiburg, 1895–) (BSt)
ATAbh	Alttestamentliche Abhandlungen	BibS(N)	Biblische Studien (Neukirchen, 1951–) (BibSt)
ATANT	Abhandlungen zur Theologie des Alten und Neuen Tetaments (AThANT)	BIES	Bulletin of the Israel Exploration Society (= Yediot)
		BIFAO	Bulletin de l'institut français d'archéologie orientale
ATD	Das Alte Testament Deutsch		
ATR	Anglican Theological Review	BJRL	Bulletin of the John Rylands University Library of Manchester
AusBR	Australian Biblical Review		
AUSS	Andrews University Seminary Studies	BK	Bibel und Kirche
		BKAT	Biblischer Kommentar: Altes Testament
BA	Biblical Archaeologist	BL	Book List
BAC	Biblioteca de autores cristianos	BLE	Bulletin de littérature ecclésiastique
BAR	Biblical Archaeologist Reader	BLit	Bibel und Liturgie
BASOR	Bulletin of the American Schools of Oriental Research	BO	Bibliotheca orientalis
		BR	Biblical Research
BASP	Bulletin of the American Society of Papyrologists	BSac	Bibliotheca Sacra
		BSO(A)S	Bulletin of the School of Oriental (and African) Studies
BBB	Bonner biblische Beiträge		
BCSR	Bulletin of the Council on the Study of Religion	BT	The Bible Translator
		BTB	Biblical Theology Bulletin
BDB	F. Brown, S. R. Driver, and C. A. Briggs, Hebrew and English Lexicon of the Old Testament	BTS	Bible et terre sainte
		BU	Biblische Untersuchungen
		BVC	Bible et vie chrétienne
BDF	F. Blass, A. Debrunner, and R. W. Funk, A Greek Grammar of the NT	BWANT	Beiträge zur Wissenschaft vom Alten und Neuen Testament
BeO	Bibbia e oriente	BZ	Biblische Zeitschrift
BETL	Bibliotheca ephemeridum theologicarum lovaniensium	BZAW	Beihefte zur ZAW
		BZNW	Beihefte zur ZNW
BEvT	Beiträge zur evangelischen Theologie (BEvTh)	BZRGG	Beihefte zur ZRGG
BFCT	Beiträge zur Förderung christlicher Theologie (BFCTh)	CAD	The Assyrian Dictionary of the Oriental Institute of the University of Chicago
BGBE	Beiträge zur Geschichte der biblischen Exegese	CAH	Cambridge Ancient History
		CAT	Commentaire de l'Ancien Testament
BGD	W. Bauer, F. W. Gingrich, and F. Danker, Greek-English Lexicon of the NT	CB	Cultura bíblica
		CBQ	Catholic Biblical Quarterly
BHH	B. Reicke and L. Rost (eds.), Biblisch-Historisches Handwörterbuch	CBQMS	Catholic Biblical Quarterly—Monograph Series
		CCath	Corpus Catholicorum

CChr	Corpus Christianorum	*EncJud*	*Encyclopaedia judaica* (1971)
CH	*Church History*	*EnchBib*	*Enchiridion biblicum*
CHR	*Catholic Historical Review*	*ErJb*	*Eranos Jahrbuch*
CIG	*Corpus inscriptionum graecarum*	*EstBib*	*Estudios biblicos*
CII	*Corpus inscriptionum iudaicarum*	ETL	*Ephemerides theologicae lovanienses* (*EThL*)
CIL	*Corpus inscriptionum latinarum*		
CIS	*Corpus inscriptionum semiticarum*	ETR	*Etudes théologiques et religieuses* (*EThR*)
CJT	*Canadian Journal of Theology*		
CNT	Commentaire du Nouveau Testament	*EvK*	*Evangelische Kommentare*
		EvQ	*The Evangelical Quarterly*
ConB	Coniectanea biblica	*EvT*	*Evangelische Theologie* (*EvTh*)
ConNT	*Coniectanea neotestamentica*	*ExpTim*	*The Expository Times*
CQ	*Church Quarterly*		
CQR	*Church Quarterly Review*	FBBS	Facet Books, Biblical Series
CRAIBL	*Comptes rendus de l'Académie des inscriptions et belles-lettres*	FC	Fathers of the Church
		FRLANT	Forschungen zur Religion und Literatur des Alten und Neuen Testaments
CSCO	Corpus scriptorum christianorum orientalium		
		FTS	Frankfurter Theologischen Studien
CSEL	Corpus scriptorum ecclesiasticorum latinorum		
CTA	*A. Herdner, Corpus des tablettes en cunéiformes alphabétiques*	*GAG*	*W. von Soden, Grundriss der akkadischen Grammatik*
CTM	*Concordia Theological Monthly* (or *CTM*)	GCS	Griechische christliche Schriftsteller
CurTM	*Currents in Theology and Mission*	GKB	Gesenius-Kautzsch-Bergsträsser, *Hebräische Grammatik*
DACL	*Dictionnaire d'archéologie chrétienne et de liturgie*	GKC	*Gesenius' Hebrew Grammar*, ed. E. Kautzsch, tr. A. E. Cowley
DBSup	*Dictionnaire de la Bible, Supplément*	GNT	Grundrisse zum Neuen Testament
DISO	C.-F. Jean and J. Hoftijzer, *Dictionnaire des inscriptions sémitiques de l'ouest*	*GOTR*	*Greek Orthodox Theological Review*
DJD	Discoveries in the Judean Desert	*GRBS*	*Greek, Roman, and Byzantine Studies*
DOTT	D. W. Thomas (ed.), *Documents from Old Testament Times*	*Greg*	*Gregorianum*
		GuL	*Geist und Leben*
DS	Denzinger-Schönmetzer, *Enchiridion symbolorum*	*HALAT*	W. Baumgartner et al., *Hebräisches und aramäisches Lexikon zum Alten Testament*
DTC	*Dictionnaire de théologie catholique* (*DTHC*)		
DTT	*Dansk teologisk tidsskrift*	HAT	Handbuch zum Alten Testament
DunRev	Dunwoodie Review		
		HDR	Harvard Dissertations in Religion
EBib	Etudes bibliques (EtBib)		
EDB	L. F. Hartman (ed.), *Encyclopedic Dictionary of the Bible*	*HeyJ*	*Heythrop Journal*
		HibJ	*Hibbert Journal*
EHAT	Exegetisches Handbuch zum Alten Testament	HKAT	Handkommentar zum Alten Testament
EKKNT	Evangelisch-katholischer Kommentar zum Neuen Testament	HKNT	Handkommentar zum Neuen Testament
EKL	*Evangelisches Kirchenlexikon*	HNT	Handbuch zum Neuen Testament

HNTC	Harper's NT Commentaries	JPOS	Journal of the Palestine Oriental
HR	History of Religions		Society
HSM	Harvard Semitic Monographs	JPSV	Jewish Publication Society Version
HTKNT	Herders theologischer Kommentar zum Neuen Testament (HThKNT)	JQR	Jewish Quarterly Review
		JQRMS	Jewish Quarterly Review Monograph Series
HTR	Harvard Theological Review	JR	Journal of Religion
HTS	Harvard Theological Studies	JRAS	Journal of the Royal Asiatic Society
HUCA	Hebrew Union College Annual		
		JRE	Journal of Religious Ethics
IB	Interpreter's Bible	JRelS	Journal of Religious Studies
ICC	International Critical Commentary	JRH	Journal of Religious History
		JRS	Journal of Roman Studies
IDB	G. A. Buttrick (ed.), Interpreter's Dictionary of the Bible	JRT	Journal of Religious Thought
		JSJ	Journal for the Study of Judaism in the Persian, Hellenistic and Roman Period
IDBSup	Supplementary volume to IDB		
IEJ	Israel Exploration Journal	JSS	Journal of Semitic Studies
Int	Interpretation	JSSR	Journal for the Scientific Study of Religion
ITQ	Irish Theological Quarterly		
		JTC	Journal for Theology and the Church
JA	Journal asiatique	JTS	Journal of Theological Studies
JAAR	Journal of the American Academy of Religion	Judaica	Judaica: Beiträge zum Verständnis . . .
JAC	Jahrbuch für Antike und Christentum		
JANESCU	Journal of the Ancient Near Eastern Society of Columbia University	KAI	H. Donner and W. Röllig, Kanaanäische und aramäische Inschriften
JAOS	Journal of the American Oriental Society	KAT	E. Sellin (ed.), Kommentar zum A.T.
JAS	Journal of Asian Studies		
JB	A. Jones (ed.), Jerusalem Bible	KB	L. Koehler and W. Baumgartner, Lexicon in Veteris Testamenti libros
JBC	R. E. Brown et al. (eds.), The Jerome Biblical Commentary		
JBL	Journal of Biblical Literature	KD	Kerygma und Dogma
JBR	Journal of Bible and Religion	KJV	King James Version
JCS	Journal of Cuneiform Studies	KlT	Kleine Texte
JDS	Judean Desert Studies		
JEA	Journal of Egyptian Archaeology	LCC	Library of Christian Classics
JEH	Journal of Ecclesiastical History	LCL	Loeb Classical Library
JEOL	Jaarbericht . . . ex oriente lux	LD	Lectio divina
JES	Journal of Ecumenical Studies	Leš	Lešonénu
JETS	Journal of the Evangelical Theological Society	LLAVT	E. Vogt, Lexicon linguae aramaicae Veteris Testamenti
JHS	Journal of Hellenic Studies	LPGL	G. W. H. Lampe, Patristic Greek Lexicon
JIBS	Journal of Indian and Buddhist Studies		
JIPh	Journal of Indian Philosophy	LQ	Lutheran Quarterly
JJS	Journal of Jewish Studies	LR	Lutherische Rundschau
JMES	Journal of Middle Eastern Studies	LSJ	Liddell-Scott-Jones, Greek-English Lexicon
JMS	Journal of Mithraic Studies		
JNES	Journal of Near Eastern Studies	LTK	Lexikon für Theologie und Kirche (LThK)

LUÅ	Lunds universitets årsskrift	NPNF	Nicene and Post-Nicene Fathers
LW	*Lutheran World*		
		NRT	*La nouvelle revue théologique (NRTh)*
McCQ	*McCormick Quarterly*		
MDOG	Mitteilungen der deutschen Orient-Gesellschaft	*NTA*	*New Testament Abstracts*
		NTAbh	Neutestamentliche Abhandlungen
MeyerK	H. A. W. Meyer, Kritischexegetischer Kommentar über das Neue Testament	NTD	Das Neue Testament Deutsch
		NTF	Neutestamentliche Forschungen
MGWJ	*Monatsschrift für Geschichte und Wissenschaft des Judentums*	*NTS*	*New Testament Studies*
		NTTS	New Testament Tools and Studies
MM	J. H. Moulton and G. Milligan, *The Vocabulary of the Greek Testament*	*Numen*	*Numen: International Review for the History of Religions*
MNTC	Moffatt NT Commentary		
MPAIBL	*Mémoires présentés à l'Académie des inscriptions et belles-lettres*	OCD	*Oxford Classical Dictionary*
		OIP	Oriental Institute Publications
MScRel	*Mélanges de science religieuse*		
MTZ	*Münchener theologische Zeitschrift (MThZ)*	OLP	Orientalia lovaniensia periodica
		OLZ	*Orientalische Literaturzeitung*
MUSJ	*Mélanges de l'université Saint-Joseph*	*Or*	*Orientalia* (Rome)
		OrAnt	*Oriens antiquus*
MVAG	Mitteilungen der vorder-asiatisch-ägyptischen Gesellschaft	*OrChr*	*Oriens christianus*
		OrSyr	*L'orient syrien*
		OTM	Oxford Theological Monographs
NAB	*New American Bible*	OTS	Oudtestamentische Studiën
NCB	New Century Bible		
NCCHS	R. C. Fuller et al. (eds.), *New Catholic Commentary on Holy Scripture*	PAAJR	Proceedings of the American Academy of Jewish Research
NCE	M. R. P. McGuire et al. (eds.), *New Catholic Encyclopedia*	PCB	M. Black and H. H. Rowley (eds.), *Peake's Commentary on the Bible*
NClB	New Clarendon Bible		
NEB	*New English Bible*	*PEFQS*	*Palestine Exploration Fund, Quarterly Statement*
NedTTs	*Nederlands theologisch tijdschrift (NedThTs)*		
		PEQ	*Palestine Exploration Quarterly*
Neot	*Neotestamentica*	*PG*	J. Migne, *Patrologia graeca*
NFT	New Frontiers in Theology	*PGM*	K. Preisendanz (ed.), *Papyri graecae magicae*
NHS	Nag Hammadi Studies		
NICNT	New International Commentary on the New Testament	*PhEW*	*Philosophy East and West*
		PhRev	*Philosophical Review*
NIDNTT	C. Brown (ed.), *The New International Dictionary of New Testament Theology*	*PJ*	*Palästina-Jahrbuch*
		PL	J. Migne, *Patrologia latina*
		PO	Patrologia orientalis
NKZ	*Neue kirchliche Zeitschrift*	*PRU*	*Le Palais royal d'Ugarit*
NorTT	*Norsk Teologisk Tidsskrift (NTT)*	*PSTJ*	*Perkins (School of Theology) Journal*
NovT	*Novum Testamentum*		
NovTSup	Novum Testamentum, Supplements	PVTG	Pseudepigrapha Veteris Testamenti graece

PW	Pauly-Wissowa, *Real-Encyclo-pädie der klassischen Altertum-swissenschaft*	*RSV*	*Revised Standard Version*
		RTL	*Revue théologique de Louvain (RThL)*
PWSup	Supplement to PW	*RTP*	*Revue de théologie et de philoso-phie (RThPh)*
QDAP	*Quarterly of the Department of Antiquities in Palestine*	*RTR*	*The Reformed Theological Review*
		RUO	*Revue de l'université d'Ottawa*
		RV	*Revised Version*
RA	*Revue d'assyriologie et d'archéolo-gie orientale*		
RAC	*Reallexikon für Antike und Chris-tentum*	SANT	Studien zum Alten und Neuen Testament
RArch	*Revue archéologique*	SAQ	Sammlung ausgewählter kir-chen- und dogmengeschicht-licher Quellenschriften
RB	*Revue biblique*		
RBén	*Revue bénédictine*	SB	Sources bibliques
RCB	*Revista de cultura biblica*	*SBFLA*	*Studii biblici franciscani liber an-nuus*
RE	*Realencyklopädie für protestan-tische Theologie und Kirche*	*SBJ*	*La sainte bible de Jérusalem*
RechBib	Recherches bibliques	SBLASP	Society of Biblical Literature Abstracts and Seminar Papers
REg	*Revue d'égyptologie*		
REJ	*Revue des études juives*	SBLDS	SBL Dissertation Series
RelArts	Religion and the Arts	SBLMasS	SBL Masoretic Studies
RelS	*Religious Studies*	SBLMS	SBL Monograph Series
RelSoc	*Religion and Society*	SBLSBS	SBL Sources for Biblical Study
RelSRev	*Religious Studies Review*		
RES	*Répertoire d'épigraphie sé-mitique*	SBLSCS	SBL Septuagint and Cognate Studies
RevExp	*Review and Expositor*	SBLTT	SBL Texts and Translations
RevistB	*Revista biblica*	SBM	Stuttgarter biblische Mono-graphien
RevQ	*Revue de Qumran*		
RevScRel	*Revue des sciences religieuses*	SBS	Stuttgarter Bibelstudien
RevSém	*Revue sémitique*	SBT	Studies in Biblical Theology
RevThom	*Revue thomiste*	SC	Sources chrétiennes
RGG	*Religion in Geschichte und Gegen-wart*	*ScEs*	*Science et esprit*
		SCR	*Studies in Comparative Religion*
RHE	*Revue d'histoire ecclésiastique*	*Scr*	*Scripture*
RHPR	*Revue d'histoire et de philosophie religieuses (RHPhR)*	*ScrB*	*Scripture Bulletin*
		SD	Studies and Documents
RHR	Revue de l'histoire des reli-gions	*SE*	Studia Evangelica I, II, III (= TU 73[1959], 87 [1964], 88 [1964], etc.) *(StEv)*
RivB	*Rivista biblica*		
RNT	Regensburger Neues Testa-ment	*SEÅ*	*Svensk exegetisk årsbok*
		Sef	*Sefarad*
RQ	*Römische Quartalschrift für christliche Altertumskunde und Kirchengeschichte*	*Sem*	*Semitica*
		SHAW	Sitzungsberichte heidelber-gen Akademie der Wissen-schaften
RR	*Review of Religion*		
RSO	*Rivista degli studi orientali*	SHT	Studies in Historical Theol-ogy
RSPT	*Revue des sciences philoso-phiques et théologiques (RSPhTh)*		
		SHVL	Skrifter Utgivna Av Kungl. Humanistika Vetenskapssam-fundet i Lund.
RSR	*Recherches de science religieuse (RechSR)*		

SJLA	Studies in Judaism in Late Antiquity	*ThA*	*Theologische Arbeiten*
SJT	*Scottish Journal of Theology*	*ThBer*	*Theologische Berichte*
SMSR	*Studi e materiali di storia delle religioni*	THKNT	Theologischer Handkommentar zum Neuen Testament (ThHKNT)
SNT	Studien zum Neuen Testament (StNT)	*TLZ*	*Theologische Literaturzeitung (ThLZ)*
SNTSMS	Society for New Testament Studies Monograph Series	TNTC	Tyndale New Testament Commentary
SO	Symbolae osloenses		
SOTSMS	Society for Old Testament Study Monograph Series	*TP*	*Theologie und Philosophie (ThPh)*
SPap	*Studia papyrologica*	*TPQ*	*Theologisch-Praktische Quartalschrift*
SPAW	Sitzungsberichte der preussischen Akademie der Wissenschaften	*TQ*	*Theologische Quartalschrift (ThQ)*
		TRev	*Theologische Revue*
SPB	Studia postbiblica	*TRu*	*Theologische Rundschau (ThR)*
SR	*Studies in Religion/Sciences religieuses*	*TS*	*Theological Studies*
		TSK	*Theologische Studien und Kritiken (ThStK)*
SSS	Semitic Study Series		
ST	*Studia theologica (StTh)*	*TT*	*Teologisk Tidsskrift*
STÅ	*Svensk teologisk årsskrift*	*TTKi*	*Tidsskrift for Teologi og Kirke*
StBibT	*Studia Biblical et Theologica*	*TToday*	*Theology Today*
STDJ	Studies on the Texts of the Desert of Judah	TTS	Trierer Theologische Studien
		TTZ	*Trierer theologische Zeitschrift (TThZ)*
STK	*Svensk teologisk kvartalskrift*		
Str-B	[H. Strack and] P. Billerbeck, *Kommentar zum Neuen Testament*	TU	Texte und Untersuchungen
		Tyn B	*Tyndale Bulletin*
StudNeot	Studia neotestamentica, Studia	*TWAT*	G. J. Botterweck and H. Ringgren (eds.), *Theologisches Wörterbuch zum Alten Testament (ThWAT)*
StudOr	Studia orientalia		
SUNT	Studien zur Umwelt des Neuen Testaments		
SVTP	Studia in Veteris Testamenti pseudepigrapha	*TWNT*	G. Kittel and G. Friedrich (eds.), *Theologisches Wörterbuch zum Neuen Testament (ThWNT)*
SWJT	*Southwestern Journal of Theology*	*TZ*	*Theologische Zeitschrift (ThZ)*
SymBU	Symbolae biblicae upsalienses (SyBU)		
		UBSGNT	United Bible Societies *Greek New Testament*
TAPA	*Transactions of the American Philological Association*	*UF*	*Ugaritische Forschungen*
		UNT	Untersuchungen zum Neuen Testament
TBI	*Theologische Blätter (ThBl)*		
TBü	Theologische Bücherei (ThBü)	*US*	*Una Sancta*
		USQR	*Union Seminary Quarterly Review*
TBT	*The Bible Today*	*UT*	C. H. Gordon, *Ugaritic Textbook*
TD	*Theology Digest*		
TDNT	G. Kittel and G. Friedrich (eds.), *Theological Dictionary of the New Testament*	UUÅ	Uppsala universitetsårsskrift
		VC	*Vigiliae christianae*
TextsS	Texts and Studies	*VCaro*	*Verbum caro*
TF	*Theologische Forschung (ThF)*	*VD*	*Verbum domini*
TGI	*Theologie und Glaube (ThGI)*	*VF*	*Verkündigung und Forschung*

VKGNT	K. Aland (ed.), *Vollständige Konkordanz zum griechischen Neuen Testament*	
VS	Verbum salutis	
VSpir	*Vie spirituelle*	
VT	*Vetus Testamentum*	
VTSup	Vetus Testamentum, Supplements	
WA	M. Luther, Kritische Gesamtausgabe (= "Weimar" edition)	
WC	Westminster Commentary	
WDB	*Westminister Dictionary of the Bible*	
WHAB	*Westminster Historical Atlas of the Bible*	
WMANT	Wissenschaftliche Monographien zum Alten und Neuen Testament	
WO	*Die Welt des Orients*	
WTJ	*Westminster Theological Journal*	
WUNT	Wissenschaftliche Untersuchungen zum Neuen Testament	
WZKM	*Wiener Zeitschrift für die Kunde des Morgenlandes*	
WZKSO	*Wiener Zeitschrift für die Kunde Süd- und Ostasiens*	

ZA	*Zeitschrift für Assyriologie*
ZAW	*Zeitschrift für die alttestamentliche Wissenschaft*
ZDMG	*Zeitschrift der deutschen morgenländischen Gesellschaft*
ZDPV	*Zeitschrift des deutschen Palästina-Vereins*
ZEE	*Zeitschrift für evangelische Ethik*
ZHT	*Zeitschrift für historische Theologie (ZHTh)*
ZKG	*Zeitschrift für Kirchengeschichte*
ZKNT	*Zahn's Kommentar zum NT*
ZKT	*Zeitschrift für katholische Theologie (ZKTh)*
ZMR	*Zeitschrift für Missions-kunde und Religions-wissenschaft*
ZNW	*Zeitschrift für die neutestamentliche Wissenschaft*
ZRGG	*Zeitschrift für Religions- und Geistesgeschichte*
ZST	*Zeitschrift für systematische Theologie (ZSTh)*
ZTK	*Zeitshcrift für Theologie und Kirche (ZThK)*
ZWT	*Zeitschrift für wissenschaftliche Theologie (ZWTh)*

D. Abbreviations for Books of the Bible, the Apocrypha, and the Pseudepigrapha

OLD TESTAMENT

Gen	2 Chr	Dan
Exod	Ezra	Hos
Lev	Neh	Joel
Num	Esth	Amos
Deut	Job	Obad
Josh	Ps(Pss)	Jonah
Judg	Prov	Mic
Ruth	Eccl	Nah
1 Sam	Cant	Hab
2 Sam	Isa	Zeph
1 Kings	Jer	Hag
2 Kings	Lam	Zech
1 Chron	Ezek	Mal

NEW TESTAMENT

Matt	1 Tim
Mark	2 Tim
Luke	Titus
John	Philem
Acts	Heb
Rom	James
1 Cor	1 Peter
2 Cor	2 Peter
Gal	1 John
Eph	2 John
Phil	3 John
Col	Jude
1 Thess	Rev
2 Thess	

APOCRYPHA

1 Esd	1 Esdras	Add Esth	Additions to Esther
2 Esd	2 Esdras	Wisd Sol	Wisdom of Solomon
Tob	Tobit	Ecclus	Ecclesiasticus (Wisdom of Jesus the Son of Sirach)
Jud	Judith		

Bar	Baruch	Bel	Bel and the Dragon
Ep Jer	Epistle of Jeremy	Pr Man	Prayer of Manasseh
S Th Ch	Song of the Three Children (or Young Men)	1 Macc	1 Maccabees
Sus	Susanna	2 Macc	2 Maccabees

E. Abbreviations of the Names of Pseudepigraphical and Early Patristic Books

Adam and Eve	Books of Adam and Eve	*Prot. Jas.*	Protevangelium of James
2–3 Apoc. Bar.	Syriac, Greek Apocalypse of Baruch	*Barn.*	Barnabas
Apoc. Abr.	Apocalypse of Abraham	*1–2 Clem.*	1–2 Clement
Apoc. Mos.	Apocalypse of Moses	*Did.*	Didache
As. Mos.	Assumption of Moses	*Diogn.*	Diognetus
Bib. Ant.	Ps.-Philo, Biblical Antiquities	*Herm. Man.*	Hermas, Mandate
		Sim.	Similitude
1-2-3 Enoch	Ethiopic, Slavonic, Hebrew Enoch	*Vis.*	Vision
		Ign. Eph.	Ignatius, Letter to the Ephesians
Ep. Arist.	Epistle of Aristeas	*Magn.*	Ignatius, Letter to the Magnesians
Jub.	Jubilees		
Mart. Isa.	Martyrdom of Isaiah	*Phld.*	Ignatius, Letter to the Philadelphians
Odes Sol.	Odes of Solomon		
Pss. Sol.	Psalms of Solomon	*Pol.*	Ignatius, Letter to Polycarp
Sib. Or.	Sibylline Oracles		
T. 12 Patr.	Testaments of the Twelve Patriarchs	*Rom.*	Ignatius, Letter to the Romans
T. Levi	Testament of Levi	*Smyrn.*	Ignatius, Letter to the Smyrnaeans
T. Benj.	Testament of Benjamin, etc.	*Trall.*	Ignatius, Letter to the Trallians
Acts Pil.	Acts of Pilate		
Apoc. Pet.	Apocalypse of Peter	*Mart Pol.*	Martyrdom of Polycarp
Gos. Eb.	Gospel of the Ebionites	Pol. Phil.	Polycarp to the Philippians
Gos. Eg.	Gospel of the Egyptians	*Adv. Haer.*	Irenaeus, Against All Heresies
Gos. Heb.	Gospel of the Hebrews		
Gos. Naass.	Gospel of the Naassenes	*De praesc.*	Tertullian, On the Proscribing of Heretics
Gos. Pet.	Gospel of Peter	*haer.*	
Gos. Thom.	Gospel of Thomas		

F. Abbreviations of Names of Dead Sea Scrolls and Related Texts

CD	Cairo (Genizah text of the) Damascus (Document)	1QapGen	*Genesis Apocryphon* of Qumran Cave 1
Hev	Naḥal Ḥever texts	1QH	*Hôdāyôt (Thanksgiving Hymns)* from Qumran Cave 1
Mas	Masada texts		
Mird	Khirbet Mird texts	1QIsa^a,b	First or second copy of Isaiah from Qumran Cave 1
Mur	Wadi Murabba ʿat texts		
p	Pesher (commentary)		
Q	Qumran	1QpHab	*Pesher on Habakkuk* from Qumran Cave 1
1Q, 2Q, 3Q, etc.	Numbered caves of Qumran, yielding written material; followed by abbreviation of biblical or apocryphal book	1QM	*Milḥāmāh (War Scroll)*
		1QS	*Serek hayyaḥad (Rule of the Community, Manual of Discipline)*
QL	Qumran literature		

1QSa	Appendix A (*Rule of the Con-gregation*) to 1QS	4QPrNab	Prayer of Nabonidus from Qumran Cave 4
1QSb	Appendix B (*Blessings*) to 1QS	4QTestim	*Testimonia* text from Qumran Cave 4
3Q*15*	Copper Scroll from Qumran Cave 3	4QTLevi	*Testament of Levi* from Qumran Cave 4
4QFlor	*Florilegium* (or *Eschatological Midrashim*) from Qumran Cave 4	4QPhyl	Phylacteries from Qumran Cave 4
4QMess ar	Aramaic "Messianic" text from Qumran Cave 4	11QMelch	*Melchizedek* text from Qumran Cave 11
		11QtgJob	*Targum of Job* from Qumran Cave 11

G. Abbreviations of Targumic Material.

Tg. Onq.	*Targum Onqelos*	*Tg. Neof.*	*Targum Neofiti I*
Tg. Neb.	*Targum of the Prophets*	*Tg. Ps.-J.*	*Targum Pseudo-Jonathan*
Tg. Ket.	*Targum of the Writings*	*Tg. Yer. 1*	*Targum Yerušalmi I**
Frg. Tg.	*Fragmentary Targum*	*Tg. Yer. 11*	*Targum Yerušalmi II**
Sam. Tg.	*Samaritan Targum*	*Yem. Tg.*	*Yemenite Targum*
Tg. Isa	*Targum of Isaiah*	*Tg. Esth I,*	
Pal. Tgs.	*Palestinian Targums*	*II*	*First or Second Targum of Esther*
		*optional title	

H. Abbreviations of Other Rabbinic Works

ʾ*Abot*	ʾ*Abot de Rabbi Nathan*	*Pesiq. R.*	*Pesiqta Rabbati*
ʾ*Ag. Ber.*	ʾ*Aggadat Berešit*	*Pesiq. Rab Kah.*	*Pesiqta de Rab Kahana*
Bab.	*Babylonian*	*Pirqe R. El.*	*Pirqe Rabbi Eliezer*
Bar.	*Baraita*	*Rab.*	*Rabbah* (following ab-breviation for biblical book: *Gen. Rab.* [with periods] = *Genesis Rabbah*)
Der. Er. Rab.	*Derek Ereṣ Rabba*		
Der. Er. Zuṭ.	*Derek Ereṣ Zuṭa*		
Gem.	*Gemara*		
Kalla	*Kalla*		
Mek.	*Mekilta*	*Sem.*	*Semaḥot*
Midr.	*Midraš*; cited with usual ab-breviation for biblical book; but *Midr. Qoh.* = *Midraš Qohelet*	*Sipra*	*Sipra*
		Sipre	*Sipre*
		Sop.	*Soperim*
		S.ᶜOlam Rab.	*Seder ᶜOlam Rabbah*
Pal.	*Palestinian*	*Talm.*	*Talmud*
		Yal.	*Yalquṭ*

I. Abbreviations of Orders and Tractates in Mishnaic and Related Literature.

ʾ*Abot*	ʾ*Abot*	ᶜ*Ed.*	ᶜ*Eduyyot*
ᶜ*Arak.*	ᶜ*Arakin*	ᶜ*Erub.*	ᶜ*Erubin*
ᶜ*Abod. Zar.*	ᶜ*Aboda Zara*	*Giṭ.*	*Giṭṭin*
B. Bat.	*Baba Batra*	*Ḥag.*	*Ḥagiga*
Bek.	*Bekorot*	*Ḥal.*	*Ḥalla*
Ber.	*Berakot*	*Hor.*	*Horayot*
Beṣa	*Beṣa* (= *Yom Tob*)	*Ḥul.*	*Ḥullin*
Bik.	*Bikkurim*	*Kelim*	*Kelim*
B. Meṣ.	*Baba Meṣiᶜa*	*Ker.*	*Keritot*
B. Qam.	*Baba Qamma*	*Ketub.*	*Ketubot*
Dem.	*Demai*	*Kil.*	*Kilʾayim*

Maʿaś.	Maʿaśerot	Qidd.	Qiddušin
Mak.	Makkot	Qod.	Qodašin
Makš.	Makširin (= Mašqin)	Roš. Haš.	Roš Haššana
Meg.	Megilla	Sanh.	Sanhedrin
Meʿil.	Meʿila	Šabb.	Šabbat
Menaḥ.	Menaḥot	Šeb.	Šebtit
Mid.	Middot	Šebu.	Šebuʿot
Miqw.	Miqwaʾot	Šeqal.	Šeqalim
Moʿed	Moʿed	Soṭa	Soṭa
Moʿed Qaṭ.	Moʿed Qaṭan	Sukk.	Sukka
Maʿas. Š.	Maʿaśer Šeni	Taʿan.	Taʿanit
Našim	Našim	Tamid	Tamid
Nazir	Nazir	Tem.	Temura
Ned.	Nedarim	Ter.	Terumot
Neg.	Negaʿim	Ṭohar.	Ṭoharot
Nez.	Neziqin	T. Yom	Tebul Yom
Nid.	Niddah	ʿUq.	ʿUqṣin
Ohol.	Oholot	Yad.	Yadayim
ʿOr.	ʿOrla	Yebam.	Yebamot
Para	Para	Yoma	Yoma (= Kippurim)
Peʾa	Peʾa	Zabim	Zabim
Pesaḥ.	Pesaḥim	Zebaḥ	Zebaḥim
Qinnim	Qinnim	Zer.	Zeraʿim

J. Abbreviations of Nag Hammadi Tractates

Acts Pet. 12		Marsanes	Marsanes
Apost.	Acts of Peter and the Twelve Apostles	Melch.	Melchizedek
		Norea	Thought of Norea
Allogenes	Allogenes	On Bap. A	On Baptism A
Ap. Jas.	Apocryphon of James	On Bap. B	On Baptism B
Ap. John	Apocryphon of John	On Bap. C	On Baptism C
Apoc. Adam	Apocalypse of Adam	On Euch. A	On the Eucharist A
1 Apoc. Jas.	First Apocalypse of James	On Euch. B	On the Eucharist B
2 Apoc. Jas.	Second Apocalypse of James	Orig. World	On the Origin of the World
Apoc. Paul	Apocalypse of Paul	Paraph. Shem	Paraphrase of Shem
Apoc. Pet.	Apocalypse of Peter	Pr. Paul	Prayer of the Apostle Paul
Asclepius	Asclepius 21–29	Pr. Thanks.	Prayer of Thanksgiving
Auth. Teach.	Authoritative Teaching	Sent. Sextus	Sentences of Sextus
Dial. Sav.	Dialogue of the Savior	Soph. Jes. Chr.	Sophia of Jesus Christ
Disc. 8–9	Discourse on the Eighth and Ninth	Steles Seth	Three Steles of Seth
		Teach. Silv.	Teachings of Silvanus
Ep. Pet. Phil.	Letter of Peter to Philip	Testim. Truth	Testimony of Truth
Eugnostos	Eugnostos the Blessed	Thom. Cont.	Book of Thomas the Contender
Exeg. Soul	Exegesis on the Soul		
Gos. Eg.	Gospel of the Egyptians	Thund.	Thunder, Perfect Mind
Gos. Phil.	Gospel of Philip	Treat. Res.	Treatise on Resurrection
Gos. Thom.	Gospel of Thomas		
Gos. Truth	Gospel of Truth	Treat. Seth	Second Treatise of the Great Seth
Great Pow.	Concept of our Great Power		
Hyp. Arch.	Hypostasis of the Archons	Tri. Trac.	Triparite Tractate
Hypsiph.	Hypsiphrone	Trim. Prot.	Trimorphic Protennoia
Interp. Know.	Interpretation of Knowledge	Val. Exp.	A Valentinian Exposition
		Zost.	Zostrianos

Commentary Bibliography

The following list of commentaries are those that have been referred to most frequently in this volume.

Alford, H. *The Greek Testament.* 4 vols. London: Longmans, Green and Co., 1894. **Barclay, W.** *The Letters to the Philippians, Colossians, and Thessalonians.* Philadelphia: Westminster Press, 1957. **Barth, K.** *The Epistle to the Philippians.* Tr. J. W. Leitch. Richmond, VA: John Knox Press, 1962. **Beare, F. W.** *A Commentary on the Epistle to the Philippians.* HNTC. New York: Harper and Bros., 1959. **Beasley-Murray, G. R.** "Philippians." *Peake's Commentary On the Bible,* ed. M. Black and H. H. Rowley. New York: Thomas Nelson, 1962. **Benoit, P.** *Les épîtres de saint Paul aux Philippiens, a Philémon, aux Colossiens, aux Ephésiens.* Paris: Éditions du Cerf, 1959. **Biggs, C. R. D.** *The Epistle of Paul the Apostle to the Philippians.* London: Methuen and Co., 1900. **Bonnard, P.** *L'épître de saint Paul aux Philippiens et l'épître aux Colossiens.* CNT 10. Neuchâtel: Delachaux et Niestlé, 1950. **Boor, W. de.** *Die Briefe des Paulus an die Philipper und an die Kolosser erklärt.* Wuppertal: Brockhaus, 1974. **Caird, G. B.** *Paul's Letters from Prison.* NClB. Oxford: The University Press, 1976. **Calvin, J.** *Commentaries on the Epistles of Paul the Apostle to the Philippians, Colossians, and Thessalonians.* Tr. J. Pringle. Grand Rapids: Eerdmans, 1948. **Collange, J-F.** *L'épître de saint Paul aux Philippiens.* CNT. Neuchâtel: Delachaux et Niestlé, 1973. E. T. *The Epistle of Saint Paul to the Philippians.* Tr. A. W. Heathcote. London: Epworth Press, 1979. **Ellicott, C. J.** *A Critical and Grammatical Commentary on St. Paul's Epistles to the Philippians, Colossians and Philemon.* Boston: Draper, 1886. **Ernst, J.** *Die Briefe an die Philipper, an Philemon, and die Kolosser, und an die Epheser.* RNT. Regensburg: Pustet, 1974. **Ewald, P., und Wohlenberg, G.** *Der Brief des Paulus and die Philipper.* ZKNT. Leipzig: Deichert, 1917. **Fitzmyer, J. A.** "Philippians." *Jerome Biblical Commentary,* ed. R. E. Brown, J. A. Fitzmyer, R. E. Murphy. Englewood Cliffs, NJ: Prentice Hall, 1968. **Friedrich, G.** *Der Brief an die Philipper.* NTD 8. Göttingen: Vandenhoeck und Ruprecht, 1962. **Gnilka, J.** *Der Philipperbrief.* HTKNT 10/3. Freiburg: Herder, 1976. **Grayston, K.** *The Epistles to the Galatians and to the Philippians.* London: Epworth Press, 1957. _____. *The Letters of Paul to the Philippians and the Thessalonians.* Cambridge: The University Press, 1967. **Haupt, E.** *Die Gefangenschaftsbriefe.* MeyerK. Göttingen: Vandenhoeck und Ruprecht, 1902. **Hendriksen, W.** *Philippians.* Grand Rapids: Baker, 1962. **Heinzelmann, G.** *Die kleineren Briefe des Apostels Paulus; Der Brief an die Philipper.* NTD 8. Göttingen: Vandenhoeck und Ruprecht, 1955. **Houlden, J. H.** *Paul's Letters from Prison.* Baltimore, MD: Penguin, 1970. **Huby, J.** *Saint Paul, les épîtres de la captivité.* VS 8. Paris: G. Beauchesne, 1935. **Jones, M.** *Philippians.* London: Methuen and Co., 1918. **Kahlefeld, H.** *Der Brief nach Philippi.* Frankfurt: Knecht, 1975. **Keck, L. E.** "The Letter of Paul to the Philippians." *The Interpreter's One-Volume Commentary on the Bible,* ed. C. M. Laymon. New York: Abingdon, 1971. **Kennedy, H. A. A.** "The Epistle to the Philippians." *Expositor's Greek Testament,* ed. W. R. Nicoll. Grand

Rapids: Eerdmans, repr. 1976. **Lightfoot, J. B.** *St. Paul's Epistle to the Philippians.* London: Macmillan and Co., 1894. **Loh, I-J. and Nida, E. A.** *A Translator's Handbook on Paul's Letter to the Philippians.* Helps for Translators, 19. Stuttgart: United Bible Societies, 1977. **Lohmeyer, E.** *Der Brief an die Philipper, an die Kolosser und an Philemon.* Göttingen: Vandenhoeck und Ruprecht, 1956. **Martin, Ralph P.** *The Epistle of Paul to the Philippians.* TNTC. Grand Rapids: Eerdmans, 1959. _____. *Philippians.* NCB. Greenwood, SC: Attic Press, 1976; Grand Rapids: Eerdmans, 1980. **Meyer, H. A. W.** *Critical and Exegetical Commentary on the New Testament.* Tr. W. P. Dickson and F. Crombie. Edinburgh: T. and T. Clark, 1875. **Michael, J. H.** *The Epistle to the Philippians.* MNTC. London: Hodder and Stoughton, 1928. **Michaelis, W.** *Der Brief des Paulus an die Philipper.* THKNT 11. Leipzig: Deichert: 1935. **Moule, H. C. G.** *The Epistle to the Philippians.* Cambridge: The University Press, 1897. **Müller, J. J.** *The Epistles of Paul to the Philippians and to Philemon.* NIC. Grand Rapids: Eerdmans, 1955. **Péry, A.** *L'épître aux Philippiens.* Paris: Delachaux et Niestlé, 1958. **Plummer, A.** *A Commentary on St. Paul's Epistle to the Philippians.* London: Robert Scott Roxburghe House, 1919. **Scott, E. F.** "The Epistle to the Philippians." *The Interpreter's Bible,* ed. G. A. Buttrick *et al.* New York: Abingdon Press, 1955. **Synge, F. C.** *Philippians and Colossians.* London: SCM Press, 1951. **Tillman, F.** "Der Philipperbrief." *Die Gefangenschaftsbriefe des heiligen Paulus,* ed. H. Meimer und F. Tillmann. Bonn: 1931. **Vincent, M. R.** *Critical and Exegetical Commentary on the Epistles to the Philippians and to Philemon.* ICC. Edinburgh: T. and T. Clark, 1897. **Weiss, B.** *A Commentary on the New Testament.* Tr. G. Schodde *et al.* New York: Funk and Wagnalls, 1906.

Introduction to Philippians

General Bibliography

Barker, G. W., Lane, W. L. and Michaels, J. R. *The New Testament Speaks.* New York: Harper and Row, 1969. **Blevins, J. L.** "Introduction to Philippians." *RevExp* 77 (1980) 311–23. **Bornkamm, G.** *The New Testament: A Guide to Its Writings.* Tr. R. H. and I. Fuller. Philadelphia: Fortress, 1973. **Cullmann, O.** *The New Testament: An Introduction.* Philadelphia: Westminster, 1968. **Delling, G.** "Philipperbrief." *Die Religion in Geschichte und Gegenwart.* Tübingen: Mohr, 1957³. **Dibelius, M.** *A Fresh Approach to the New Testament and Early Christian Literature.* New York: Scribners, 1936. **Enslin, M. S.** *Christian Beginnings: The Literature of the Christian Movement.* New York: Harper, 1956. **Feine, P., Behm, J. and Kümmel, W. G.** *Introduction to the New Testament.* Tr. A. J. Mattill Jr. Nashville: Abingdon, 1966; revised ed. See below under **Kümmel, W. G. Fuller, R. H.** *A Critical Introduction to the New Testament.* London: Duckworth, 1966. **Grant, R. M.** *Historical Introduction to the New Testament.* New York: Harper and Row, 1963. **Guthrie, D.** *New Testament Introduction.* Chicago: Inter-Varsity Press, 1963 (2nd ed.); 1970 (3rd ed.). **Harrison, E. F.** *Introduction to the New Testament.* Grand Rapids: Eerdmans, 1964. **Hunter, A. M.** *Introducing the New Testament.* Philadelphia: Westminster, 1957². **Kümmel, W. G.** *Introduction to the New Testament,* rev. ed. Tr. H. C. Kee. Nashville: Abingdon, 1975. **Martin, R. P.** *New Testament Foundations.* Vol. 2. Grand Rapids: Eerdmans, 1978. **Marxsen, W.** *Introduction to the New Testament.* Tr. G. Buswell. Philadelphia: Fortress, 1968. **McNeile, A. H.** *Introduction to the New Testament.* Rev. ed. C. S. C. Williams. Oxford: Clarendon, 1953. **Michaelis, W.** *Einleitung in das Neue Testament.* Bern: Buchhandlung der Evangelischen Gesellschaft, 1946. **Moffatt, J.** *An Introduction to the Literature of the New Testament.* New York: Scribners, 1911. **Perrin, N.** *The New Testament: An Introduction.* New York: Harcourt Brace, 1974. **Riddle, D. W. and Hutson, H. H.** *New Testament Life and Literature.* Chicago: University of Chicago Press, 1946. **Robert, A. and Feuillet, A.** *Introduction to the New Testament.* Tr. P. W. Skehan. New York: Desclée, 1965. **Wikenhauser, A.** *New Testament Introduction.* Tr. J. Cunningham. New York: Herder and Herder, 1958. **Zahn, T.** *Introduction to the New Testament.* Tr. J. M. Trout *et al.* Edinburgh: T. and T. Clark, 1909.

1. Authorship

Baur, F. C. *Paul, the Apostle of Jesus Christ.* London: Williams and Norgate, 1875. **Morton, A. Q. and McLeman, J.** *Christianity in the Computer Age.* New York: Harper and Row, 1965. ———. *Paul, the Man and the Myth: A Study in the Authorship of Greek Prose.* New York: Harper and Row, 1966.

Paul claims to be the author of the letter to the Philippians (1:1), a claim that rarely has been challenged since it was first made. And for good reason. In disclosing his innermost feelings (1:18–24), sharing autobiographical information (3:5, 6), describing his present situation (1:12, 13), naming his friends and co-workers (2:19–24) and referring to gifts sent him from Philippi to Thessalonica and elsewhere (4:15, 16; cf. Acts 17:1–9; 2 Cor 8:1–5), the author unconsciously and naturally draws a picture of himself that coincides precisely with what can be known of Paul from other sources (e.g. Acts and Galatians). In style and language, too, "no letter can make a stronger claim to be from Paul" (Enslin, *Beginnings*, 3.280). An abundance of special Pauline vocabulary appears throughout Philippians. Phrases, ideas and allusions to opposition of false teachers that show up here also appear in letters unquestionably written by Paul (Romans, 1 and 2 Corinthians, Galatians). "In this epistle surely, if anywhere, the two complementary aspects of St. Paul's person and teaching . . . both appear with a force and definiteness which carry thorough conviction" (Lightfoot, 74).

Echoes of Philippians may be heard in the writings of Clement (*ca.* A.D. 95), Ignatius (*ca.* A.D. 107), Hermas (*ca.* A.D. 140), Justin Martyr (d. *ca.* A.D. 165), Melito of Sardis (d. *ca.* A.D. 190) and Theophilus of Antioch (later second century). Polycarp of Smyrna (d. *ca.* A.D. 155) addresses himself to the Philippians and directly mentions Paul as having written them (3.2). Irenaeus (d. *ca.* A.D. 200), Clement of Alexandria (d. *ca.* A.D. 215), Tertullian (d. *ca.* A.D. 225) and the later Fathers not only quote from Philippians, but assign it to Paul as well. Philippians appears in the oldest extant lists of NT writings—the Muratorian Canon (later second century) and the special canon of Marcion (d. *ca.* A.D. 160). There apparently never was a question in the minds of the Fathers of the Church as to the canonical authority of Philippians or about its authorship.

A few modern-day scholars, however, have questioned the Pauline authorship of Philippians, in whole or in part. Edward Evanson (1731–1805) was the first to do so (*The Dissonance of the Four Generally Received Evangelists* [Ipswich: G. Jermym, 1792] 263), followed later by F. C. Baur (1792–1860) and the Tübingen school he founded. Baur's historical studies led him to the conclusion that Paul wrote none of the epistles that bear his name except Romans, 1 and 2 Corinthians and Galatians. This radical view, though ably set forth by men of learning, was not convincing and disappeared, only to be revived in recent years by A. Q. Morton and J. McLeman.

With the aid of sophisticated computers, Morton and McLeman are able to do intricate and detailed studies. For example, they claim that they can readily count the number of sentences in each epistle that bears Paul's name and at the same time the frequency of *καί* in each sentence. On the basis of such analysis they can show, to their satisfaction, which of the letters were written by Paul and which were not. Their conclusions harmonize with those of Baur. Philippians is not among the genuine Pauline letters. The validity of Morton's and McLeman's methodology and the quality of their work have been severely criticized (see H. K. McArthur, "Computer Criticism," *ExpTim* 76 [1965] 367–70; "*Καί* Frequency in Greek Letters," *NTS* 15 [1969] 339–49; M. Whittaker, "A. Q. Morton and J. McLeman," *Theology* 69 [1966] 567–68). Therefore, their conclusions have not been widely adopted, nor are they likely to be.

It is safe to say that the great majority of contemporary NT scholars considers that Paul did write Philippians and that the question of its genuineness only has historical significance (Gnilka). This statement, however, does not mean that all scholars agree that Paul wrote all of Philippians. For example, W. D. Völter attempted to excise non-Pauline insertions in Philippians ("Zwei

Briefe an die Philipper," *TT* 26 [1892] 10–44; 117–46). Phil 1:1*b*, with its mention of bishops and deacons is looked upon by some as an addition to the original letter (Riddle and Hutson, *Life and Literature,* 123). Still others consider that 2:6–7 is a Marcionite interpolation (E. Barnikol, *Der Marcionite Ursprung des Mythossatzes Phil 2, 6–7,* [Kiel: W. G. Mühlau, 1932]. Many see the whole of 2:6–11 as a song to Christ, not originally written by Paul, but modified and used by him as the supreme example for humility and service (see R. P. Martin, *Carmen Christi* [Cambridge: Cambridge University Press, 1967; rev. ed. Grand Rapids: Eerdmans, 1983] and *New Testament Foundations,* vol. 2, 256–68 for details. See also M. D. Hooker, "Philippians 2:6–11," in E. E. Ellis and E. Grasser [eds.], *Jesus und Paulus* [Göttingen: Vandenhoeck und Ruprecht, 1975] 151–64 to become aware of the problems involved in discovering pre-Pauline fragments in the Pauline letters). J. H. Michael (*Philippians,* 112) suggests the possibility that 2:19–24 was a brief Pauline note "written to correspondents whose identity can no longer be determined."

2. The Integrity of Philippians

Bahr, C. J. "The Subscriptions in the Pauline Letters." *JBL* 87 (1968) 27–41. **Bornkamm, G.** "Der Philipperbrief als paulinische Briefsammlung." *Neotestamentica et Patristica, Freundesgabe für O. Cullmann,* Leiden: Brill, 1962, 192–202. **Bruce, F. F.** "St. Paul in Macedonia: 3. The Philippian Correspondence." *BJRL* 63 (1981) 260–84. **Buchanan, C. O.** "Epaphroditus' Sickness and the Letter to the Philippians." *EvQ* 36 (1964) 157–66. **Dalton, W. J.** "The Integrity of Philippians." *Bib* 60 (1979) 97–102. **Delling, G.** "Der Philipperbrief." *Die Religion in Geschichte und Gegenwart,* 1957, Cols. 333–36. **Furnish, V.** "The Place and Purpose of Phil. III." *NTS* 10 (1962–63) 80–88. **Jewett, R.** "The Epistolary Thanksgiving and the Integrity of Philippians." *NovT* 12 (1970) 40–53. **Jones, M.** "The Integrity of the Epistle to the Philippians." *Expositor,* 8th Series 8 (1914) 457–73. **Köster, H.** "The Purpose of the Polemic of a Pauline Fragment (Philippians III)." *NTS* 8 (1961–62) 317–32. **Mackay, B. S.** "Further Thoughts on Philippians." *NTS* 7 (1960–61) 161–70. **Michael, J. H.** "The Philippian Interpolation: Where Does it End?" *Expositor,* 8th Series 19 (1920) 49–63. **Michaelis, W.** "Der zweite Thessalonicherbrief kein Philipperbrief." *TZ* 1 (1945) 282–86. ———. "Teilungshypothesen bei Paulusbriefen." *TZ* 14 (1958) 321–26. **Mitton, C. L.** *The Formation of the Pauline Corpus of Letters.* London: Epworth Press, 1955. **Müller-Bardorff, J.** "Zur Frage der literarischen Einheit des Phil." *Wissenschaftliche Zeitschrift der Universität Jena* 7 (1957–58) 591–604. **Pollard, T. E.** "The Integrity of Philippians." *NTS* 13 (1966–67) 57–66. **Rahtjen, B. D.** "The Three Letters of Paul to the Phil." *NTS* 6 (1959–60) 167–73. **Refshange, E.** "Literaerkritiske overvejelser til Filipperbrevet." *DTT* 35 (1972) 186–205. **Schmithals, W.** *Paul and the Gnostics.* Tr. J. E. Steely. Nashville: Abingdon, 1972. ———. "Zur Abfassung und ältester Sammlung der paulinischen Hauptbriefe." *ZNW* 51 (1960) 225–45. **Schweizer, E.** "Der zweite Thessalonicherbrief ein Philipperbrief?" *TZ* 1 (1945) 90–105. **Völter, D.** "Zwei Briefe an die Philipper." *TT* 26 (1892) 10–44; 117–46.

Although most interpreters agree on the question of authorship, that Paul wrote Philippians, by no means do all these agree about the question of integrity: Is Philippians a single letter or a compilation of several letters? The suggestion that Philippians is a composite letter was first made in the seventeenth century (so Collange), and this suggestion has gained an increasing number of supporters through the years (see Bornkamm, Köster, Müller-Bardorff, Rahtjen, Schmithals in the articles cited above; Beare, Collange, Gnilka). The reasons for believing that Philippians is actually one document compiled from two or more letters are many and plausible: (1) If Romans 16 was originally a note addressed to Ephesus and 2 Corinthians was composed of at least two letters, then it is not an incredible thing to think of Philippians as a composite of previously existing letters. (2) One can readily imagine that Paul wrote more than a single letter to a community he loved as dearly as he loved the church at Philippi. If he did, were all these letters lost but one? (3) An ancient Syriac stichometry mentions two letters to the Philippians (E. Preuschen, *Analecta*, 1910, 68, noted by J. A. Fitzmyer, "Philippians," *JBC* 2.248). (4) Polycarp, in his letter to the Philippians also states that Paul had written them letters (ἔγραψεν ἐπιστολάς: 3.2). (5) Polycarp's own letter may itself be the end-product of a compilation. If so, here is further confirmation of the practice of composing one letter out of several (P. N. Harrison, *Polycarp's Two Epistles to the Philippians* [Cambridge: University Press, 1936]). (6) The disjointedness of Philippians itself raises the question of original unity. This is especially noticeable in the abrupt transition from 3:1 to 3:2 which introduces a section whose tone is markedly different from the rest of the letter. Since the letter as a whole is a model of warmth and friendliness, the furious attack launched in 3:2 against Paul's opponents, whom he calls "dogs," "evil doers," "mutilators" seems out of place (J. Weiss, *Earliest Christianity* [New York: Harper, 1952²] 1.387; Schmithals, *Paul*, 71–72). (7) "Verses 3:1 and 4:4 fit together so exactly that upon sober reflection one must come to the conclusion that a later hand has pulled the two verses apart." This was done to insert a harsh letter (3:2–4:3) written by Paul at a different time (so Schmithals, *Paul*, 72–3). (8) The question of unity is further raised by the fact that Paul did not turn to thanking the Philippians for their gift until the end of the letter (4:10–20). Does this seem likely? Hardly. From this then arises the argument that 4:10–20 must be a separate earlier letter sent soon after Epaphroditus brought the gift, but carried back to Philippi by someone else since Epaphroditus fell ill (Müller-Bardorff, "Zur Frage," 596–98).

These, then, are the major reasons for seeing the letter to the Philippians as a composite, the work of an anonymous editor, who, aware of the existence of several modest notes from Paul to the Philippians, put them all together to form a more imposing whole, and thereby to increase the importance of the Philippian correspondence at a time when Paul's letters "were acquiring an eminently respectable status" (Collange; Feine-Behm-Kümmel, *Introduction*, 236). Belief that Philippians is one letter composed of two or more earlier letters leads naturally to an attempt to isolate these letters and to exegete accordingly. Some scholars see Philippians made up of only two letters: Letter A = 1:1–3:1a; 4:2–7, 10–23, and Letter B = 3:1b–4:1, 8–9 (Gnilka; cf. Bruce, *BJRL* 63 [1981], 260–84). Other scholars see Philippians made up of three letters: Letter A = 4:10–20 (or 4:10–23); Letter B = 1:1–3:1a; 4:2–7, 21–23, and Letter C = 3:1b–4:1, 8–9 (Collange). Few scholars, however, can agree on the number of "letters" or on precisely what sections go to make up these "letters" (Beare, K. Lake, *Introduction*, 1937, 143; Michael, *Expositor*,

8th Series 19 [1920] 46–63; Rahtjen, *NTS* 6 [1959–60] 167–73; Refshange, *DTT* 35 [1972] 186–205; Schmithals, *Paul,* 79, n. 58).

The case, then, for believing that Philippians is one letter made up from several letters is considerable, but not wholly convincing:

(1) The fact that Romans and 2 Corinthians may be composite letters proves nothing about the composition of Philippians.

(2) It is easy to imagine that Paul wrote more than one letter to the church at Philippi and that Paul himself may have alluded to this fact when he said: "It is no trouble for me to write the same things to you again" (3:1). But attempts to recover these letters remain wholly in the realm of conjecture (see Delling, Mackay, Schweizer and Michaelis in the articles cited above).

(3) Polycarp's use of the plural, "letters" (ἐπιστολάς), when he reminded the Philippians of the apostle's having written them, may not in itself be strong proof that Paul wrote more than one letter to the church at Philippi. The plural may mean simply "a letter of importance" (Lightfoot, 140–42), or it may refer to a collection of Paul's letters that were sent to *all* churches including the church at Philippi (Mitton, *Formation*), or it may simply be the guess on Polycarp's part inferred from his reading of Philippians 3:1 (Wikenhauser, *Introduction,* 437; Martin, *Philippians,* 1976, 11, 12).

(4) The reference of the Syriac stichometry, *Catalogus Sinaiticus,* to two Philippian letters may be the result of accidental repetition (so A. Souter, *Text and Canon of the New Testament* [London: G. Duckworth, 1954] 209) and thus may offer no corroborating proof of a plurality of Pauline letters to Philippi.

(5) P. N. Harrison's thesis that the one letter of Polycarp is in reality a composite of two earlier letters has not gone unchallenged (see B. Altaner, *Patrology* [Freiburg: Herder, 1960] 111 for bibliography).

(6) There is certainly a disjointedness about Philippians, and Paul does interrupt himself at 3:1*b.* But this should not be surprising in a personal, almost conversational, letter written by a man accustomed to abrupt shifts in style (cf. Rom 16:16–19; 1 Thess 2:13–16. See E. Strange, "Diktierpausen in den Paulus-Briefen," *ZNW* 18 [1917–18] 115–16, cited by Martin, *Philippians,* 1976, 13). The change in tone from warmth and friendliness to harshness is startling only if one assumes that the opponents Paul denounces were fellow Christians, identical with those opponents already mentioned in 1:15–17. But 3:1*b*–21 makes it clear that they were Jews who were hostile to the gospel and who were attempting to turn the Philippians away from faith in Jesus Christ—reason enough for Paul to be indignant and to assert his authority (3:4–6; see A. F. J. Klijn, *Introduction* [Leiden: E. J. Brill, 1967] 109–10, and "Paul's Opponents in Phil III," *NovT* 7 [1964–65] 278–84; Schmithals, *Paul,* 82–122; Köster, *NTS* 8 [1961–62] 317–32). It should also be noted that the harsh tone of 3:2–6 leads up to and gives way before the most eloquent personal confession of faith and hope found anywhere within the writings of Paul—a confession which is totally consistent with Paul's other intimate expressions found elsewhere in his letter to the Philippians. In addition it is difficult to separate chapter 3 from the rest of the letter because the same terms, word-roots and motifs pervade all of its so-called separate parts (see Furnish, Mackay, Pollard, Dalton, articles cited above, and more recently,

R. A. Culpepper, "Co-workers in Suffering: Philippians 2:19–30," *RevExp* 77 [1980] 349–57).

(7) If it is true that verses 3:1 and 4:4 fit together so perfectly that chapter 3 must be viewed as a later insertion from another Pauline letter, one cannot help asking why any intelligent scribe, bent on unifying the fragments would have placed it here. And the same question may also be asked about the so-called letter of thanks (4:10–20). Why would a scribe wishing to put the Philippian "letters" together into an ordered whole place this "letter" at the end? Is not Bahr's suggestion just as reasonable—that Paul, in the custom of his day, dictated the early part of the letter, but picked up the pen to sign it in his own hand, and in doing so wrote his own personal "thank you" for their gift (*JBL* 87 [1968])?

Compilation theories, therefore, solve nothing. They merely shift the problem of order and organization from Paul to an unknown editor, and raise questions impossible to answer: Why should three original letters be combined at all (Michaelis, *TZ* 14 [1958])? Were these earlier letters complete letters with salutations and signatures, or merely fragments? If they were complete letters why were they not allowed to stand without modification, since apparently length was not a criterion for preservation (e.g. Paul's letter to Philemon)? If they were complete letters what right did any editor have to eliminate their prescripts and postscripts? (8) From the beginning of its manuscript history there has been only one canonical letter to the Philippians. Admittedly, however, the earliest manuscript that includes Philippians is the Chester Beatty Papyrus (P[46]), dated about A.D. 200.

There is, then, no compelling reason to doubt the integrity of Philippians. As Dibelius has noted "all the peculiarities of the sequence of thought are comprehensible without assuming editorial work or interpolations. . . . The style of the whole corresponds not with the desire to express a homogeneous conception, but with the requirement proper to private speech" (Dibelius, *Fresh Approach*, 166–67). As a consequence Philippians will be treated in this commentary as a single letter written by Paul. The exegesis of the text that follows will, therefore, be governed by this assumption, for any claim to be able to isolate separate letters and to identify the theology and *Sitz im Leben* of each meets only with disagreement and proves to be a critical exercise in futility (see P. Richardson, *Israel in the Apostolic Church* [Cambridge: University Press, 1969] 111, n. 4).

3. The Recipients and Their City

Collart, P. *Philippes, ville de Macédonie depuis ses origines jusqu' à la fin de l' époque romaine.* Paris: E. de Boccard, 1937. **Conzelmann, H.** *History of Primitive Christianity.* Tr. J. E. Steely. Nashville: Abingdon Press, 1973. **Foakes-Jackson, F. J.** *The History of the Christian Church from Earliest Times to A.D. 461.* Cambridge: Deighton Bell, 1947[6]. **Henle, F. A.** "Philippi und die Philippergemeinde." *TQ* 75 (1893) 67–104. **Kennedy, H. A. A.** "The Historical Background of the Philippians." *ExpTim* 10 (1898–99) 22–24. **Lemerle, P.** *Philippe et la Macédonie orientale à l' époque chrétienne et byzantine.* Paris: E. de Boccard, 1945. **McDonald, W. A.** "Archaeology and St. Paul's Journeys in Greek Lands." *BA* 3 (1940) 18–24. **Picard, C.** "Les dieux de la Colonie de Philippes vers le Ier siècle de notre ère, d' après les ex voto rupestres." *RHR* (1922) 117–201. **Ramsay,**

W. M. *St. Paul the Traveller and the Roman Citizen.* New York: G. P. Putnam, 1898. **Schmidt, J.** "Philippoi." PW (1938) 19, 2.2206–44. **Schürer, E.** *The Jewish People in the Time of Jesus Christ.* New York: Chas. Scribners, 1891. **Selwyn, E. C.** "The Christian Prophets at Philippi." *Expositor*, 6th series, 4 (1901) 29–38. **Sherwin-White, A. N.** *Roman Society and Roman Law in the New Testament.* Oxford: Clarendon Press, 1963. **Thomas, W. D.** "The Place of Women at Philippi." *ExpTim* 83 (1971–72) 117–20. **Weiss, J.** *Earliest Christianity.* New York: Harper, 1959.

Paul addressed his letter to the Christians who resided in Philippi and to their bishops and deacons (1:1). At the time he wrote, Philippi was already an ancient and historic city. It was built and fortified in 358–57 B.C. by Philip II of Macedon (the father of Alexander the Great) and named after himself. The site Philip chose for his new fortification was the old Thracian city of Crenides (or Daton) in northeast Greece (Macedonia). It was located about eight miles from the sea in a very fertile region that was enriched by an abundance of springs and by the gold that was mined there (ἀρίστην ἔχει χώραν καὶ εὔκαρπον καὶ ναυπήγια καὶ χρυσοῦ μέταλλα: Strabo, *Geogr.* 7.331, frg. 33: see Schmidt, PW, 2212).

After the Roman victory over the Persians in 168 B.C. Philippi became part of the Roman Empire and belonged to the first of the four *regiones* (μερίδες) of Macedonia (Schmidt, PW, 2213; cf. Acts 16:12). It also gained in importance because it was made one of the stations along the *Via Egnatia*, the main overland route connecting Rome with the East, stretching from the Adriatic Coast to Byzantium.

Philippi became world-prominent, however, as the place where the battle between Brutus and Cassius, the assassins of Julius Caesar, and Antony and Octavian took place in 42 B.C. Antony and Octavian emerged as the victors. When Octavian later defeated Antony at Actium (31 B.C.) and took to himself the title of Augustus, he rebuilt Philippi, established a military outpost there, filled it with Roman soldiers, veterans of his wars and Antony's partisans evicted from Italy, made it a colony (*Colonia Iulia Augusta Philippiensis;* see Schmidt, PW 2233–34), and gave it the *ius italicum* (Lemerle, *Philippe,* 7–10) which represented the legal quality of Roman territory in Italy—the highest privilege obtainable by a provincial municipality (*OCD* 559). Colonists, therefore, could purchase and own or transfer property and had the right to civil lawsuits. They also were exempt both from the poll tax and land tax.

Thus when Paul made his first visit to Europe he purposely neglected the port city of Neapolis to begin preaching the gospel in the small but more important city of Philippi of the first district of Macedonia (Acts 16:12, GNB, contra NIV. See Nestle-Aland, *Novum Testamentum Graece,* 26th ed., for the textual data about this translation problem, and Sherwin-White, *Roman Society,* 93–95 for a good explanation and solution of the difficulty. See also B. M. Metzger, *A Textual Commentary on the Greek New Testament* [New York: United Bible Societies, 1971] 444–46 and G. Zuntz, "Textual Criticism of Some Passages of the Acts of the Apostles," *Classica et Mediaevalia* 3 [1940] 36, 37). This city was inhabited predominantly by Romans (Dio Cassius, *Rom. Hist.* 47.42–49), but many Macedonian Greeks and some Jews lived there as well. They were a people proud of their city, proud of their ties with Rome, proud to observe Roman customs and obey Roman laws, proud to be Roman citizens (cf. Acts 16:21). Philippi was a reproduction of Rome.

The story of Paul's arrival in Philippi and the beginning of the Church there is told in dramatic fashion by Luke to underscore heavily the significance of the transition of the gospel mission from Asia Minor to Europe (Acts 16:6–40; see Conzelmann, *Primitive Christianity*, 96). For some scholars this story is so heavily obscured by legends that it cannot be trusted as an historical source for details concerning Paul or the founding of the church at Philippi (see E. Haenchen, *The Acts of the Apostles* [Philadelphia: Westminster Press, 1971] 504; Perrin, *Introduction*, 106). For others "this episode contains nothing unworthy of credence" (Weiss, *Earliest Christianity*, 1.282), and their research has shown the essential trustworthiness of the information Luke provides here (Sherwin-White, *Roman Society*, *passim;* Ramsay, *St. Paul*, 221 and the excellent summary by Martin, *Philippians*, 1976, 7–9).

In any case, whatever historical value one places on the account, Acts does say that Paul made his journey to Philippi along with Silas, Timothy and Luke (note the "we"-section that begins at 16:10) as the result of a night vision he had. In it Paul saw someone standing and saying, "Come across to Macedonia and help us" (Acts 16:9). Upon reaching Philippi, these missionaries spent several days in the city before the first Sabbath came round. Luke gives no hint of what they did in the interim, or where they stayed. Were they looking for work? Studying the town? Getting acquainted with the customs and practices of the people? Sizing up the composition of the population? Observing evidences of religious interest? (Apparently the religion of the Philippians at this time was distinctively syncretistic. Indigenous Thracian deities coexisted with the imperial cult, the classical Greco-Latin gods as well as those from Egypt, Syria and elsewhere. See Collart, *Philippes*, 389–486; Collange, 2.)

When the Sabbath did come, however, Paul and his companions went out of the city to the riverside where they expected to find a Jewish place of prayer (Acts 16:13). Some have understood these words to mean that there were too few Jews in Philippi to have a synagogue of their own, and that what Jews there were held their services in the open air beside the Gangites River (Blevins, *RevExp* 77 [1980] 312; Harrison, *Introduction*, 319; Scott). Others see in these remarks quite a different meaning—almost certainly "a house of assembly, in fact a synagogue, [for] there is evidence elsewhere that such places were usually, for convenience of religious ablutions, built close to water" (Weiss, *Earliest Christianity*, 1.281, but see also Collart, *Philippes*, 1.319–22; McDonald, *BA* 3 [1940] 20).

The first convert to Christianity was Lydia, a Godfearer (σεβομένη τὸν θεόν), a pagan woman who had been impressed with the lofty teachings of the Jewish religion, and who had attached herself to the synagogue. She was in Philippi to sell cloth which had been dyed in her home town of Thyatira in north Lydia (Asia Minor). Guild workers and dyers (βάφεις) at Thyatira are mentioned in inscriptions (*RE* 5.550). It is conceivable that this woman's real name was not Lydia, but that she bore the title "the Lydian" as a surname to some other name (Weiss, *Earliest Christianity*, 1.281). She is not mentioned in Paul's letter to the Philippians, unless Euodia or Syntyche (Phil 4:2) is this Lydian woman.

Nevertheless, responding to the gospel, and putting her faith in Christ, Lydia was baptized. She and her family became the first Christians in Europe (Acts 16:14, 15) and the fledgling Christian church of Philippi began to meet in her home (16:15, 40). How many others were added to the church before Paul was forced to leave Philippi is not indicated. But quite likely Paul and his companions stayed on in Philippi, in spite of the pain and insults they had to face (cf. 1 Thess 2:2), and preached and taught for a longer period of time than one might expect from reading the Acts account. If this is so, then the number of converts may have been many (see Acts 16:40) and their growth in the knowledge of the faith considerable. Certainly Paul left behind a strong church which continued to show its fidelity to God and its love and concern for the apostle.

The other Philippian converts mentioned in Acts were the jailer and his family (16:30–33). At the climax of Luke's dramatic story this Roman soldier rushed into the prison where Paul and Silas had been bound and tremblingly begged them to tell him what he must do to be saved. Their answer was, "Believe in the Lord Jesus." The jailer responded positively to this initial message and the teaching that followed it (cf. Acts 16:32), was baptized and demonstrated his faith by deeds of kindness (Acts 16:33, 34). Other names of members of this Philippian community that are mentioned—Epaphroditus, Euodia, Syntyche and Clement (2:25; 4:2, 3)—indicate that the first church on European soil was made up largely of Gentiles (see W. H. Schinz, *Die christliche Gemeinde zu Philippi* [Zürich: Orelli, Füssli & Co., 1833]).

Women seem to have played a major role in the Philippian church, not only in meeting the physical needs of the missionaries, but also in working side by side with them in the proclamation of the gospel (αἵτινες ἐν τῷ εὐαγγελίῳ συνήθλησάν μοι [Phil 4:3]; see Thomas, *ExpTim* 83 [1971–72] 117–120). Lydia, who welcomed Paul into her home and first provided for him in those earliest days, probably should get the credit for rallying these women and for keeping alive the cordial and intimate relations that existed between Paul and the rest of the Philippian Christians.

Paul stayed in touch with the Macedonian churches through Timothy (Acts 19:21–23; Phil 2:19, 20), and he himself visited them on at least two other occasions—probably the autumn of 54–55 and again a short time later in the spring of 55–56 (Acts 20:1–3: see Feine-Behm-Kümmel, *Introduction*, 228). Surely he made every effort on these trips to visit his friends at Philippi (Acts 20:6) in order to instruct and encourage them. In any case, they remained loyal to Paul, sent him gifts on several occasions (Phil 4:15, 16) and, long after his death, continued strong in the faith he preached (see Pol. *Phil.*).

Paul's trouble at Philippi began when he freed a slave girl from an evil spirit that enabled her to predict the future and so make money for her owners (Acts 16:19–21). Furious, these men seized Paul and Silas, dragged them before the authorities (στρατηγοί), and charged them with teaching customs that were against Roman law. Then, in case their charge should fail, they took advantage of an apparent pervasive anti-Jewish sentiment (see

F. F. Bruce, *New Testament History* [Garden City: Doubleday, 1971] 291–304) by adding, "These men are Jews," (Acts 16:19–21). Paul and Silas were whipped publicly without a trial and thrown into prison where the jailer fastened their feet between heavy blocks of wood.

This incident highlights several significant things: (1) The Christian church was not yet distinguished from Judaism by outsiders so that hostile feelings against the Jews were readily transferred over to Christians. (2) Paul could have appealed to his Roman citizenship in order to avoid a flogging. He did not. Theodore Mommsen's suggestion that a Jew who was a Roman citizen might well be reluctant, on ethnical grounds, to insist overmuch on his Roman privileges may be the reason (*Gesammelte Schriften,* 1907, 3.440, cited by Sherwin-White, *Roman Society,* 66). Paul at this time may have considered that he was a Jew before he was a Roman. (3) Although Paul would not claim Roman citizenship to spare himself physical suffering, he would and did claim it to clear Christianity from any possible reproach by the Roman government. Personal preferences must now be sacrificed to make sure that future contacts between Christianity and Rome might be positive and the gospel not impeded.

4. Place and Date of Writing

Bowen, C. R. "Are Paul's Prison Letters from Ephesus?" *AJT* 24 (1920) 112–35; 277–87. **Buchanan, C. O.** "Epaphroditus' Sickness and the Letter to the Philippians." *EvQ* 36 (1964) 157–66. **Cadoux, C. J.** "The Dates and Provenance of the Imprisonment Epistles of St. Paul." *ExpTim* 45 (1933–34) 471–73. **Coppieters, H.** "Saint Paul fut-il captif à Ephèse pendant son troisème voyage apostolique?" *RB* 16 (1919) 408–18. **Dacquino, P.** "Data e provenienza della lettera ai Filippesi." *RevistB* 6 (1958) 224–32. **Deissmann, A.** "Zur ephesinischen Gefangenschaft des Apostels Paulus." *Anatolian Studies Presented to Sir William Ramsay,* ed. W. H. Buckler and W. M. Calder. Manchester: Manchester University Press, 1923, 121–27. **Dockx, S.** "Lieu et date de l' épître aux Philippiens." *RB* 80 (1973) 230–46. **Dodd, C. H.** *New Testament Studies.* Manchester: University Press, 1953. **Duncan, G. S.** "Chronological Table to Illustrate Paul's Ministry in Asia." *NTS* 5 (1958–59) 43–45. ———. "A New Setting for Paul's Epistle to the Philippians." *ExpTim* 43 (1931–32) 7–11. ———. "Paul's Ministry in Asia—The Last Phase." *NTS* 3 (1956–57) 211–18. ———. *St. Paul's Ephesian Ministry.* London: Hodder and Stoughton, 1929. ———. "Were Paul's Imprisonment Epistles Written from Ephesus?" *ExpTim* 67 (1955–56) 163–66. **Feine, P.** *Die Abfassung des Philipperbriefes in Ephesus.* BFCT 20. Gütersloh: C. Bertelsmann, 1916. **Ferguson, J.** "Philippians, John and the Tradition of Ephesus." *ExpTim* 83 (1971) 85–87. **Harrison, P. N.** "The Pastoral Epistles and Duncan's Ephesian Theory." *NTS* 2 (1955–56) 250–61. **Hinshaw, V.** "The Provenance of Philippians: A Problem of Critical Introduction." Ph.D. dissertation, Vanderbilt University, 1964. **Johnson, L.** "The Pauline Letters from Caesarea." *ExpTim* 68 (1957–58) 24–26. **Knox, W. L.** *St. Paul and the Church of the Gentiles.* Cambridge: University Press, 1939. **Lisco, H.** *Vincula Sanctorum; Ein Beitrag zur Erklärung der Gefangenschaftsbriefe des Apostels Paulus,* 1900. **Malherbe, A. J.** "The Beasts at Ephesus." *JBL* 87 (1968) 71–80. **Manson, T. W.** "St. Paul in Ephesus: The Date of the Epistle to the Philippians." *BJRL* 23 (1939) 182–200. **Michaelis, W.** *Die Datierung des Philipperbriefes.* Gütersloh: C. Bertelsmann, 1933. ———. *Die Gefangenschaft des Paulus in Ephesus und das Itinerar des Timotheus.* Gütersloh: C. Bertelsmann, 1925. **Ogg, G.** *The Chronology of the Life of Paul.* London: Epworth Press, 1968. **Reicke, B.** "Caesarea, Rome and the Captivity Letters." *Apostolic History and the Gospels,* ed.

W. W. Gasque and R. P. Martin. Grand Rapids: Eerdmans, 1970. **Robinson, J. A. T.**
Redating the New Testament. Philadelphia: Westminster Press, 1976. **Rowlingson,**
D. T. "Paul's Ephesian Imprisonment." *ATR* 32 (1950): 1–7. **Schmid, J.** *Zeit und Ort*
der paulinischen Gefangenschaftsbriefe. Freiburg im Breisgau: Herder, 1931. **Stanley,**
D. M. *Christ's Resurrection in Pauline Soteriology.* Rome: Pontificio Instituto Biblico, 1960.
Suggs, M. J. "Concerning the Date of Paul's Macedonian Ministry." *NovT* 4 (1960–
61) 60–68.

From the second century Marcionite prologues attached to Paul's epistles
(cf. J. Knox, *Marcion and the New Testament* [Chicago: University of Chicago
Press] 170; see also the *subscriptio* to some Greek MSS in Nestle-Aland, *Novum*
Testamentum Graece, 1979[26], Phil 4:23) until the eighteenth century, everyone
accepted without question the "fact" that the Philippian letter was written
from Rome. Now, in the words of a contemporary writer, it seems impossible
to decide the place where the Philippian epistle originated with any degree
of certainty (Wikenhauser, *Introduction,* 436). For in addition to the traditional
location (Rome), Caesarea, Ephesus and even Corinth have been suggested
as cities from which Paul wrote Philippians, and each of these suggestions
is supported by substantial arguments.

There are, however, certain fundamental factors that must be considered
before even a tentative conclusion as to place and date can be reached. Some
of these include (1) the fact that Paul was in prison when he wrote (Phil
1:7, 13, 17); (2) the fact that Paul faced a trial that could end in his death
(1:19–20, 2:17) or acquittal (1:25; 2:24); (3) the fact that from wherever it
was that Paul wrote there was the *praetorium* (τὸ πραιτώριον, 1:13), and there
were "those who belonged to Caesar's household" (οἱ ἐκ τῆς Καίσαρος οἰκίας,
4:22); (4) the fact that Timothy was with Paul (1:1; 2:19–23); (5) the fact
that extensive evangelistic efforts were going on around Paul at the time he
wrote to the Philippians (1:14–17); (6) the fact that Paul soon planned to
visit Philippi if he were acquitted (2:24), and (7) the fact that several trips
were made back and forth between Philippi and the place from which Paul
wrote Philippians—all within the time-span of his imprisonment: (*a*) news
traveled to Philippi of Paul's arrest, (*b*) the Philippians therefore sent Epaphroditus to Paul with a gift to aid him in his distress, (*c*) news of Epaphroditus'
illness was sent back to Philippi, (*d*) word that the Philippians were greatly
concerned about Epaphroditus reached Paul (see 2:25–30) and (*e*) Paul hoped
to send Timothy to the Philippians and get encouragement back from them
through him before he himself set off for Philippi (2:19, 24).

Rome, as the place from which Philippians was written (*ca.* A.D. 60–62)
meets most of these fundamental facts and thus today still has many advocates
(Buchanan, Dodd, Harrison, W. L. Knox, Reicke, Schmid, articles cited above,
and most of the commentators). In Rome Paul was a prisoner under house
arrest (*custodia libera*) for at least two years (Acts 28:30; but see Johnson,
ExpTim 68 [1957–58] 24). He had soldiers guarding him (28:16), yet he was
free to send letters, to receive Jewish leaders and anyone else who came to
see him or bring him gifts (28:17, 30). He was also free to preach the gospel
and he readily took advantage of this opportunity so that evangelism thrived
in Rome under Paul's direction (28:31). From Rome Paul had no higher

court of appeal; here he would stand trial before Caesar and his fate would ultimately be decided—death or acquittal. The expressions, "the praetorium" (Phil 1:13) and "those of Caesar's household" (4:22), are most easily and naturally understood if Rome is assumed as the birth place of Philippians— the Imperial or Praetorian Guard, on the one hand (cf. Tac. *Hist.* 4.46; Suet. Nero 9; MM 553) and the large number of people, slaves and free, in the employ (not in the family) of the Emperor, on the other hand (see BGD 557). In Rome there was a church sufficiently large and of sufficiently diverse composition to divide up into factions over Paul and his teaching (Phil 1:14– 17).

The strongest objection to a Roman origin for Philippians (so Collange) is the distance between Rome and Philippi. It would have been difficult to fit all the known trips back and forth between these cities into the two-year time-span of Paul's imprisonment in Rome. It is also difficult to understand how Paul could speak so easily about sending Epaphroditus, a recently very ill man, back to Philippi (2:25–30) and about dispatching Timothy there as well with the expectation of his quick return (2:19) if the distance was really as great as the distance between Rome and Philippi. Other objections to a Roman origin stem (1) from the fact that there is no indication that Timothy was with Paul in Rome (but see Phil 1:1), (2) from the fact that Paul planned to visit Philippi upon his release from prison (2:24), when earlier his expressed intent was to be finished with the East and to focus his attention on new mission fields in the West, especially Spain (Rom 15:24–28; but see Grant, *Introduction,* 90), and (3) from the assumption drawn from Phil 1:30 and 4:15, 16 (cf. also 1:26; 2:12, 22) that Paul is here stating that he had not been back to Philippi since he and Timothy founded the church there (so Michaelis, cited by Feine-Behm-Kümmel, *Introduction,* 230)—an impossible statement if Paul were writing from Rome, since he had in fact twice been to Philippi between its founding (Acts 16) and his trip to Rome (Acts 20:1–6).

In 1900 H. Lisco (*Vincula Sanctorum*) first suggested that Paul may have written his letter to the Philippians from Ephesus (*ca.* A.D. 54–57). Since then many serious scholars have followed his lead and developed his suggestions with detailed arguments (Bowen, Deissmann, Duncan, Ferguson, Hinshaw, Michaelis, Rowlingson, articles cited above, and a few commentators, Bonnard, Collange, Gnilka). Some of these arguments are the following: (1) The references to the "praetorium" can refer to the residence of any provincial governor (and does so exclusively in the rest of the New Testament: Matt 27:27; Mark 15:16; John 18:28, 33; 19:9; Acts 23:35), and "those of Caesar's household" can refer to slaves or freedmen in the imperial service located in Rome, Ephesus or elsewhere (J. T. Wood, *Discoveries at Ephesus* [London: Longmans, Green, 1877] App. 7, 18; McNeile, *Introduction,* 182, n. 3). (2) Timothy was with Paul in Ephesus as he was when Paul wrote Philippians (Acts 19:22; Phil 1:1), and the projected trip of Timothy to Philippi (Phil 2:19) from Ephesus harmonizes with his recorded itinerary in Acts (19:22). (3) The relatively short distance between Ephesus and Philippi favors an Ephesian origin for Philippians. The distance between the two cities could have been traversed in a week's time so that the mention of several journeys in the letter to the Philippians is no longer a problem. (4) It is certain that extensive evangelistic activity went on in and around Ephesus during Paul's long stay there (Acts 19:10, 25, 26; cf. Phil 1:12–14), and that contention over Paul and his teaching was intense, especially on the part of the Jews (Acts 19:8–9). (5) Acts does not say that Paul was imprisoned in Ephesus, but this fact does not tell against the possibility that he was: (*a*) Acts makes no attempt to record every imprisonment Paul experienced, citing only three of these (Acts 16, Philippi; Acts 23, Caesarea; and Acts 28, Rome); (*b*) Paul says he was often in prison (1 Cor 11:23) and Clement of Rome specifies how often this was—seven times (*1 Clem.* 5:6); (*c*) 2 Cor 1:8–10 coupled with Acts 20:18–19 indicates that in Asia Paul suffered extreme hardships even to the point of despairing of life: (*d*) the mysterious reference to Paul fighting with wild beasts (ἐθηριομάχησα) in Ephesus (1 Cor 15:32), if it is not to be taken literally, ought to be taken figuratively of his imprisonment (so Marxsen, *Introduction*, 65); (*e*) a rupture occurred in Paul's relations with the Jews at Ephesus because he preached the gospel (Acts 19:8–9), and the motive for Paul's imprisonment, hinted at in Phil 1:12–13, 16, was the preaching of the gospel—this, plus the fact that Paul's sharp attack on the Jews in Phil 3:2–6 makes it conceivable that Paul's Jewish adversaries were the ones who had him put in jail; (*f*) Acts 19:11–12 tells of miracles of healing taking place at Ephesus as the result of handkerchiefs and scarves being carried from Paul's body to the sick. This can more easily be understood on the hypothesis that Paul was in jail at the time, and so unable to heal the sick personally (so Stanley, *Christ's Resurrection*, 66, n. 23). (6) The language, style and ideas of Philippians are closer to those epistles in the central section of Paul's ministry—Corinthians and Galatians, those written from Ephesus— than to his other prison epistles written either from Caesarea or Rome at a later date—Ephesians, Colossians and Philemon.

The fatal flaw in the Ephesian imprisonment hypothesis is that it is totally built on conjecture. And Hinshaw, who has provided the most recent thorough historical survey for the provenance of Philippians, and who himself decides for Ephesus, is forced to admit that the attempts to show how the data of Philippians fit into an Ephesian milieu better than into a Roman are mostly of neutral value ("Provenance of Philippians").

Other objections to the Ephesian origin of Philippians are as follows: (1) The silence of the letter about the "collection" for the poor in Jerusalem, a matter of supreme importance to Paul when his ministry in Ephesus was drawing to a close, is most difficult to explain. It is mentioned in every other letter known to have been written from this period. Thus it is hard to imagine that Paul, so ardent and single-minded in soliciting funds for the needy, would say nothing at all about this project to the Philippians, but would, on the other hand accept their personal gift to him (Phil 2:26; 4:10–20; see Schmid, *Zeit und Ort*, 114). (2) Paul speaks harshly about the Christians who are around him, with the exception of Timothy (Phil 2:19–21). But this seems strange when most likely his best friends, Aquila and Priscilla, were in Ephesus when he was (Acts 18:2, 18, 24–26; 1 Cor 16:19). (3) The church in the city from which Paul writes to the Philippians is a divided church—some standing with him and others against him (Phil 1:15–17)—a factor that does not answer to the situation in Ephesus, a church founded by Paul and under his control (Scott: but see E. Käsemann, "Die Johannesjünger in Ephesus," *ZTK* 49 [1952] 144–54: E.T. in *Essays on NT Themes* [London: SCM 1964] 136–48). (4) If Paul were imprisoned in Ephesus, how could he be facing the possibility of immediate death for his crime (Phil 1:19, 20) when he had the right as a Roman citizen to appeal his case to the Emperor—a right he exercised in Caesarea (Acts 25:10)? (5) Finally, C. L. Mitton has demonstrated clearly that parallel ideas, phrases and vocabulary are spread throughout all of Paul's letters, so that it is difficult, if not impossible, to say what letter is early and what letter is late simply on this basis alone (*The Epistle to the Ephesians* [Oxford: Clarendon Press, 1951] 322–32).

That Paul wrote Philippians from Corinth (*ca.* A.D. 50) was first hinted at by G. L. Oeder in 1731 (see Martin, *Philippians*, 1976, 44), but it was a suggestion that did not gain widespread support. Recently it has been revived and championed by Dockx (*RB* 80 [1973] 238–43). His argument includes the following elements: (1) There was a proconsul in Corinth (Acts 18:12) and consequently a "praetorium" and "a household of Caesar" ("des gens de la maison de César"; cf. Phil 1:13; 4:22). (2) Corinth is not as far from Philippi as is Ephesus. Therefore the frequency of journeys back and forth that are hinted at in Philippians is still more easily accounted for. (3) Seemingly Paul wrote Philippians before his polemic with the Jews from James (note that there is no reference to his apostleship in Philippians). Therefore, it is likely that it was written before 1 Corinthians which was written at the beginning of Paul's stay in Ephesus—written likely while he was still in Corinth. (4) One can understand the fact that the Philippians wanted to continue regular gifts to Paul but were prevented from doing so (Phil 4:10) because of Paul's rapid flight from Thessalonica to Berea to Athens and the winter stop in Corinth. Winter conditions would have prevented the Philippians from reaching Paul with assistance until the opening of the sea and the resumption of regular travel. Since the Philippians then came to Paul's aid as soon as possible, the quick arrival of Epaphroditus and his companions ought therefore to be placed in Corinth and not in Ephesus. (5) 2 Cor 11:9 is seen as an allusion to the arrival of Epaphroditus with the gift from the Philippians for Paul and to Paul's "thank you" note sent to them in return (cf. Phil 4:15). (6) Paul, meeting severe opposition in Corinth and in mortal danger, received divine encouragement and the promise of safety through a dream (Acts 18:10). The parallels between this nocturnal call to courage and that which came to Paul in prison in Jerusalem (Acts 23:11) are so similar that one is permitted to suppose that Paul's enemies in Corinth had arrested him, put him in prison and threatened him with death (*RB* 80 [1973] 243). Comforted by this night vision, however, he could be confident of release and could write to the Philippians these words: "I know that I shall remain and continue with you all" (1:25). According to Dockx, the Corinthian hypothesis is far more plausible than the Roman one and is at least as plausible as the Ephesian hypothesis.

Again, the major difficulty with placing the writing of Philippians in Corinth is that the theory is wholly based on speculation with no facts to support it. There is no mention anywhere of a Corinthian imprisonment for Paul, nor is there sufficient correlation between the other parts of Dockx's thesis and the facts called for by the statements in Philippians. Again, as against the

Ephesian hypothesis, Paul's harsh remarks about those around him (Phil 2:19–20) make no sense when one realizes that during his time in Corinth Priscilla and Aquila, his most trusted friends (cf. Rom 16:3, 4), were with him there (Acts 18:1–2, 18).

In 1779 H. E. G. Paulus proposed for the first time that Caesarea was the place of the origin of Philippians. In modern times his proposal has been taken up and developed by F. Spitta, *Zur Geschichte und Literatur des Urchristentums* (Göttingen: Vandenhoeck und Ruprecht, 1907); E. Lohmeyer, *Der Brief an die Philipper* (Göttingen: Vandenhoeck und Ruprecht, 1930) 3–4, 15–16, 40–41; J. J. Gunther, *Paul: Messenger and Exile* (Valley Forge: Judson Press, 1972) 98–120; Johnson, *ExpTim* 68 (1957–58) 24–6; and most recently by Robinson, *Redating*, 60–61. These are the more important arguments:

(1) Luke specifically states that Paul was imprisoned in Caesarea in the praetorium of Herod (Acts 23:35). This was a palace built by Herod the Great, but used in New Testament times as the residence of the Roman procurator and as the headquarters of the Roman garrison in Palestine. This specific statement corresponds, then, with Paul's phrase in Phil 1:13, ἐν ὅλῳ τῷ πραιτωρίῳ καὶ τοῖς λοιποῖς πᾶσιν, "in the whole praetorium and to all the rest." One is not compelled to believe, however, that the phrase ἐν ὅλῳ τῷ πραιτωρίῳ can only mean a body of people and not an official residence (so Reicke, "Caesarea," 283). It is rather a hyperbolic statement by which Paul triumphantly asserted that the news of his imprisonment for Christ had become known in the entire (ὅλῳ) palace, i.e. it had not escaped the notice even of the procurator himself. And indeed it had not (Acts 24:24–26). The phrase καὶ τοῖς λοιποῖς πᾶσιν, "and to all the rest," could easily refer to the soldiers garrisoned in Caesarea who were attached to the praetorium. Furthermore, this statement of Luke's, that Paul was put in the praetorium of Herod, harmonizes with Phil 4:22 where the expression, "those of Caesar's household," meaning any number of administrative staff in the employ of the emperor, refers to those administrative personnel involved in the governing of Judea from Caesarea.

(2) It is clear also from Acts that Paul's imprisonment was a long one, at least two years (Acts 24:27), allowing time for several communications to pass from Philippi to Caesarea and back.

(3) Luke says, too, that the Roman governor, Felix, gave orders that the centurion should keep Paul in custody, but allow him some liberty (ἄνεσις, "open arrest"? See Josephus *Ant.* 18.235, and F. J. Foakes-Jackson and K. Lake, *The Beginnings of Christianity* [London: Macmillan, 1920–23] 4, 304), and prevent none of his friends from attending to his needs (Acts 24:23). This is in complete accord with the statements in Phil 2:25–30 and 4:10–20.

(4) Furthermore, Phil 1:7 implies that Paul had already been given a hearing and that he had made a defense (ἀπολογία) of himself and his preaching of the gospel, while Phil 1:16 indicates that Paul still lay in prison (κεῖμαι) in spite of his defense. This harmonizes with the events that took place in Caesarea. There Paul defended himself before the Roman governor Felix for preaching the gospel (Acts 24:20–21), yet remained a prisoner for two years subsequent to this defense. The story of Paul in Rome, on the other hand, concludes by describing him as a prisoner without even hinting that

he had made any defense before any government official (Acts 28:16–31). (5) At the time Paul wrote to the Philippians he was confident he would be released from prison (1:24–26), and would soon visit them on his journey west (2:24; cf. Rom 1:13–15; 15:23–29). Here again is a close correlation between the statements in Philippians and those in Acts (19:21; 23:11). Paul's projected westward journey loomed extremely large in his thinking because he believed that there was no more place for him to work in the East (Rom 15:20, 23, 24). Thus, to assume that Paul later changed his mind and made plans to return east from Rome would be a most perplexing assumption, and one entirely without foundation in fact (see Robinson, *Redating*, 6). It is not unreasonable, however, to assume that Paul would want to stop off on his way west to see old friends, especially those as loyal and as generous as the Philippians had been to him.

(6) Paul's bitter attack in Phil 3:2–6 was probably directed against Jews (see the discussion below, p. xliv–xlvii). The tone here is markedly different from the tone Paul used against those fellow Christians who opposed him and who preached the gospel for the purpose of adding to his troubles (Phil 1:15–18). The bitterness of his attack, therefore, harmonizes with the "fanatical and unrelenting Jewish opposition Paul encountered in Jerusalem and Caesarea" (Acts 21:37–26:32; cf. 28:19) rather than with his experience with the Jews in Rome. The only statements Luke makes about the Jews in Rome indicate that they treated Paul fairly, although they did not all believe his message (Acts 28:21–28; see Robinson, *Redating*, 61).

(7) The fact that there is no mention in the Philippian letter about the "collection" and the fact that Paul was now willing to accept a personal gift from the Philippians argues for a period after the collection was completed and delivered to the poor in Jerusalem.

If distance from Philippi is the major objection for considering Rome as the site for the origin of Philippians (so Collange), then there exists no possibility for suggesting Caesarea in its place. Caesarea is farther from Philippi than Rome. But as E. F. Scott pointed out, too much can be made of this matter of distance and of the number of trips assumed to be required by statements in the epistle (*Philippians*, 7; cf. Reicke, "Caesarea," 284, who contends that the epistle presupposes only two journeys!). But even if the journeys are as numerous as suggested, all of them could be fitted into a two-year time-span (Guthrie, *Introduction*, 147; cf. Pliny, *Hist.* 19.19, 3–4, who says that the distance from Puteoli [the Port of Rome] to Corinth was crossed in a record-breaking five days). The most difficult aspect of this matter of distance, however, is the supposition that Paul planned to send Timothy to Philippi with the expectation that he would return in a short time bringing news about the Philippians—a return that would take place even before Paul made his own trip to Philippi (Phil 2:19; 2:24). The flaw in this argument lies in the fact that though Paul expected to send Timothy to Philippi soon, there is no statement in the text that requires the interpretation that he expected him back *soon*. If Paul were still in prison, he could wait; time was no factor. If he were released, it may be assumed he would go himself and join Timothy in Philippi.

W. Marxsen (*Introduction*, 64) makes the statement that there is no evidence of a church in Caesarea as proof against its being the city from which Paul's letter to the Philippians originated. But this statement seems not to fit the facts: (1) Caesarea was a large, beautiful and new city, built by Herod the Great in 25–13 b.c. Josephus describes its palaces, temples, theaters, hippodrome, aqueducts and other monumental structures (*Ant.* 15.9.6; see PW 3.1, 1291–94). It is hard to imagine, therefore, that Christian missionaries would have neglected this key city in their strategy to spread the gospel. (2) This apart, Luke does record the fact that Peter preached to the Gentiles in Caesarea at the invitation of the Roman centurion, Cornelius (Acts 10). (3) In addition, Philip the evangelist first visited Caesarea (Acts 8:40) and later settled there to live and preach with his virgin daughters who themselves were active in the Christian proclamation (Acts 21:8, 9). (4) Furthermore, Luke records that some of the disciples from Caesarea accompanied Paul as he journeyed toward Jerusalem (Acts 21:16). This last statement in itself could imply (*a*) that the church in Caesarea was of a fair size, (*b*) that some of its members were extremely loyal to Paul and (*c*) that some may have been less than enthusiastic about him.

A major objection to Caesarea is the fact that wherever Paul was when he wrote Philippians, he was facing the possibility of death (Phil 1:20; 2:17). This, however, could not be true, so it is assumed, if he were in any place but Rome. As a Roman citizen he had the right of appeal to Caesar and he could easily have staved off the death penalty in the provinces by such an appeal. Yet as Robinson points out, the Acts account makes clear that Paul's life was in constant danger in Caesarea (cf. Acts 21:31, 36; 22:22; 23:30; 25:3, 24; 26:21), and that he was protected from death only because he was in Roman custody. But if the Jews could have proved that he had really brought a Greek into that part of their temple that was forbidden to Gentiles (cf. Acts 21:28; see Reicke, "Caesarea," 281 and n. 3), "then, even as a Roman citizen, he would, under Jewish law, have been liable to death" (Robinson, *Redating*, 60; see Josephus, *Wars* 5.193, 94; *Ant.* 15.417; note Paul's own words to Festus: "If, however, I am guilty of doing anything deserving death, I do not refuse to die" [Acts 25:11]). But since he knew he was innocent of this charge and he knew the authorities were convinced of his innocence, he could confidently expect release in order to go about his business of strengthening the churches and preaching the gospel.

That no plans for missionary journeys, such as those anticipated in Phil 2:24, were possible after Paul appealed to Caesar (see G. R. Beasley-Murray, "Philippians," *PCB* 985) is hardly an argument against the Caesarean origin of Philippians. Paul, up until the last moment, expected to be set free. Therefore, he planned missions and wrote of his plans. Only at the last moment, when he feared that Festus would hand him over to the Jews did he finally make his appeal to the Emperor.

Not all questions can be answered or all problems solved, and to paraphrase Origen, "Only God knows where Philippians was really written." Yet it seems best for the sake of the understanding and explanation of Philippians to make a decision about where it was written and to exegete the text in the light of that decision. Hence, the assumption made in this commentary is that Philippians was written by Paul from prison in Caesarea about a.d. 59–

61. Robinson is correct in thinking that Caesarea, as the place of origin for Philippians, has been too quickly abandoned; it is certainly preferable to Ephesus, and "Rome has little to be said against it, precisely because the evidence is so thin" (*Redating*, 61; see Kümmel, *Introduction*, 329).

5. Paul's Opponents and the False Teachers at Philippi

Baumbach, G. "Die Frage nach den Irrlehren in Philippi." *Kairos* 13 (1971) 252–66. ———. "Die vom Paulus im Philipperbrief bekämpften Irrlehren." *Gnosis und NT*, ed. K. W. Tröger. Gütersloh: Mohn, 1973. **Friedrich, G.** "Die Gegner des Paulus im 2. Korintherbrief." *Abraham unser Vater, Festschrift für O. Michel*, ed. O. Betz, M. Hengel, P. Schmidt. Leiden: Brill, 1963, 181–215. **Georgi, D.** *Die Gegner des Paulus im 2. Korintherbrief.* Neukirchen-Vluyn: Neukirchener Verlag, 1964. **Gnilka, J.** "Die antipaulinische Mission in Philippi." *BZ* 9 (1965) 258–76. **Gunther, J. J.** *St. Paul's Opponents and Their Background. NovTSup* 35. Leiden: Brill, 1973. **Holladay, C. R.** "Paul's Opponents in Phil. 3." *Restoration Quarterly* 3 (1969) 77–90. **Jewett, R.** "The Agitators and the Galatian Congregation." *NTS* 17 (1970–71) 198–212. ———. "Conflicting Movements in the Early Church as Reflected in Philippians." *NovT* 12 (1970) 362–90. **Klijn, A. F. J.** "Paul's Opponents." *NovT* 7 (1964–65) 278–84. **Koester, H.** "The Purpose of the Polemic of a Pauline Fragment (Philippians III)." *NTS* 8 (1961–62) 317–32. **Linton, O.** "Zur Situation des Philipperbriefes." *ConNT* 2 (1936) 9–21. **Richardson, P.** *Israel*, 111–17. **Schmithals, W.** *Paul*, 58–122. **Tyson, J. B.** "Paul's Opponents at Philippi." *Perspectives in Religious Studies* 3 (1976) 82–95.

Paul was facing opposition to himself while in prison. Strangely, this opposition came from fellow-Christians. Paul called them "brothers" and said that they spoke the Word of God and preached Christ (Phil 1:14–17). But these "brothers" did so with impure motives—envy (φθόνος), rivalry (ἔρις) and selfish partisanship (ἐριθεία)—hoping thereby to add to Paul's suffering (1:15–17). Although Paul could joyfully accept the results of their conduct—the fact that Christ was being preached (1:18)—it is impossible to imagine that he could have believed their attitude and actions were right. Perhaps, then, the force of Paul's personal feeling against his opponents came to the surface in his harsh words contained in 2:21: "All seek their own interests, not the interests of Jesus Christ."

One cannot say with certainty who these opponents were. Some have suggested that they were Christian missionaries with a divine-man theology, who believed that humility, meekness, imprisonment, suffering, and so on, were proofs that Paul was no apostle (or divine-man), since these weaknesses which Paul experienced showed that he knew nothing of the triumphant power of Christ. ("The divine-man concept in the Hellenistic world assumed a correspondence between the missionary and the god he served," Jewett, *NovT* 12 [1970] 368; see also Georgi and Friedrich, articles cited above.) This particular identification of Paul's opponents assumes (1) that the divine-man idea in the Hellenistic world has been satisfactorily demonstrated (but see Baumbach, *Kairos* 13 [1971] 252–66; *Gnosis und NT*, and D. L. Tiede, *The Charismatic Figure as Miracle Worker* [SBLDS 1. Missoula, MT: Scholars Press, 1972]), (2) that this divine-man concept was sufficiently well formulated within the Christian church so as to be considered a theology adopted by a band of itinerant missionaries and (3) that Ephesus was the place of Paul's imprisonment, because these missionaries were surely the same as those Paul contended with when he wrote the Corinthian letters (Jewett, *NovT* 12 [1970] 364).

Others have suggested that Paul's opponents while he was in prison were Judaizers, Jewish Christians, who taught that in addition to believing in Christ one must also keep the Jewish law including regulations about food and drink and especially the rite of circumcision (cf. Meyer, Lightfoot; but see Beare). Paul had been hard on these teachers from James and even on Peter who was influenced by them (cf. Gal 2:11–3:5), saying that they preached "another gospel" which was not good news (Gal 1:6, 7), they frustrated the grace of God (Gal 2:21), they bewitched people (Gal 3:1), they sought their own interests, not those of Christ (Phil 2:21). They in turn would surely have been hard on Paul, seeking, whenever possible, to stop him from proclaiming a partial gospel. They would likely, therefore, have taken advantage of Paul's imprisonment, seeing it as a means to achieve their goal. If he had been put in prison because of the gospel, they would proclaim the gospel in order to keep him there and curtail his activities. It is true that Paul's most intense struggle with the Judaizers was much earlier (*ca.* 54–57), but the virility of this movement kept it alive as an active force for years beyond the Apostolic Conference. It could still have been strong in Caesarea in A.D. 59.

Although it may not be possible to identify with certainty those who opposed Paul while he was in prison, it is certain, however, that Paul was not concerned about himself and the threat to his own life. He would gladly accept the consequences of Christians preaching Christ for whatever motive they might do this, if only Christ would be preached (Phil 1:18). What concerned him was the threat to his friends at Philippi and to their faith. It was this concern that caused Paul to promise destruction (ἀπωλεία, 1:28; cf. 3:19) for those who opposed the Philippians, who made them afraid and who attempted to undermine their firmness in the gospel (1:27–29). It was this concern that caused him to turn on these same persons so suddenly and fiercely in 3:2 (see Klijn, *Introduction*, 109 and *NovT* 7 [1964–65] 278–84; Martin, *Philippians*, 1976, 22, however, does not think that the opponents mentioned in 1:28 have any relation to the ones in chapter 3).

Who were these false teachers? Paul calls them "dogs" (κύων, 3:2), a word not intended to describe but to insult (Koester, *NTS* 8 [1961–62] 317–19). To a Jew it meant the ignorant, the godless, the heathen, "die Nichtisraeliten" (Str-B 3,621–22). Paul also says that they are "those who do evil" (τοὺς κακοὺς ἐργάτας, 3:2). This is an expression too vague to be helpful in identifying the false teachers, since it could refer to any number of adversaries. Paul's next remark, however, narrows the field. The false teachers are people who were urging, or who were intending to urge upon the Philippians the necessity of circumcision: βλέπετε τὴν κατατομήν. ἡμεῖς γάρ ἐσμεν ἡ περιτομή ("watch out for the incision. For we are the circumcision," 3:2–3). In a bitter, aggressive, ironic play on words—κατατομή/περιτομή—Paul claims circumcision for Christians, denies it to Jews and supplies the latter instead with a new "jeering title of his own coinage" (Beare; Koester, *TDNT* 8, 109–11; see C. E. DeVries,

"Paul's 'Cutting' Remarks about a Race: Galatians 5:1–12," in G. F. Hawthorne [ed.], *Current Issues in Biblical and Patristic Interpretation* [Grand Rapids: Eerdmans, 1975] 115–20). The three titles together—"dogs," "evil-doers," "mutilators"—seem heavy with irony and thus seem to point toward Jewish missionaries "who think they are clean, and do good and are inborn members of God's people (cf. Rom 2:17–29), but who have converted these features into the opposite through their opposition to the gospel" (Richardson, *Israel,* 114). Certainly Paul's difficulties in Thessalonica, Berea, Corinth and Ephesus after he left Philippi (Acts 16) came from Jews who were not convinced by his message and who considered him a menace to their own religion (Acts 17:5, 13; 18:6; 19:9). It is reasonable to assume, then, that the most likely source of the trouble threatening the Philippians was Jews, possibly from Thessalonica (Richardson, *Israel,* 113; Klijn, *Introduction,* 109–110).

Paul attempts to combat this threat from the Jews by claiming that a right-standing before God (δικαιοσύνη) is not achieved through human effort, by painstakingly obeying the law and practicing circumcision, but rather by abandoning all confidence in these external things and staking one's life wholly upon Jesus Christ. The passionate autobiographical section, which begins with "circumcised the eighth day" (3:5), is Paul's way of proving the validity of his claims: "I personally have found this to be true! I had all the advantages of a Jew. I appraised their real value. I found them to be less than nothing when compared to Christ" (3:5–9).

The middle part of chapter 3 (vv 12–16) has been used to develop a theory that the Philippians also faced a second set of opponents, Gnostics (G. Friedrich, "Gnostische Schwärmerei," *NTD* 8 [1962] 120). They believed and taught that perfection could be attained on earth without waiting for, or without any need for, the resurrection. It is not necessary, however, to see in these verses opponents different from those already mentioned in 3:2–3. The idea of "perfection" was not foreign to Judaism, "which states repeatedly that a person who has been circumcised and is true to the law can reach perfection" (B. Rigaux, "Révélation des mystères et perfection à Qumran et dans le Nouveau Testament," *NTS* 4 [1957–58] 237–62, cited by Klijn, *Introduction,* 109). Paul, therefore, continues his attack against the Jews. Though they may offer immediate perfection, it is an earth-bound (ἐπίγεια) perfection (3:19) and comes to an end with the earth without any prospect of bodily transfiguration. Christ, however, offers true perfection and the promise of a new body, like his own glorious body, although this perfection cannot be attained this side of the resurrection (3:21; cf. 3:11).

Paul began his attack against these Jewish adversaries who would undermine the faith of the Philippians with bitterly harsh words (3:2). He concludes his opposition to them with tears (3:18; Lohmeyer is wrong in saying that Jewish agitators would not deserve Paul's grief; cf. Rom 9:1, 2). He weeps for these enemies of the cross (cf. Rom 11:28), for their end will be destruction (ἀπώλεια, 3:18; cf. 1:28). The expressions, "their god is their belly," and "their glory is their shame," are expressions that need not mean Paul is addressing still another set of adversaries, i.e. "heretical libertinists with gnostic tendencies," who arose out of the Philippian church itself (Jewett, *NovT* 12 [1970] 376–82). Rather it is possible to see these remarks as allusions to Jewish practices involving foods for the belly that could and could not be eaten, on the one hand, and, on the other hand, circumcision which on occasion was considered a mark of shame and disgrace (cf. Hab 2:16 [LXX]; Hos 4:7; Mic 1:11; Nah 3:5; Ecclus 4:21).

Paul, then, set his face against a single opponent in chapter 3, Jews, who had their own missionaries proclaiming a message of righteousness and perfection that was attainable *now* simply by submitting to circumcision and complying with certain laws. Theirs was a seductive message, because it offered visible and tangible tokens of God's favor in the present, not in the future and invisible world.

The apostle continues and concludes his polemic against the Jews by contrasting the Christians' "colony" (πολίτευμα) with that of Judaism (3:20–21). Πολίτευμα, "commonwealth," "state," "colony," refers to "a group of people who live surrounded by an ethnologically different population and lead a more or less independent existence." The Jews outside of Jerusalem had their own πολιτεύματα in the many cities of the Greco-Roman world where they were permitted to live according to their own laws (Klijn, *Introduction*, 110). But theirs were earthly "colonies" and time-bound as a consequence. The Christians' πολίτευμα, by contrast, is in heaven and is thus eternal. Hence, there should be no incentive to turn to Judaism, because the one who knows God through Jesus Christ is the "circumcision," will achieve perfection and bodily transfiguration at the resurrection, and is presently a citizen of a heavenly colony that is eternal. (Bornkamm, *New Testament*, 104; Fuller, *Introduction*, 37; Koester, *NTS* 8 [1961–62]; Schmithals, *Paul*, all agree that Paul fights against only one group of adversaries. They do not agree, however, that this group was composed of Jews.)

6. Paul's Purposes for Writing Philippians

In assuming that the letter to the church at Philippi is a unity (see above pp. 5–8), one is not thereby forced to conclude that Paul had only one purpose in mind when he wrote this letter. Indeed his purposes were many: (1) The simplest purpose to imagine is that, having a deep affection for the Philippians (cf. 4:1), he *wanted* to write them. So when an opportunity came to have a letter taken to them (2:25–28), he wrote.

(2) Paul wrote also to bring them up to date on the news about himself, about his present situation and the prospects for his future, namely that he was in danger and was suffering, but was at the same time rejoicing and optimistic (1:12–26; 2:24).

(3) Paul wrote to inform them of the erroneous but seductive tenets of the Jewish religion and to plead with them to follow him and his teaching as a pattern for living rather than to follow Judaism (3:2–21).

(4) Paul wrote to encourage the Philippians to stand firm for the faith of the gospel, to inspire in them complete dedication to the will of Christ in spite of any crucible of suffering they might find themselves in—whether because of persecution that might come upon them for rejecting the message of fanatical Jewish missionaries, or because of the possibility of experiencing a martyr's death for refusing to bow before any Lord but Jesus (cf. 1:27–

30; Lohmeyer saw this purpose as *the* overriding purpose for Paul's writing to the Philippians and as a consequence considered the letter addressed to them as a tractate on martyrdom written by a martyr to a community of martyrs. Although Lohmeyer's contribution had a profound impact on such Christians as Dietrich Bonhoeffer and perhaps other modern Christian martyrs, it is a thesis that cannot be wholly maintained without straining the exegesis of the text. Cf. Gnilka 95, n. 12).

(5) Paul wrote the Philippians to tell them about Epaphroditus their messenger, whom they sent to minister to his needs. Epaphroditus had been desperately ill; he had now recovered; he had not failed in his mission although he was returning home; he was worthy of a place of very great honor among them, perhaps a place of leadership, for risking his life to carry out their orders and fulfill the work of Christ (2:25–30).

(6) Paul wrote them to correct division within their ranks. He was proud of the Philippians and asked "for nothing better than to have his work judged by the record of this one church" (2:16; 4:1; Scott, 12). Yet he was keenly aware that all was not well within it. The fellowship was fractured, not by doctrinal but by personal differences—differences arising out of rivalry, vanity, selfishness and animosity. Repeatedly, therefore, Paul encourages them to unity (1:27; 2:2–4; 4:2).

(7) Paul wrote to exhort the Philippians to rejoice irrespective of circumstances (2:18; 3:1; 4:4). He could do this for he himself rejoiced although in prison facing the possibility of an unnatural death (1:18–20). "Joy" (χαρά) and "rejoice" (χαίρω) occur sixteen times in this letter. Bengel summarizes Paul's intent in his wondrously succinct phrase: *"Gaudeo, gaudete"* ("I rejoice; do you rejoice").

(8) Paul wrote them to express his thanks for their gift of money (?) to ameliorate his situation in prison (4:10–20). This, however, surely cannot be the sole purpose for writing the letter, or even the chief purpose, because Paul leaves it to the last to mention, and then expresses his gratitude, as Dibelius remarked, "in that form of thankless thanks" (*Fresh Approach*, 164). Perhaps Paul's words here comprise a delicate way of saying, "I did not need your gift, but I appreciate the Christian love that prompted it."

Philippians bears all the characteristics of a very personal letter, where the reasons for writing are various and numerous. It is like a chat, the subject matter changing without notice as in an informal conversation between friends. For this reason an outline of the letter is not easy to make. The letter follows no logical progression. Swift changes of topic and even of tone come as no surprise. Philippians is the antithesis of Romans (or Galatians; see H. D. Betz's elaborate discussion of the literary composition of Galatians in his commentary on that epistle [Philadelphia: Fortress Press, 1979] 14–25).

7. Outline of Philippians

I. Introductory Section (1:1–11)
   A. Salutation (1:1–2)
   B. Thanksgiving and Prayer (1:3–11)

8. *Aspects of the Christology of Philippians*

Barrett, C. K. *From First Adam to Last.* New York: Scribners, 1962. **Bornkamm, G.** *Paul.* Tr. D. M. G. Stalker. New York: Harper and Row, 1971. **Bultmann, R.** *Theology of the New Testament.* Tr. K. Grobel. New York: Scribners, 1951, 1, 185–352. **Cerfaux, L.** *Christ in the Theology of St. Paul.* New York: Herder and Herder, 1959. **Conzelmann, H.** *An Outline of the Theology of the New Testament.* New York: Harper and Row, 1969. **Cullmann, O.** *The Christology of the New Testament.* Tr. S. C. Guthrie and C. A. M. Hall. Philadelphia: Westminster, 1959. **Davies, W. D.** *Paul and Rabbinic Judaism.* London: SPCK, 1948. **Ellis, E. E.** *Paul and His Recent Interpreters.* Grand Rapids: Eerdmans, 1961. ———. *Paul's Use of the Old Testament.* London: Oliver and Boyd, 1957. **Feine, P.** *Die Theologie des neuen Testament.* Berlin: Evangelische Verlag, 1950. **Fitzmyer, J. A.** "Pauline Theology." *JBC* 2, 800–22. **Klausner, J.** *From Jesus to Paul.* Tr. W. F. Stinespring. New York: Macmillan, 1943. **Knox, W. L.** *St. Paul and the Church of the Gentiles.* Cambridge: The University Press, 1939. **Kümmel, W.** *The Theology of the New Testament.* Tr. J. E. Steely. Nashville: Abingdon, 1973. **Ladd, G. E.** *A Theology of the New Testament.* Grand Rapids: Eerdmans, 1974. **Longenecker, R. N.** *Paul, Apostle of Liberty.* New York: Harper and Row, 1964. **Moule, C. F. D.** *The Origin of Christology.* Cambridge: The University Press, 1977. **Munck, J.** *Paul and the Salvation of Mankind.* Tr. F. Clarke. Richmond: John Knox Press, 1959. **Nock, A. D.** *St. Paul.* New York: Harper and Row, 1963. **Pfitzner, V. C.** *Paul and the Agon Motif.* Leiden: Brill, 1967. **Ridderbos, H. N.** *Paul: An Outline of His Theology.* Tr. J. R. DeWitt. Grand Rapids: Eerdmans, 1975. **Schoeps, H.** *Paul.* Tr. H. Knight. Philadelphia: Westminster, 1961. **Schweitzer, A.** *The Mysticism of Paul the Apostle.* Tr. W. Montgomery. London: A. and C. Black, 1931. **Stauffer, E.** *New Testament Theology.* Tr. J. Marsh. London: SCM

Press, 1955. **Whiteley, D. E. H.** *The Theology of St. Paul.* Philadelphia: Fortress Press, 1964.

Paul's writings in general do not provide a systematic presentation of his thought. And this is especially true of his letter to the Philippians. Intensely intimate, it lacks formality. Paul sets down his ideas as they come to him, and they are primarily concerned with personal matters—himself, his friends, Timothy and Epaphroditus, and the problems and generosity of the Philippian community. It is a far cry from being a theological treatise. And yet unconsciously he writes theologically, or Christologically, for his mind is saturated with thoughts of Christ, God, man, salvation, Spirit, end times: resurrection, Parousia, the new world, and so on.

The background for Paul's thought was not primarily Hellenistic philosophy or Hellenistic mystery religions, as has been believed and taught for a long while (see Fitzmyer, *JBC* 2, 802–803; Nock, *Paul;* Stauffer, *Theology,* 35, 36; Whiteley, *Theology,* 1–8, and more recently I. H. Marshall, "Palestinian and Hellenistic Christianity," *NTS* 19 [1972–73] 271–87; M. Hengel, *Judaism and Hellenism,* 2 vols., Tr. J. Bowden [Philadelphia: Fortress, 1974]; E. E. Ellis, "Dating the New Testament," *NTS* 26 [1980] 497). Paul was born into a Jewish home that rigidly adhered to orthodox Jewish beliefs and customs (Phil 3:5). He was sent "to the holy city of his people to attend the law school, before the world outside the ghettos could gain possession of his affections" (Stauffer, *Theology,* 35). He attended the school of Hillel, studied under Rabbi Gamaliel (Acts 22:3), joined the order of strict observance of the law, the Pharisaic order (cf. Phil 3:5–6), and earned the confidence of his superiors. Paul had a promising career as a teacher of the law until the Damascus Road experience. While on a mission to Damascus to persecute the church he encountered—or better, in his own words, he "was seized by" (Phil 3:12)—the exalted Lord of the church, Jesus (Acts 9:1–8), and the whole course of his life was radically altered. He who had persecuted Jesus now preached Jesus.

The effects of this encounter never wore off. When Paul wrote to the Philippians many years later, and perhaps near the end of his career, he still stressed the overwhelming and life-shattering importance of Christ. Never once did he himself regret giving up everything to gain Christ and he had no compunction about urging others to follow his example (Phil 3:7–8). One might say that Paul was obsessed with Christ, because for him Christ was everything (1:20–21). He was divine and preexistent, humble to the point of becoming human and of dying on a cross, exalted to heaven, adored by the universe and all its powers, and given a new name that is above all names, Lord (κύριος, 2:6–11).

This centrality of Jesus Christ in the universe, in the world, in an individual's life, vibrates throughout the letter to the Philippians, but not in any formal way. Rather, even the great Christological hymn (2:6–11) is introduced simply as an illustration of what the Christian's life should be like—humble, self-giving, a life-for-others. And the intimate personal testimony of what Christ meant to Paul is seemingly the inevitable outcome of a passionate denunciation of false teachers. Had he not become so agitated, the curtain of his inner life might not have been drawn aside so completely, so that the dramatic encounter between Christ, an individual, and the world of human experience might become clearly visible.

A life of goodness, that is, one filled with the fruit of righteousness, is possible because of Jesus Christ (1:11; cf. 2:5–11), but Paul does not elaborate on how Jesus Christ effects this in a believer. Christ died a death on a cross (2:8), but Paul does not say here that it was for "our sins" that he died as in the traditional gospel (1 Cor 15:3). Rather he says that death was the supreme display of obedience on Christ's part as an example for Christians to follow (2:12). Incorporate in Christ by faith, the Christian is found to be "right with God," that is, not having a righteousness of his own earning as a "legal rectitude, but the righteousness which comes from faith in Christ given by God in response to faith" (3:9). Christ alone is sufficient to put men and women right with God. Jesus Christ, now in heaven, will come again to deliver the Christian and transfigure his body making it like his own resplendent body (3:21). The day of Christ's return, the day of transfiguration, is near (4:6).

Jesus Christ was the central "fact" of Paul's life from the Damascus experience to the experience of his death, and this reality can be seen cropping up everywhere in his brief letter to the Philippians. Jeremias wrote that "the hour of Damascus is the key to Pauline theology" (*ExpTim* 76 [1964–65] 30). Yet there are some interesting restraints here as well that are characteristic of Paul elsewhere: (1) Paul never addresses Jesus Christ directly, either in a prayer or in thanksgiving. He does not call on him to bear witness to any aspect of his own conduct, nor does he direct his doxology to him. Even Paul's final salutation: "May the grace of our Lord Jesus Christ be with your spirits" (4:23) seems to be a studied avoidance of any kind of direct address to Jesus. Only God the Father is the object of prayer and thanksgiving (1:3; 4:6). Only God is called on to bear witness (1:8). Only God receives the doxology of praise (4:20); only God is directly addressed. (2) Paul is careful to distinguish between God the Father and the Lord Jesus Christ (1:2). Jesus is never called "God" (θεός) in Philippians (but see 2:6 and cf. Rom 9:5 and 2 Thess 1:12). The "fruit of righteousness" is produced *through* Jesus Christ, but it is *for* the glory and praise of God (1:11; cf. 2:11). Christians are called "children of God" (2:15), not of Christ. Righteousness comes from (ἐκ) God through (διά) faith in Christ or through the faithfulness of Christ (3:9). God calls men by Christ (3:14). God is the God of peace (4:9) who brings peace to men in/by Christ (4:7). Why this distinction? Why this restraint in vocabulary on the part of a man so obviously committed to the Lordship of Jesus Christ? Perhaps it was due to the influence of Jewish monotheism on Paul, the former Pharisee (cf. 1 Cor 8:5–6). Convinced as Paul was from the "Christ-encounter" on the Damascus Road that Jesus was divine, on a par with God himself (cf. Phil 1:1; 2:6, 11) and one to be worshiped (2:10), he, nevertheless, could not quickly or easily bring himself to transfer to Jesus a title that he regarded to be exclusively the Father's (see Moule, *Origin* and D. R. de Lacey, "Image and Incarnation in Pauline Christology—A Search for Origins," *TynB* 30 [1979] 1–28 for helpful suggestions in this difficult area of names for Jesus).

9. The Text

Aland, K. *Kurzgefasste Liste der griechischen Handschriften des NT,* 1963, 1929–33. ────. *Studien zur Überlieferung des NT und seines Textes,* 1967, pp. 58–60, 91–136. *The Greek New Testament,* ed. K. Aland, M. Black, *et al.* New York: United Bible Societies, 1975.[3] Metzger, B. M. *The Text of the New Testament.* New York: Oxford University Press, 1968.[2] *Novum Testamentum Graece,* ed E. Nestle and K. Aland. Stuttgart: Deutsche Bibelstiftung, 1979[26].

There are no major difficulties posed by the textual tradition of Philippians. The oldest witness to the Greek text of this letter is the Chester Beatty Papyrus (P[46]), dating from about A.D. 200, now kept in Dublin. It contains Phil 1:1, 5–15, 17–28, 30–2:12, 14–27, 29–3:8, 10–21; 4:2–12, 14–23. The other papyri, P[16] and P[61], are later, the former dating from the third or fourth centuries, and the latter about A.D. 700. P[16] contains Phil 3:9–17; 4:2–8, and P[61] contains Phil 3:5–9, 12–16. There are eighteen uncial witnesses to Philippians, the three oldest of which (א B, A) provide a complete text dating from the fourth and fifth centuries. Six other uncial manuscripts also contain the whole of the Philippian text. The minuscule manuscripts stand in contrast to the eighteen uncials in that there are no less than 626 of them as of September 20, 1967 (so Gnilka). The commentary that follows will note significant textual matters, if any, at the beginning of each section.

I. Introductory Section (1:1-11)

A. Salutation (1:1, 2)

Bibliography

Baur, F. C. *Der Ursprung des Episkopats.* Tübingen: L. F. Fues, 1838. Beare, F. W. "The Ministry in the New Testament Church: Practice and Theory." *ATR* 37 (1955) 14–17. Berger, K. "Apostelbrief und apostolische Rede: Zum Formular frühchristlicher Briefe." *ZNW* 65 (1974) 190–231. Best, E. "Bishops and Deacons: Phil 1:1." *TU* 102 (1968) 371–76. Bousset, W. *Kyrios Christos.* Tr. J. E. Steely. Nashville: Abingdon, 1970. Bouttier, M. En Christ. *Etude d'exégèse et de théologie pauliniennes.* Paris: Presses Université de France, 1962. Brooke, D. *Private Letters Pagan and Christian.* New York: E. P. Dutton and Co., 1930. Brun, L. "Zur Formel 'In Christo Jesu' im Brief des Paulus and die Philipper." *SO* 1 (1922) 19–38. Büchsel, F. " 'In Christus' bei Paulus." *ZNW* 42 (1949) 146–52. Campenhausen, H. von. *Kirchliches Amt und geistliche Vollmacht in den ersten drei Jahrhunderten,* 1953. ET *Ecclesiastical Authority and Spiritual Power in the Church of the First Three Centuries.* Tr. J. A. Baker. Stanford: Stanford University Press, 1969. Conzelmann, H. *An Outline of the Theology of the New Testament.* Tr. J. Bowden. New York: Harper and Row, 1969. Deissmann, A. *Light from the Ancient East.* Tr. L. R. M. Strachan. New York: George Doran, 1927. ———. *Die neutestamentliche Formel "in Christo Jesu."* Marburg: Elwert, 1892. ———. *Paul, A Study in Social and Religious History.* Tr. W. E. Wilson. New York: George Doran, 1962. Dix, G. *Le ministère dans l'Eglise ancienne.* Paris: Delachaux, 1955. Doty, W. G. *Letters in Primitive Christianity.* Philadelphia: Fortress Press, 1973. Driver, G. R. *Aramaic Documents of the Fifth Century B.C.* Oxford: Oxford University Press, 1900. Ernst, J. "From the Local Community to the Great Church, Illustrated from the Church Patterns of Philippians and Ephesians." *BTB* 6 (1976) 237–57. Fitzmyer, J. A. "New Testament Epistles." *JBC* 2, 223–26. Hort, F. J. A. *The Christian Church.* London: Macmillan and Co., 1897. Hunt, A. S. and Edgar, E. E. *Select Papyri,* 2 vols. New York: G. P. Putnam's Sons, 1932–34. Jeremias, G. *Der Lehrer der Gerechtigkeit.* SUNT 2. Göttingen: Vandenhoeck und Ruprecht, 1963. Kennedy, H. A. A. *The Theology of the Epistles.* New York: Scribners, 1920. Koskenniemi, H. *Studien zur Idee und Phraseologie des griechischen Briefes bis 400 n. chr.* Helsinki, 1956. Lauerer, H. " 'Diakonie' im NT." *NKZ* 42 (1931) 315–26. Lemaire, A. *Les ministères aux origines de l'Eglise, Naissance de la triple hiérarchie: evêques, presbytres, diacres.* Paris: Éditions du Cerf, 1971. Lightfoot, J. B. "The Christian Ministry." *St. Paul's Epistle to the Philippians.* Grand Rapids: Zondervan, repr. 1953, 181–269. ———. "The Synonyms 'Bishop' and 'Presbyter.' " Ibid. 96–99. Longenecker, R. N. *Paul, Apostle of Liberty.* New York: Harper and Row, 1964. Loofs, F. "Die urchristliche Gemeindeverfassung." *TSK,* 619–57. Malherbe, A. J. "Ancient Epistolary Theorists." *Ohio Journal of Religious Studies* 5 (1977) 3–77. Martin, R. P. *New Testament Foundations.* Vol. 2, 241–47. Moule, C. F. D. *Origin.* Neugebauer, F. *In Christus. Eine Untersuchung zum paulinischen Glaubensverständnis.* Göttingen: Vandenhoeck und Ruprecht, 1961. Ridderbos, H. N. *Paul.* Roberts, C. H. "Elders: A Note." *JTS* 26 (1975) 403–405. Rohde, J. *Urchristliche und frühkatholische Ämter.* Berlin: Ost, 1976. Roller, O. *Das Formular der paulinischen Briefe. Ein Beitrag zur Lehre von antiken Briefen.* BWANT 58. Stuttgart: Kohlhammer, 1933. Sass, G. "Zur Bedeutung von δοῦλος bei Paulus." *ZNW* 40 (1941) 24–32. Schweizer, E. *Church Order in the New Testament.* Naperville,

IL.: A. R. Allenson, 1961. **Stauffer, E.** *New Testament Theology.* **Sykutris, J.** "Epistologra-phie." *PWSup* 5. 187. **Thiering, B. E.** *"MEBAQQER* and *EPISKOPOS* in Light of the Temple Scroll." *JBL* 100 (1981) 59–74. **Thraede, K.** *Grundzüge griechisch-römischer Brief-topik.* Munich: Beck, 1970. **Weber, H. E.** "Die Formel, 'in Christo Jesu' u. d. paul. Christusmystik." *NKZ* 31 (1920) 213.

Translation

¹ *Paul and Timothy, slaves of Christ Jesus,*ᵃ *to all God's people incorporate in Christ Jesus who are in Philippi, with the overseers*ᵇ *who serve:* ² *Grace to you and peace from God our Father and the Lord Jesus Christ.*

Notes

ᵃ Χριστὸς Ἰησοῦς: There is no textual variant here, but in several MSS of Paul's other letters the formula appears both as Ἰησοῦς Χριστός as well as Χριστὸς Ἰησοῦς (Rom 1:1; 1 Cor 1:1; Eph 1:1). In Philippians the following variations of this title appear: Ἰησοῦς Χριστός (1:6), 11, 19; κύριος Ἰησοῦς Χριστός 1:2; 2:11; 3:20; 4:23; Χριστός 1:10, 13, 15, 17, 18, 20, 21, 23, 27, 29; 2:1, 16, (30); 3:7, 8, 9, 18; Χριστὸς Ἰησοῦς ὁ κύριός μου 3:8; Ἰησοῦς 2:10.

ᵇ B² K 33 *al.* and Cassiodorus read συνεπισκόποις "to the fellow-bishops" (i.e. co-bishops with Paul and Timothy), for σὺν ἐπισκόποις, "with the bishops."

Form/Structure/Setting

This section follows a set pattern that Paul uses as an introduction to all his letters. It has three basic parts to it, and each part always appears in the same order: (1) the sender's name, (2) the name of the person or persons to whom the letter is sent, and (3) the greeting.

Although quite unlike the twentieth-century style of letter writing, this pattern, nevertheless, conforms closely to that of the letter-form of the first century and earlier. It is reminiscent, on the one hand, of ancient Near Eastern letters (cf. Dan 4:1: "King Nebuchadnezzer to all peoples, nations, and lan-guages that dwell in all the earth: Peace be multiplied to you"; Ezra 7:12; 2 Baruch 78:2)—a fact that points to the possibility of Aramaic influence on Pauline epistolography, especially if one considers "seriously the proposal that the Captivity Letters . . . were composed in Caesarea Maritima" (Fitz-myer, *JBL* 93 [1974] 201–25; see above, xli–xliv). It also recalls, on the other hand, the personal letters of the Greco-Roman period published and discussed by Deissmann (see *Light*, 148–217 and note this example: "Asclepiades, the son of Charmagon, to Portis, the son of Peramis, greeting (χαίρειν)," ibid. 152–53; see also Hunt and Edgar, *Papyri*, 2.549–601; cf. Acts 15:23; James 1:1). Thus Hellenism also had an influence on Paul's letter-form.

Although Paul may have owed much to both East and/or West for the basic form of his letters, so that the introductions of his letters, like their models, invariably followed the pattern, "A to B, greeting," yet Paul's own contribution to the history of letter writing should not be overlooked. He often expanded these conventional formulas and infused them with deep theological or christological meaning (cf. Rom 1:1–7).

It is important to recognize this "literary" form, the letter-form, for what it is. When Paul chose to express his ideas in this form, one can only surmise that he did so with a limited audience in mind—friends, for the most part, whom he knew personally and whom he knew were facing particular problems of faith and life. The content of his letters shows that Paul wrote with a keen awareness of apostolic authority, but the letter-form seems to indicate that he had no intention of leaving behind him masterpieces of literature or theological treatises for the world (but see Malherbe, *Ohio Journal of Religious Studies,* 5 [1977] 3–77, who notes that rhetorical theorists discussed the letter-form).

Comment

1. Παῦλος καὶ Τιμόθεος δοῦλοι Χριστοῦ Ἰησοῦ, "Paul and Timothy, slaves of Christ Jesus." The unique feature here is not that Paul links Timothy's name with his own, for Timothy was Paul's "son in the faith" (1 Cor 4:17), his close associate in the gospel (2 Cor 1:19) and his trusted emissary (Phil 2:19). Besides, Paul names other co-senders with him of his letters (1 Cor 1:1; 1 Thess 1:1; 2 Thess 1:1). Rather, the uniqueness lies in the fact that Paul permits the noun δοῦλοι ("slaves") to stand in apposition both to his own name *and* Timothy's, a unique feature in the literary legacy left by Paul. In all other letters he puts a distance between himself and his colleagues by describing only himself as "slave," or "apostle," or "prisoner" of Christ Jesus—never anyone else. If ever he does add a descriptive title to a fellow worker, he does so only with the word ἀδελφός ("brother"; 1 Cor 1:1; 2 Cor 1:1; Gal 1:2; Col 1:1; Philem 1).

From this observation it is clear that Paul always was conscious of his own supreme authority within the churches he founded and of his unique relationship to the risen Christ, a relationship so singular that no other person could share it. The fact that it *is shared* only this once demands explanation.

The explanation cannot lie in the fact that Timothy was associated with Paul in his imprisonment (Martin, 1976), for why then is the familiar distance again put between the apostle and Timothy in two of the other Prison Epistles (Col 1:1; Philem 1)? Nor can the explanation be that Timothy was co-author of the letter (Meyer, 11), or any part of it, because it is throughout far too personal for that. Paul's use of "I," "me," "my" pervades Philippians (51 times), while Timothy's name appears again only in 2:19, and then "in clear distinction from the author of the letter" (Collange). That Timothy was Paul's secretary or amanuensis (Müller) is not the explanation either. In Rom 16:22 Paul's secretary is named, and if it can be assumed that this chapter is an integral part of the Roman letter, it becomes obvious that for one to have been Paul's secretary was not, therefore, sufficient reason to have his name linked with that of the apostle in the salutation. Furthermore, to assume that Paul regularly dictated his letters to secretaries is a valid assumption (cf. 1 Cor 16:21; Gal 6:11; Col 4:8; 2 Thess 3:17; see Bahr, *JBL* 87 [1968] 27–41). But there is no evidence that will permit the assumption that Timothy was one of these secretaries. Nor can one say that Paul shared the title δοῦλος with Timothy because Timothy was a co-founder with him of the church at Philippi (Gnilka). It is true that Timothy was indeed with Paul when this

church began (Acts 16:1–15). But he was only a minor member of the missionary team, who apparently escaped the serious trouble Paul and Silas experienced because of his unobtrusiveness (Acts 16:16–40). What is more, it seems
that Paul even had to remind the Philippians of Timothy's worth and reliability,
of the quality of his character and the validity of his credentials (Phil 2:19–
24). Nor can the explanations that Paul wished to be courteous to a loved
associate (Keck, Caird), or to give wider scope and a more solid basis to
what he was going to say (Michael) be adequate explanations for such a
radical departure from Paul's standard procedure. Why then did the apostle
dare to share, for this one time only, his otherwise carefully and jealously
guarded uniqueness? The best explanation seems to be that Paul, by such
condescension, was most effectively able to teach the Philippians a lesson
they needed to learn—"that relationships in the bosom of the church between
collaborators were not those of authority, superiority or inferiority but of
humble equality" (Collange; cf. Phil 2:5–11).

Δοῦλοι Χριστοῦ Ἰησοῦ. The word δοῦλοι often translated "servants," literally
means "slaves," a word that carries the normally negative ideas of abasement,
subservience and total submissiveness. Slavery was a commonplace feature
of the Roman world of the first century and a fact of life seldom questioned
or challenged (OCD 843–44). There was no autonomy for the slave. His
own will was totally subject to the will of another so that he was a person
with "no right of personal choice" (Rengstorf, TDNT 2,261). The service
he provided was not voluntary but forced. He was totally in bondage to the
claims of his master. He had no rights and no freedoms.

It is possible then that Paul understood δοῦλοι in terms of this contemporary
cultural practice. He, therefore, would have viewed himself and Timothy as
persons bound over to Christ Jesus, owned by Christ Jesus (1 Cor 6:20),
possessing no rights of their own, totally at the service of their master. But
δοῦλοι Χριστοῦ Ἰησοῦ ("slaves of Christ Jesus") would not have been a repugnant
expression to Paul, as it would have been for his contemporaries—none of
whom would ever have described his own relationship to deity in terms of
slavery (Rengstorf, TDNT 2,262–65) but rather a liberating idea. For Paul
viewed himself and Timothy as slaves of One who was divine. Κύριος ("Lord"),
the common term for the master of slaves (Col 4:1) was also the Septuagint
word for Yahweh. It was this title, "Lord," that Paul regularly used as the
most important christological term to describe Jesus (cf. Phil 2:10–11). And,
paradoxically, for Paul to be a slave of this divine master was the only way
to be a truly free person—free from the tyranny of sin (Rom 6:18–22), of
fear (Gal 4:8–9), and of the law (Rom 7:1–6).

Δοῦλος, however, was used frequently in the Septuagint to describe Yahweh's special servants (Exod 14:3; Num 12:7; Jer 25:4; Ezek 38:17; Amos
3:7; Zech 1:6). It is possible, therefore, that this title may have had a quite
different meaning for Paul from that outlined above. Understood in the context of the OT, δοῦλος may have conveyed to Paul the idea of leader or prophet,
and he may have understood it as a title of esteem (Gnilka) to be used to
inform his readers of the fact that he and Timothy were two of the select
few who had the "God-given authority to speak and act in his name, as his
accredited (representatives)" (Martin, 1976). If so, δοῦλος consequently carried

for Paul not "the thought of unconditional vassalage and bodily ownership, but the thought that God is acting through" him. "Not servitude but instrumentality" stands in the foreground. The word then takes on a new theological meaning "in which the emphasis no longer rests on . . . the unfree condition of the man, but wholly upon the work and actions of God" (Sass, *ZNW* 40 [1941] 24–32, as quoted by Beare).

If one must choose between these two ideas, it appears that the better choice is to affirm that Paul derived the meaning of δοῦλος from his Hellenistic-Roman environment. For here at the outset of his letter to the Philippians Paul uses it to strike the note of devoted service and its consequent idea of subordination first and foremost to Christ Jesus (note that "Christ Jesus," or "Lord Jesus Christ" occurs three times in the salutation alone, vv 1, 2. See A. Escande, *Kyrios, Iésous, Christos. Notes exégetiques* [Paris: Librairie Protestante, 1970]), and second, to the church and its needs. Paul is going to stress throughout this letter a very Christian concept, the greatest person must be the servant (διάκονος) and the most important the slave (δοῦλος) of all (cf. Mark 10:43–44), a lesson the Philippians apparently were slow to learn.

Πᾶσιν τοῖς ἁγίοις ἐν Χριστῷ Ἰησοῦ, "to all God's people in Christ Jesus." Paul rarely uses the all-inclusive word πᾶς ("all") to address the readers of his letters (only in Rom 1:7 and Phil 1:1). He does so here, one suspects, because there was dissension in Philippi and not everyone was convinced that he was included in the apostle's concern. The startling frequency of the expression, "all of you," with which Paul continually addresses the Philippian Christians (1:4, 7 [twice], 8, 25; 2:17, 26; cf. 4:21, 23 ᵐᵍ) indicates that he is subtly but forcefully calling them to unity, assuring them all of his love and prayers, and telling them that he was writing not only to those who continually brought him joy (4:1), but also to those whose actions tended to fracture the church (4:2, 3). None was excluded.

ἅγιοι is often translated "saints." With this word Paul regularly addresses the Christians to whom he is writing, not to draw attention primarily to the ethical character of their lives (i.e. "saintly," "pious"), but to their special relationship to God; not here to their moral qualities as if there were no longer any sinners at Philippi, but to the new ground of their existence (Gnilka).

Ἅγιος has a long history of meaning. Originally it was applied only to the gods as beings who commanded religious awe (ἅγιος) or were worthy of veneration (ἄζεσθαι). Later it was also applied to persons and things, because of their special relation to the gods. By virtue of this special relationship, therefore, they were separated from the profane world about them so as to be ceremonially pure enough to perform special service for, or be used in special rites pertaining to, the worship of these gods.

In the LXX ἅγιος is used chiefly to translate קֶדֶשׁ (q-d-š), a Hebrew word with essentially the same meanings as the Greek word. Yahweh God is holy (Lev 19:2), and as such is different from, over against, set apart from, transcending, every created thing and the one who rightly commands awe and veneration (Isa 6:1–5). Because of God's special relation to parts of his creation, things also can be holy, e.g. the ground around a burning bush (Exod 3:5), Jerusalem (Isa 48:2), the temple (Isa 64:10), the Sabbath, garments, candlesticks, oil, swords, etc., and persons can be holy, even a whole nation. Yahweh God makes a covenant with Israel and as a result Israel is called holy, God's elect people, a nation separated from all the other nations of the world (Exod 19:5, 6; Lev 11:44, 45). Israel was holy because of God's gracious choice (A. Asting, *Die Heiligkeit im Urchristentum* [FRLANT 46. Göttingen: Vandenhoeck und Ruprecht, 1930] 133–51; see also Kuhn and Procksch, *TDNT* 1, 89–110; G. F. Moore, *Judaism in the First Centuries of the Christian Era* [Cambridge: University Press, 1927–30] 2, 102–103). These same ideas still cling to ἅγιος in the NT (see Matt 24:15; Mark 1:24; Luke 1:49; John 17:11; Acts 9:13; 1 Pet 2:9, 10). Therefore, to translate ἅγιοι as "God's people" rather than the traditional and often misunderstood "saints," is fully justified, capturing better the root meaning of the word, and showing more clearly that Paul viewed the members of the Christian church as the New Israel, the new community separated and dedicated to God, the eschatological people, the people of the end-times, to whom God will make good his promises (cf. Dan 7:18, 27).

This is not to say, however, that ethical ideas are totally foreign to ἅγιος (קָדֹשׁ, q-d-š). Quite the contrary. They were present in the OT (Lev 19:2–18), and they are present in the NT (1 Pet 1:16; cf. Matt 5:8; 1 Tim 1:15; 2 Tim 2:22). Since God is holy, that is to say that among other things God is perfect in purity and goodness and justice and love, it is expected that his special people will also possess personal purity and practice goodness, justice and love. Hence, ethics and religion belong together; relationship to God requires a moral response; God's people must live like God. But the point to be' made is that Paul used the word ἅγιοι here as a technical term to refer to people who are in a special relation to God (cf. ἅγιοι in 1:1; 4:21, 22 with ἁγνῶς in 1:17 ["purely," "from pure motives"] and ἁγνά in 4:8 ["pure"]).

Ἐν Χριστῷ Ἰησοῦ ("in Christ Jesus") modifies τοῖς ἁγίοις. The Philippians were holy, not through any merit of their own, but because they were "in Christ Jesus." The expression, ἐν Χριστῷ, first appears in the letters of Paul where it is used 164 times (not counting its appearances in the Pastorals). Other NT writers, interestingly, rarely use it. For Paul, then, ἐν Χριστῷ (also ἐν Χριστῷ Ἰησοῦ, ἐν κυρίῳ) seems to have been the key phrase by which he was able to describe the essence of the Christian life (cf. 1 Cor 1:30, 31).

The words are simple—"in Christ"—but their meaning is profound and elusive. Does this expression refer to some mystical ecstatic experience that follows some sacramental initiation rite resulting in the Christian becoming absorbed into Christ, just as the pagan initiate was absorbed into the divinity in the Greek mystery religions (Bousset, *Kyrios*, 164–69; but see Neugebauer, *In Christus*)? Does it mean that Christ must be understood as a semiphysical ethereal spirit that permeates the Christian and in which the Christian lives as air is in him and he in air (Deissmann, *Die neutestamentliche Formel*, 1892, 98)? Does it mean that instead of the Christian being in Christ (ἐν = location), Christ is the source, cause and power of the Christian's life (ἐν = instrument), that is, " 'in Christ' . . . means that . . . in him and not in me, salvation has taken place: therefore it is true for me. Christ is the instrument of God" (Conzelmann, *Outline*, 210; Büchsel, *ZNW* 42 [1949]; Bouttier, *En Christ*)? Is it a metaphor of personal communion with Christ, an expression for the most intimate relation between the believer and Christ (Kennedy, *Theology*, 121, 124; cf. the translation of the GNB: "To all God's people . . . who are in union with Christ Jesus")? Is it a phrase that "often simply replaces the adjective 'Christian' which (had) not yet been found" (Conzelmann, *Outline*, 209; cf. the translations of LB and Phillips)?

A more helpful way of getting at the meaning of ἐν Χριστῷ derives from recognizing that the early church viewed Christ as a universal person (Oepke, *TDNT* 2,542). Christ was indeed a single self who lived in space and time, but to Paul the risen Christ was more than an historical human being. Paul understood and experienced him to be cosmic Man. Just as Adam was a single self and yet corporate Man, one who embodied the whole world of mankind and included his descendants in himself and under himself, so for Paul Christ was the Last Adam, the progenitor of a new race of men (Rom 5:12–21; 1 Cor 15:22, 45–49; cf. Phil 1:1 [NEB]: "God's people incorporate in Christ Jesus"). "Paul had religious experiences in which the Jesus of Nazareth who had recently been crucified—this same person . . . was found to be more than individual. He was found to be an 'inclusive' personality. And this means, in effect, that Paul was led to conceive of Christ as any theist conceives of God: personal, indeed, but transcending the individual category. Christ is like the omnipresent deity 'in whom we live and move and have our being.' " "Jesus Christ . . . actually *is*, or constitutes that ideal society: He is the ultimate Adam, to be incorporated in whom is to belong in the renewed society" (Moule, *Origin*, 95, 126; see also Barrett, *First Adam to Last*, 73, 77, 78 and *passim;* E. E. Ellis, *Recent Interpreters*, 31–33; Longenecker, *Paul*, 160–70; Ridderbos, *Paul*, 58–62).

Σὺν ἐπισκόποις καὶ διακόνοις, "with the bishops and deacons." It is striking to observe that in Paul's lists of officers of the church—apostles, prophets, teachers, evangelists (1 Cor 12:28; Eph 4:11)—there is no mention made of bishops or deacons (unless, of course, they are referred to by different names, e.g. "helpers" and "administrators": ἀντιλήμψεις and κυβερνήσεις, 1 Cor 12:28). And nowhere else in Paul's letters do these two terms, "bishops and deacons," appear so coupled together. Hence, it has been thought difficult to determine whether they refer to administrative officers within the church at Philippi (cf. Ign. *Trall.* 2.1.2; 3.1; 7:2; *Phld.* 6.2) or simply to any person who might at any time be called upon to perform a particular function important to the welfare of the church.

The following general matters should be noted, however, before reflecting on the specific terms themselves: (1) The phrase ἐπίσκοποι καὶ διάκονοι may be explained grammatically as referring to two distinct groups of people, bishops *and* deacons, or it may also be correctly explained as referring to a single group of people, bishops, who are also deacons (see Moulton, *Grammar*, 3,335 on the epexegetical καί). (2) Paul mentions the ἐπίσκοποι καὶ διάκονοι in such a way as to distinguish them from the congregation. This implies that he considered them to be persons with some kind of official status. (3) Paul did not address himself to these "officers" over the head of the congregation. Rather, as was his custom elsewhere in his letters, he addressed the congregation; he addressed the bishops and deacons second and only in conjunction with the congregation (cf. also Acts 15:4, but contrast LB: "to the pastors and deacons and all the Christians in the city of Philippi"). One can infer from this that Paul did not perceive these as "lords" over Christ's church, but as individuals designated for special service within the church and perhaps subject to the church. (4) The terms are plural: "bishops and deacons." This means at least, then, that at the time Paul wrote there was no single chief officer (bishop) with his assistant (deacon) at Philippi (contrast this with Ign. *Smyrn.* 8. 1–2; 9. 1).

The word ἐπίσκοπος ("bishop") had a long history of usage before Paul employed it here, reaching far back into antiquity where the gods (cf. Job 20:29 LXX) were described as "watchers over" (ἐπίσκοποι) men and things that were committed to their protection (see LSJ for references). In Classical and Septuagint Greek ἐπίσκοπος also was used of humans who had functions to perform or who filled established offices—tutors, inspectors, scouts, army officers, watchmen, superintendents, officials associated with the temple, treasurers, and so on, were called ἐπίσκοποι (See LSJ; Num 4:16; 31:14; 2 Kings 11:18; 12:11; Neh 11:9; 1 Macc 1:51). Although this single word could describe so many different offices and functions, yet the one idea of "oversight" consistently ran as a common thread through all these various titles.

One also learns with interest that each of the Essene communities (Jewish ascetic communities existing in Palestine from about the second century B.C. to about the second century A.D.) was administered by a supervisor (*mᵉbaqqēr*) who had to be at least thirty years old, who was viewed as a shepherd of his sheep and spiritual father of his people, and who was responsible, among other things, for receiving gifts for charity from the community and overseeing the distribution of these gifts (CD 13.7–9; 14.8, 9, 13: See J. Jeremias, *Jerusalem in the Time of Jesus* [Tr. F. H. and C. H. Cave. Philadelphia: Fortress Press, 1969] 260–61). Jeremias notes that the title *mᵉbaqqēr* ("supervisor") "corresponds literally with the Greek ἐπίσκοπος," and that "the position and the functions of the *mᵉbaqqēr* are identical with those of a bishop in the Syrian *Didaskalia.*" He suggests, therefore, that the *mᵉbaqqēr* might have been the model for the NT ἐπίσκοπος (*Jerusalem,* 261; see also B. Reicke, "Constitution of the Primitive Church," in K. Stendahl [ed.] *The Scrolls and the NT* [New York: Harper and Bros., 1957] 143–56, and most recently B. E. Thiering, *JBL* 100 [1981] 59–74, who concludes that now there is "even better reason for supposing that the earliest Christian church adopted the office of bishop from the Essene lay communities," 74).

In light of this it is by no means unthinkable that from its inception, even in that early period when the Spirit was everything (Collange), the Christian church developed some sort of organizational structure, most likely along the lines of its Jewish counterparts. This development may have taken place, for reasons unknown (but see Beare), more rapidly in Philippi than elsewhere. If so, then ἐπίσκοποι in Phil 1:1 probably do not refer to functions that just any Christian on any required occasion could be led to fulfill (see Schweizer, *Church Order;* von Campenhausen, *Ecclesiastical Authority;* M. A. Chevallier, *Espirit de Dieu, Paroles d'hommes* [Neuchâtel: Delachaux et Niestlé, 1966] 148–50), but to officials, that is specific individuals who were appointed by the apostle and his companions (cf. Acts 14:23) and whose duties were fairly well defined. They were in some sense to govern, to administer, to oversee the affairs, both material and spiritual, of the community (cf. Acts 20:28). The idea of "supervision" or "protective care" still lay at the heart of the meaning of ἐπίσκοπος, even after centuries of usage (Beyer, *TDNT* 2,610, 615–16).

Διάκονος ("deacon") like ἐπίσκοπος ("bishop") was commonly employed by the Greeks. They used it to describe one who was a servant or responsible for certain welfare duties within the city, or a messenger, or an attendant in a temple or religious guild (LSJ). Often the negative ideas of servility or meniality were present when διάκονος was used—ideas repugnant to the Greeks. They believed that ruling, not serving, was the proper activity for mankind (Beyer, *TDNT* 2,88). Service, to be sure, is seen in a better light when rendered to the state or to God (Epict. *Diss.* 3.22.69), but in such instances, service to people faded almost into obscurity.

Διάκονος appears infrequently in the LXX, but there it is used to describe a loftier kind of service—adviser to the king, for example (Esth 1:10; 2:2) or the king's bodyguards (4 Macc 9:17). In the New Testament, διάκονος is elevated to the ultimate of titles to describe those involved in beneficent activity. Here value-systems are completely reversed, and Jesus is responsible for this change. He consciously opposed the world's idea of values and substituted his own: greatness lies not in freedom from serving, but in serving (Mark 10:43), in being the servant (διάκονος) of all. Hence, Paul sees rulers as servants (διάκονοι) of God (Rom 13:4), distinguished Christian persons as servants of the church or of Christ (Rom 16:1; 1 Cor 3:5; Eph 6:21; Col 1:7), Christ as the servant of the Jews (Rom 15:8) and himself as a servant of the gospel (Col 1:23).

Service or ministering to others, then, lies at the heart of the word διάκονος. Thus if here in Phil 1:1 the διάκονοι refer to people appointed to religious office (see MM, διάκονος) and are to be distinguished from the ἐπίσκοποι, they would quite likely be assistants to the bishops, people primarily responsible for the more menial tasks such as taking care of the needs of the poor and the sick in the community, and those in prison (cf. Rom 12:7; 16:1–2; 1 Cor 12:28).

It is possible, however, to translate the expression, ἐπίσκοποι καὶ διάκονοι, as "bishops who are deacons" or "overseers who serve." This is an ancient interpretation (Chrysostom) but it has been rejected, perhaps too hastily, by most scholars. Yet notice the following things: (1) "Bishops and deacons" looks very much like a ready-made, stock phrase (Lemaire, *Les ministères*, 97–103). (2) This same coupling of terms not only appears in Phil 1:1 but also in two other early Christian texts, *1 Clem* 42:4–5 and *Did* 15.1, whereas in Timothy bishops are discussed separately (1 Tim 3:1–7) from deacons (1 Tim 3:8–13). (3) It is worth noting that Clement speaks of the apostles appointing their first converts as "bishops and deacons" and then he legitimizes this action by a free quotation from Isa 60:17, where in typical Hebrew parallelism bishops and deacons are equated: "For the Scripture says . . . 'I will establish their bishops (ἐπισκόπους) in righteousness and their deacons (διακόνους) in faith' " (42:4–5). (4) The conjunction καὶ in ἐπίσκοποι καὶ διάκονοι legitimately may be used to point to a *single* group of people known as ἐπίσκοποι καὶ διάκονοι (see above, 7). (5) Ἐπίσκοπος ("bishop") and πρεσβύτερος ("elder") were synonymous terms in NT times, the latter, perhaps, the title of the office and the former a description of the duties of the officer (Acts 20:28; Tit 1:5–7; see Lightfoot, 95–99). (6) Polycarp speaks about πρεσβύτεροι ("elders") καὶ διάκονοι ("deacons") in a way that does not seem to distinguish them from mere deacons (Pol. Phil. 5.2,3). (7) Although certain early Christian writers did view "bishops," "deacons," and "elders" as separate and distinct offices (cf. 1 Tim 3:1–10; Ign. Smyrn. 8.1–2), this was not universally so. Thus it is reasonable to assume that at one stage of the tradition elders may have been called "bishops and deacons," or "bishops and elders" may have been referred to as "deacons."

If there were not two groups of officers in Phil 1:1, why then the double title, ἐπίσκοποι καὶ διάκονοι? The answer lies "in Pauline Theology and also in the particular circumstances presented by the Philippian community at the time when the letter was written," i.e. dissension, lack of humility, and self-serving attitudes (cf. Phil 2:1–5)—circumstances that perhaps had their origin among the leaders of the community. So in beginning his letter Paul "tried gentleness and persuasion—and at once he started by giving a title to the leaders of the church, something he normally avoided. At the same time he reminds them that authority before all else means responsibility, and he addresses them only after 'all the saints' whose edification (as 'diakonoi') they have been called to serve" (Collange).

If this interpretation can be sustained, no further inquiry needs to be made into why Paul, contrary to his custom, singled out certain officers of the church for address at the beginning of his letter. It was not, then, because they had control of the treasury and were chiefly responsible for the gift of money sent to Paul, nor because Paul felt a special need of bringing his commendation of Epaphroditus (Phil 2:25–30) to the attention of the leaders of the church, nor because the members of the church lacked due respect for these leaders, but simply because by using this stock expression, ἐπίσκοποι καὶ διάκονοι, "overseers who serve," Paul was articulating an idea that the Philippian officials needed to learn and adopt, one that is wholly consistent with Paul's own understanding of office within the Church (Rom 1:1; Phil 1:1), and with the teaching and practice of his Lord (Mark 10:45; John 13:3–17; Phil 2:5–11).

Translators, however, differ considerably on how to render ἐπίσκοποι καὶ διάκονοι: "Bishops and deacons" (AV, ASV, RSV, NEB), "overseers and deacons," (NIV, NASB), "church leaders and helpers" (GNB), "overseers and assistants" (Williams), "ministers of the Church and their assistants" (Weymouth), "superintendents and assistants" (Goodspeed), "overseers and ministers" (Darby), "presidents and assistant officers" (Twentieth Century NT).

2. Χάρις ὑμῖν καὶ εἰρήνη, "grace to you and peace." The salutation of the letter-form current in the Greco-Roman world of Paul's day invariably concluded with the word χαίρειν ("greetings") or the phrases πλεῖστα χαίρειν or πολλὰ χαίρειν ("abundant greetings"; cf. also Acts 15:23; 23:26; James 1:1; see Edgar & Hunt, Papyri 1,269–395; E. Lohmeyer, "Briefliche Grussüberschriften," ZNW 26 [1927] 158–73). Paul follows this form. But in a clever play on the sound of the standardized and expected χαίρειν (chairein, "greet-

ings") he deliberately substitutes χάρις (*charis*, "grace"; see J. Weiss, *Der erste Korintherbrief* [Göttingen: Vandenhoeck und Ruprecht, 1910] 4). This latter word is a definitely Christian word used 155 times in the NT and a key term in Paul's letters, used by him approximately 100 times. Through it he conveys to his readers more than his own personal greetings. He stresses each time the enormous idea of the free, spontaneous, unmerited favor of God. God is now "for them," having acted in grace toward them on the basis of the death of Christ (cf. Gal 2:15–21; see Conzelman, *TDNT* 9,394; H. Küng, *On Being a Christian* [Tr. E. Quinn. Garden City: Doubleday, 1976] 249–77).

But Paul changes the standardized Greco-Roman formula of salutation still further. Correspondence of that period generally limited the greeting to a single word (χαίρειν) with its appropriate modifiers. Paul, however, not only replaces χαίρειν with χάρις but regularly adds to it the word εἰρήνη ("peace"). Χάρις καὶ εἰρήνη, then, is his most frequently used formula of greeting (Rom 1:7; 1 Cor 1:3; 2 Cor 1:2; Gal 1:3; Eph 1:2; Phil 1:2; Col 1:2; 1 Thess 1:1; 2 Thess 1:2; Philem 3; but cf. 1 Tim 1:2; Tit 1:2, many MSS of Tit 1:4 and 2 John 3, where the greeting χάρις, ἔλεος, εἰρήνη ["grace, mercy and peace"] appears). He thus combines western and eastern salutations in his new formula, "peace" being the standard Jewish or Oriental form of greeting (cf. Gen 43:23; Ezra 4:17; Dan 3:98 [4:1]; 2 Apoc Bar 78:2; see Fitzmyer, *JBL* 93 [1974] 214–16). But once again the commonplace is used in an uncommon way—an ordinary salutation is elevated into a benediction (Michael), for εἰρήνη, like the word "grace" is linked up with the activity of God. As a result "peace" comes to mean in Paul "harmony," "tranquillity," "wholeness," "well-being," "salvation" of the total person, reconciliation of that person to God—peace at the deepest level. The whole greeting, χάρις καὶ εἰρήνη, therefore, states that the OT dream for the future is being fulfilled (Isa 11:1–9; Houlden, 50), and, therefore, it "becomes an epitome of all that is central and essential in the christian religion" (Jones; Foerster *TDNT* 3,411–16).

Ἀπὸ θεοῦ πατρὸς ἡμῶν καὶ κυρίου Ἰησοῦ Χριστοῦ, "from God our Father and the Lord Jesus Christ." This phrase, never found in Greco-Roman correspondence, now carries the salutation on to extraordinary heights of meaning. Commonplace to Christians today, it must surely have been striking to those who first received such an address. For by this modification of the traditional letter-form Paul says, in effect, that it is God who ultimately salutes them, and he does so with grace and peace. God greets them as the ultimate source of all that is good. From now on no evil "destiny has power, validity or meaning. . . . Words like εἱμαρμένη ("destiny") or μοῖρα ("fate") are never found in the New Testament [because God] has overcome both the cosmic anxiety of the world of antiquity, and the very concept of fate itself" (Stauffer, *TDNT* 3,118).

The expression, πατρὸς ἡμῶν ("our Father"), echoing the Lord's prayer (cf. Matt 6:9), indicates (1) Paul's acquaintance with the gospel tradition, (2) the intimacy of the relationship that now exists between God and man, and (3) the reality of personal faith on the part of writer and reader—a faith that makes it possible for both to think of God as "our Father."

The phrase καὶ κυρίου Ἰησοῦ Χριστοῦ ("and the Lord Jesus Christ") on the surface seems open to more than one interpretation. The καί ("and") could coordinate κυρίου Ἰησοῦ Χριστοῦ with ἡμῶν in order to emphasize the *subordination* of Christ to the Father—"From God the Father *of* us and *of* the Lord Jesus Christ." (1) This idea is not foreign to the NT, for the very expression, "The God and Father of our Lord Jesus Christ" is found in the writings attributed to Paul (Rom 15:6; 2 Cor 1:3; 11:31; Eph 1:3; Col 1:3) and to others (1 Pet 1:3; cf. 1 John 1:3). (2) Had Paul wished to say something different from this, i.e., had he wished to say *"from* God and *from* our Lord Jesus Christ" (cf. κJV and JB) and not "from God the Father of Christ," he might have been expected to repeat the preposition ἀπό ("from") before κυρίου Ἰησοῦ Χριστοῦ (cf. 2 John 3 and Rev 1:4-5).

More likely, however, Paul intended the καί to couple κυρίου Ἰησοῦ Χριστοῦ with θεοῦ πατρός to emphasize the *coordination* of Christ with God the Father as the co-source with him of grace and peace, and for the following reasons: (1) One must not think of the ἡμῶν as a separate entity that could in any way be construed as a coordinate with κυρίου Ἰησοῦ Χριστοῦ. As has been pointed out above, ἡμῶν is such an integral part of the traditional formula "our Father" that the two words, πατρὸς ἡμῶν must be treated as a single phrase, with πατρός the significant substantive. For all practical purposes then ἡμῶν is grammatically nonexistent, and thus in no way is it able to be a coordinate with κυρίου Ἰησοῦ Χριστοῦ.

(2) In the majority of instances in a nonliterary style of writing the preposition is not repeated, although we might wish it were. So although Paul truly meant *"from* God our Father and *from* the Lord Jesus Christ" by his phrase ἀπὸ θεοῦ πατρὸς ἡμῶν καὶ κυρίου Ἰησοῦ Χριστοῦ, it is to be expected, on the basis of contemporary unofficial documents, that he would quite naturally and quite unconsciously omit the second preposition before the phrase connected by καί (see Moulton, *Grammar,* 3, 275).

(3) Those modifications of the Pauline formula, ἀπὸ θεοῦ πατρὸς ἡμῶν καὶ κυρίου Ἰησοῦ Χριστοῦ (*a*) that either omit ἡμῶν altogether (several important MSS of 2 Thess 1:2), (*b*) that remove it from its place after πατρός and place it at the end of the phrase (1 Tim 1:2; 2 Tim 1:2; Tit 1:4), or (*c*) that add a second preposition before κυρίου (2 John 3) seem consciously designed to remove any possibility of coordinating κυρίου Ἰησοῦ Χριστοῦ with the wrong word, and to make crystal clear that Paul fully intended to make κυρίου Ἰησοῦ Χριστοῦ coordinate with θεοῦ πατρός. The Lord Jesus Christ is, therefore, as much the source of "grace and peace" as is "God the Father." Thus, in the words of Moule, "The position here occupied by Jesus in relation to God, as well as in many other opening formulae of the New Testament letters, is nothing short of astounding—especially when one considers that they are written by monotheistic Jews with reference to a figure of recently past history" (*Origin,* 150)—for it appears to put Jesus Christ and God the Father on an equal basis.

Explanation

The introduction to Paul's letters follows a basically uniform structure that corresponds closely to a contemporary, widespread, stereotyped letter-form involving three elements: sender, addressee and greeting. But Paul is never content to shut himself up to just these three elements when he writes, e.g. "Paul, to the Church at Philippi, greetings!" On the contrary, he fills them with matters of great mutual concern to himself and the community to which he writes, and raises them to the level of theological statements to match individual needs, always, however, centering in Christ (notice, the name Christ Jesus occurs three times in the opening two verses). Hence, the precise contents of the prescripts in Paul's letters vary. Here two important features, unique among the Pauline letters, appear: (1) Paul allows Timothy to share the same "platform" with him, and (2) Paul addresses the "bishops and deacons" within the Church. Both of these speak to the concrete situation at Philippi: How is one to begin to attack selfishness and disunity? By subtly showing from the very beginning that in the Church seniority and high calling do not put one Christian leader above another (Paul and Timothy together are one—they are slaves of Christ Jesus) and that "church supervisors" are not above serving, but are by virtue of their office, called to serve (to be *diakonoi*) ministering to the needs of their fellows.

B. Thanksgiving and Prayer (1:3–11)

Bibliography

Bultmann, R. *Der Stil der paulinischen Predigt und die Kynisch-Stoische Diatribe.* FRLANT 13. Göttingen; Vandenhoeck und Ruprecht, 1910. **Davies, J. L.** "St. Paul's χάρις." *Expositor,* 4th series, 5 (1892) 343–46. **Deissmann, A.** *Light.* **Dewailley, L. M.** "La part prise à l'Évangile (Phil I. 5)." *RB* 80 (1973) 247–60. **Doerne, M.** *Die alten Episteln; homiletische Auslegung.* Göttingen: Vandenhoeck und Ruprecht, 1967. **Eichholz, G.** "Bewahren und Bewähren des Evangeliums: der Leitfaden von Phil 1–2." *Hören und Handeln. Festschrift für E. Wolf,* ed. H. Gollwitzer and H. Traub. Munich: C. Kaiser, 1962. **Gaide, G.** "L'amour de Dieu en nous (Ph 1. 4–6. 8–11)." *Assemblées du Seigneur* 6 (1969) 62–69. **Garland, D. E.** "Philippians 1:1–26: The Defense and Confirmation of the Gospel." *RevExp* 77 (1980) 327–36. **Harder, G.** *Paulus und das Gebet.* Gütersloh: Bertelsmann, 1936. **Holzmeister, U.** " 'Viscera Christi.' " *VD* 16 (1936) 161–65. **Hunt, A. S. and Edgar, E. E.** *Select Papyri.* 1,289–395; 2,549–601. **Kennedy, G. A.** *Classical Rhetoric and Its Christian and Secular Tradition from Ancient to Modern Times.* Chapel Hill, NC: University of North Carolina Press, 1980. **O'Brien, P. T.** "The Fellowship Theme in Philippians." *Reformed Theological Review* 37 (1978) 9–18. ———. *Introductory Thanksgivings in the Letters of Paul.* NovTSup 49. Leiden: Brill, 1977. **Ogara, F.** " 'Socios gaudii mei omnes vos esse': notae in Phil 1:6–11." *VD* 15 (1935) 324–30. **Omanson, R. L.** "A note on the Translation of Philippians 1:3–5." *BT* 29 (1978) 244–45. **Schubert, P.** "Form and Function of the Pauline Thanksgivings." *ZNW* 20 (1939) 71–82. **Weiss, J.** *Beiträge zur paulinischen Rhetorik.* Göttingen: Vandenhoeck und Ruprecht, 1897. **White, J. L.** *The Form and Function of the Body of the Greek Letter.* Missoula, MT: Scholars Press, 1972.

Translation

[3] *I thank my God*[a] *every time I mention you in my prayers.* [4] *Always in every prayer I pray, I pray for all of you with joy* [5] *because you have been partners with me in the gospel from the first day until now.* [6] *And I am sure that God who began this good work through you will bring it to completion at the day of Christ Jesus.*[b]

⁷ *Indeed it is only right that I should feel like this about all of you, because you hold me in such affection, and because all of you are sharers together with me in the privilege*ᶜ *that is mine both of being in prison and of defending and vindicating the gospel.* ⁸ *For God is my witness that I yearn for all of you with deep affection that comes from Christ Jesus.* ⁹ *And I pray that your love may keep on increasing*ᵈ *still more and more in deeper knowledge and broader perception,* ¹⁰ *in order that you may approve what is excellent, be pure and harmless in preparation for the day of Christ,* ¹¹ *and be filled with the fruit of righteousness that Jesus Christ produces— and all this for the glory and praise of God.*ᵉ

Notes

ᵃ D F G b Ambrosiaster have ἐγὼ μὲν εὐχαριστῶ τῷ κυρίῳ ἡμῶν ("I for my part thank our Lord"). This reading has little MSS support and no theological support. Paul never "gives thanks to the Lord"—only "to God," yet it is adopted by K. Barth and others.

ᵇ ℵ A pm read Ἰησοῦ Χριστοῦ ("Jesus Christ").

ᶜ Eberhard Nestle's brilliant conjectural reading—χρείας ("need"), for χάρις ("grace")—"All of you have been sharers with me in my need"—has not been adopted.

ᵈ B D pc read the aorist, περισσεύσῃ for the present tense, περισσεύῃ. The present tense better fits the context.

ᵉ D has the curious reading καὶ ἔπαινον Χριστοῦ ("and praise of Christ"); F G have καὶ ἔπαινόν μοι ("and my praise"); P ⁴⁶ has θεοῦ καὶ ἔπαινόν μοι ("(for the glory) of God and my praise"). Could one of these ill-supported readings be original? It is hard to imagine how they came into existence if the original reading was "(for the glory) and praise of God."

Form/Structure/Setting

Although the major part of Paul's education was under the direction of Jewish Rabbis (see above, xlix–xli), it is inconceivable that the rhetorical schools common in the Hellenized cities of the East played no part in his intellectual development. If only indirectly, through the Rabbis, Paul became familiar with the rhetorical conventions of speeches in the law courts, the oral teachings of Greek philosophers and the conventions of Greek letter-writing. Some of his letters seem even to indicate the influence on them "of the arrangement of contents, argumentation, and figures of speech of classical rhetoric" (Kennedy, *Classical Rhetoric,* 130; Betz, *Galatians,* 14–23; cf. Bultmann, *Der Stil* and Weiss, *Paulinische Rhetorik*).

Paul's letter to the Philippians, though far less formal and less carefully developed than his letters to the Galatians or to the Romans, nevertheless anticipates the parts of the Classical oration which were later adapted into a standard five-part epistolary structure: (1) The *salutatio* or greeting, (2) the *captatio benevolentiae* or exordium, which secured the good will of the recipient; (3) the *narratio* (4) the *petitio* or specific request, demand of announcement, and (5) the *conclusio* which was usually relatively simple (see Kennedy, *Classical Rhetoric,* 186; cf. also White, *Form and Function*).

The form of this section (1:3–11) seems to answer to the *captatio benevolentiae,* for Paul here formally secures the good will of the Philippians by letting them know how thankful to God he is for them (1:3), how deeply he loves them (1:7, 8) and how regularly he prays for them (1:9).

As in the salutation (1:1, 2) Paul again seems consciously to be following the Hellenistic letter-writing conventions of his day—conventions that he developed and enriched, to be sure, from the piety and liturgy of Judaism on the one hand (2 Macc 1:3–5), and his own Christian ideas and practices on the other. But it is incorrect to imply, as does Gnilka (42), that the Jewish community-letters (*jüdische Gemeindebriefe*) were the only, or even the primary, models that Paul used to construct his own epistles. The following pagan letter, dated in the second century A.D., reveals close parallels to Phil 1:1–11: "Apion to Epimachus his father and lord (τῷ πατρὶ καὶ κυρίῳ), very many greetings (πλεῖστα χαίρειν). Before all else I pray (εὔχομαι) for your health . . . I thank (εὐχαριστῶ) the Lord Serapis . . ." (Edgar & Hunt, *Papyri*, 1,305; see also 1,274, 283, 303, 307, 317, 319. See Schubert, *Form and Function*, for a survey of all the surviving parallels; C. K. Barrett, *The New Testament Background: Selected Documents* [New York: MacMillan, 1957] 27–29; O'Brien, *Introductory Thanksgiving;* Roller, *Das Formular*, 63).

Recognizing the carefully structured nature of this section (1:3–11), confined as it is by liturgical idiom and epistolary convention, Wiles nevertheless sees it functioning as a prologue that sets the tone of the letter and anticipates the major themes that bind the whole letter together (*Paul's Intercessory Prayers* [Cambridge: University Press, 1974] 206–207): gratitude, affection, joy, thanksgiving, the importance of fellowship (κοινωνία), growth in Christ, the Day of Christ, perfection, Paul's imprisonment, and so on (see also Garland, *RevExp* 77 [1980] 328–32 and Schubert, *Form and Function*, 71–82). Thus Paul acknowledges the rhetorical patterns of his day, welcomes their availability, and ably adapts them to and employs them in the cause of Christ.

Comment

3. Εὐχαριστῶ τῷ θεῷ μου, "I thank my God." Adhering to a beautiful secular custom, Paul begins his letter with thanks to God (Deissmann, *Light*, 168, n. 3). But only in Rom 1:8; 1 Cor 1:4 (?) and Philem 4 is the form as personal and intimate as it is here: "*I* thank *my* God." The apostle stands alone before his God in prayer (contrast Col 1:3; 1 Thess 1:2; 2 Thess 1:3). The joint relationship with Timothy that was so apparent in the salutation (1:1) has disappeared.

In thus expressing his gratitude, Paul shows (1) that this prayer is not a community-prayer for the church at Philippi, but his own—one that reveals his personal state of mind toward the Christians there—that of complete thankfulness for each one of them (Gnilka), (2) that he keenly senses a close personal and vital relationship with and dependence upon God—"my God" (cf. Acts 27:23), and (3) that he feels at liberty freely to supplement a common Hellenistic letter-form with expressions of religious piety derived from his Jewish background (cf. Pss 22:1; 63:1; 1 QH 11.3 in A. Dupont-Sommer, *Essene Writings from Qumran* [Tr. G. Vermes. New York: World Publishing Co., 1962] 236). Thus Paul takes a colorless, customary convention, reworks it and makes it express the intensity of his devotion to God and of his feelings for his friends.

Ἐπὶ πάσῃ τῇ μνείᾳ ὑμῶν, "every time I mention you in prayer." Several exegetical difficulties present themselves in this brief expression. (1) The first has to do with the meaning of ἐπί with the dative. Does it mean "because of," as it may, especially when it follows a verb that expresses feelings or emotions (εὐχαριστῶ), or does it convey, as it also may, the idea of time and thus mean, "at the time of"? (2) The second difficulty has to do with the phrase πάσῃ τῇ μνείᾳ: (a) Paul alone of the NT writers uses the word μνεία (Rom 1:9; Eph 1:16; Phil 1:3; 1 Thess 1:2; 3:6; Philem 4). Does he do so to convey the idea of "recollection" or "remembrance," or the idea of "mentioning someone (in prayer)"? (b) How is πάσῃ τῇ μνείᾳ to be translated? Usually when πᾶς means "all" or "every" it stands outside the article-noun unit (C. F. D. Moule, *An Idiom Book of the New Testament* [Cambridge: University Press, 1963] 93). Can the phrase ἐπὶ πάσῃ τῇ μνείᾳ be as general, then, as *"whenever* someone mentions/remembers another" (cf. JB, NEB, Phillips)? Or must it mean "every mention/remembrance of another" (cf. AV, NIV)?

(3) The third problem has to do with the genitive, ὑμῶν. Is it objective—"I remember/mention *you,"* or subjective—"You mention/remember (me)"? Both are grammatically possible.

Towards a solution: To translate the expression ἐπὶ πάσῃ τῇ μνείᾳ ὑμῶν as *"for* all your remembrance of me" and to link it with verse 5, seemingly solves all difficulties and results in a translation that makes excellent sense: "I thank my God because of your every remembrance of me (v 3) . . . and because of (ἐπί) your partnership in the gospel from the first day until now" (v 5). Verse 4 must, therefore, be understood as a parenthesis. "There is everything to commend this interpretation, not the least the fact that it shows how Paul expresses his thanks for the Church's love-gift right at the head of the letter. He does not . . . leave his 'Thank you' until a final section (in ch 4)" (Martin, 1976; so Ewald-Wohlenberg).

Attractive as this interpretation is, the data do not seem to support it: (1) Martin claims that Paul Schubert (*Form and Function,* 71–82) has demonstrated that "in the other Pauline letters *apart from Philippians* [italics mine] the construction *epi* (for) with the dative case . . . invariably introduces the cause for which thanks are offered" (Martin, 1976). But can this be so? In only *one* other letter does Paul express his reason for giving thanks (εὐχαριστεῖν) in the opening part of his letter by using ἐπί with the dative (1 Cor 1:4; cf. also 2 Cor 9:15). Everywhere else this idea is expressed either by the conjunction ὅτι (Rom 1:8; 1 Cor 1:14; 1 Thess 2:13; 2 Thess 1:3; 2:3) or by the prepositions περί or ὑπέρ with the genitive (Eph 1:16; Col 1:3; 1 Thess 1:2). Hence, although ἐπί with the dative *may* express the reason for Paul's gratitude it does not of necessity do so here.

(2) In the OT there were set times when the pious prayed (Ps 5:3; Ezra 9:5; Ps 55:17; Dan 6:10; 1 Chron 23:30). And it is evident from Rabbinic literature that this practice continued on beyond NT times (Ber.4.1; see "Prayer," in *Encyclopedia Judaica,* 13,982; E. P. Sanders, *Paul and Palestinian Judaism* [London: SCM Press, 1977] 223). Hence, the expression ἐπὶ πάσῃ τῇ μνείᾳ suggests not so much the possibility that Paul was giving thanks *for* something, but that he was giving thanks *at* those formal times of prayer which accorded with the customs of his Jewish heritage, and to which he adhered even as a Christian. At every one (ἐπὶ πάσῃ) of these prayer times he was compelled by love to mention his Philippian friends. This means,

then, that Paul gave thanks not whenever he happened to remember them, but that he regularly gave thanks for them and mentioned them to God at set times of prayer.

(3) It is unambiguously clear from Paul's use of μνεία with the genitive elsewhere in his letters that it is *he* (or he and his companions) who does the remembering or mentioning of someone else and *not* the other way around (Rom 1:9; Eph 1:16; 1 Thess 1:2; Philem 4).

4. Although Paul never allowed elegance of speech to detract from his message (1 Cor 2:1), it is clear, nonetheless, that he was aware of the rhetorical elegances current in his day. On occasion he even made use of them. Here in vv 3–4 he indulges in alliteration in π (P) and in a play on related sounds by a deliberate repetition of the same word in different forms—πάσῃ . . . πάντοτε . . . πάσῃ . . . πάντων (vv 3, 4). Thus it is clear that v 4 is so closely tied to v 3 by these figures of speech that it must not be thought of as a parenthesis as some have suggested (see Martin, 1959, following Lightfoot; see also Omanson, *BT* 29 [1978] 244–45). The rhetorical flare Paul employs here serves forcibly to arrest the attention of his readers and focus it upon several important points: (1) The intense personal nature of his prayer (δέησίς μου ὑπὲρ ὑμῶν, *"my* prayer for *you"*). (2) the constancy of his prayer (πάντοτε, and the present participle ποιούμενος), (3) the all-inclusiveness of his prayer (ὑπὲρ πάντων ὑμῶν)—none of the Philippian Christians for any reason whatsoever was excluded from the apostle's love and concern, and (4) the spontaneousness of his prayers. He prayed for them with joy (μετὰ χαρᾶς). Paul's attitude toward the Philippians made his praying for them a delight, not a chore.

Δέησις, "prayer." This word appears twice in v 4 and it is most often translated as given above (RSV, NEB, NIV). But it is not the usual word for prayer (προσευχή, cf. 1:9) that Paul uses in the beginning sections of his letters (cf. Rom 1:10; 1 Thess 1:2; Philem 4). The original meaning of δέησις is "lack" or "need." It comes therefore to be used for specific prayers in specific situations for God to fulfill a real need that only God can (Luke 22:32; Heb 5:7; Rom 1:10—a meaning it retains even when "the object of the prayer is not mentioned and the situation provides no clue" (Greeven, *TDNT* 2,41). Thus the idea of intercession is always close at hand (cf. Rom 10:1—someone pleading with God to fill up that which is lacking in another. Paul knowing what the Philippians have need of—unity, humility, mutual concern, etc.— prays (δέησις) for them. The Philippians, on the other hand, knowing what Paul needs—release from prison—pray (δέησις) for him (1:19). There exists then between the apostle and his beloved congregation a mutual understanding and affection, which prompts each to plead that God will meet the particular needs of the other. Intercession indeed is the fundamental response of love within the brotherhood of believers (cf. 1 John 5:16, 17; see Gnilka, 44; Stauffer, *Theology,* 194).

Μετὰ χαρᾶς, "with joy." The theme of joy that pervades Philippians begins here, linked with prayer. It may be easy enough to translate the words χαρά and χαίρειν as "joy" and "rejoicing," but it is not as easy to understand the concept. Whatever it is, seemingly it cannot be affected by external happenings. Personal hostilities against himself, imprisonment or the prospect of a violent death cannot rob Paul of joy (1:18; 2:17). To quote Karl Barth, joy "is a defiant 'nevertheless,' which Paul sets like a full stop against" resentment and fear that might otherwise well up within him (*Philippians*, 120). And yet, at the same time, joy seems to be something that *can* be affected by external happenings: (1) The Philippian church was Paul's joy, or the source of his joy, *if they continued to "stand firm in the Lord"* (4:1). (2) The Philippians were at least capable of increasing, if not diminishing the amount of Paul's joy. Their positive response to his plea for unity, for example, would make his joy complete (2:2). (3) Had Epaphroditus' illness resulted in his death, it would have brought down upon Paul sorrow upon sorrow (λύπη, the opposite of χαρά, 2:27; see 2 Cor 2:3). Epaphroditus' recovery, however, was grounds for rejoicing (2:28, 29).

What then would the Philippians have understood by Paul's use of χαρά and χαίρειν, "joy" and "rejoicing"—words that recur fourteen times in this brief letter (more times than in any other of Paul's writings) and with apparently conflicting meaning? The Philippians' resolution of this conflict and their understanding of "joy" came about by listening to what else Paul had to say to them about the subject. They thus came to realize that when he talked of joy he was, in reality, describing a settled state of mind characterized by εἰρήνη ("peace"), an attitude that viewed the world with all of its ups and downs with equanimity, a confident way of looking at life that was rooted in faith (τῆς πίστεως), that is, in a keen awareness of and trust in the living Lord of the Church (1:25, notice the definite article with "faith"). Again and again the command is, "Rejoice *in the Lord!*" (3:1; 4:4, 10). Hence, for Paul joy is more than a mood or an emotion. Joy is an understanding of existence that encompasses both elation and depression, that can accept with creative submission events which bring delight or dismay because joy allows one to see beyond any particular event to the sovereign Lord who stands above all events and ultimately has control over them. Joy, to be sure, "includes within itself readiness for martyrdom" (Lohmeyer), but equally, the opportunity to go on living and serving (2:27–29; see Conzelmann, *TDNT* 9,369–70).

5. Ἐπὶ τῇ κοινωνίᾳ ὑμῶν εἰς τὸ εὐαγγέλιον, "because you are partners with me in the gospel." Some interpreters claim this expression must be taken with εὐχαριστῶ ("I give thanks," v 1), (1) because εὐχαριστῶ, would otherwise be left without an object, (2) because εὐχαριστεῖν and similar verbs are used by Paul with ἐπί (cf. 1 Cor 1:4; 2 Cor 9:15), and (3) because to construct ἐπὶ τῇ κοινωνίᾳ with μετὰ χαρᾶς ("with joy") would require the definite article τῆς before ἐπί—μετὰ χαρᾶς τῆς ἐπί . . . (Vincent; Omanson, *BT* 29 (1978) 244–45; cf. Gnilka, Lightfoot, Martin, 1976, Müller). But the Greek is not so clear and precise as to be so certain! (1) εὐχαριστῶ is used without an object when the object can be inferred from the context (cf. Matt 15:36; 26:37). Here in v 5 it is possible to infer that the Philippians themselves are the object of Paul's gratitude. (2) Only once does Paul use εὐχαριστεῖν with ἐπί and the dative to express the object of his thanks (1 Cor 1:4; but cf. 2 Cor 9:15). He uses other constructions much more frequently. (3) To demand that the definite article be present before ἐπί in order to connect ἐπὶ τῇ κοινωνίᾳ with μετὰ χαρᾶς is to demand the unreasonable, for it is to

place classical requirements on a writer of nonliterary Koine Greek (cf. τὸ κρίμα ἐξ ἑνός, Rom 5:16; οἱ νεκροὶ ἐν Χριστῷ, 1 Thess 4:16; see BDF 272). Hence, it is possible to take this prepositional phrase with χαρᾶς—"I pray for you with joy *because* you are partners with me" (cf. AV, NIV, GNB, LB, NEB, Phillips).

Κοινωνία ("to have something in common") is a distinctively Pauline word, used by him thirteen of the nineteen times it appears in the NT. The frequent use of this word and its cognates in Philippians is striking (1:5, 7; 2:1; 3:10; 4:15) and provides further proof of the intimate relationship that existed between Paul and the Christians at Philippi. The word carries a wide range of ideas, from being an expression to describe the marital relationship as the most intimate between human beings (POxy. 1473, 33; 3 Macc 4:6), to indicating generosity or altruism (2 Cor 9:13), to providing proof of brotherly unity, i.e. a gift or contribution (Rom 15:26), to referring to a participation or sharing in something (see BGD; J. Y. Campbell, "Κοινωνία and its Cognates in the NT," JBL 51 [1932] 352–80; H. Seesemann, *Der Begriff κοινωνία im Neuen Testament* (Giessen: Töpelmann, 1933); H. W. Ford, "NT Conception of Fellowship," *Shane Quarterly* 6 [1945] 188–215).

Here in v 5, modified as it is by εἰς τὸ εὐαγγέλιον, κοινωνία ὑμῶν may refer to the fact that the Philippians and Paul share together in a common faith that is brought about by the preaching of the gospel (ὑμῶν, seen as an objective genitive, "fellowship *with you.*" (See Seesemann, *Der Begriff Κοινωνία*, 73–83 and Lohmeyer as noted by Martin [1976] 64–65). Even if this interpretation is admissible (and it may not be—see Vincent, 7), nevertheless, this "sharing in the faith" results in tangible assistance. Paul, therefore, can and does use κοινωνία to describe the "collection" for (εἰς) the poor in Jerusalem (Rom 15:26; 2 Cor 8:4; 9:13)—a sharing of one's material goods for (εἰς) the physical benefit of others (cf. Heb 13:16). Hence, it is easy to see in this expression, κοινωνία ὑμῶν εἰς τὸ εὐαγγέλιον, a clear reference to the gift(s) that the Philippians had sent to Paul (ὑμῶν, understood now as a subjective genitive) in order to make it possible for him to spread the gospel. The same preposition, εἰς, follows κοινωνία here as in Rom 15:26 and 2 Cor 9:13. The Philippians were partners (κοινωνοί) with the apostle in the proclamation of the good news, not in the sense that they shared the same faith with him, or were co-evangelists with him, but that they supported him financially in his mission work.

This understanding of κοινωνία does not exclude, however, reference to the Philippians' faith, their own efforts at evangelism, nor to their intercession for the progress of the gospel in the world. In its fullest extent κοινωνία means whole-hearted, active participation in every imaginable way with Paul in the "labor and suffering" that was necessary to spread the good news (Vincent; see Collange, Gnilka, Hauck, TDNT 3,798; Martin, Lightfoot).

Τὸ εὐαγγέλιον, "the gospel." Εὐαγγέλιον is still another distinctively Pauline word, used by the apostle approximately 60 of the 76 times it appears in the NT. Originally it meant "a reward for good news" and then simply "good news." In the NT and especially in Paul's letters, its meaning narrows down to the specific sense of the "good news" that God has acted to save people from their sins and to reconcile them to himself in or through Jesus Christ (cf. Matt 1:21; 1 Cor 15:1–3; 2 Cor 5:19). For Paul, the gospel is not merely good news in the sense of words spoken and heard, i.e. a good story, but is itself God's power by which people are changed (cf. Rom 1:16)—"effective power which brings to pass what it says because God is its author" (Friedrich, *TDNT* 2,731; J. Schniewind, *Die Begriffe Wort und Evangelium bei Paulus* [Bonn: C. Georgi, 1910] 64–117).

In Philippians, as also in the other letters of Paul, εὐαγγέλιον appears most frequently without modifiers of any kind (1:5, 7, 12, 16, 27b; 2:22; 4:3, 15), a fact which indicates that its contents, its message and meaning, were well-known to writer and reader alike so that no explanation was necessary. The gospel as a message was at the center of Paul's thought and the force behind his mission (see Friedrich, *TDNT* 2,729). The churches to which he wrote came into existence as a result of their response to the gospel he preached (cf. 1:5).

The gospel was the good news about Jesus Christ that was constantly being proclaimed (1:15, 27a), a body of teaching that had been and could be defended (1:7, 16), a message that was being spread abroad, helped along, furthered, caused to progress by what people said about it or by how they behaved in respect to it (1:12, 27; 2:22). It is this last idea that is prominent in the expression εἰς τὸ εὐαγγέλιον (cf. 1:5), where the Philippian church is commended for making a turning (*Wendung*) toward the gospel message and taking an active part with Paul in passing it along (Gnilka).

Ἀπὸ τῆς πρώτης ἡμέρας ἄχρι τοῦ νῦν, "from the first day until now." This phrase does not so much mark in time the precise moment when the gospel reached Philippi and was accepted by the community, as it indicates (1) the constant loyalty of the Philippians to the gospel and to Paul who brought it, and (2) Paul's rare willingness to continue to accept gifts from a particular church. It had been his policy not to take money from those groups he preached to, for fear that someone should accuse him of charging for that which in reality was free—the grace of God (cf. 1 Cor 9:15–18; 2 Cor 11:7–9). The Philippians, however, had sufficiently gained Paul's affection and confidence so as to persuade him to waive this rule in their case. They, therefore, sent more than one gift to him for the advancement of the gospel while he was in Thessalonica (Phil 4:16) and at least one gift while he was in Corinth (2 Cor 11:9). Now, again at this critical time, they sent additional funds in the hopes that they could thereby alleviate his suffering in prison (4:10, 18) or perhaps secure his release. Here, then, is an excellent example where "the beginning has value only in so far as it involves the enlightening and revitalizing of the present" (Collange).

6. Πεποιθὼς αὐτὸ τοῦτο, "And I am sure." This translation must not be allowed to obscure the fact that the participle πεποιθὼς (literally, "being confident") is attendant on εὐχαριστῶ making clear that Paul's thanks to God are accompanied closely by his confidence in God. Confidence permeates Philippians, much like joy. Paul's fellow Christians are made confident by his imprisonment and thus daringly preach the gospel without fear (1:14). Paul himself is confident that he will be released from prison (2:24); he is confident *that he* thus will continue to be around to stimulate the church at Philippi to joy and faith (1:25). But the basis for such confidence is the Lord; it is a confident certainty about life that does not find its locus in human

abilities or achievements (3:3, 4), but in the character and acts of God. Here in 1:6 Paul is confident about the church of Philippi because he is confident in God who is at work in the church (cf. 2:13).

The phrase αὐτὸ τοῦτο (lit. "this very thing") need not be made much of, as though it might be important to identify its antecedent. For such universal adjectives as τοῦτο were popular in Koine as in Classical Greek and had a strong tendency simply to pass over to the accusative of general reference. Thus πεποιθὼς αὐτὸ τοῦτο = "confident with just this confidence" = "I am sure" (BDF 154).

Ὅτι ὁ ἐναρξάμενος . . . Χριστοῦ Ἰησοῦ, "that he who began this good work through you will finish it at the Day of Christ Jesus." Ὅτι ("that") introduces the object of Paul's certainty: "I am sure *that* God will finish what he started!" What God started Paul describes as ἔργον ἀγαθόν ("a good work"), a phrase that cannot be shaken loose from its immediate context and be interpreted primarily in terms of "God's redeeming and renewing work" in the lives of the Philippians (Martin, 1959; see also Barth, Caird, Hendriksen, Jones, Müller). Rather ἔργον ἀγαθόν finds its explanation in the fact that the Philippians were partners with Paul in the gospel (v 5), and shared their resources with him to make the proclamation of the gospel possible. This "sharing in the gospel" *is* the good work referred to here (cf. 2 Cor 8:6).

The word ἔργον may have brought to Paul's mind the creative activity of God. For he very likely stood in that tradition of thinkers who referred to creation as God's ἔργον, God's work (cf. Gen 2:2, 3; 2 Esd 6:38, 43; Bertram, *TDNT* 2,629, 30). If so, then Paul would have viewed this "good work" he mentions here not as some accomplishment that the Philippians could justly take credit for by themselves. Rather he would have seen it as the creative activity of God, something God initiated (ἐναρξάμενος), and which he alone would bring to completion (ἐπιτελέσει) by means of (ἐν) the Philippians (ἐναρξάμενος ἐν does not demand the idea of "in" or "within" [cf. Gal 3:3], for ἐνάρχεσθαι simply means "to make a beginning," and ἐν can be instrumental as well as local [BDF 219.1]). As in the first creation God accomplished his work (ἔργον) by his word—"His word went out and the work of creation was done forthwith" (2 Esd 6:38, 43; see J. M. Myers, *I & II Esdras* [Garden City: Doubleday, 1974] 204)—so now in the new creation God will accomplish this "good work" (ἔργον ἀγαθόν), that of advancing the gospel by human means, and in this instance by the Philippian church.

Paul envisioned that the good work, which God started and which was now being carried on by the Philippians, would reach its completion at the Day of Christ Jesus. That is to say, Paul was certain that the Philippians would never waiver in their generosity, would never cease sharing their good gifts to help spread the gospel, until the Parousia, the return of Christ took place—that final event of history which he believed was near at hand (Phil 4:5). This "Day of Christ Jesus" (also referred to as the Day of Christ, Phil 1:10; the Day of our Lord Jesus, 1 Cor 1:8; the Day of the Lord, 1 Thess 5:2; the Day of Judgment, 1 John 4:17; the Day, 1 Thess 5:4; that Day, 2 Tim 1:12; the Day of Wrath, Rev 2:5; cf. W. Kramer, *Christ, Lord, Son of God.* [Tr. B. Hardy. Naperville: A. R. Allenson, 1966] 139) very likely brought the idea of judgment to Paul's attention, since it was an expression that had its origin in the OT concept of the Day of Yahweh, a day of darkness and gloom and wrath (Joel 2:2; Amos 5:20). This Day would test the deeds of men with fire (1 Cor 3:13), and the works of the Philippian church as well. But Paul anticipated that day without alarm. Knowing the Philippians, he was confident that when their "work" (ἔργον) was examined it would be pronounced "good" (ἀγαθόν; cf. 2:16; 4:1).

Other interpretations of v 6 such as those that apply its words to "a more comprehensive work of grace in the hearts of the believers (in general), affecting both (their) inner disposition and (their) outward activity" (Müller), must be considered secondary interpretations to that given above. The context does not permit any of them to be primary. It does not follow, however, that they cannot be right by extension. For when God is involved, whatever he begins already has the end in sight. The completed state already exists in the divine initiation. It is the nature of God that this be so. For what God creates he brings to completion (cf. Isa 48:12, 13; 44:6). So if God calls the community to faith, He stands also at the end of the call to bring each member to the desired goal of their faith—the salvation of their souls (cf. 1 Thess 5:24; see also 1 Cor 1:8, 9; 2 Cor 1:8; 2 Thess 3:3; cf. Gnilka).

7. Καθώς ἐστιν δίκαιον ἐμοὶ τοῦτο φρονεῖν ὑπὲρ πάντων ὑμῶν . . . , is usually translated, "Indeed it is only right that I should feel like this about all of you. . . ." These words begin a difficult section to translate. Καθώς ("as" or "just as") usually calls for its correlative, οὕτως ("so"). But Paul frequently begins a sentence with καθώς not followed by οὕτως, and in so doing gives to καθώς something of the meaning of "because" (Rom 1:28; 1 Cor 1:6; 5:7; Gal 3:6; Eph 1:14; Phil 3:17. See BDF 453.2). He does that here and thus connects v 7 with vv 3–6 to show that his gratitude to God for each one of the Philippians, his joy over them, his confident expectation of their constant fidelity, are feelings on his part (ἐμοί) that are justly and rightly (δίκαιον) due them. To have such thoughts about the Philippians is *just as* it should be for Paul, and *just as* the Philippians would have expected of him.

The verb φρονεῖν, translated "feel" is a distinctively Pauline word. Paul uses it twenty-three of the twenty-six times it occurs in the NT, and ten of these twenty-three are found in his letter to the Philippians (1:7; 2:2 [twice], 5; 3:15 [twice], 19; 4:2, 10 [twice]). It is a difficult word to translate, for in addition to ideas of attitude and feeling on the one hand, such as "interest in," "sympathetic attention to," "concern for," φρονεῖν also includes such ideas as "to think," "to form or hold an opinion" about someone or something, "to set one's mind on, to be intent on something." It therefore is a word that embraces both feeling and thought, emotions and mind. Paul not only *feels* deeply for the Philippians, but as a consequence he *plans*, or *schemes* how best his concern for them can be actualized in tangible ways. "He cannot and need not send them money . . . , but he can cherish great and good hopes of their religious prospects" and work towards those ends (Moffatt, as quoted by Michael, 15; see also Bertram, *TDNT* 9,220–35; Martin, 1976).

The rightness (δίκαιον) of Paul's feelings for the Philippians is explained in the next phrase, διὰ τὸ ἔχειν με ἐν τῇ καρδίᾳ ὑμᾶς, usually translated, "because I have you in my heart," meaning, "because you are very dear to me." But again the Greek is so ambiguous that one cannot be certain that this interpretation is correct. (1) There is no personal pronoun modifying καρδίᾳ ("heart"); hence, the definite article could mean *"my* heart," or *"your* heart." (2) The word order με . . . ὑμᾶς is not itself a guarantee that the flow of thought must be *"I* have *you* in my heart," and not the opposite. First, there are no other examples of διὰ τὸ ἔχειν in Paul's writings. Hence, it is not possible to determine a pattern of word order for this construction based on Pauline usage. Second, on examining διὰ τὸ ἔχειν elsewhere, one notices that the so-called (accusative) subject of the infinitive stands outside the prepositional phrase as many times as it does within the phrase (cf. Matt 24:12; Luke 2:4; 6:48; 19:11; Acts 18:2; Heb 7:23; James 4:2; contrast Mark 5:4; Acts 27:9). Where subject and object are both clearly denoted, sometimes the subject is within the phrase and the object outside (John 2:24; Acts 27:4); sometimes the object is within the phrase and the subject outside (Heb 10:2), and sometimes both subject and object (as here) are outside the phrase with object first and then subject (Luke 18:5) or subject first and then object (Acts 4:2). (3) The context seems fairly neutral as well. Verse 8 may favor the interpretation, *"I* have *you* in my heart," but the content of v 7 favors the opposite: Paul says, "I am justified in thanking God for you, rejoicing over you, having confidence in you, because *you* have me in your heart and *because you* are partners with me in my imprisonment, etc." Since the construction is ambiguous and since it is yet necessary to make a choice between the two interpretations, the translation of the NEB is judged to best fit the facts—"because you hold me in such affection." Justification for the way Paul feels about the Philippians has its basis, then, in their affection for him, καρδία ("heart") being understood as the seat of one's emotions.

It also finds its basis in the fact that all (πάντας) members of the Philippian community are (ὄντας, taken as a causal participle) Paul's partners (συγκοινωνούς; cf. the echo here of κοινωνία in v 5) in the grace given him by God. Χάρις ("grace"), in this context does not mean the general favor of God—God's salvation-grace (*Heilsgnade*)—extended to everyone through Christ's death and resurrection, but to the special favor of God (τῆς χάριτος) in the form of a spiritual gift or an ability given to individuals to accomplish certain specific tasks (see BGD). Here "grace" refers to Paul's apostolic commission to preach the gospel handed him by God (cf. Rom 1:5; 12:3, 6; 1 Cor 3:10; Gal 2:9; Eph 3:2; see Benoit, Caird, Heinzelmann) and in which the Philippians have shared by making it financially possible for him to carry out this work of evangelism.

But "grace," as Lightfoot has pointed out, "applies equally to Paul's 'bonds,' and to his 'defense and confirmation of the gospel' " (85). Paul's present situation of suffering for the gospel and of defending and confirming the gospel is but the result of his commission. And in this also the Philippians are partners. If Paul suffers, so do they; if he defends and vindicates the gospel, so do they. Paul sees himself as an extension of the Philippian Christians, and them as joint-participants with him in his troubles and triumphs, co-sharers with him of the divine grace (τῆς χάριτος).

When Paul mentions his "defense and confirmation of the gospel" (ἡ ἀπολογία καὶ βεβαίωσις τοῦ εὐαγγελίου) he does not have in mind that general defense and vindication of the gospel—that overcoming of objections to the

Christian message, on the one hand, and the confirming of it by straightforward preaching, on the other, which he customarily gave when he was able
to proclaim the gospel as a free man (so Lightfoot, and see the misleading
translation of the GNB). Rather Paul had in mind a particular defense that
he had already made, or was in the process of making before his judges
subsequent to his arrest for the sake of the gospel (cf. Acts 22:1).
"Defense"
(ἀπολογία) and "vindication" (βεβαίωσις) are technical, legal terms common
in the law courts of the first century (cf. Acts 25:16; 2 Tim 4:16. See especially
A. Deissmann, *Bible Studies* [Tr. A. Grieve. Edinburgh: T. and T. Clark, 1923]
104–106, and MM, 108). The picture that emerges, therefore, is the following.
Paul, the prisoner, gave evidence in his own case. This allowed him the opportunity to defend not only himself but also the gospel and, in the process,
to vindicate it. His defense-speech was an extraordinary opportunity to proclaim the gospel. The proclamation of the gospel was the means by which
people were won to the faith (cf. Acts 26:29). Their conversion showed that
the gospel was a creative, life-imparting power (Gnilka). This beneficial effect
of the gospel cleared it of slander and proved to the world that it did not
and does not ever deserve to be on trial. Paul, in making his own defense,
therefore, acts as advocate for the gospel, and he congratulates the Philippians
on being his partners in the privilege (Caird, 108). He now waits for the
verdict confident that he has made a good case for himself (cf. 1:19; 2:24)
as well as for the gospel.

8. Μάρτυς γάρ μου ὁ θεός . . . ("For God is my witness . . ."). By means
of the conjunction γάρ ("for") Paul emphatically calls on God to bear witness
to the genuineness of his feelings for the Philippians, *all of them* (cf. 1:4, 7
[twice], 8)—those feelings of gratitude, joy and confidence that he had articu-
lated in vv 3–6, and the feeling of yearning that he mentions now. Why did
Paul think it necessary to employ such an extreme statement, even employing
the name of God which the rabbis studiously avoided (Str-B 1,330–32; 3,26),
especially since such oaths are relatively infrequent in his other letters (Rom
1:9; 2 Cor 1:23; 1 Thess 2:5, 10)? Was it because Paul was incapable of
expressing his own feelings so he calls on God to help—"I cannot tell how
deeply I long for you all, but *God knows*"(so Chrysostom as quoted by Vincent)?
Was it because the enormity of Paul's love deserved more than his own testimony to its genuineness could provide? Perhaps (so Caird, Müller, Vincent).
More likely, however, Paul took this solemn oath because he was aware that
within the church that he founded and for which he cared so deeply there
were those who were not at all convinced of his right to lead them nor certain
of the reality of his love for them. What more could he do to convince them
than swear before God that they all (πάντας ὑμᾶς) had the same great place
in his affections? Nothing. In his day and in his culture a solemn oath was
the end of every dispute (cf. Heb 6:16).

Ὡς ἐπιποθῶ πάντας ὑμᾶς,"that I yearn for all of you." Ὡς, though a word
with more than one meaning, here introduces the content of the divine witness—"God witnesses *to the fact that* (ὡς) I yearn for you" (cf. Rom 1:9, AV,
RSV, GNB, JB), rather than to the degree of Paul's yearning ("How greatly,"
AV, RSV, JB). This latter idea is already fully expressed by the modifying phrase

ἐν σπλάγχνοις Χριστοῦ Ἰησοῦ ("with the deep affection of Christ Jesus") and needs no additional word such as ὡς to explain it qualitatively.

Ἐπιποθῶ ("I yearn") is a Pauline word used by the apostle seven of the nine times it appears in the NT. It is a strong word, and registers Paul's intense longing for his friends (see C. Spicq, "Epipothein, Désirer ou Chérir?" *RB* 64 [1957] 184–95). Here he uses it to describe his longing for the Philippians—probably his longing to be with them, to enjoy their presence and to help them in their Christian faith (cf. 4:1). But it is a longing that is not only intense but unique in that it is rooted in a love (ἐν σπλάγχνοις) that originates in and is fostered by Christ Jesus (Χριστοῦ Ἰησοῦ is a subjective genitive). Paul loves them as Christ loves them and because Christ loves them through him. Bengel: *in Paulo non Paulus vivit, sed Jesus Christus; quare Paulus non in Pauli sed Jesus Christi movetur visceribus* ("In Paul it is not Paul that lives, but Jesus Christ; wherefore Paul is moved not by Paul's but by Jesus Christ's affection"; quoted by Barth).

The phrase Paul uses to describe his "deep affection" is striking and powerful. Literally it is, "in the viscera, entrails of Christ Jesus" (ἐν σπλάγχνοις Χριστοῦ Ἰησοῦ). In Greek the viscera (τὰ σπλάγχνα) were the nobler organs of the body—the heart, liver and lungs—not the intestines (τὰ ἔντερα), and were regarded as the seat and origin of the deeply felt emotions such as anger and love (see Köster, *TDNT* 7,548). So Paul is saying, in effect: "If it is true that you hold me *in your heart* (v 7), and this is the measure of your affection for me, I wish to assure you that I long for you. I hold you *in the heart of Christ Jesus!* This is the measure and meaning of my affection for you." Surely this astonishing metaphor powerfully drove home to the Philippians the depth and reality of Paul's love for them!

9. Love leads to prayer. Once more Paul reminds the Philippians that they are constantly in his prayers (προσεύχομαι is present tense). Now, however, he not only states the *fact* that he prays for them (cf. v 4), but he reveals the *content* of his prayer—καὶ τοῦτο προσεύχομαι ἵνα . . . ("and I pray this, namely, *that*"). The ἵνα here is a conjunction that introduces a clause explaining or expounding on τοῦτο ("this"), the grammatical object of προσεύχομαι ("I pray"), and not one that offers the purpose of his prayer. (For similar uses of ἵνα see Luke 1:43; John 15:8, 13; 17:3; 1 John 3:11, 23; 4:17, 21; 5:3; 3 John 4; cf. also 1 Cor 9:18; 2 Cor 2:9; Phil 2:2; Herm *Sim* 9.28.4; see BDF 394 and Moule, *Idiom-Book*, 145, 146, who calls this, "ἵνα denoting content".) The content of his prayer, then, is that the Philippians' love may increase.

It is interesting to note that Paul does not qualify or limit this love for which he prays by adding an object to it—it is not love for others (LB), nor for each other (JB), nor yet their love for him. Rather, it is love unlimited, "the inward state of the soul" (Lightfoot), "love in the most comprehensive sense as the central element of the Christian life" (Beare)—God's love poured out in their hearts by the Holy Spirit (Rom 5:5). In effect, Paul prays that the Philippians increasingly may *be* persons characterized by love, even as God their Father, *is* himself characterized by love (cf. 1 John 4:3). Paul knows that if the love they already possess increases steadily (μᾶλλον καὶ μᾶλλον) and continues to abound (περισσεύῃ:—the total context indicates that the present tense is preferred to the aorist περισσεύσῃ), it will overflow into deeds of kindness; wrong attitudes and actions toward each other will disappear and the problems at Philippi will be resolved (2:3, 4; 4:2, 3). Paul's prayer, therefore, borders on exhortation (Collange).

Περισσεύειν ("to abound, overflow, be more than enough, be extremely rich") is a Pauline word, used by Paul twenty-six of the thirty-nine times it appears in the NT. Perhaps no other word so characterized for him the new age opened up by Christ as did this word. For this new age is no meagre age but one marked by an overflowing and rich abundance of good things—grace overflows (Rom 5:15–17), the Church richly overflows in hope (Rom 15:13), in faith, in word, in knowledge, in zeal (2 Cor 8:7) and in wisdom (Eph 1:8). The new ministry (διακονία)) overflows in edification (1 Cor 14:12) and in excellence in contrast to the old (2 Cor 3:9), Christians overflow in ability to comfort (2 Cor 1:4, 5), in generosity (2 Cor 8:2), in thanksgiving (2 Cor 4:15), in every good work (2 Cor 9:8) in the work of the Lord (1 Cor 15:58), in everything (2 Cor 8:7; see Gnilka). So it is not surprising, then, that Paul's aspiration for the Philippians, people of the new age, is that they might be so rich in love that they have no room to store it. Love must not only characterize them, it must well up and flow out from them in an ever-increasing degree (ἔτι μᾶλλον καὶ μᾶλλον: "still more and more") toward each other and toward all (cf. 1 Thess 3:12).

With the word "still more and more" Paul quietly thrusts in the idea that the Philippians have not yet become "perfect" (cf. 3:12–15) in love, and gently opens up the subject of the problems that exist in this community through a lack of love—problems he intends to deal with more directly later on (2:1–5; 4:2, 3; see Garland, RevExp 77 [1980] 330).

But their ever-increasing love is also to be a discriminating love. It is to be accompanied by knowledge (ἐπιγνώσει) and understanding (αἰσθήσει), intellectual and moral insight—a new awareness of God as revealed in Jesus Christ, on the one hand, and the ability to make moral decisions, on the other (Grayston, 1967). "Nothing perhaps is more harmful than the easy good nature which is willing to tolerate everything; and this is often mistaken for the Christian frame of mind. Love must fasten itself on the things which are worth loving, and it cannot do so unless it is wisely directed" (Scott).

One of the things that directs love is ἐπίγνωσις ("knowledge"). This is still another of Paul's favorite words, used by him fifteen of the twenty times it appears in the NT. Over against the simple γνῶσις it may refer to a deeper, fuller, or more advanced type of knowledge (cf. 1 Cor 13:12). Since ἐπίγνωσις is limited in usage to religious and moral things (BGD) it follows that for Paul ἐπίγνωσις is that advanced knowledge, that full appreciation of the real meaning of the Christian gospel that is the result of instruction and experience. It is practical knowledge that "informs Christian love as to the right circumstances, aims, ways and means" in which it is to be applied in the concrete situations of life (Vincent). Without ἐπίγνωσις ("knowledge") love easily may be misdirected.

Πάσῃ αἰσθήσει ("in extensive perception") is still another control set on love by Paul. This is the only time αἴσθησις appears in the NT, although it is frequent in Proverbs (Prov 1:4, 7, 22; 3:20; 5:2, LXX), where it sets forth the ideas of "sensation," i.e. sense perception, and "insight," and denotes moral understanding and discernment (BGD). The adjective ("all") that modifies αἰσθήσει ("perception") does not so much mean *total* perception as it means a *breadth* of perception. Hence πᾶσα αἴσθησις is the ability to make proper moral decisions in the midst of a vast array of differing and difficult choices that are constantly presenting themselves to the Christian (cf. Heb 5:14). Love, therefore, although constantly expanding, is nevertheless regulated by knowledge and discernment (ἐπίγνωσις καὶ αἴσθησις). Both of these words and the phrase τὰ διαφέροντα ("the things that really matter," v 10) were frequently used by moral philosophers contemporary with Paul (see A. Bonhöffer, *Epiktet und das Neue Testament* [Stuttgart: F. Enke, 1890] 105, 298, 299). Paul, therefore, is not averse to taking up ideas and traditions from the intellectual world around him in order to put them to good use in developing a truly Christian morality, based not on human striving, on the one hand (Hellenistic moral philosophy), nor on the Law, on the other hand (Judaism; cf. Rom 2:18), but on love (see Gnilka).

If one were to ask from whence come these regulatory agents of knowledge and perception, the answer would be, "from God," and hence, they are legitimately included in Paul's prayer for the Philippians as is the request for love. Yet this is not a complete answer, for although knowledge ultimately is the revelation of God, it is nevertheless passed on from generation to generation by the teachers of the Church. "Knowledge," therefore, which controls love is that which is learned by hearing and responding to the truth of God as God's ministers, such as Paul, constantly and carefully expound it. And "perception," though it too may be considered a gift of God for which one can pray, yet it in a sense is a "moral taste" that can only be acquired and developed by experience—a sensitivity to and desire for what is right as over against what is wrong. This can only be the result of determined and strenuous moral exercise on the part of each individual Christian (Heb 5:14).

10. Paul prays that the Philippians' love may be a controlled and developing love for two reasons: (1) that they might know how to make the best choices possible and (2) that they themselves might be the best people possible.

He expresses the first of these purposes with the phrase εἰς τὸ δοκιμάζειν ὑμᾶς τὰ διαφέροντα, which is yet another of Paul's difficult expressions to understand. The verb δοκιμάζειν may mean either "to test or examine, to prove by testing" as one would assay metals or test the genuineness of coins (Plato *Tim.*, 656), or "to accept as proved" hence "to approve" (1 Cor 16:3). And the verb διαφέρειν from which τὰ διαφέροντα comes may mean either "to differ" (1 Cor 15:41) or "to be superior" (Matt 6:26; see BGD and MM). Hence, the phrase has been variously understood to mean, "in order that you may put to the proof things that differ" (Alford, Weiss, Vincent), or "in order that you may accept as proved the things that really matter" (Collange, Houlden, Lightfoot, Martin, 1976, Meyer). Since one must choose between these two interpretations he should choose the latter, because to distinguish between things that differ significantly is a relatively easy task. But great powers of insight and perception are needed "to decide with sureness what things are really excellent and worthy of adoption in practice" (Plummer). To distinguish *ex bonis optima* (Bengel) is the truly difficult task. Hence, love sharpened by knowledge and discernment is for Paul the ultimate requirement for acquiring "a sense of what is vital" (Moffatt), and choosing from among those things which in themselves may be morally indifferent—"that small things should as small be seen, and great things great to us should seem" (Barth).

It should be noted, in passing, that the majority of the early Greek Fathers understood the "distinguishing" of v 10 to mean the ability to distinguish between what was orthodoxy and what was heresy, what was true and what was false teaching (Collange, Vincent).

Paul's second goal in praying for the Philippians is that they might be the best people possible. This simple idea is expressed by three adjectives (vv 10*b*–11), each of which is filled with imagery. The first is εἰλικρινεῖς usually translated "sincere" or "pure." Although the etymology of this adjective is not certain (cf. Moulton, *Grammar*, 2,105) it appears to be derived from εἵλη (ἥλιος), a word that means "the warmth and light of the sun," and κρίνειν, "to judge" (Lightfoot). If this is so, then the picture it conjures up is of someone bringing something, a garment or the like, out into the sunlight so as to see clearly if it is unsoiled, free of stains. Through usage, therefore, the word came to mean, "spotless," and from Plato's day (cf. *Phaed.* 66a; 81C; *Symp.* 211e) onwards this idea of spotlessness or cleanness in the physical realm moved over into the idea of purity in the moral realm. In the NT εἰλικρινής and its cognates always denote moral purity (cf. 2 Pet 3:1; 1 Cor 5:8; 2:17; see Büchsel, *TDNT* 2,397–98; cf. also Gnilka, 52, n. 14; MM, 184). Hence, Paul's goal for the Philippians is that they may be people of sincerity, honesty, cleanness of mind, who live lives that are transparent before God and other people.

The second adjective is ἀπρόσκοποι, usually translated "blameless." Derived as it is from προσκόπτω, a verb that can mean either "causing someone to stumble" or "stumbling" (Abbott-Smith, *Lexicon*), ἀπρόσκοπος is equally as colorful a word as εἰλικρινής. It pictures either a person who carefully avoids (ἀ-) putting anything in another's way that would cause that person to trip and fall, or one who is equally careful to avoid tripping over obstacles that may be placed in his own way. Chrysostom takes ἀπρόσκοπος in both senses (Beare). Yet in light of 1 Cor 10:32 (the only other place it is used in Paul's writings), it seems best to understand the adjective here as meaning "not causing another to stumble." Paul's aspiration for the Philippians, then, is that they may be harmless and that their conduct may be such as to give no offense either towards those within the church or to those outside it. Paul reminds the Philippians with the accompanying phrase—εἰς ἡμέραν Χριστοῦ ("in view of the day of Christ") that the quality of their lives and the character of their behavior toward others are vital as preparation for the final judgment (cf. Matt 25:31–46; Michael). The Day of Christ will be a day of scrutiny (see comments on v 6 above), and it is Paul's hope that the conduct of the Philippians will be such as to fend off or stand against (εἰς) possible punishment (cf. 1 Cor 3:10–15). The Day of Christ thus "lends direction and seriousness to ethics" (Collange).

11. The third adjective Paul uses is a participle with its accompanying

direct object. Paul's imagery here is drawn from an orchard setting. The Philippians are now graphically pictured as trees loaded down with, bearing a full crop of (πεπληρωμένοι), good fruit (καρπὸν δικαιοσύνης) ready to be harvested.

What is this "good fruit" (lit. "the fruit of righteousness") that Paul has in view here? Is it that "divine righteousness" about which he has so much to say elsewhere in his letters—that "right standing" with God which cannot be achieved by keeping the Law (cf. Phil 3:4–9), that righteousness that is imputed, that righteousness which is God's free, unearned gift based solely on the work of Christ, and obtained by faith? (Caird, Collange).

The answer is, "No." Since the expression, "fruit of righteousness" (καρπὸν δικαιοσύνης: δικαιοσύνης, a genitive of apposition) is a familiar biblical phrase for conduct pleasing to God (LXX: Prov 11:30; Amos 6:12; cf. James 3:12), since the participial phrase πεπληρωμένοι καρπὸν δικαιοσύνης is parallel to the two previous adjectives, εἰλικρινεῖς ("pure") and ἀπρόσκοποι ("harmless"), and since the previous adjectives describe the Philippians in relationship to others as being transparent before them and having no inclination to harm anyone in any way, it is but natural to see here an extension of this same idea. The "fruit of righteousness," therefore, must be understood in an ethical sense as referring collectively to those "truly good qualities" (GNB) in the Philippians that result in all kinds of noble acts and worthwhile deeds done toward each other and their neighbors (Michael, Scott).

Paul makes it clear, however, that this crop of goodness is not self-generated. Nor can it be, for the "fruit" he has in mind is supernatural and is produced through Jesus Christ (καρπὸν . . . τὸν διὰ Ἰησοῦ Χριστοῦ). Hence, although Paul uses the vocabulary of the OT, i.e. "fruit of righteousness" (Prov 11:30; Amos 6:12), he recognizes, as the OT writers seemed not to recognize, that no man is capable of producing this by himself. So in exactly the same way as he told the Galatians that love, joy, peace, and so on are the fruit (καρπός) of the Spirit (Gal 5:22), so here he tells the Philippians that their rich harvest of good deeds is in reality the product of Jesus Christ, the source of all life and goodness (cf. John 15:4; see J. A. Zeisler, *The Meaning of Righteousness in Paul* [Cambridge: University Press, 1972] 151, 203; Martin, 1976).

Paul concludes this section with the phrase, εἰς δόξαν καὶ ἔπαινον θεοῦ ("for the glory and praise of God"). He does so to indicate (1) that the Philippians are to recognize and openly acknowledge God's power and grace at work in their community, and (2) that their neighbors are to do the same upon seeing evidence of this power and grace in the way the Philippians live. For it should be clear to all that their love which abounds in knowledge and moral perception, their ability to choose the things which really matter, their good qualities which result in an abundance of noble deeds point beyond themselves, to God, God as the source and origin of goodness and truth, of justice and mercy, and so on—ἐξ αὐτοῦ καὶ δι᾽ αὐτοῦ καὶ εἰς αὐτὸν τὰ πάντα (the "Source, Guide and Goal of all that is," Rom 11:36, NEB).

The fact that this phrase, "for the glory and praise of God," and others like it, seems to have been a common phrase of doxology regularly used to conclude Jewish prayers (2 Sam 22:50; Pss 35:28; 41:13; Ecclus 39:10; Pr

Man 15; 1QSb 4:25; see Martin, 1976; Collange, Gnilka), must not detract from its meaning here. Paul did not merely use it by habit, unthinkingly, to bring his prayer to a close, but with full comprehension of what he wrote. God is the utter finality of the Christian life (*"die letzte Finalität des christlichen Leben,"* Gnilka), and as such he alone is to be honored and praised by all. In this connection it is instructive to observe that in exactly the same way as the life of Jesus and its influence on men were ordained for the glory of the Father (Phil 2:11; Fitzmyer, *JBC* 2,249), so the life and influence of the Philippian community on its environs are also ordained for the glory and praise of God. Paul can see it no other way: as the master, so must the servant be.

Explanation

This section (1:3-11) also follows the conventions of first-century letter-writing as did the earlier section (1:1-2). It begins with the customary thanksgiving (1:3-8), and is followed by the prayer (1:9-11). Although stylized in form there is here nothing perfunctory about Paul's words nor any hint of insincerity in them. Rather, every word and phrase breathes out (1) the genuine gratitude of the apostle for the Philippians and their continued partnership with him in the gospel, (2) his utter confidence that they will not let up in this good work until the Day of Christ Jesus simply because God will not permit them to, and (3) his deep affection for them generated in turn by their love for him—a love that is demonstrated by their stand with him and their continued support of him even while he is in prison defending and vindicating the gospel.

And his prayer, though brief, is profound in its implications; it is a prayer for a Christian community (1) that it might overflow in an intelligent and perceptive love, (2) that it might have the ability to recognize and choose the truly essential things of life, (3) that it might be pure and never the means of hurting others, (4) that it might allow Jesus Christ to generate through it all kinds of good deeds, and (5) that thus it might be a community committed to honoring and praising God, and at the same time the cause of God being honored and praised by others.

II. News and Instructions (1:12-2:30)

A. News about Paul (1:12-26)

Bibliography

Antin, P. "Mori lucrum et Antigone 462, 464." *RSR* 62 (1974) 259–60. **Bartlett, V.** "Philippians 1:22." *ExpTim* 4 (1892–93) 177. **Bertram, G.** "Ἀποκαραδοκία (Phil. 1, 20). *ZNW* 49 (1958) 264–70. **Bigaré, C.** "Soit que je vive, soit que le meure! Ph 1,20c–24, 27a." *AsSeign* 56 (1974) 9–14. **Bonnard, P.** "Vivre et mourir avec Jésu Christ selon saint Paul." *RHPR* 36 (1956) 101–12. **Cullmann, O.** *Immortality of the Soul or Resurrection of the Dead?* London: Epworth, 1958. **Deissmann, A.** *Die neutestamentliche Formel "in Christo Jesu."* Marburg: Elwert, 1892. **Dupont, J.** ΣΥΝ ΧΡΙΣΤΩΙ. *L'union avec le Christ suivant Saint Paul.* Bruges: Editions de l'Abbaye de Saint-André, 1952. **Ellis, E. E.** "II Cor. v 1–10 in Pauline Eschatology." *NTS* 6 (1960) 211–24. **Feuillet, A.** "Mort du Christ et Mort du chrétien d'après les épîtres pauliniennes." *RB* 66 (1959) 481–513. **Gappert, G.** "Aufbrechen und Bleiben." *BibLeb* 8 (1967) 63–67. **Garland, D. E.** "Philippians 1:1–26: The Defense and Confirmation of the Gospel." *RevExp* 77 (1980) 327–36. **Hawthorn, T.** "Philippians 1:12–19, with Special Reference to vv 15, 16, 17." *ExpTim* 62 (1950–51) 316–17. **Hoffmann, P.** *Die Toten in Christus.* Münster: Aschendorff, 1966; see especially "Das mit-Christus-sein im tode nach Phil 1, 21–26," 286–320. **Johnston, G.** "The Life of the Christian in the World: An Exposition of Phil. 1:1–2:4." *CJT* 3 (1957) 248–54. **Lee, G. M.** "Philippians I,22–3." *NovT* 12 (1970) 361. **Lohmeyer, E.** "Σὺν Χριστῷ." *Festgabe für Adolf Deissmann zum 60. Geburtstag.* Tübingen: Mohr, 1927. **Michael, J. H.** "Two Brief Marginal Notes in the Text of Philippians." *ExpTim* 35 (1923–24) 139–40. **Moule, C. F. D.** "The Influence of Circumstances on the Use of Eschatological Terms." *JTS* 15 (1964) 1–15. ———. "St Paul and Dualism: The Pauline Conception of Resurrection." *NTS* 12 (1965–66) 106–23. **Omanson, R. L.** "A Note on the Translation of Philippians 1:12." *BT* 29 (4, 1978) 446–48. **Palmer, D. W.** "'To Die is Gain' (Philippians 1:21)." *NovT* 17 (3, 1975) 203–18. **Perret, J.** "Notes bibliques de prédication sur trois péricopes de l'Epître de Saint Paul aux Philippians." *Verbum Caro* 19 (1965) 278–84. **Pesch, R.** "Zur Theologie des Todes." *BibLeb* 10 (1969) 9–16. **Sanders, J. T.** "The Transition from Opening Epistolary Thanksgiving to Body in the Letters of the Pauline Corpus." *JBL* 81 (1962) 348–62. **Schmidt, O.** "Zum Verständnis vom Philipper 1, 21." *Neutestamentliche Studien. G. Heinrici zu seinem 70. Geburtstag*, 1914, 156–58. **Schütz, J. H.** *Paul and the Anatomy of Apostolic Authority.* Cambridge: University Press, 1975. See especially "The Normative Character of the Gospel: Philippians and II Corinthians," 159–86. **Streider, I.** "Salvação Pessoal e Engrandecimento de Christo em Fil 1, 19f. Perspectiva Teologica 5 (1973) 59–72. **Urquhart, W. S.** "Glorifying Christ: A Meditation (Phil. 1, 20f.)." *ExpTim* 34 (1922–23) 548–50. **Vogel, C. J. de.** "Reflexions on Philipp. i 23–24." *NovT* 19 (4, 1977) 262–74. **Vorster, W. S.** "Concerning Semantics, Grammatical Analysis and Bible Translation." *Neot* 8 (1974) 21–41. **Wiles, G. P.** *Paul's Intercessory Prayers*, 1974, 276–81. **Wulf, F.** "Denn Leben ist für mich Christus und Sterben ist Gewinn (Phil 1, 21)." *Geist und Leben* 30 (1957) 241–45.

Translation

¹² *Now I want you to know, my brothers, that the things that happened to me have advanced the progress of the gospel rather than retarded it.* ¹³ *As a result it has become clear throughout the entire praetorium and to everyone else that I am a*

prisoner because I am a Christian. [14] *Furthermore, my being a prisoner has made most of the brothers confident in the Lord, so that they dare all the more to preach the gospel* [a] *without fear.* [15] *And yet some of these preach Christ out of envy and a desire to stir up trouble; but surely some do so out of good intentions.* [16] *Some preach Christ because they love me. They know that I am put here to defend the gospel.* [17] *Others preach Christ without sincerity moved by selfish ambition. They think that they will stir up trouble* [b] *because I am in prison.* [c] [18] *What then comes of all this except that* [d] *in every way, whether with false motives or true, Christ is being preached?* [e] *This surely makes me glad.*

Yes, and I will continue to be glad, [19] *for* [f] *I know that everything that has happened to me will result in my release because of your prayers and the help which comes from the Spirit of Jesus Christ.* [20] *And all of this is in harmony with my one eager hopeful expectation.* [g] *I know, too, that I will not be put to shame by anything, but rather that with full courage now as always Christ will be praised because of me, whether by my life or by my death.* [21] *For to me, living is Christ and dying is gain.* [22] *But if to live on in the body means fulfilling some good purpose, then I cannot tell what I would choose.* [h] [23] *Indeed, I am torn between two desires. I desire to break camp and to be with Christ, which is a very much better thing for me,* [24] *and I desire to remain alive* [i] *in this body, which is a more urgent need for you.* [25] *Therefore, since I am convinced that this need exists, I know that I am going to stay, to remain on with all of you in order that you may make progress and be glad in the faith,* [26] *and in order that your boasting in Christ Jesus might increase because of me through my presence with you once again.*

Notes

[a] τὸν λόγον ("the word"), adopted by Nestle-Aland is supported by P[46] D[2] the majority text and Marcion; τὸν λόγον τοῦ θεοῦ ("The word of God") by ℵ A B D*P ψ 33.81. *aliq.* some OL MSS, some Syr MSS, the Coptic and Clement of Alexandria; τὸν λόγον κυρίου ("The word of the Lord") by F G and Cyprian. The latter two readings, as the translations show, reflect attempts to make clear the meaning of τὸν λόγον.

[b] For the difficult ἐγείρειν ("to raise up") the majority text has the easier reading ἐπιφέρειν ("to bring to," "to inflict upon").

[c] Except for the position of οἱ μὲν . . . οἱ δέ the majority text puts v 17 before v 16 (cf. AV), making the order here coincide with the order in v 15, but thereby destroying the chiastic structure of this section.

[d] πλὴν ὅτι ("except that"), although supported by P[46] ℵ A F 33.81. *aliq.*, looks like a conflation of πλήν ("except") supported by the majority text, and ὅτι ("that") supported by B and Syr[p].

[e] P[46] adds ἀλλά ("but") at this point, which likely is dittography for the ἀλλά that appears again almost immediately.

[f] The γάρ here is weakened to δέ ("and," "but") in P[46] B.

[g] The compounded form ἀποκαραδοκία ("eager expectation"), found only in Christian writings, was returned to its earlier better known form, καραδοκία by only a few MSS.

[h] P[46] B 2464 have the subjunctive αἱρήσωμαι for the indicative, αἱρήσομαι, which looks like an attempt to improve on the Greek.

[i] A few MSS, including B, have the aorist infinitive ἐπιμεῖναι ("to remain") for the present infinitive ἐπιμένειν ("to be remaining").

Form/Structure/Setting

Paul moves now from the introductory sections, which contain the customary salutation, thanksgiving and prayer, to the body of his letter. He does so by using a formula not found elsewhere among his other writings at this particular point of transition—γινώσκειν ὑμᾶς βούλομαι ("I want you to know"; other like-formulas appear in his epistles, but not in the same location or with the same function: Cf. Rom 1:13; 11:25; 1 Cor 10:1; 1 Thess 4:13).

What is interesting is that Paul here is either establishing a new model that was to be followed by later second- and third-century letter-writers (for Paul's formula does not show up in letters before the second century A.D.), or he and they both were adhering to a standard formula seemingly characteristic only of personal, intimate letters written in the first century or earlier. (This latter statement is the more likely. See Roller, *Das Formular*, 65, 467 and J. L. White, *The Form and Function of the Body of the Greek Letter* [Missoula, Montana: Scholar's Press, 1972] 121, 122). Edgar and Hunt collected and published letters dating from the second century A.D. onward in their *Select Papyri*. The following is but a single example taken from among many in their collection: "Apollinarius to Taesis, his mother and lady, many greetings. Before all, I pray for your health . . . I wish you to know (γινώσκειν σε θέλω) . . . that I arrived in Rome in good health . . ." (1,303; see also 1,307, 317, 327, 329, 341; Deissmann, *Light*, 167, 178).

Invariably this formula directs attention to and gives important information about the safety, the activities, the feelings, and so on of the sender. Paul, too, uses this formula in the customary way. With it as an introduction he begins to share personal information about himself. He does not tell his friends precisely what has happened to him (perhaps they already know the details, or to write the details would be too dangerous), but he informs them that everything is working out the way he wants it to: Christians are becoming more bold, the gospel is being preached by all kinds of people, for right reasons and wrong, and he is glad. He also lets them in on some of the other emotions at work within him: a confidence that he will be released from prison, a fear of himself being shamed or bringing shame on Christ, a longing to be released from this body, but a still greater longing to live on, if by doing so he can be useful in helping them, his friends, to joyfully move forward in the faith.

One wishes that Paul had been more specific about the troubles he alludes to—what they were, when and where they happened to him, and so on— for historical reasons. But one cannot help but be grateful for the deep insights gained from the statements found here into the person of the apostle himself. It is a moving passage written by Paul that though personal does not focus attention upon Paul. Rather, it draws attention to his mission, to the progress of the gospel. All of Paul's anxiety is for the work he is engaged in. "As long as it goes forward he cares nothing for himself" (Scott).

The emotions of joy, confidence, fear, desire, and so on, that vibrate through this passage are heightened by Paul's rhetoric. Figures of speech abound: metaphor, alliteration, paronomasia, and especially chiasm. He chooses the rare word, or the compounded word, or plays with different words having similar meanings. He effectively makes his readers share his personal dilemma by skillful use of the rhetorical question, helping them focus on the alternatives by employing antitheses. Form, setting and structure combine to show how deeply personal this letter to the Philippians is, and how deeply Paul felt about the success of the gospel and the spiritual welfare of his friends.

Comment

12. In spite of the fact that the expression γινώσκειν ὑμᾶς βούλομαι, "I want you to know," is a trite formula of transition apparently a standard part of personal letters of the first century, Paul nevertheless uses it here sincerely to inform his friends about himself and how he fares, or rather, about his mission and how it progresses.

He greets them affectionately as "brothers/sisters" (ἀδελφοί; see also 3:1, 13, 17; 4:1, 8, 21). He does so because he sees himself with them as belonging to the same family, closely and lovingly related to each other not by birth, but by faith in Jesus Christ and by commitment to doing the will of God (cf. Mark 3:34, 35; see also MM 9). ἀδελφοί ("brothers") is a favorite word with Paul (used by him 133 times), and its significance must not be forgotten. Later when he tells the Philippians about those who preach Christ for wrong reasons (1:15–18), he nevertheless calls them "brothers" (cf. 1:14 with 1:15). By doing so he says in effect that, although he regrets their motives, he does not reject them.

Paul wants the Philippians to understand that what happened to him did not hinder the progress of the gospel, but advanced it. Unfortunately, however, the apostle is silent about what exactly it was that had happened to him. He refers to it in the briefest possible way—τὰ κατ' ἐμέ ("my affairs"; cf. Eph 6:21; Col 4:7). Whatever it was—whether a change of mind on Paul's part from a desire for martyrdom to a determination to secure release for himself, a change of mind that may have angered and alienated his radical followers (Collange), or a lengthy prison term—it was something, however, that could rightly be assumed by some to injure the cause of the gospel and prompt Christians to remain silent out of pique or fear. But Paul writes to tell his friends at Philippi that the reverse of this was true. With the introduction of μᾶλλον ("rather") he announces the unexpected (Omanson, BT 29 [1978] 446–48). Rumors to the contrary, Paul assures them that his "present situation," which should have hindered the spread of the gospel, in fact caused it to spread more than (μᾶλλον) it otherwise would have without this supposed hindrance.

Far from hurting the gospel's cause, his "sufferings and restraints" (Lightfoot) actually helped it; far from slowing it down, they really advanced it (εἰς προκοπήν—a metaphorical word that pictures "pioneers cutting a way before an army and so furthering its march"; Vincent; Stählin, TDNT 6.703–19; Bonhöffer, Epiktet, 128; see also 1 Tim 4:15; Ecclus 51:17; 2 Macc 8:8).

13–14. Proof that this is so lies in tangible results. Therefore, Paul now proceeds to name these results in the long sentence structured as follows, ὥστε . . . γενέσθαι . . . τολμᾶν. These results are: (1) It has now become clear that Paul is a prisoner, not for any crime he committed, political or otherwise, but simply because he is a Christian. (2) Most of his fellow believers are inspired by his imprisonment to speak the word daringly and fearlessly.

(ὥστε and the infinitives, as used here, contrary to Classical idiom, indicate actual result, not mere potential or intended result; Moulton, *Grammar*, 3,136.4.)

When Paul was arrested in Jerusalem (Acts 21) and shut away in prison in Caesarea (Acts 23, 24), one could easily imagine that this was the end of his ministry, especially as his imprisonment dragged on month after month (Acts 24:27). But in the providence of God the place of his imprisonment, the Praetorium of Herod (Acts 23:35), and the length of his imprisonment, both served to thrust the gospel up into higher levels of Roman society than it had ever reached before. Roman military officers, chiliarchs and centurions (Acts 23:24, 26), as well as Roman soldiers, in Jerusalem and Caesarea, heard the gospel. Two Roman governors, Felix and Festus, along with King Herod Agrippa and their wives heard Paul speak about faith in Christ Jesus (Acts 24:24–27; 25:1–26:32). One of these governors, over a span of two years, often sent for Paul to converse with him (Acts 24:26). News of this celebrated prisoner and his teaching must have spread through the Praetorium, the barracks and out into the surrounding community. Thus, what appeared at first to be the fatal blow to the Christian mission, the arrest of Paul, turned out to be the means of its revitalization, the key to preaching the gospel before governors and kings (cf. Mark 13:9) and their staff personnel. It became evident, therefore, to those in all parts of the residence of the provincial governor of Caesarea (ἐν ὅλῳ τῷ πραιτωρίῳ) and to all outside it (τοῖς λοιποῖς πᾶσιν) that Paul was a prisoner because he was a Christian. (On the wide range of meanings of "praetorium" see BGD; R. Brown, *The Gospel According to John* [AB, 29A. New York: Doubleday, 1966] 2,845; Collange, Gnilka; on the location of this praetorium see Lohmeyer; Introduction, above, xxxvii–xxxviii; contrast Reicke, "Caesarea," 283.) Christianity, therefore, gained public notice because of Paul's bonds. His imprisonment produced notoriety as being for Christ (φανεροὺς ἐν Χριστῷ) and provided extraordinary opportunity for bearing witness to the saving power of Christ in the gospel (Benoit, Hendriksen, Lightfoot, Lohmeyer, Vincent).

Paul's affairs had yet a second result which advanced the gospel still more—the majority (πλείονας; cf. BDF 224.3), though not all, of his fellow Christians (τῶν ἀδελφῶν) somehow gained confidence in the Lord or were somehow infused with courage by the Lord because of Paul's imprisonment and they dared to preach more than they had ever dared to preach before. (It is best to take ἐν κυρίῳ ["in the Lord"] with πεποιθότας ["confident"] rather than with ἀδελφῶν ["brothers"] since by ἀδελφῶν Paul already means "brothers in the Lord"; to add ἐν κυρίῳ to it would be tautological; cf. also 2:24.)

Paul does not intend to suggest by this statement that these people, most likely his fellow Christian workers in Caesarea, had ever lacked courage, or had ever failed in their preaching mission. His use of περισσοτέρως ("all the more") merely indicates that their courage and efforts, while continuing, were now heightened to a much greater degree. And these renewed efforts were directed toward preaching the word without fear. "The word" (ὁ λόγος), used here absolutely (cf. Gal 6:6; 1 Thess 1:6), but explained by its variants—"the word of God," and "the word of the Lord," refers to the totality of the Christian message (so Collange, 55, n. 3; Kittel, *TDNT* 4,114–19), against which all the hatred of the world concentrated itself. The "Tempter," the "Opponent" puts everything into action so as to make the gospel ineffective by intimidating those who proclaim it. The history of the church then as later was a history of the church under the cross (Euseb. *Hist. Eccl.* 5, Prol.). "But the people of God withstood this general attack of God's enemies in the fearlessness of those who fear God" (Stauffer, *Theology,* 187).

15–18*a*. These verses form a unit as is clear from the double chiasm (a crisscross structure) that binds them together:

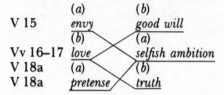

And their purpose is to provide yet more information about Paul's fellow-Christians (ἀδελφῶν) who had grown confident in the Lord so as to preach the gospel quite daringly (v 14). Paul says that they were all active in preaching, but surprisingly they were not all preaching with the right motives. Some were driven by jealousies, others by love and good will.

There is no grammatical reason for viewing this section as an excursus independent of its context and especially independent of v 14 as several scholars suggest (Barth, Dibelius, Gnilka, Hendriksen, Vincent). τινές ("some"), which immediately begins v 15, is a pronoun whose antecedent most logically and naturally is taken to be ἀδελφῶν ("brothers," v 14). The καί, although it can be adversative, expressing the idea of contrast, setting one group off against another (Vincent), is, nevertheless, the common connective between nouns, adjectives, clauses, and so on (Moulton, *Grammar,* 3,334; BGD), sometimes expressing surprise at something unexpected or noteworthy, and can be translated "and yet" (cf. Matt 3:14; 6:26; 1 Cor 5:2; Heb 3:9). Paul's language, therefore, points to the fact that he has in mind, in vv 15–18*a* some of those "brothers" he mentioned in v 14. Were it otherwise, surely he would have stated his intent more clearly. For "it would have been easy for Paul, had he so desired, to say, 'These indeed act in such and such a way, but there are other preachers who act in a different manner' " (Michael). True, it is difficult to imagine that Christian brothers, "made confident in the Lord," could be prompted to act by motives of envy and selfish ambition. But the history of the Christian church makes plain that such a contradiction, though distressing (καί), is not rare. Wesley, for example, urged his preachers "by prayer, by exhortation, and by every possible means, to oppose a party spirit," adding that "this has always, so far as it has prevailed, been the bane of all true religion" (*Letters,* 252, as quoted by Michael, 38).

There are several important things to notice in this section: (1) Whatever Paul might say later about his "brothers," he affirms first and foremost that all of them preach Christ. To emphasize this fact he uses three different verbs successively and synonomously—λαλεῖν (v 14, "speak"), κηρύσσειν (v 15, "preach") and καταγγέλλειν (vv 17, 18, "proclaim"). Christ himself, or the message (λόγος) about Christ, including the account of his death, burial and resurrection (cf. Acts 4:29–31; 1 Cor 1:23; Col 1:27–28; 4:3), is the gospel that they were preaching, and this pleased the apostle (v 18*a*). The content of their message was sound. Therefore, it is impossible to say with Lightfoot that the group whose motives Paul questioned were of the Judaizing party. For the Judaizers preached a different gospel, which to Paul really was not a gospel at all. Rather to him it was a distortion of the gospel of Christ and contrary to the gospel he approved and preached (Gal 1:6–9).

(2) How Paul was able to judge the motives of these two groups he does not disclose. But he confidently asserts that one group preached Christ motivated by "good intentions" out of "benevolence" (εὐδοκία, v 15) and from love (ἀγάπη, v 16). Both of these terms are relational and mean that such attitudes as they describe are directed toward someone. Here Paul, not Christ, is the object. Some of these brothers preached Christ simply because they had feelings of good will toward Paul, knowing that, irrespective of the consequences, this is what Paul wanted them to do. They knew for a fact (εἰδότες) that the apostle had been commissioned (κεῖσθαι—"to be appointed," "to be destined"; see Luke 2:34; 1 Thess 3:3) by God to provide a full defense (ἀπολογίαν) for the gospel (v 16). They knew also that, if because of their preaching he should more quickly or more frequently be brought before the tribunal to defend himself, this would only serve a good end—namely, to provide a forum for the defense of the gospel. Therefore, they were not hesitant to speak the word boldly for they worked together with the apostle in a spirit "of understanding and collaboration" (Bonnard, Dibelius, Collange).

But Paul also asserts that others preached Christ for less noble reasons: φθόνος καὶ ἔρις ("envy and strife" v 15) and ἐριθεία ("selfish ambition," v 17; see BGD who relate this word not to ἔρις but to ἔριδος, which originally meant a "day laborer," then "sordid work" of any kind, then in politics "a hired canvasser," and finally, "a partisan worker" or a "partisan spirit"). What does this mean? Were these preachers really directing their hostilities against Roman authority, rather than against Paul? Was their aim to stir up strife by preaching and thus incur the anger of Rome, in order to bring down upon themselves and Paul suffering, persecution, even martyrdom, in the belief that tribulation (θλῖψις) was necessary to hasten the end of the world and the return of Christ? (Hawthorn, *ExpTim* 62 [1950–51] 316–17). Or were they preachers who were motivated by envy and strife against the Jews, whose intrigues had landed Paul in jail? Were they using the preaching of the gospel as a counterattack against these Jews, preaching out of a contentious spirit that was aimed at arousing friction (θλῖψιν ἐγείρειν) against them *by* Paul's bonds, not at adding affliction *to* his bonds (Synge, 25)?

These answers are attempts to ease what otherwise is the contradiction of Christian brothers behaving in a less than Christian way toward an apostle of Jesus Christ. But these answers cannot be correct, (*a*) since, similar to "good will" and "love" the words "envy" "strife," and "selfish-ambition" are relational words, (*b*) since these latter words are exactly parallel to the former words, and (*c*) since Paul was the object of those former words—"love" and "good will"—therefore one is forced to conclude that, for whatever reason, he is also the object of the latter words—people reacted against Paul himself and thought to hurt him by their preaching.

Could it be that these were Christians who believed that for an apostle of the cross martyrdom was the true vocation, and were they thus disappointed with Paul "for the steps he (had) taken to secure his imminent release" (Collange)? Or were they Christians with a divine-man theology, who believed that any sign of weakness on Paul's part, such as imprisonment, showed that he knew nothing of the triumphant power of the Christ he presumed to serve? Thus they acted in a hostile manner toward him because to them he had placed the Christian message in jeopardy by his inability to throw off his chains. They were his rivals because, contrary to him, they had a mission strategy that preached a gospel of success, and they proved their claim by triumphing over all opposition (Jewett, *NovT* 12 [1970] 362–90). Irrespective of the difficulty one faces in identifying this group precisely, it seems clear that it was made up of people who opposed Paul out of personal animosity and rivalry. And as Barth has pointed out the grounds for such feelings were manifold for "there were 'Christian' persuasions which were so publicly and vigorously combatted by Paul that their supporters can hardly be blamed if they saw in him more their *opponent* than their Christian 'brother' " (Barth, 29).

(3) Why Paul felt it necessary to disclose to the Philippians the weaknesses of some of the brothers who were with him in Caesarea is a mystery. Was it simply because he could not contain his own vexation at this personal attack? Was his spirit "fretful as he wrote"? Does the splendid magnanimity of v 18 blind one to "the signs of annoyance" in vv 15, 16 and 17, and make it difficult to see a man who was unable to curb his agitated mind? Was Paul so hurt that "words escape him which in a calmer mood he would scarcely have uttered" (Michael)? Perhaps so, for Paul, though an apostle was human and as susceptible to the range of human emotions as anyone else. The fact, however, that he could conquer his indignation with forgiveness, and could replace his irritation with joy (v 18) provides a model for Christian living and thus is a sufficient reason for allowing this exposure of the darker side of Christian conduct to stand.

Yet it is more likely that Paul writes about these people who had wrong motives to make clear that such people do exist even within the Christian community, and therefore the Philippian Christians should not be taken by surprise if such should arise in their midst. At the same time he wishes to show that the nature of these base motives is truly malevolent. For the particular words Paul chose to describe them—φθόνος, ἔρις and ἐριθεία—are words frequently found in lists of other vices that always adversely affect, even endanger, the life of the church (Rom 1:29; 2 Cor 12:20; Gal 5:20–21; 1 Tim 6:4). Therefore, although Paul rejoices over the objective fact that men preach Christ (v 18a—ἐν τούτῳ χαίρω, "in *this* I rejoice") he cannot restrain himself from pointing out the subjective motives, false (πρόφασις) or true (ἀλήθεια), that prompt people to do so. It is not to be imagined, however, that Paul took any delight in those who preached with impure motives (οὐχ ἁγνῶς, v 17), or who used their preaching as a pretext for attacks on himself. His joy was in knowing that the Christian gospel was being preached. The "how" of preaching is not the object of Paul's joy; the "fact" of the preaching is. For when the Word of God is preached it overcomes all hindrances and moves on to its goal; its contents are irresistible (Isa 55:10–11; 1 Kings 2:27;

13:2, 5, 9, 17, 32; 2 Kings 1:17; 9:36; 22:16). The power of the gospel, therefore, does not depend on the character of the preacher.

18*b*–20. ἀλλὰ καὶ χαρήσομαι, "Yes, and I will continue to be glad." καί coupled with ἀλλά makes ἀλλά progressive and not adversative, to be translated, "And what is more," rather than "but" (see M. E. Thrall, *Greek Particles in the New Testament* [NTTS 3. Grand Rapids: Eerdmans, 1962] 11–16; BDF 448.6). Thus ἀλλά moves the letter on to a new topic: "I am glad because Christ is being preached. *And in addition* I will be glad for still another reason." This reason Paul discusses in vv 19 and 20, and it has to do with his expected fate as a prisoner.

19. Paul's future joy is based on (γάρ) what he knows (οἶδα). To some interpreters εἰδέναι, as distinguished from γινώσκειν, is "the knowledge of intuition or satisfied conviction or absolute knowledge" (Vincent; cf. NEB: "knowing well"). But the usage of these two verbs does not justify such fine distinctions (cf. John 21:17; 1 Cor 8:1–3; 2 Thess 1:8). Although Paul prefers εἰδέναι to γινώσκειν, he nevertheless uses them synonymously.

How Paul came to know what he did is not completely clear. Information about his future state may have filtered down to him through friends in high places. More likely, however, his knowledge was simply a deep inner conviction based on the words of Scripture. Paul's words, τοῦτό μοι ἀποβήσεται εἰς σωτηρίαν ("this will turn out for my deliverance," RSV), are exactly the words of Job (Job 13:16, LXX). Although this OT text is not introduced as a quotation, and it may not have been noticed as such by the Philippians (Gnilka), yet surely the verbal identity between the two passages strongly indicates that Paul understood and interpreted his situation in terms of Job's experience. As Job was ultimately "saved" from his plight and vindicated, so he, Paul, would ultimately be saved from his plight and vindicated. Thus, he was able to say "I know" with a conviction originating in sacred scripture.

There are two things here that Paul knew, each of which is introduced by the conjunction ὅτι ("that"): (1) that things would turn out well for him (v 19), and (2) that he on the one hand would not be ashamed, and Christ on the other hand would be honored (v 20*a*).

The first of these convictions is expressed in ambiguous language: ὅτι τοῦτό μοι ἀποβήσεται εἰς σωτηρίαν, which the RSV translates with equal ambiguity, "this will turn out for my deliverance." By τοῦτο ("this") Paul refers back to all the things that had happened to him, good and bad, "perplexities and annoyances," and so on that had come to him as the result of his preaching the gospel.

But what does Paul mean by σωτηρία ("deliverance")? It is true that σωτηρία is the special word that he uses to refer to the ultimate salvation which people will experience at the last judgment (Rom 1:16; 10:10; 13:11; 2 Cor 7:10; 1 Thess 5:8–9; 2 Thess 2:13). Thus, many interpreters feel compelled to give to σωτηρία its full eschatological sense here. They insist, therefore, that Paul means that he is confident he will endure to the end and so be saved in the Day of Christ (Beare, Collange, Gnilka, Houlden; see Foerster, *TDNT* 7,992–94).

Σωτηρία also has a lesser meaning, especially in the papyri, with the general sense of "health" or "well-being" (MM, 622). Such an understanding of σωτηρία for the present passage shows up in several modern translations: "all this will turn out for my highest welfare" (Goodspeed), "my good" (LB), "my soul's health" (Knox).

Σωτηρία seems also to have the meaning of "vindication," and thus some interpreters suggest that σωτηρία here is "equivalent to (Paul's) vindication at court. He hopes that his trust in God will be honored and his witness to divine faithfulness will be attested by the turn of events" (Martin, 1976).

Several things, however, argue for the fact that when Paul spoke of σωτηρία here he had in mind his release from prison: (1) The primary meaning of σωτηρία is deliverance from impending death (BGD). (2) Although Paul does indeed use σωτηρία regularly for the ultimate cosmic saving act of God to be completed at the end of the world, it is wrong to say he must always give this meaning to the word (cf. Paul's use of σωτηρία as quoted by Luke in Acts 27:34; and see 2 Cor 1:6 where "salvation" coupled with "encouragement" seems simply to refer to the general welfare or profit of others). (3) Paul, in reflecting on the Job story, seeing in it parallels to his own sufferings and the misunderstandings of these sufferings by others, and knowing that God saved Job out of all his troubles and vindicated him, was led to the conviction that he too would be "saved," released from prison, and vindicated in the eyes of Jew and Roman. (4) Finally, Paul repeats this same verb οἶδα ("I know") later on when he states, "I know that I am going to stay and remain on with all of you" (vv 25, 26). He uses an even stronger verb when he assures the Philippians that he will soon come to see them (2:24). How could this be unless he knew that his release was certain?

Paul believed that some important things would contribute to his being set free from prison. One of these was prayer (δέησις). As he prayed for the Philippians (see notes on 1:4 for the meaning of δέησις) so he now depends on them to pray in his behalf. Whenever Paul asks the church to pray for him, it is that he might be delivered from disobedient and evil men (Rom 15:30–31; 2 Thess 3:2), that he might be released from prison and brought safely again to his friends (Philem 22), that he might remain true to God in the face of opposition (2 Cor 1:9–11; 1 Thess 5:25), and that his ministry might be effective (Col 4:3; 2 Thess 3:1–2). Paul knew that God effected changes in history through prayer and therefore he counted heavily on his churches to carry out this ministry on his behalf.

Another thing that Paul believed would contribute to his release is phrased in a way difficult to understand—ἐπιχορηγίας τοῦ πνεύματος Ἰησοῦ Χριστοῦ, which has been translated as "the supply of the Spirit of Jesus Christ" (AV). The difficulty arises from the ambiguity of the genitives Paul uses here, an ambiguity that is perpetuated in the translation of these genitives into English by the preposition "of"—"of the Spirit of Jesus Christ."

There are at least two possibilities of interpretation for the first of these genitives, τοῦ πνεύματος ("of the Spirit"). On the one hand, πνεύματος could be an objective genitive, meaning that the Spirit is the object of the action implied in the noun ἐπιχορηγία ("supply"). Such an interpretation leads naturally to a translation such as Moffatt's—"The outcome of all this . . . will be my release as I am *provided with the Spirit*" (cf. NEB).

On the other hand, and more likely, τοῦ πνεύματος could be a subjective genitive. So understood, the Spirit is not that which is given, but is himself the giver of the needed help or assistance to bring about his release. "The help which comes from the Spirit," or "is given by the Spirit" (GNB, NIV), are the logical translations from such an interpretation. This idea of the Spirit bringing assistance to Christians, especially as they bear witness to their faith when they are brought before judges, is an idea firmly anchored in early Christianity, although not particularly in Paul (Collange; cf. Mark 13:11; Matt 10:20; Luke 12:12).

The other difficulty is in understanding the genitive, Ἰησοῦ Χριστοῦ ("of Jesus Christ"). It could be a genitive of apposition, indicating that the Spirit of Jesus Christ means "the Spirit which is Jesus Christ" (cf. Rom 8:1–11). It could also be a subjective genitive, meaning that Jesus Christ is the giver of the Spirit in accord with the promise he made to his disciples (Luke 12:11–12; cf. John 16:7). Or, since in Paul the Spirit is usually said to be given by God the Father, not by Jesus Christ (1 Cor 6:19; 2 Cor 1:21–22; 5:5; Eph 1:17; Gal 3:5; 1 Thess 4:8), and since the Spirit is referred to alternatively as the Spirit of Christ (Rom 8:9; 1 Pet 1:11) and the Spirit of his Son (Gal 4:6), perhaps it is best to understand this expression as just another name for the Holy Spirit, the Spirit who animated Jesus in his human life and who, in the risen Christ, is the life principle of believers (Vincent; cf. 1 Cor 15:15 and see also J. D. G. Dunn, *Jesus and the Spirit* [Philadelphia: Westminster, 1975] 318–26; Schweizer, *TDNT* 6,415–36).

20. Paul's confident conviction that he would be released from prison harmonized with (κατά and the accusative) his own aspirations (τὴν ἀποκαραδοκίαν καὶ ἐλπίδα μου). In effect he told the Philippians, "Things will turn out just as I expected and hoped!" The word Paul used to describe his expectation, ἀποκαραδοκία, is a rare word, perhaps coined by him and used elsewhere in the NT only in Rom 8:19. Etymologically it envisions both an outstretched head (κάρα, "head," and the Ionic δέκεσθαι, "to stretch"), and the averting of the eyes from (ἀπό) other objects. As it has been explained, ἀποκαραδοκία is "the concentrated hope which ignores other interests . . . and strains forward as with outstretched head" (Kennedy; see also BDF 119.1; Delling, *TDNT* 1,393; G. Bertram, "ΑΠΟΚΑΡΑΔΟΚΙΑ (Phil.1,20)," *ZNW* 49 [1958] 264–70). Ἐλπίς, although regularly used by Paul to describe the Christian's hope for the eternal future (Gnilka; Bultmann, *TDNT* 2,530–33), is here used with the lesser meaning of simple human expectation (cf. Rom 4:18; 1 Cor 9:10; cf. Acts 16:19). Since these two nouns, ἀποκαραδοκία and ἐλπίς are bound together with only one article—τὴν ἀποκαραδοκίαν καὶ ἐλπίδα μου—it is possible to treat them as a hendiadys and translate, "my hope-filled eager expectation" (cf. NEB).

Why was Paul so eager to be released from prison and so filled with the expectation that he would be? Certainly the reasons were not because he could not stand suffering, although he might wish to be freed from it (cf. 2 Cor 4:17), or that he feared death (cf. Phil 1:21–23). Rather it was because release would demonstrate that he was innocent of any crime and especially prove that the gospel he preached was not a subversive element in society aimed against the Roman government. Release would mean not only his vindication but that of the gospel as well.

Paul knew, then, that he would be set free. This is the first thing he was convinced of (οἶδα ὅτι . . . vv 19–20a). The second conviction he had is also introduced in the same way, with ὅτι ("that," v 20b). Most commentators (but see Michaelis) and translators, however, attach this ὅτι-clause with ἐλπίδα and not with οἶδα, making it the object hoped for rather than the object known—"my hope is *that* I will not be ashamed," rather than, "I know *that* I will not be ashamed." The majority notwithstanding, it seems more correct to link this second ὅτι with οἶδα and not with ἐλπίδα: (1) It should be clear from the discussion above that the prepositional phrase, κατὰ τὴν ἀποκαραδοκίαν καὶ ἐλπίδα μου ("according to my eager expectation and hope") is grammatically dependent on τοῦτό μοι ἀποβήσεται εἰς σωτηρίαν ("this will result in my release"), and therefore it follows that Paul's hope is not that he will not be ashamed, but rather that he will be set free. (2) Many times in the NT ἐλπίς is used absolutely, that is without any object, when it refers to the Christian hope (Acts 2:16; Rom 5:5; 8:24; 1 Cor 13:13; 2 Cor 3:12; Col 1:5, etc.). But when ἐλπίς does have an object, that object is almost always expressed by the genitive case (Acts 16:19; 23:7; 26:6; Rom 5:2; 2 Cor 10:15; Gal 5:5; Col 1:27; 1 Thess 5:8; Titus 1:2; 3:7) even when the object is a verbal form (1 Cor 9:10). Ἐλπίς followed by ὅτι to express the object of hope occurs only once in the NT (Rom 8:20). Thus, to take the ὅτι here in Phil 1:20b with ἐλπίδα, although possible, is not very probable. (3) Finally, the ideas that follow ὅτι, namely that Paul will not be ashamed and that Christ will be glorified, so partake of the nature of certainty for the apostle that οἶδα ("know") is a more appropriate term to govern these ideas than ἐλπίς ("hope").

The verb αἰσχύνεσθαι ("be ashamed") is rarely used in the NT and only twice by Paul, here and in 2 Cor 10:8. Αἰσχύνεσθαι, however, is found often in the Psalms, the prophetic literature and in the documents of the Dead Sea Community (LXX Pss 24:3; 34:26–27; 39:15–17; 68:7; 118:80; Isa 1:29; 45:17; 49:23; 50:7; Jer 12:13; Zeph 3:11; 1QH 4:23–24; 5:35; 9:20, 22; 1QS 4:23). These texts describe the humble pious, who, in the proper relationship of trust in God, count on him not to let them be disgraced, disappointed, disillusioned, or brought by him into judgment and thus be covered with shame before their enemies (see Bultmann, *TDNT* 1,189–90).

Hence, when Paul says, "I know that I will not be ashamed by anything," his words may mean that since in the final analysis only God has the power to cover anyone with disgrace (αἰσχυνθήσομαι, a "divine passive"? cf. J. Jeremias, *New Testament Theology* [London: SCM Press, 1971] 1, 9), and since those who trustingly wait for God will never be confounded (LXX Ps 24:3; Isa 49:23), and since Paul's own relationship with God was one of trusting dependence, he knew that in no way would it be possible for God to bring shame down upon him by disappointing his expectations.

Or these words, "I will not be ashamed," may mean that, because of Paul's obedient trust in God, he could count on the fact that God would never permit the "false brethren," who challenged his conduct, to cover him with disgrace, or force him to repent in shame for the course of action he had chosen (Collange).

Or, as is more likely, these words may mean that Paul, having his release from prison (σωτηρία) in mind, and realizing that he must first be brought to trial, and knowing that he must then give an account (ἀπολογίαν) of his involvement with the gospel (1:7, 16), viewed this trial not as a cause for personal embarrassment or as a threat to his life, but as an unexpected but welcomed platform for proclaiming the gospel. Instead of seeing the gospel as something that would bring shame upon him personally, Paul could say, now as always he had said before, "I am not ashamed (οὐκ ἐπαισχύνομαι) of the gospel for it is the power of God unto salvation" (εἰς σωτηρίαν; Rom 1:16), and again, "having therefore such a message to preach I am very bold (πολλῇ παρρησίᾳ) in proclaiming it" (2 Cor 3:12). It is with this same vocabulary and with this same ring of confidence that Paul now tells the Philippians, "I know I will in no way be ashamed (ἐν οὐδενὶ αἰσχυνθήσομαι), but now as always, I will publicly and very boldly (ἐν πάσῃ παρρησίᾳ) speak out not only in my own defense but in the defense of the gospel" (εἰς ἀπολογίαν τοῦ εὐαγγελίου, vv 20b, 16). His trial before the Roman tribunal, therefore, could never succeed in embarrassing him, but only in providing him with the occasion for his most important public (παρρησίᾳ) testimony to Christ.

Thus Paul can proceed to say, "Christ will be praised because of me" (v 20b), i.e. because of my open witness to his person and power. The verb translated, "be praised," (μεγαλυνθήσεται), literally means "to make" something "large," such as increasing the number of one's enemies (Thuc. 5.98), or the size or length of the tassels on one's garments (Matt 23:5). But when Paul uses this verb here he does not mean that his trial will succeed in making Christ greater, but rather that it will serve to make Christ, who *is* great, known to a larger audience. Thus many more will praise him who otherwise would have been silent, having known little or nothing about him. (For the meaning of μεγαλύνω as "praise," see Ps 68:31; Ecclus 43:31; Luke 1:46; Acts 10:46.)

Paul uses the passive form of the verb μεγαλύνω with Christ as the subject (μεγαλυνθήσεται Χριστός), not merely for rhetorical purposes to balance one passive (αἰσχυνθήσομαι) with another (μεγαλυνθήσεται) and to keep the sounds agreeably similar, nor because he found this pair of verbs in their passive forms coupled together in the Psalms—"Let the enemy be ashamed" (αἰσχυνθείησαν), "Let the Lord be praised" (μεγαλυνθήτω; LXX Pss 34:26–27; 39:15–17; cf. 1QH 4:23–24), but because he cannot bring himself to say, "*I* will magnify Christ." With characteristic humility he makes Christ the subject of the verb and himself the means by which the action of the verb will be achieved. Paul wants his whole life (σῶμα; see Schweizer, *TDNT* 7,1065–66) to be the instrument Christ will use "for the extension of his power and glory" (Barth; cf. 1 Cor 6:20; 2 Cor 4:10; see also Caird, and G. B. Caird, "The Glory of God in the Fourth Gospel; an Exercise in Biblical Semantics," *NTS* 15 [1968–69] 265–77).

It is difficult to see in Paul's phrase εἴτε διὰ ζωῆς εἴτε διὰ θανάτου ("whether by life or by death") anything more than an emphatic, perhaps stock expression that means "totally," or "all-encompassingly" (cf. Rom 8:38; 1 Cor 3:22; see also 2 Sam 15:21; Ecclus 11:14; 37:18), somewhat like the modern expression "for dear life," or "on your life." The apostle has already stated that he knows he will be released from prison (v 19), and in a moment he will state with confidence that he will go on living and remain with the Philippians for their spiritual welfare (v 25). Thus this phrase carries in it no suspense regarding the outcome of his trial (Moule), nor does it suggest the possibility of death as an alternative to life as a means of bringing glory to Christ (Gnilka, Hendriksen, Martin, and most commentaries; see also C. Bigaré, *AsSeign* 56 [1974] 9–14). Rather, the expression simply means that Paul's *entire existence*, as that of a responsible human being (σῶμα), is aimed at one goal, that of bringing praise to Christ.

21–24. And yet the mere mention of these words, "life or death," triggers a reverie within Paul on the subject of living or dying. But his musings were not due to the fact that he was actually facing the immediate possibility of death (see above). Rather, the long, hard struggles of his life as a slave of Jesus Christ (2 Cor 11:23–27), the constant emotional strain on his soul arising from his concern for the welfare of the churches he founded (2 Cor 11:28–29), and the debilitating effects of a lengthy imprisonment (Acts 24:27), have wearied him and have forced him to think in a new way about the meaning of life and death, about their relative importance to him, and about which of the two he would prefer *for himself*. Notice the emphatic position of ἐμοί ("for me") which begins this excursus (v 21).

This section (vv 21–24) is tied together, as Gnilka has pointed out, around the alternating ideas already begun in v 20 of life and death whose differing expressions serve to support and explain each other:

21a   Life (τὸ ζῆν) is Christ
21b   Death (τὸ ἀποθανεῖν) is gain
22   Life (τὸ ζῆν ἐν σαρκί) is worthwhile work
23   Death (τὸ ἀναλῦσαι) is to be with Christ
24   Life (τὸ ἐπιμένειν ἐν τῇ σαρκί) is for the benefit of others

Such an alternation underscores the inner turmoil of the apostle as he wrestles with these ultimate issues, leaning now in favor of one, now in favor of the other. But it ends with a call to live in order to serve.

21. Ἐμοί, "to me," is the very first word in this new section. Paul purposely places it here in the emphatic position to draw special attention to his own personal understanding of life and death, irrespective of what others may think or say about them. *"To me* living is Christ, dying is gain!" His sentences in Greek are short, perfectly balanced, concise, verbless, powerful. τὸ ζῆν, "living," is a present infinitive accentuating the *process* of living. It answers to the τὸ ἀποθανεῖν, "dying," an aorist infinitive accentuating the *act* of dying. The verb "to be" is absent from both sentences, but can and should be supplied, for Χριστός and κέρδος stand in the predicate position to τὸ ζῆν and to τὸ ἀποθανεῖν respectively. Χριστός ("Christ"), in the first sentence, there-fore, answers to κέρδος ("gain") in the second.

By saying τὸ ζῆν Χριστός ("living is Christ") Paul does not mean that Christ is the source of his physical existence (cf. Acts 17:28), or even of his spiritual life (Rom 8:2–11; 2 Cor 5:17). Nor does he mean that Christ is his life (Luther, Tyndale), in the sense that Christ lives in him—Gal 2:20 is *not* an explanation of this statement (see the comments of Betz, *Galatians*, 124; cf. Bultmann,

TDNT 2, 868–70). He does not even mean that living is to be with Christ (cf. Phil 1:23). Rather, without rejecting these ideas, but including them and embracing them in his thinking, Paul nevertheless puts the emphasis now in quite a different place. To say "living is Christ" is to say that for him "life *means* Christ" (Goodspeed, Knox, Moffatt, Phillips). Life is summed up in Christ. Life is filled up with, occupied with Christ, in the sense that everything Paul does—trusts, loves, hopes, obeys, preaches, follows (Vincent), and so on—is inspired by Christ and is done for Christ. Christ and Christ alone gives inspiration, direction, meaning and purpose to existence. Paul views his life in time (against Dibelius) as totally determined and controlled by his own love for and commitment to Christ. Overpowered by Christ on the Damascus Road and overwhelmed by his majesty and love and goodness and forgiveness, Paul can see no reason for being except to be "for Christ" (Rom 14:7–9). "To me to live is Christ!"

But for Paul to say this "does not thereby mean that his life [was] a carefree or blissful absorption into a transcendent realm of being" (Palmer, *NovT* 17 [1975] 217). It does not mean that from henceforth his life was problem-free. Quite the contrary. Precisely because Christ was the goal of Paul's life he felt constrained (ἀνάγκη), not by external pressure, but by the inner compulsion of love, to take up the tough task of preaching the gospel (Phil 1:7, 12, 16, 27; 2:16; 4:3). As a result his life was marked by imprisonment (1:7, 13, 17), afflictions (1:17; 4:14), sufferings (1:29; 3:10), struggles (1:30), beatings, stonings, weariness, pain, privation and dangers of every sort (2 Cor 11:23–27). Precisely because Paul's life was so occupied with Christ, so totally given over to Christ, to doing the will of Christ, he found life a very heavy load to carry. Thus, he was led to say, τὸ ἀποθανεῖν κέρδος ("dying is gain"). These words are not the words of the brave martyr, like Ignatius of Antioch, crying out for "fire and cross and struggles with wild beasts" to come upon him in order that he may attain to Jesus Christ (Ign *Rom* 5.3), or in order that he might be carried up straight away from the place of execution into heaven without passing through any intermediate state (see Lohmeyer; Stauffer, *Theology*, 186). They are the words of the very human Paul giving vent to a very human and universal sentiment: death is a gain to those whose life has become weighed down with well-nigh unbearable burdens.

The universality of this sentiment can be demonstrated by numerous quotations drawn from lyric poetry, drama, philosophy and rhetoric spread over several centuries of Greek and Latin literature. Interestingly, the vocabulary used to express this sentiment is almost identical with that which Paul used here in Phil 1:21. Antigone, for example, says: "Whoever lives in as many ills as I—how does this one not get gain by dying?" (πῶς ὅδ' οὐχὶ κατθανὼν κέρδος φέρει; Sophocles *Ant.* 463–64). And Io, upon being told by Prometheus of sufferings still to come, cries out, "What gain (κέρδος) have I then in life? Why did not I hurl myself from this rugged rock . . . ? Better it were to die (κρεῖσσον θανεῖν) once for all than linger out all my days in misery" (Aeschylus, *PV* 747–51; cf. Euripides, *Med.* 145–47; Plato, *Ap.* 40c–e; see Gnilka and Palmer, *NovT* 17 [1975] 203–18 for the best collection of similar expressions see also Ecclus 41:2*b*–4, a reference they do not cite).

If it is true that Paul by his statement τὸ ἀποθανεῖν κέρδος ("dying is gain")

is echoing the universal longing of a human being to be released by death
from the burden life has placed upon him, (1) how does it square with his
first statement, τὸ ζῆν Χριστός ("living is Christ"), and (2) how, if at all, does
he make any advance in thinking over his pagan counterparts?

The answers to these questions seem to be as follows. Since for Paul "living
is Christ," meaning that life for Paul had no significance whatsoever without
Christ, it follows that he never would have renounced Christ to save himself
from those things that wearied him and hurt him and made life a burden
for him. Therefore, for him to go on and say that "dying is gain" required
a firm belief on his part that death, although it had the power to free him
from "lingering out his days in misery," could not in any way separate him
from Christ (see Rom 8:38–39). He was certain that even in death the Christian
was still in vital relation with Christ. So certain was he that he put the two
ideas together in one phrase, τὸ ἀναλῦσαι καὶ σὺν Χριστῷ εἶναι ("to depart
[=to die] and to be with Christ"). It is also this belief that spells the fundamental difference between Paul's thinking and that of his non-Christian counter-
part. The pagan viewed death as a release from earthly troubles and no more.
It was for the pagan a walking away from present ills out into the unknown,
perhaps into nonexistence, and hence a "gain" (κέρδος) in that sense (cf.
Plato, Ap. 29a–c; 40c–e). Paul also viewed death as a release from earthly
troubles. But he saw death as more than this: in death there was a continuing
relationship with Christ. Life which is Christ is thus not destroyed by death;
it is only increased and enriched by death (GNB, Phillips). Hence, for Paul
τὸ ἀποθανεῖν is κέρδος, in the ultimate sense of this word (cf. Antin, RSR 62
[1974] 259–60 for a somewhat different interpretation; cf. also Ridderbos,
Paul, 498–99).

22. At this point, for whatever reason (see Martin, 1959, for a suggested
reason) Paul's sentence structure becomes quite broken and difficult to piece
together. It is so difficult that Michael wishes to emend the text saying that
none of v 22 except the last clause belonged to Paul's original sentence.
Michael's reconstruction of vv 21 and 22 certainly makes everything flow
smoothly—"as life means Christ to me, so death means gain; and which to
choose I cannot tell"—but there is not a shred of evidence to support this
radical treatment of excision to resolve a difficult problem. So it is necessary
to try to make sense out of the verse as it stands.

Literally translated v 22 reads as follows: "but if to live in the flesh, this
to me fruit of work, and what I shall choose I do not know." Apparently
this verse is an elliptical sentence, a not uncommon phenomenon in Paul's
writings (Rom 4:9; 1 Cor 4:6; 2 Cor 1:6; Gal 2:9, etc.). Something, then,
must be supplied in order for the translated sentence to be intelligible. The
simplest and easiest thing to do is to add a second "if" immediately before
"this," so that the "this" (τοῦτο), then, clearly refers back to and explains
the "to live." It also means that the "and" (καί) introduces the main clause
and must be translated "then" (cf. Luke 2:21; Acts 1:10; 2 Cor 2:3; BDF
442.7). The result of this slight addition gives a perfectly understandable
translation in harmony with the context: "but if to live in the flesh—if this
is the fruit of my work, then I do not know what I would choose," meaning,

that if to live is going to result in productive effort for Paul, then he is in a dilemma—he cannot tell which to choose, life or death (cf. Bonnard, Collange, Dibelius, Goodspeed, GNB, JB).

Looking more closely at the text, one notices that the "if" clause, introduced as it is by εἰ, may not really be conditional in meaning at all, but may border on causal, "since" (BDF 372.1). If so, then by using this construction, Paul underscores the idea already expressed (see v 19 and the comments there). He assumes that he will be released from prison and that fruitfulness will be the natural consequence of his release.

Ἐν σαρκί ("in the flesh") is an expression often found in Paul with very negative overtones describing one's sinful lower nature (cf. Rom 8:5; see A. Sand, *Der Begriff 'Fleisch' in den paulinischen Hauptbriefen* [Regensburg: Pustet, 1967]). Here, however, linked as it is with ("to live") it means nothing more than life in the body, Paul's physical life lived here on earth.

"Fruit of my work" (μοι καρπὸς ἔργου) is also an ambiguous phrase. It may mean that as a result of his release Paul was confident that he would be able to reap the fruit of his efforts which had been interrupted by his imprisonment. More likely, as Martin points out, by using this phrase Paul envisions "a further extension of his missionary labours and a greater opportunity to prove that Christ is his life." Ἔργον ("labor") is a frequent word used by Paul to describe his missionary activity (Martin, 1959; cf. Rom 15:18; 2 Cor 10:11; Phil 2:30, LB).

Finally, in the last part of this verse, Paul admits to not knowing which to choose, death or life. The Greek verb translated "know" is neither εἰδέναι or γινώσκειν but γνωρίζειν. Γνωρίζειν is a Pauline word, used by him eighteen of the twenty-six times it appears in the NT, and always in the sense of "to make known" or "to reveal" (Rom 9:22–23; 1 Cor 12:3; 15:1; Gal 1:11; Phil 4:6, etc.). Hence, there is no good reason to translate it here, "I do (not) know" (cf. AV, LB, NIV, JB AND BGD). The selection of this particular word reflects the reality of the dilemma Paul faced. "I dare not reveal" my preference and "I cannot tell" what I would choose (cf. NEB, RSV, Goodspeed, Knox, Moffatt) are translations that come closer to the force of the Greek than the translation "I do not know." "The Apostle will not venture to decide between the alternatives, and the choice must be left in his Master's hands" (Jones).

23. The verb συνέχομαι serves to highlight the magnitude of Paul's dilemma. It is a powerful word that can describe a person who is hemmed in on both sides so that he has no room to move (Luke 8:45), or a city encircled by enemies who are closing in on it from every side (Luke 19:43). It can describe those who are attacked or tormented by pain or grief or terror (cf. Job 3:24; Luke 8:37). It can also describe those who are totally controlled or dominated by some external power (Köster, *TDNT* 7, 882–85). Paul uses συνέχειν in this last sense in 2 Cor 5:15, the only other time he uses it, where he speaks of being completely controlled by the love of God. Hence, upon seeing this word one can easily picture the stress Paul felt with two desires like two equally strong external forces pressing in on him viselike from both sides (ἐκ τῶν δύο).

Paul names these desires, and at the same time accentuates how equal they are in terms of the pressure they place on him in a perfectly balanced construction obscured by punctuation and by most, if not all, translations. It is best to set them out clearly as follows:

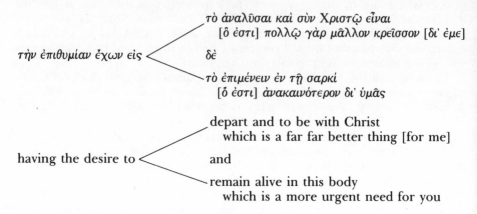

The first of these desires is "to depart and to be with Christ." Interestingly, Paul now refrains from boldly saying, "I desire to die" (ἀποθνῄσκειν), preferring rather to use a euphemism (ἀναλῦσαι) for death. The verb ἀναλῦσαι, although it does mean "to die," nevertheless is a highly picturesque word that paints death in brighter colors. Ἀναλῦσαι is used to describe an army "striking camp" and moving on (2 Macc 9:1; cf. Haupt who sees in this word an allusion to the wilderness generation of Israel and to the tents in which they lived). Or it is used to refer to a ship "being released from its mooring," "weighing anchor" and sailing off (Polyb. 3.69.14). Or it is used to speak of the "solution" of a difficult problem (see LSJ). Hence, with any or all of these images in mind, Paul says, "I wish to depart this life" (see Lee, NovT [1970] 361, for a note on the possible origin of this remark by Paul).

Now the reason for his longing "to depart" did not lie in the desire for immortality such as the ancient Greeks had. Paul did not yearn simply for a state in which his soul would live on freed at last from the hampering shackles of his body (cf. Plato, Phd.). The idea of a disembodied soul was intolerable to him (2 Cor 5:1–5; see M. J. Harris, "Paul's view of Death in 2 Corinthians 5:1–10," in R. N. Longenecker and M. C. Tenney [eds.] New Dimensions in New Testament Study [Grand Rapids: Eerdmans, 1974] 317–28). Rather Paul's longing to leave this earthly life lay in the belief that he would "be with Christ" (καὶ σὺν Χριστῷ εἶναι). He could not possibly desire the one without the other, that is, death without Christ, even if death did bring him relief from all his troubles. Paul's grammar here indicates that for him, although "leaving this life" and "being with Christ" are not necessarily identical (against Stauffer, Theology, 211–12), the latter being an advance over the former, yet they are nevertheless inextricably interwoven. He makes the two infinitives share one article in Greek—τὸ ἀναλῦσαι καὶ σὺν Χριστῷ εἶναι—thus binding the two together.

But what did Paul mean by the phrase σὺν Χριστῷ εἶναι ("to be with Christ")? As simple as these words seem they nevertheless have been the catalyst for many lengthy and bewildering discussions (see the select bibliography at the beginning of this section). The discussion arises from seeing in Paul a consistent doctrine of life after death, namely, that Christians who die "sleep" until the second coming of Christ, at which time they will be awakened, raised to life again, and given new incorrruptible bodies in exchange for their old corruptible physical bodies, a view that sees Paul insisting on the resurrection as essential in order for one to be a complete person (1 Cor 15:35–55; 1 Thess 4:13–5:10; see Caird; Moule, NTS 12 [1965–66] 120–23; Cullmann, Resurrection; Ellis, Paul, 35–48 and NTS 6 [1960] 211–24). Here in Phil 1:23, however, Paul seems to suggest quite a different view, namely that the Christian, upon dying, goes immediately into the presence of the Lord, where he enjoys conscious personal fellowship with him, a view that leads some to believe that a future resurrection is superfluous, to see the "resurrection" as taking place at death (cf. W. D. Davies, Paul and Rabbinic Judaism [London: SPCK, 1948] 319; K. Barth, as quoted by Cullmann, Resurrection, 49).

No completely satisfactory resolution to the problem posed by these seemingly contradictory views has as yet been given, and perhaps none can be given. But there are several important things to notice before making a final decision: (1) The phrase "with Christ" is a unique formula coined by Paul (Grundmann, TDNT 7, 782), and is of fundamental importance in his thinking. Yet he is not always consistent in the meaning he attaches to it. (a) Sometimes he lets the expression σὺν Χριστῷ convey the idea of "incorporation" (cf. the interchange of ἐν Χριστῷ with σὺν Χριστῷ in Rom 6:11 and context), building on the concept of corporate solidarity—Christ is not only a single self but the last Adam, the new Man (1 Cor 15:45, 47), the embodiment of a new humanity. What happened to him happened also to that humanity: it was crucified with Christ (Χριστῷ συνεσταύρωμαι, Gal 2:20; cf. Rom 6:6), put to death with Christ (ἀπεθάνομεν σὺν Χριστῷ, Rom 6:8; cf. Col 2:2), buried with Christ (συνετάφημεν αὐτῷ, Rom 6:4), and made alive (i.e. resurrected) with Christ (Col 2:13; cf. Rom 6:4). Death, burial and resurrection have already taken place for the Christian because the Christian is "with Christ," incorporate in Christ (but see also 2 Cor 4:14; 13:4; Col 3:4 where some of these ideas are expressed by the future tense). (b) At other times Paul uses σὺν Χριστῷ to express the simple notion of "association." For example, notice 1 Thess 4:13–17. Here Paul states that the dead in Christ, those who sleep in him (διὰ τοῦ Ἰησοῦ), will be resurrected, and God will bring them with Jesus (σὺν αὐτῷ) when he comes from heaven with a shout. They will join Jesus in his triumphal return. And what is more, those who are still alive at the Parousia of Jesus will be caught up to meet him in the air, and so, Paul concludes, "we will be with the Lord" (σὺν κυρίῳ), i.e. we will be in his company forever. (c) And there are other, though fewer, instances where Paul used the expression σὺν Χριστῷ to stress the idea of "fellowship with Christ." Following hard on the heels of the clearest futurist eschatological passage in Paul's writings (1 Thess 4:13–17), come these words of the apostle: Christ "died for us so that whether we are awake or asleep, we may live together with him" (σὺν αὐτῷ, 1 Thess 5:10; see BGD on καθεύδω; also Oepke TDNT

3, 436). As in those Psalms where prepositions, such as σύν, convey the idea of vital communion with God (LXX Pss 138:18; 139:14), so here the idea of conscious personal fellowship with Christ looms large, whether one is alive or dead (cf. 1 Thess 5:10, JB, Moffatt). Thus it is clear that there is no single idea expressed by Paul's important phrase "with Christ."

(2) The context of Phil 1:23 and the very wording of the verse itself favors the idea of "fellowship with Christ" as belonging to the phrase σὺν Χριστῷ found here. In fact, Paul, musing about death, his own death, and the meaning of death, comes to combine the words, "to live is Christ and to die is gain," and the words "to depart and to be with Christ" in such a way as to emphasize his growing conviction that death cannot in any way deprive believers of this "fellowship with Christ" (Rom 8:38–39)—it can only provide them with the opportunity to enjoy this fellowship to a degree never before experienced. Paul's focus on the supreme importance of Christ and of fellowship with Christ, and his own understanding of fellowship as living communion with Christ, based perhaps on his reflections on the Psalms (cf. Pss 72:23–24 and 15:11 with the valuable comments on this Ps by A. Weiser, *Die Psalmen* [ATD 14–15. 5th ed. Göttingen: Vandenhoeck und Ruprecht, 1959]; see also Luke 16:22–26; 23:43) seem to lead him to envision an intermediate existence in which any deceased Christian, not just the martyred Christian as Lohmeyer suggests, is "with Christ" after death and before the resurrection in a state of companionship with Christ in glory (2 Cor 5:2–8; Dupont, ΣΥΝ ΧΡΙΣΤΩΙ, 182, although it is not necessary to see with Dupont the origin of this idea in Hellenism. A more satisfactory view is that expressed by Moule, *JTS* 15 [1964] 1–15; see also G. E. Ladd, *A Theology of the New Testament* [Grand Rapids: Eerdmans] 463–64, 552; S. Laeuchli, "Monism and Dualism in Pauline Anthropology," *BR* 3 [1958] 15–27; C. J. De Vogel, "Reflexions on Philipp, i.23–24," *NovT* 19 [1977] 262–74; Whiteley, *Theology of St Paul;* see Ellis, *NTS* 6 [1959–60] 211–24 for a different interpretation of 2 Cor 5:1–11).

(3) But Paul does not speculate on the nature of this "interim condition." He goes no further than to say that it exists and that it signifies union with Christ (Cullmann, *Resurrection*, 51, n. 7). Nor will he allow this intermediate state to substitute for a future resurrection. When Paul wrote the Philippians he had in no way surrendered his futurist eschatology. That is to say, his doctrine of a bodily resurrection at the last day (1 Thess 4:13–17) was still intact—the exchange of the Christian's humiliating and humiliated body for a glorious body does *not* take place at death, but only at the Parousia of Jesus Christ (Phil 3:20–21). Thus Phil 1:23 (and 2 Cor 5:1–10) cannot at all indicate a development in Paul's thinking away from the expectation of a physical resurrection in the future, toward a spiritual "resurrection" in the present coincident with one's departing from this life (so C. H. Dodd, "The Mind of Paul: Change and Development," *BJRL* 18 [1934], 69–70; A. Schweitzer, *The Mysticism of Paul the Apostle* [London: A. and C. Black, 1931] 135–36; Stanley, *Christ's Resurrection;* Moule argues for a basic consistency in Paul's various eschatological formulations, *JTS* 15 [1964] 1–15 and *NTS* 12 [1966] 106–23). The two apparently conflicting views must be understood, as Kümmel has succinctly pointed out, in terms of Paul's basic interest: "Paul obvi-

ously is interested only in the fact that the Christian always remains in fellowship with his heavenly Lord" (*Theology*, 242; see E. P. Sanders, *Paul and Palestinian Judaism* [London: SCM Press, 1977] 432 and n. 9). What Paul longs for, then, is the hope of the resurrection. "But though that day should not yet dawn, he would nevertheless be of good courage . . . to surrender his life in death." This was in fact to be preferred in light of his trials, persecutions, sufferings, and so on, "for then he might already take up his abode with the Lord." Hence, "the idea of the 'intermediate state' is no *Fremdkörper* here. It comes to the fore of itself . . . when the future is still waiting and death is nevertheless an immediate reality." And yet the intermediate state is not in itself a separate ground for comfort (cf. 1 Thess 4:18); it has no independent existence apart from the resurrection. Without the resurrection there is no hope at all for believers who have died (cf. 1 Cor 15:18; 1 Thess 4:13–16). Thus "to be with Christ" after death and before the resurrection "does not have the full redemptive significance in Paul's epistles that the resurrection has" (Ridderbos, *Paul*, 505–507).

24. The other desire that Paul had pressing in on him with equal force as the desire to depart and be with Christ was the desire to go on living and be with the Philippian Christians. Both desires are equally balanced grammatically by their respective comparative expressions. The one has "very much better" (πόλλῳ μᾶλλον κρεῖσσον), the other, "much more necessary" (ἀναγκαιότερον). It is wrong, therefore, to say that "the desire weakens before the necessity" (Gnilka) or that Paul's "personal desire 'to be with Christ' in glory" was "subordinated to his pastoral responsibility to the Philippians," as though Paul himself decided through some sort of "pastoral altruism" to say "No" to himself and "Yes" to "the down-to-earth needs of his fellow-believers" (Martin, 1959, 1976; Collange, etc.). Paul has already made clear that both of these desires are equal in intensity, so much so that he himself was incapable of making a choice—τί αἱρήσομαι οὐ γνωρίζω: "I cannot say what I would choose!" (v 22). Hence, it is not Paul who, martyrlike, sacrifices his personal desire on the altar of service to others, and decides to keep on living, but God who chooses for him.

25. Because Paul is convinced that the Philippians need him (τοῦτο πεποιθώς, the τοῦτο pointing back to the very great necessity, and the πεποιθώς taken as a causal participle), a conviction that perhaps grew out of things he had learned about problems at Philippi (cf. 2:1–4, 14; 4:2–3), he knows (οἶδα) what God's choice for his immediate future will be. As an apostle, "part of the divine plan of salvation is committed to him, and its seriousness consists in the fact that he cannot evade it" (Grundmann, *TDNT* 1, 346–47). Ἀνάγκη ("necessity"), therefore, characterizes Paul's apostolic office (1 Cor 9:16). Need determines the direction his life is to take. In this instance the need of the Philippian church constitutes the divine call for Paul to go on living, a call to which he cannot say "No," and which he accepts with cheerfulness (against Lohmeyer). There is, thus, no need to debate the question, "How can someone who has just been affirming the utter uncertainty of his fate now convincingly and without more ado make plans for the future?" (Collange; see also Bonnard, Dibelius, Gnilka, Lohmeyer, Martin, Michael, Vincent). For Paul was never uncertain about his fate. He was, however, uncertain

about which choice to make, had he the chance to make it, whether to depart or to stay, to live or to die. He wanted the one equally as much as the other. Therefore, it must be repeated, Paul did not make the choice—he could not make the choice. God made it for him. Caught up in God's redemptive plan which is marked by healing and wholeness Paul was certain that he would stay with (μενῶ) and stand fast alongside (παραμενῶ) his friends. (For similar word-plays as μένω/παραμένω see Rom 1:20; 5:19; 2 Cor 4:8; 5:4; Phil 3:2-3; 2 Thess 3:11.)

One purpose for Paul's staying on is expressed by the phrase εἰς τὴν ὑμῶν προκοπὴν καὶ χάραν τῆς πίστεως ("in order that you may make progress and be glad in the faith"). For the meaning of προκοπή, see the comments on v 12, and for the meaning of χάρα, see those on v 4. Both of these nouns share one article and thus should be associated closely with πίστεως ("faith"). It was important to Paul that the Philippians not only make progress in the Christian faith, growing in their appreciation for and in their understanding and practice of those things taught by him as the truth of God (ἡ πίστις is used absolutely in the sense of the Christian creed; cf. Phil 1:27; 1 Tim 3:9; 4:1, 6; 5:8; 6:10, 21; Jude 3), but that they also be glad while doing so. Joy for Paul was an indispensable element of the Christian faith.

26. The other purpose Paul had in mind for his stay in Philippi is now expressed by ἵνα and the subjunctive—ἵνα τὸ καύχημα ὑμῶν περισσεύῃ ἐν Χριστῷ Ἰησοῦ ἐν ἐμοὶ . . . ("so that in me you may have ample cause to glory in Christ Jesus . . ." RSV). The word translated "to glory in" is καύχημα, a very strong word which carries the idea of "boasting." Καύχημα, to be sure, stresses the *object* of one's boasting rather than the *act* of boasting (καύχησις) but the idea of "pride" is present nonetheless.

There are again some grammatical and lexical difficulties involved in this sentence: (1) the ὑμῶν (lit. "of you") is probably a subjective genitive rather than objective. The Philippians are doing the boasting, rather than someone else boasting in them or about them.

(2) But in whom were they boasting? The expressions ἐν Χριστῷ Ἰησοῦ ("in Christ Jesus") and ἐν ἐμοί ("in me") are prepositional phrases that stand side by side in identical constructions. Forced to make a choice, some interpreters take the first phrase to be the object of καύχημα—"and so you will have another reason to give praise *to Christ Jesus* on my account" (JB: Moffatt; cf. NIV). Others, however, understand the second phrase to be the immediate cause of pride—"so that when I am present with you again, your pride in *me* may be unbounded in Christ Jesus" (NEB; cf. GNB; Phillips). But the striking parallel in Phil 3:3—καυχώμενοι ἐν Χριστῷ Ἰησοῦ ("our pride is in Christ Jesus")—tips the scales in favor of the former of the two interpretations given here. Apparently, then, the Philippians were tempted to boast in other people or things than in Christ Jesus alone, and Paul purposed to be present with them so that by his efforts (ἐν ἐμοί) he might direct their pride toward the right person (cf. Bultmann, *TDNT* 3, 646-54; D. Genths, "Der Begriff des καύχημα bei Paulus," *NKZ* 38 [1927] 501-21).

(3) His efforts would be brought to bear on the problem not by letter but by his presence (παρουσία) among them again. This word, παρουσία, is the same word Paul uses of the second coming of the Lord Jesus Christ (1

Thess 3:13). In Classical Greek it referred to the pomp and pageantry that accompanied the arrival of a king or governor in a city. By using this special word Paul may indicate that he expects to receive a "king's welcome" from the Philippians when he comes to their town (Beare).

Explanation

Paul still adheres to the standard form of letter-writing. His phrase, "I want you to know," is a typical expression used to introduce the personal, intimate parts of a letter. And yet, unexpectedly he immediately turns attention away from himself to the gospel. The things that happened to him personally, however painful they may have been, are not worth detailing. Their effects, however, are of major consequence to him and to the cause of Christ: (1) every one in the praetorium and those nearby learned that he was in prison simply because he was a Christian, not because he was a criminal, and (2) the majority of his fellow workers in Caesarea took heart because of his own courage and they preached the word more earnestly and fearlessly than they had ever done before.

Some of these, unfortunately, preached for less than pure motives. For whatever reason—jealousy, envy, or party spirit—there were some who preached specifically to make added trouble for Paul already in prison. But others preached because they loved the apostle and knew he wanted them to preach irrespective of what might happen to him as a result. And so, whether from good motives or bad, the gospel of Jesus Christ was being proclaimed abroad, and that fact made Paul very glad.

His gladness is boundless as he lets the Philippians know that he will soon be released from prison because of their prayers and because of the help the Holy Spirit will give him when he gets to make his defense before the Roman tribunal. He knows that, as he is questioned about his part in spreading the gospel, he will not be ashamed of it, but will boldly use the opportunity to let still more people hear about the saving power of Christ.

Paul then permits the Philippians to have a unique look into his own innermost being, to see the turmoil of his soul as he yearns equally for death on the one hand, because life has become a very heavy burden and death would bring him into a closer more intimate fellowship with Christ, and for life, on the other hand, because to go on living would mean for him continued productive work in general and in particular would serve to meet the very great need of the Philippian church. He cannot make up his mind. So God makes the choice for him. Need dictates direction. Thus because of the need of the Philippians, he knows he will be released to come and be with them, to help them forward in the faith, to stimulate their joy and to direct their boasting and pride increasingly toward Christ and Christ alone.

B. *Instructions for the Church* (*1:27–2:18*)

1. *To Stability in the Faith* (*1:27–30*)

Bibliography

Brewer, R. R. "The Meaning of *Politeuesthe* in Phil. 1:27." *JBL* 73 (1954) 76–83. **Güttgemanns,** E. *Der leidende Apostel und sein Herr.* FRLANT 90. Göttingen: Vandenhoeck und Ruprecht, 1966. **Hall, D. R.** "Fellow-workers with the Gospel." *ExpTim* 85 (1974) 119–20. **Johnston, G.** "The Life of the Christian in the World: An Exposition of Philippians 1:1–2:4." *CJT* 3 (1957) 248–54. **Kümmel, W. G.** "πάρεσις und ἔνδειξις." *ZTK* 49 (1952) 154–67. (Eng. Tr. in *JTC* 3 [1967] 1–13) **Pfitzner, V. C.** *Paul and the Agon Motif.* Leiden: E. J. Brill, 1967. **Roberts, R.** "Old Texts in Modern Translations: Philippians 1:27." *ExpTim* 49 (1937–38) 325–28. **Stagg, Frank.** "The Mind in Christ Jesus: Philippians 1:27–2:18." *RevExp* 77 (1980) 337–47. **Walter, N.** "Christusglaube und heidnische Religiosität in paulinischen Gemeinden." *NTS* 25 (1979) 422–42.

Translation

²⁷ *Only and always show yourselves to be good citizens, worthy of the gospel of Christ. Then, whether I come and see you or am separated from you by distance, I may hear*[a] *good things about you—that you stand firm with one spirit, struggling together with one mind to preserve the faith brought about by the gospel,* ²⁸ *in no way letting your opponents intimidate you. For although your loyalty to the faith is proof to them*[b] *that you will perish, it is in fact proof to you that you*[c] *will be saved—saved by God.* ²⁹ *For God has graciously given you*[d] *the privilege both of believing in Christ and of suffering in his stead.* ³⁰ *This is the meaning of the struggle you are in. It is the same sort of struggle you saw me once engage in and now hear that I*[e] *am still engaged in it.*

Notes

[a] The majority text reads the aorist subjunctive (ἀκούσω) for the present, but this looks like a grammatical improvement on the original.

[b] To the expression ἐστὶν αὐτοῖς the majority text adds μέν or rearranges the word order and adds μέν. This has the appearance of a stylistic improvement to balance the δέ that follows.

[c] The majority text has ὑμῖν for ὑμῶν; a few MSS have ἡμῖν. These are further attempts to make the two phrases parallel to each other in every way possible (see comments below).

[d] A few MSS read ἡμῖν for ὑμῖν.

[e] P⁴⁶ 81 omit the phrase, ἐν ἐμοί.

Form/Structure/Setting

After having discussed his own affairs and their consequences, and after having disclosed his own innermost feelings, Paul turns now, as is his custom, to give instructions to the entire community. The transition from personal matters to matters of encouragement is quite sudden, with simply the word μόνον ("only and always") given as an introduction. Immediately one is in the middle of a parenetic section. Words of exhortation now control the thought. The musings about life and death are gone. Hesitation between two decisions is past, and everything is now directed toward life—the rigorous life of a Christian who is called to be loyal to the faith, to fight for the faith and to live worthily of the faith. Battle terms, or terms from the athletic games, are present: "stand firm," "struggle" [twice], "suffer" (στήκειν, συναθλοῦν, ἀγών, πάσχειν) characterize this section. One is tempted to compare Paul with a commanding officer or a coach who is determined to inspire his troops, or to encourage his contestants, as he sends them into the fray, with the hope of getting back a good report about how they conducted themselves in the fight (Gnilka).

This section is highly rhetorical. Some see Paul lapsing into a particular strophic pattern or metrical style of speech (Lohmeyer, Michaelis); chiasm is present in abundance (vv 27–28); even an unusual number of the words used here are metaphorical. Thus, although such rhetoric drives home the need for concerted action it also makes it difficult to decide definitely what the historical situation was really like in which the church at Philippi found itself. Apparently, however, the Philippian Christians, like Paul, faced some sort of hostile opponents who were set on their destruction (ἀπωλεία, v 28). The apostle sees a united firmness on behalf of the gospel, and a disciplined life of self-sacrifice as the sure and certain way to overcome all adversaries. These twin themes bind this section (1:27–30) together with that which follows it (2:1–11).

Comment

27. Paul introduces this new section with the adverb μόνον (translated here "only and always"). In so doing he stresses that "the one essential thing" (see Gal 1:23; 2:10; 3:2; Bonnard, Collange) for the Christian is to live in a manner worthy (ἀξίως) of the gospel of Christ. But what does it mean to live in a manner worthy of the gospel of Christ? Paul answers this question in part by the special verb he uses to issue his command—πολιτεύεσθε ("live!"), and in part by the subordinate ideas he attaches to this verb.

Vv 27–30 constitute a single sentence in Greek that contains only one main verb—πολιτεύεσθε. This verb is an unusual one, appearing only twice in the NT, here and in Acts 23:1, where it means little more than to live out one's life. Originally, however, it meant "to live as a citizen of a free state" (πόλις), "to take an active part in the affairs of the state" (LSJ). Paul seems here to go back to this earlier meaning.

To the ancient Greek the state (ἡ πόλις) was by no means merely a place to live. It was rather a sort of partnership (κοινωνίαν τινά) formed with a view to having people attain the highest of all human goods (so Arist. *Pol.* A 1252a). Here in the state the individual citizen developed his gifts and realized his potential not in isolation, but in cooperation. Here he was able to maximize his abilities not by himself or for himself, but in community and for the good of the community (see Beare). As a consequence, mutuality and interdependence were important ideas inhering in the concept of πόλις. "To live as a citizen" (πολιτεύεσθαι), therefore, meant for the Greek (and later the Roman) rights and privileges but also duties and responsibilities.

To the Jew the idea of πόλις had as its focal point the "city of the great king" (Ps 48:2; cf. Matt 5:32). Originally Jerusalem was this ideal city, localized and restricted in scope. But under the influence of psalmist and prophet the concept "city" was expanded until Jerusalem was not only home for every member of the Commonwealth of Israel, but a spiritual fellowship into which the nations of the world eventually would enter (cf. Ps 87), a universal center of worship of Israel's God, the God of the whole earth (Isa 66:20 LXX; Amos

9: 11–12; Zech 14:8–11; see B. F. Westcott, "On the Social Imagery in the Epistle," in B. F. Westcott *The Epistle to the Hebrews* [Grand Rapids: Eerdmans, repr. 1965] 384–90).

Both these ideas appear to be combined in Paul's studied choice (against Gnilka) of this rare verb, πολιτεύεσθαι, over his customary verb for "living," περιπατεῖν (Rom 6:4; 1 Cor 3:3; 2 Cor 5:7; Gal 5:16; Eph 2:2; Phil 3:17; 1 Thess 2:12, etc.). Thus, to live in a manner worthy of the gospel of Christ means to live as a good citizen of an earthly state, fully discharging one's duties and responsibilities to that state (cf. Brewer, *JBL* 73 [1954] 76–83). But there is more. Through the gospel which proclaims Christ as Savior, the Christian is made a citizen of the heavenly Jerusalem (cf. Heb 12:22–23; Rev 21:2–3), a partner in a spiritual fellowship, a member of a new community, the Christian commonwealth, the Church (Phil 3:20; cf. Eph 2:19). To live worthily of the gospel, then, also means that the Christian lives as a good citizen of this new state, governing his actions by the laws of this unique *politeuma*—righteousness, peace, faith, hope, love, mutuality, interdependence, good deeds, service to one another, worship of the living God, and so on (cf. the use of this word in *1 Clem* 3:4; 21:1; Pol *Phil.* 5:2; see also Lightfoot, "St Paul and Seneca," *Philippians*, 270–333, especially 305–308).

Furthermore, to live in a manner worthy of the gospel of Christ means that the Philippians, it is hoped, will live in harmony with each other, a meaning that springs quite naturally from the fact that they are fellow citizens of a heavenly state, partners in a new community. Thus Paul expects to hear that his friends at Philippi are standing firm in one spirit (ἐν ἑνὶ πνεύματι), struggling together in one mind (μιᾷ ψυχῇ). Both of these expressions are intended to remind the Philippians that as Christians they are in a battle and that a united front is the best strategy for victory.

"Stand firm" translates one Greek word (στήκετε), a verb found first in the NT, newly formed from the perfect tense of ἱστάναι ("to stand"; BDF 73; Moulton, *Grammar* 2,220, 259). It conveys the idea of firmness or steadfastness, or unflinching courage like that possessed by soldiers who determinedly refuse to leave their posts irrespective of how severely the battle rages (cf. 1 Cor 16:13; Gal 5:1; Phil 4:1; 2 Thess 2:15; cf. Also Eph 6:13–17; see Lohmeyer who has gathered evidence for this metaphorical meaning of στήκω). Paul does not say who it is the Philippians are to stand firm against, but it is clear from the verses which follow that the Christians at Philippi are being challenged by adversaries, perhaps Jews (see chap 3), and are in danger of being shaken.

They can, however, resist the challenge and overcome the adversary by joint effort, by a community spirit. Thus, it is incorrect to say that the phrase ἐν ἑνὶ πνεύματι ("in one spirit") refers to the Holy Spirit (Bonnard, Collange, Dibelius, Gnilka, Jones, Martin); only the human spirit is in view here. The context, with its strong appeal to unity, and the carefully constructed chiastic form of this sentence that brings the phrase μιᾷ ψυχῇ ("in one mind") immediately up against the phrase ἐν ἑνὶ πνεύματι ("in one spirit"), combine not merely to show that these two expressions are equivalent in meaning, but to show that it is of extreme importance for Christians to coexist in community, work together in harmony, resist the common enemy with common intention.

Nor is it necessary to maintain that the phrase ἐν ἑνὶ πνεύματι refers to *both* the human spirit *and* the divine Spirit (Scott), as though Paul intended to convey by this single expression the twin ideas that "the Holy Spirit strengthens the human spirit under trial" (Martin, 1959). It is true, of course that Paul does use this exact expression to refer to the Holy Spirit (1 Cor 12:13; Eph 2:18). It is also true that he clearly teaches that Christian unity or Christian fellowship is the product of the creative activity of the Holy Spirit (Phil 2:1; cf. Eph 4:3). But here there is no signal to indicate that he means anything similar to this, or that he intends anything more by πνεῦμα than he does by ψυχή. The two parallel phrases, ἐν ἑνὶ πνεύματι and μιᾷ ψυχῇ therefore, serve strictly to heighten the idea that Christian harmony, "a common spirit" (Moffatt), which believers themselves must strive for, is essential if the church at Philippi, or anywhere else, is to maintain a courageous witness against hostile opposition (see Beare, Lohmeyer, Michaelis, Schweizer, *TDNT* 6,435).

The verb στήκειν ("to stand firm") is now explained by two participial phrases. The Christian best stands his ground (1) when he is struggling and (2) when he is showing a certain kind of bravado.

"To struggle" again is a verb that underscores the ideas that play such an important part in this section and throughout the entire letter, that of fellowship and community, of camaraderie and mutual understanding. Συναθλοῦν not only means "to struggle," but "to struggle along with someone" (BGD). It is a rare word, even in Classical Greek, found in the NT only here and in Phil 4:3. With it Paul quickly changes the picture from soldiers at battle stations to athletes working as a team, side by side, playing the game not as several individuals but together as one person with one mind (μιᾷ ψυχῇ), for one goal (see Pfitzner, *The Agon Motif*, 116–18). Here that goal is to preserve the faith brought into existence by the gospel (τῇ πίστει τοῦ εὐαγγελίου).

This interpretation of the expression τῇ πίστει τοῦ εὐαγγελίου understands (1) that τῇ πίστει ("the faith") here is an early example of the tendency for the word πίστις ("faith") to become a technical term for "creed," those things which the Christian believes (cf. also 1 Tim 3:9; 4:1, 6; 5:8; 6:10, 21; Jude 3). (2) It understands that the dative, τῇ πίστει, is a dative of interest or advantage, to be translated "for the faith," and not a dative of association governed by the preposition σύν in the compound word συναθλοῦντες, to be translated, "with the faith" (as does Hall, *ExpTim* 85 [1974] 119–30; see also Jones, Lightfoot). The context, with its stress on community, demands that ἀλλήλοις ("with one another") be mentally supplied if one needs to see a substantive governed by συναθλοῦντες. (3) It also understands that τοῦ εὐαγγελίου is a subjective genitive, meaning that the gospel is the generative power of the Christian's creed, that the good news that God has acted in Christ for man's salvation is the source and origin of the faith, the essence of what a Christian believes.

The issue here then is the Christian faith. The faith is being threatened. There are those who would nullify this faith, perhaps by proclaiming a message that is not founded on the free grace of God (Collange) and the finished work of Christ to which nothing can be added by way of human effort. Thus the plea for unity is no small matter. Only by the total cooperation of Christians striving unitedly together with each other in this fierce contest for the minds of men can the true gospel be preserved against distortion or destruction by its opponents.

The Christian also stands his ground by showing a certain kind of bravado, by not allowing himself to be intimidated in any way by his opponents (v 28). The verb here translated "to be intimidated" (πτύρεσθαι) is extremely rare, found nowhere else in the entire Greek Bible. But it is used on occasion in Classical Greek of timid horses that shy upon being startled at some unexpected object (LSJ). Perhaps by the choice of this unusual word Paul shows himself anxious that his friends should not "break loose in disarray" (Martin, 1976) or lose control of themselves as a result of the attacks of their adversaries.

It is not clear who these adversaries were. True, Paul's own sufferings at Philippi had been caused by pagan Gentiles (Acts 16). It is also true that Paul's plea here to united action against the enemy is reinforced by reminding the Philippians of the suffering he himself had experienced while at Philippi, and which the Philippians had witnessed (v 30). But these facts do not of themselves prove that the present opposition facing the Philippian church came only from the pagan world (as Loh and Nida, Martin, Michael suggest). Rather the threat to the faith of the gospel which figures so prominently in this section, a threat which arose from the proclamation of a false "gospel," or from persecution promoted by the champions of that false gospel, seems to argue more forcefully for the view that these adversaries were evangelistically fervent Jews who either resided in Philippi or who had come from Thessalonica (see Introduction, xxxiv, xlv–xlvii; cf. Acts 17:1–5, 10–13) to attack the growing church. These adversaries, then, would be the same as those Paul speaks so sharply against in ch. 3.

The words which now follow—ἥτις ἐστὶν αὐτοῖς ἔνδειξις ἀπωλείας, ὑμῶν δὲ σωτηρίας (lit. "which is to them a sign of destruction, but of your salvation")— are extraordinarily difficult to interpret. This difficulty is reflected in the translations, which either leave one still puzzled over their meaning, or add details hard to justify textually in order to try to make sense of them (cf. Phillips, GNB). Westcott and Hort found these words so disconcerting that they suggested that they and the words in v 29 be put in a parenthesis, thus enabling v 30 to be attached directly to v 28a. Such a suggestion provides a smooth flow of thought, and treats the parenthesis as a Pauline aside that gives a theological explanation of Christian suffering.

Perhaps the difficulty can be resolved in a different, less radical way, resulting in a quite different interpretation of the text from the one generally accepted today.

First, τῇ πίστει ("the faith," v 27) is a reasonable antecedent for the relative pronoun ἥτις ("which"). It is certainly as reasonable as making the idea of fearlessness in v 28 the antecedent. This latter idea was suggested by Lightfoot, and is reflected in most translations. But τῇ πίστει easily accounts for the form of ἥτις, which agrees with its antecedent in number and gender (singular and feminine) as normally it should (H. W. Smyth, *Greek Grammar* [Cambridge: Harvard University Press, 1956] 562.2501). There is no need then to search for a less normal, though also possible grammatical explanation, i.e. that ἥτις gets its number and gender not from its antecedent, but from attraction to some noun (ἔνδειξις) within its own clause (so Lightfoot; cf. Eph 3:13). Thus the Philippians' adherence to the faith, not their courage, is the ἔνδειξις ἀπωλείας . . . ("the sign of destruction . . .").

Second, ἥτις may in fact introduce two clauses that, although compressed, are nevertheless parallel to each other. With a minimal amount of reconstruction it is possible to make this parallelism obvious:

ἐστὶ (μὲν) αὐτοῖς ἔνδειξις ἀπωλείας (ὑμῶν)

ἥτις

(ἐστὶ) δὲ (ὑμῖν ἔνδειξις) σωτηρίας ὑμῶν

is (on the one hand) a sign to them of (your) destruction

which

(is) on the other hand (a sign to you) of your salvation

To justify this reconstruction the following things should be noted: (a) In the NT it is possible to find antithetic parallel clauses with or without μέν ("on the one hand") as a correlative to δέ ("on the other hand," Rom 16:19; Gal 2:9; see BDF 447.2, 5). To insert μέν into the reconstruction for the sake of the obvious is, therefore, grammatically legitimate. (b) The verb ἐστίν is frequently omitted from parallel phrases in Classical and NT Greek. Its presence, though not visible, is always understood (BDF 127.1). This is the case here in Phil 1:28. The reconstruction, however, merely inserts ἐστί for the sake of clarity, although it is superfluous to do so. (c) It is the same with ἔνδειξις ("sign"). Ἔνδειξις clearly is modified by σωτηρίας ("of salvation") as well as by ἀπωλείας ("of destruction"). Thus, to include ἔνδειξις in the reconstruction, although it too is superfluous, nevertheless increases the visibility of the parallelism. (d) Ὑμῶν ("your") in Paul's text is placed directly between ἀπωλείας and σωτηρίας in an amphibolous position that permits one to see it as modifying both of these nouns, in spite of the fact that ὑμῶν is followed by δέ. If the postpositive δέ were intended to limit the ὑμῶν only to the second clause, one would expect the word order to have been αὐτοῖς . . . ἀπωλείας/σωτηρίας δὲ ὑμῶν, resulting in a neat chiastic construction such as Paul is fond of. Therefore, to add it to the reconstructed text after ἀπωλείας ("of your destruction") is grammatically defensible, more so than importing αὐτῶν ("of their destruction"), with no basis, as the great majority of translators do. (e) The only real addition to the text, then, is ὑμῖν ("to you"). But this is now demanded by the clear antithetic parallelism of the two clauses. The dative αὐτοῖς ("to them") of the first clause is answered now by the dative ὑμῖν ("to you") of the second. (f) The manuscript tradition supports this reconstruction, supplying μέν and altering ὑμῶν to ὑμῖν (ἡμῖν). It is interesting and instructive to note that never was the αὐτοῖς altered to αὐτῶν in order to find a parallel for ὑμῶν—never was the contrast understood as being "their destruction" over against "your destruction." These variants, though rightly rejected as secondary, nevertheless indicate how early Greek scribes understood what Paul was saying.

The result of this reconstruction shows that the real contrast is not between *"their* destruction" and *"your* salvation," as is generally understood today, but between the different perceptions of two groups of people: the adversaries, on the one hand, perceive the willingness of the Philippians to fight for the faith of the gospel (v 27) as an indication of their destruction. The Philippians on the other hand perceive this as a sure sign (see Kümmel, *ZTK* 49 [1952] 134–67) of their salvation (cf. 2 Cor 2:15–16, and see Pss Sol 16:5).

Third, ἀπωλεία is generally used of eternal destruction (Oepke, *TDNT* 1,397) and σωτηρία of eternal salvation (Foerster, *TDNT* 7,992–94). But both words can and are used with less than such ultimate meanings (cf. Matt 26:8; Phil 1:19). Hence, here, in these highly rhetorical phrases that appear in a context where the imagery of battle and contest is prominent, it may be that these words should be understood in the lesser sense of "defeat" or "victory," of "winning" or "losing" (so GNB, JB). It is even more likely that Paul, in making a play on these words, especially on their sounds—ἀπωλείας /σωτηρίας—may also be making a play on their meanings, going to the extreme with one and holding back on the other, seeing in ἀπωλείας the immediate destruction of the body and in σωτηρίας the ultimate salvation of the soul (cf. 1 Cor 5:5).

Fourth, a free translation of v 28 will serve as a summary: "In no way let your adversaries strike terror in you. For although they see your loyalty to the truth as inevitably leading to your persecution and death (ἀπωλείας), you see it as leading through persecution to the salvation of your souls (σωτηρίας)."

29. One is led on by this saying of Paul, if understood in the fashion just explained, quite easily to the next saying. A Christian who is willing to stand up together with other Christians for the faith of the gospel (v 27) can expect to suffer. It has always been so. Redemptive history teaches that those who believe the Word of God, who uncompromisingly speak this Word and unyieldingly live in accordance with it often pay for their courage and resolution with their lives—from the ancient prophets to Jesus (Matt 5:12; 23:29–37; cf. 21:33–46). "Believing" (πιστεύειν) and "suffering" (πάσχειν), therefore, go together now as they have in the past (cf. 4 Macc 5–6; 9–15, especially 15). Paul reminds his friends at Philippi of this fact. At the same time he encourages them by telling them, twice over, that their suffering is "for Christ" (ὑπὲρ Χριστοῦ, ὑπὲρ αὐτοῦ).

This prepositional phrase, ὑπὲρ Χριστοῦ ("for Christ") may mean simply that the Philippians are suffering because they are on Christ's side (BGD). They have believed the gospel of Christ (v 27a). They have set themselves to preserve and propagate this gospel (v 27b). They have taken their stand with Christ. As a consequence they have put themselves on a collision course with hostile forces abroad in their world that are opposed to Christ. It is inevitable then that they suffer.

Ὑπὲρ Χριστοῦ can also mean "for the sake of Christ." If this is the sense here, then Paul is saying that the Philippians are willing to suffer because of their love for and devotion to Christ. Christ is the moving cause or reason for their willingness to endure. Like earlier disciples these newer ones are able to view suffering for the sake of Christ as an honor and privilege (cf. Acts 5:41; so Moule, *Origin*, 120–21).

But this prepositional phrase can also mean "in place of," "instead of" (BGD). If this is the idea, then the phrase has reached its most profound meaning. Πάσχειν ὑπὲρ Χριστοῦ then would indicate that the Philippians are in some way permitted to suffer in Christ's stead. To use the apostle's own words, in that the Philippians, as he himself, are suffering, they actually are filling up "what is still lacking in regard to Christ's sufferings" (Col 1:24–25). They, by having joined the "fellowship of his sufferings" (Phil 3:10), have chosen to be Christ's replacements on earth in order to suffer in his place in his absence. It is not that anyone dares put himself on the same level with Christ in this respect. Yet there apparently is a very real sense in which Christ needs people who are willing to take upon themselves the burden of his suffering in history that still remains to be borne. Paul, on the one hand, wishes to be such a person (Col 1:24–25)—to suffer in Christ's stead that others may be consoled (2 Cor 1:4–6), to die that others might live (2 Cor 4:12), to endure hardships that others might be saved (1 Cor 4:13; note that the word περικάθαρμα used in 1 Cor 4:13 is found in the LXX in the sense of "ransom" [Prov 21:18]; it was also used in the atonement rites of the Grecian Thargelium. See Stauffer, *Theology*, 307–308). The Philippians, on the other hand, can also share in this privilege. They, too, may suffer "in Christ's place" (ὑπὲρ Χριστοῦ).

Thus it is that Paul dares say that suffering ὑπὲρ Χριστοῦ ("in Christ's stead") is a divine gift offered to them in love. The verb he uses, ἐχαρίσθη ("it was given"), though far less common than διδόναι ("give"), is, nevertheless, one of his special verbs. It is used by him sixteen of the twenty-three times it appears in the NT. Formed from the same root as χάρις ("grace"), it conveys the idea of the free, unmerited favor or kindness of God (Eph 4:32). It denotes privilege, therefore, and this idea is made explicit in many translations: "you have (graciously) been granted the privilege of suffering for Christ" (BGD; cf. GNB, JB, NEB, Phillips). The passive form of this verb, "it was given" (ἐχαρίσθη), is a "divine passive" and can be changed into an active statement with God as the subject (see Jeremias, *Theology*, 1.9). This use of the passive indicates Paul's belief that "God is in control of all events. Therefore, the Philippians should not be upset by their bitter experience as if God had forgotten them or were angry with them. On the contrary, the verb . . . would remind them that even this trial comes to them as a gift of his grace" (Martin, 1976; cf. Beare). "God rewards and indorses believers with the gift of suffering" (Vincent; cf. Heb 12:5–11 for a similar Christian understanding of suffering).

The idea of suffering, and suffering "for Christ," is preeminent here. But it should be noted in passing that Paul incidentally says that the act of believing in Christ (εἰς αὐτὸν πιστεύειν) is also a gift of God (cf. Eph 2:8). Πιστεύειν εἰς ("to believe in") is a NT grammatical invention and is the most emphatic way of expressing absolute trust in Christ, infrequently used by Paul, but often by John (see G. F. Hawthorne, "The Concept of Faith in the Fourth Gospel," *BSac* 116 [1959] 116–26).

30. Paul concludes this section with a participial phrase that further explains the meaning of the Philippians' suffering. Their struggle is an extension of the suffering he himself had experienced when he was at Philippi (Acts 16:16–24; cf. 1 Thess 2:2), which they then had seen at close hand, and which he is even now enduring at Caesarea (Acts 24–25), about which they have only heard through Epaphroditus. It is a battle that results from preaching and defending the gospel, and in this battle the Philippians have joined. They together with him have formed a "fellowship of Christ's suffering" (3:10), since the gospel is itself "the word of the cross" (1 Cor 1:18; see A. Richardson, *An Introduction to the Theology of the NT* [London: SCM Press, 1958] 29; Güttgemanns, *Der leidende Apostel*). The word Paul uses here for "fight" or "battle" is the word ἀγών. Originally it applied to athletic contests in the arena. Eventually it came to mean any inward or outward struggle (Col 2:1; 1 Thess 2:2; cf. 1 Tim 6:12; 2 Tim 4:7; Heb 12:1; see Loh and Nida). The nominative participle, ἔχοντες ("having") agrees, not in form, but in sense with the dative ὑμῖν ("you"; cf. Eph 3:18; 4:2; Col 3:16; see Moulton, *Grammar*, 1,225). There is thus no reason for going back to στήκετε ("you stand firm" v 27) to find a "proper" word for the participle to modify, and therefore, there is no reason for treating vv 28b–29 as a parenthesis in order to save the grammar. The relative pronoun οἷον ("which") that is used here by Paul, instead of the more usual ὅν, indicates that he knew the Philippians were pitted against the same foe as he was, but that their sufferings had taken a different form from his. He gives no indication that the Philippians or any of their leaders were in prison, but he makes clear that they were nonetheless hurting, and for the same reason as he—both his sufferings and theirs were the direct result of a determination to preach the gospel and make sure of its advancement (προκοπή, 1:12, 25) throughout the world. And this determination stood firm in spite of strong opposition from aggressive adversaries (1:28; cf. 1 Thess 2:14–16).

Explanation

Paul encourages the Philippians to live in a manner worthy of the gospel of Christ at all times. This means, among other things, that they will be good citizens both of the earthly state in which they live and of the heavenly state to which they ultimately belong. It also means that the Philippians must present a united front. They must be one in spirit and intent, fighting side by side for the preservation of the faith brought about by the gospel, those things most surely believed by the Church. It means loyalty to this faith which, in the eyes of their opponents, seems a foolhardy allegiance to something that can only bring them persecution and death. In their own eyes, however, such loyalty is to something that will bring them salvation. They believed that in response to their faith God would bring them safely to their desired end. Finally, living in a manner worthy of the gospel means that they must not fear their adversaries or grow discouraged because of the trouble heaped upon them. For suffering for Christ, as believing in Christ, is a gracious gift to them from God, for which they should be thankful. They and Paul form a community of sufferers with the suffering Christ. Because of their whole-hearted allegiance to the gospel, and their total commitment to Christ, they can fully expect to share in the sufferings of Christ. "The disciple is not above his teacher, nor a servant above his master; it is enough for the disciple to be like his teacher and the servant like his master" (Matt 10:24–25: cf. Phil 3:10).

2. To Harmony and Humility (2:1–4)

Bibliography

Barclay, W. "Great Themes of the New Testament: Phil 2:1–11." *ExpTim* 70 (1958) 4–7, 40–44. **Campbell, J. Y.** "Κοινωνία and its cognates in the New Testment." *JBL* 51 (1932) 352–80. **Ford, H. W.** "The New Testament Conception of Fellowship." *Shane Quarterly* 6 (1945) 188–215. **George, A. R.** *Communion with God in the New Testament.* London: Epworth Press, 1953. **Glombitza, O.** "Mit Furcht und Zittern," *NovT* 3 (1959) 100–106. **Hill, D.** *Greek Words and Hebrew Meanings.* London: Cambridge University Press, 1967. **Neugebauer, F.** *In Christus,* 'EN ΧΡΙΣΤΩ. *Eine Untersuchung zum paulinischen Glaubensverständnis.* Göttingen: Vandenhoeck und Ruprecht, 1961. **Reicke, B.** "Unité chrétienne et diaconie: Phil 2:1–11." *Neotestamentica et Patristica: Eine Freundesgabe O. Cullmann.* NovTSup 6. Leiden: Brill, 1962, 203–12. **Seesemann, H.** *Der Begriff* Κοινωνία.

Translation

¹ *Therefore, if in any way* ᵃ *I have given you encouragement in Christ, if in any way my love has consoled you, if in any way you have enjoyed the fellowship created by the Spirit, if in any way you have experienced the tenderness and compassion of God in Christ,* ² *then make my joy complete: Think alike. Love alike. Be of one soul. Be of one* ᵇ *mind.* ³ *Do not act out of a spirit of rivalry, nor out of empty conceit. Act rather with humility and consider others better than yourselves.* ⁴ *Each* ᶜ *of you must look to* ᵈ *the interests of others as well as to the interests of yourselves.*

Notes

ᵃ εἰ τις or εἰ τι appears four times in v 1. The MSS tradition, in some instances, is uncertain as to whether the text should read εἰ τις or εἰ τι. BDF conjecture that εἰ τι was intended throughout, τι being understood as the stereotyped adverbial τι, "in any way" (137.2; see also Haupt; Moulton, *Grammar,* 1,59).

ᵇ The MSS tradition is divided between ἐν and αὐτό. αὐτό, however, appears to be secondary, an attempt to harmonize τὸ ἐν φρονοῦντες with τὸ αὐτὸ φρονῆτε which one finds earlier in v 2.

ᶜ ἕκαστος at the beginning of v 4 is read as ἕκαστοι by A B F G 33 81 and a few other MSS. Since ἕκαστος was the form more widely used by Greek writers even with a plural subject (BDF 305) it seems that ἕκαστοι should be considered original and ἕκαστος secondary, a change made to conform the text to that which was grammatically more familiar. It is possible to take the ἕκαστοι at the end of v 4 with the beginning of v 5.

ᵈ Some MSS attempt to make the long sentence beginning at v 2 less awkward by changing the participle σκοποῦντες into imperative forms: σκοπεῖτε or σκοπείτω.

Form/Structure/Setting

This new section is closely joined to that which precedes it, not only by the conjunction οὖν ("therefore"), but by Paul's emphatic reiteration of the one idea that harmony is essential for Christian community and for an effective effort to defend the gospel (cf. 1:27; 2:2). Other concepts such as humility and self-sacrifice (2:3–4) are added, not to divert attention away from the fundamental concept of unity, but to show that unity of spirit flows from humility of spirit, and self-sacrifice flows from a willingness to restrain one's own desires in order to satisfy the desires of others. And Paul's appeal is based on the deepest experiences common to every Christian—encouragement in Christ, incentive of love, fellowship of the Spirit, tenderness and compassion.

Unity, then, dominates the thinking of the apostle in this section, and he makes full use of his skill as a writer to convey to the Philippians its consummate importance. He uses words big in meaning, compacted into brief verbless phrases; rare words; and words never found anywhere else in the NT. He piles clause on top of clause, beginning each clause with the same word. He does all this as if searching for ways to make his readers both think and feel deeply about the essential nature of harmony and its necessity within the Christian community. Even the exalted solemn speech-pattern of this section adds to the magnitude of this idea. As Paul writes, his words have been seen to fall into three strophes. The first is recognized by the fourfold εἰ τις/εἰ τι introducing four phrases, each of which is composed of two nouns and no verbs (v 1). The second strophe also has four parts. The first half is composed of two imperatives (ἵνα with the subjunctive is taken imperatively; cf. Moulton, *Grammar*, 3,94–95), the second half of two participles, with the verb φρονεῖν marking the end of each half (v 2). The third strophe has six parts. The first half is discerned by three important nouns and the last half by two participles and the twice-used ἕκαστος (vv 3–4; so Gnilka; see also Lohmeyer, who was the first to recognize the metrical speech-form of this section). Whether this strophic pattern can be demonstrated to the satisfaction of everyone is doubtful, but unimportant. For it is clear in any case that Paul puts the force of fine rhetoric to work to impress upon his audience the importance of fundamental Christian ideas—unity based on humility and self-sacrifice.

Comment

1. This verse contains four brief clauses, each of which begins with εἰ ("if"), contains two nouns and no verbs. As a result it presents the translator with unusual difficulties and the commentator with a bewildering number of possibilities of interpretation.

For example, to translate these expressions into English as conditional clauses, beginning each with the word "if," does retain something of the rhythm and the rhetorical repetitiveness of the Greek, but it may convey the wrong idea. When Paul introduced each of these clauses with εἰ ("if"), he did not intend by this to cast doubt at all on what he was saying. Just the opposite. The construction of these clauses in Greek, introduced by εἰ, is such that it becomes equivalent in meaning to an affirmative statement: "Since there is . . ." Some modern speech translations attempt to make this clear. Thus Goodspeed translates, "By whatever appeal there is in our relation to Christ . . ." (see also Moffatt, NAB; cf. Matt 6:30; 12:27; Rom 2:17–20; 1 Cor 9:11 for other examples of εἰ used in this way; BDF 372.1).

A much greater difficulty, however, arises from attempting to understand exactly what Paul meant by the nouns he used in each of these four clauses, and how each noun in a given pair of nouns relates to the other. A further problem arises from the fact that the personal character, which is so much a part of this letter, is obscured by the compressed nature of these four expressions, leaving one to ask, "Who is doing what to whom?" And yet that personal element is present, nonetheless.

What then does Paul mean by παράκλησις ἐν Χριστῷ (lit. "encouragement in Christ")? The noun παράκλησις is capable of conveying at least two very different ideas: (1) "comfort" or "consolation," on the one hand, and (2) "exhortation" or "encouragement," on the other. But since the verb from which this noun comes (παρακαλεῖν) is used especially by Paul for the exhortation he himself gives based on the Word of God and in the power of the Holy Spirit (Schmitz, *TDNT* 5,794–95; cf. Rom 12:1; 15:30; 16:17; 1 Cor 1:10; 4:16; 16:15; Eph 4:1; Phil 4:2; 1 Thess 2:11–12; 5:14), it seems best to understand the noun παράκλησις here in the same sense (against Barclay, *ExpTim* 70 [1958] 4–7, 40–44, and Collange). Thus this compact expression seems to picture Paul as the one who has given the Philippians exhortations, words of encouragement "in Christ," in the power of the Holy Spirit. His παρακλήσεις were not commands but appeals to Christians (those ἐν Χριστῷ) by a fellow Christian (one who is himself ἐν Χριστῷ)—moral strengthenings by one who is strong in the faith (see Caird). "If this is true, as indeed it is," Paul says, "and if my words of encouragement have in any way helped you stay true to the faith in the past, then respond accordingly in the present."

εἰ τι παραμύθιον ἀγάπης, "if any comfort of love," is the second clause. Its first noun, παραμύθιον, used only here in the NT (cf. παραμυθία, 1 Cor 14:3), has as its fundamental idea "to speak to someone," or "to speak to someone by coming close to his side," and always in a friendly way. Its meaning, like that of παράκλησις, has also developed along two lines: with reference to what ought to be done, "to admonish," and with reference to what has already happened, "to console" (Stählin, *TDNT* 5,815–16). Thus the words παράκλησις and παραμύθιον (παραμυθία) cannot be sharply distinguished. Notice how the verbs from which these nouns derive are regularly coupled together (1 Thess 2:12; cf. also 1 Cor 14:3; Phil 2:1). Since this is so and since παράκλησις was used in the first clause to convey the idea of "exhortation," it seems likely that here in the second clause the idea of "consolation" comes to the fore in παραμύθιον (cf. Wisd Sol 3:18). The noun ἀγάπης ("of love") is a subjective genitive, so the "consolation" is that consolation generated by love. But by whose love? Paul's or God's? In this letter where Paul's affection for the Philippians seems so obvious and so much in the foreground, and since the verb παραμύθεσθαι is never used directly for God's comfort (so Stählin, *TDNT* 5,821), it is but natural to suppose that it is Paul's love that provided consolation for the Philippians and is in view here now (so Michael; but see Barth, Martin, 1976 contrasted with Martin, 1959). "If my love has provided you with any consolation in your suffering, as indeed it has," Paul says, "then please now respond properly to my request."

εἰ τις κοινωνία πνεύματος, "if any fellowship of spirit," is the third clause
piled up in rhetorical fashion on the preceding clauses. In the NT κοινωνία
is that fellowship or that close relationship which exists between believers,
and here especially between Paul and the Philippians (cf. Phil 1:5, 7). It is
that community made up of people who are fellow members of the heavenly
politeuma (cf. Aristotle's definition of πόλις as κοινωνία; see comments on 1:27
and Reicke, *NovTSup* 6 [1962] 203–12), and who share the common life
of God (cf. 1 John 1:3; 2:6, NEB). But what is the meaning of πνεύματος in
this expression and what is the connection between κοινωνία ("fellowship")
and πνεύματος ("of spirit")? Since πνεύματος has no definite article in Greek,
some interpreters understand it merely as "spirit" or "mind." The expression,
κοινωνία πνεύματος, thus means no more than a "fellowship of kindred spirits,"
"mutual harmony," or perhaps "spiritual fellowship" (see F. F. Bruce, *The
Letters of Paul: An Expanded Paraphrase* [Grand Rapids: Eerdmans, 1965]; Hendriksen). The genitive πνεύματος then is a descriptive genitive.

It is more likely, however, that πνεύματος refers to the Holy Spirit: (*a*)
κοινωνία itself as it is used in the NT conveys the idea of "*spiritual* fellowship."
Hence, to add πνεύματος as an adjectival modifier is unnecessary. (*b*) On occasion when Paul clearly refers to the Holy Spirit, he will omit both the definite
article and the adjective "holy" (Rom 7:6; 1 Cor 2:4; Gal 3:3; 5:16, 18, 25).
(*c*) The "presence or absence of the article is a precarious index of reference
when the substantive is a great and familiar word; context or parallels must
be brought in" (Moule). (*d*) The words of 2 Cor 13:14—ἡ κοινωνία τοῦ ἁγίου
πνεύματος ("the fellowship of the Holy Spirit")—is a parallel so unusually
close to the expression found in Phil 2:1 that one is fairly forced to admit
that here πνεύματος can only refer to the Holy Spirit.

Most interpreters proceed then to interpret the genitive, πνεύματος, which
modifies κοινωνία, as an objective genitive, "fellowship *in* the Holy Spirit,"
a fellowship "which comes about through his indwelling presence in the
church and the Christian's personal communion with him" (Martin, 1976,
who follows Seeseman, *Der Begriff* κοινωνία). But the threefold benediction
of 2 Cor 13:13—"The grace of our Lord Jesus Christ, and the love of God,
and the fellowship of the Holy Spirit"—where the closest and only parallel
to κοινωνία πνεύματος occurs, argues against this interpretation and for interpreting πνεύματος instead as a subjective genitive. Thus, κοινωνία πνεύματος
here, as in 2 Cor 13:13, refers to that fellowship created by the Spirit (cf.
Eph 4:3 and see the comments there by T. K. Abbott, *Ephesians* [ICC: New
York: Scribners, 1905] and M. Barth, *Ephesians* [AB 34A; New York: Doubleday, 1974]). So Paul pleads, "If you belong to that community brought into
existence by the Holy Spirit, and enjoy any fellowship with one another as
a result, then live accordingly."

The final clause, εἰ τις σπλάγχνα καὶ οἰκτιρμοί (lit. "if any bowels and mercies," AV), is the most difficult of the four clauses to understand. The noun
σπλάγχνα ("bowels") has occurred already in 1:8 and was translated there
as "deep affection." Τὰ σπλάγχνα, the viscera, were thought of as the seat
of one's deep feelings such as "affection" (RSV, NEB), "tenderness" (JB), "compassion" (NAB), "kindness" (Phillips, GNB), etc. Οἰκτιρμοί ("mercies") used
only five times in the NT, and almost exclusively by Paul, overlaps somewhat

in meaning with σπλάγχνα, describing similar feelings such as pity, mercy and compassion. These two nouns together then may be translated correctly into English with the words, "affection and compassion" (cf. NEB). But whose affection and compassion are in view and toward whom are these feelings directed? Some interpreters understand these nouns to be referring to human emotions exhibited on the strictly human plane (Moule), either the feelings of the Philippians for one another (GNB) or for Paul (Beare; Bultmann, *TDNT* 5,161; Michael), or the feelings of Paul for the Philippians (cf. Collange). However, since Paul employs οἰκτιρμοί twice over (out of the four times he uses this word) to describe God's tender mercies (Rom 12:1; 2 Cor 1:3), since σπλάγχνα itself is sometimes used of divine compassion (Luke 1:78; Phil 1:8; cf. Col 3:12), and since σπλάγχνα and οἰκτιρμοί are so closely associated here as to be taken for a hendiadys, translated "affectionate sympathy" (Dibelius, cf. Col 3:12), it is probable that Paul has in mind God's or Christ's warmth of affection and tenderness toward the Philippians. Thus the four clauses divide into two distinct parts. The first focusing on the human side of things—Paul's encouragement of and love for the Philippians, the second on the divine—the unity among the Philippians created by the Holy Spirit, and God surrounding them with the warmth of his affection. "If then," says Paul, "you know anything of the mercy and compassion shown you by God in Christ, as you most certainly do, then please respond by saying 'Yes' to my request."

2. Πληρώσατέ μου τὴν χάραν, "make my joy complete," appears at first glance to be the climax toward which the rhetorical clauses of v 1 were building. True, πληρώσατε ("make complete") is the only main verb in a very long sentence (2:1–4), but in reality it is simply prefatory to the main *idea* expressed through many subordinate constructions which repeat this idea in a variety of ways. Paul is concerned with his own feelings only as a by-product. His main concern, his supreme request of the Philippians, is that they strive for unity coupled with humility.

Ἵνα τὸ αὐτὸ φρονῆτε (lit. "that you think the same") strikes the theme. Grammatically it is difficult to explain this clause: (1) It may be functioning as the direct object of a verb that must be supplied—"I ask (παρακαλῶ) that . . ." (BDF 392.1c). (2) It may be seeking to describe what Paul means by completing his joy (Moule, *Idiom-Book*, 145, n. 3; 145–46, and most translations). Or (3) it may be substituting for an imperative (Moulton, *Grammar*, 3,94–95).

The expression τὸ αὐτὸ φρονεῖν is common enough in Paul (Rom 12:16; 15:5; 2 Cor 13:11; Phil 4:2), but it is not for this reason any easier to understand or translate accurately. The verb φρονεῖν (used ten times in Philippians, twenty-three times in Paul, twenty-six times in the NT) means "to think," but not only, or even primarily in the intellectual sense. It equally involves one's emotions, attitudes and will (cf. Bertram, *TDNT* 9,220–35; Collange; Lohmeyer). Hence, this expression cannot mean that Paul here pleads for drab uniformity of thought or that he insists on everyone holding in common a particular opinion—a demand that by its very nature would contribute to dissension. Rather by his choice of the verb φρονεῖν he is asking for a total inward attitude of mind or disposition of will, that strives after that one thing (τὸ αὐτό, τὸ ἕν) which is greater than any human truth—"mine, yours, his" (Barth), a unity of spirit and sentiment in which powerful tensions are held together by an overmastering loyalty to each other as brothers and sisters in Christ. "Such unity will only come when Christians are humble and bold enough to lay hold on the unity already given in Christ and to take it more seriously than their own self-importance . . . , and to make of those deep differences of doctrine, which originate in our imperfect understanding of the Gospel and which we dare not belittle, not an excuse for letting go of one another or staying apart, but rather an incentive for a more earnest seeking in fellowship together to hear and obey the voice of Christ" (C. E. B. Cranfield, *The First Epistle of Peter* [London: SCM Press, 1950] 75–76).

This theme is reinforced by the words τὴν αὐτὴν ἀγάπην ἔχοντες ("having the same love"), where the adjective αὐτήν ("same") stresses the mutuality of love that is to pervade the Christian community, identical with the self-sacrificing love of Christ for the church (2 Thess 1:3; 1 John 3:16). The participle ἔχοντες may also function here with imperatival force, as may the other participles which follow or must be supplied for sense (cf. Moule, *Idiom-Book*, 31, 179; Moulton, *Grammar*, 3,303).

The theme of unity is pressed even further both by σύμψυχοι and the repetition, slightly strengthened now, of the initial clause—τὸ αὐτὸ φρονῆτε becomes τὸ ἕν φρονοῦντες. Σύμψυχος, found only here in the Greek Bible, perhaps coined by Paul, recalls the expression μιᾷ ψυχῇ ("with one soul") in 1:27. But by its very uniqueness it underscores the idea that the Philippians are to share one soul, possess a common affection, desire, passion, sentiment for living together in harmony—"harmony of feeling" (Weymouth). Finally, Paul, so emphatic in his own longing for unity, repeats himself—τὸ ἕν φρονοῦντες ("mind this one thing") is almost identical in wording to the clause he used earlier (ἵνα τὸ αὐτὸ φρονῆτε). Thus in four different ways Paul repeats the same idea over and over again, hoping that the Philippians will get the point. Unity is essential for the spiritual growth of the church, the progress of the gospel and the victory of believers over their adversaries.

3–4. But unity is impossible if each is out for himself, each is promoting his own cause, each is seeking his own advantage. Thus in these verses Paul emphasizes certain attitudes and actions that must stop as well as those that must continue.

Μηδὲν κατ᾽ ἐριθείαν μηδὲ κατὰ κενοδοξίαν (lit. "nothing according to selfish-ambition, nor according to conceit"). This phrase has no verb, yet it carries within itself the force of a negative command (cf. Gal 5:13). Some interpreters wish to connect it with φρονοῦντες from the preceding verse—"being in nothing factiously or vaingloriously *minded*" (Vincent, cf. Barth). Others wish to supply some verb of action to give the command greater force—"Never *act* for selfish ends . . ." (cf. Ign. *Phld.* 8:2: μηδὲν κατ᾽ ἐριθείαν πράσσετε and most translations). Both ἐριθεία and κενοδοξία belong to the traditional stock-words in ancient catalogs of vices (see Gnilka, 105, n. 19 for references).

Paul already has used ἐριθεία in 1:17. There as here it carries overtones of a party-spirit generated by selfish ambition (cf. Büchsel, *TDNT* 2,660–61). "Rivalry" is guaranteed to destroy unity. Therefore, it must go.

Κενοδοξία, used only here in the NT, is found several times in the OT

(LXX; Wisd Sol 14:4; 4 Macc 2:15; 8:18; cf. 4 Macc 5:9 and Gal 5:26), and frequently in the writings of the Cynic philosophers (see A. Malherbe, *The Cynic Epistles* [Missoula, MT: Scholars Press, 1977] 58:11; 176:15). It has as its root idea "empty opinion," "error" (cf. Ign. *Magn.* 11). A person, then, who is motivated by κενοδοξία is a person who assertively, even arrogantly, claims to have the right opinion (δόξα), but who is in fact in error (κένος). He is a person who is conceited without reason, deluded (Oepke has no basis for saying this sense of the word is not found in the NT, *TDNT* 3,662), ambitious for his own reputation, challenging others to rivalry, himself jealous of others (cf. Gal 5:26, where the corresponding adjective, κενόδοξοι is used). Consequently he is a person who will fight to prove his idea is right. "This all-too-human element *could* be behind the inability of the Philippian Christians to be united" (Barth). Was this in fact so? Paul, by asking that no one do anything from a cheap desire to boast (cf. GNB), is in reality asking that each look to himself and reflect on this possibility. For where such "empty conceit" (BGD) is present, unity is absent.

Still a third negative factor that must go if the Philippian church, or any Christian community, is to live in harmony is a selfish looking out for one's own interests, or those of his special group, to the exclusion of the interests of others (v 4). Paul on more than one occasion speaks out against this practice (1 Cor 10:24; Phil 2:21) reminding his readers that it is divisive (2:4) and that it is contrary to the nature of the God they worship (cf. 1 Cor 13:5 with 1 John 4:7–8). The normally recurring verb, ζητεῖν, that he generally uses to warn against this "seeking of one's own," he here replaces with the verb σκοπεῖν, "to look (out) for," "notice," "keep one's eyes on." Since the difference in meaning between these two verbs is slight, and since the construction involving them is exact—τὰ ἑαυτῶν σκοπεῖν/τὰ ἑαυτῶν ζητεῖν (cf. Phil 2:4 with 2:21; 1 Cor 10:24, 33; 13:5), it seems unnecessary, therefore, to see here a different and more subtle meaning from what would be expected, namely that the Philippians are to keep their eyes fixed on the good points of others rather than to concentrate each on his own spiritual endowments (so Beare, Bonnard, Martin). The problem at Philippi was not the same as the problem at Corinth. It was not that people were overvaluing spirit-inspired manifestations and glorying in these (Collange), but simply that people (ἕκαστος), or groups of people (ἕκαστοι), were selfishly interested only in themselves or their parties. Unity cannot coexist with individualism or partisanship. So underneath the negative form in which this warning comes, Paul in reality is making the appeal for each to pay concerned attention to the things that interest and deeply concern the other (Gnilka).

Alongside the negative commands is the one positive encouragement to "humbly consider others better than yourselves" (v 3). This is the linchpin that guarantees the success of the Christian community. "Humility," today as in ancient times, tends to be regarded *in sensu malo*. The noun used here, ταπεινοφροσύνη, is apparently not found in any Greek writing before the NT (Moule). But the adjective related to it (ταπεινός) was frequently employed, and especially so, to describe the mentality of a slave. It conveyed the ideas of being base, unfit, shabby, mean, of no account. Hence "humility" could not have been regarded by the pagan as a virtue to be sought after (see

Grundmann, *TDNT* 8,1-27). This same understanding of ταπεινός survives in the LXX. But already in the OT a new note is struck: God chooses the unimportant and the small for his plans (LXX I Kings 18:23; Ps 118:67; Jud 9:11; Wisd Sol 2:3). God saves the lowly and humble (Ps 17:28). God looks upon the lowly (Ps 112:4-6); God pays attention to the prayers of the lowly (Ps 101:18); God gives grace to the lowly while he opposes the scoffers (cf. Isa 2:11; Ezek 17:24). Lowliness and humility are thus evaluated as positive virtues by the Bible, especially as they affect the way in which people behave toward others and in which they approach God (cf. Isa 57:15).

In the Qumran community humility is valued as a virtue because it carries within itself the ingredients for unity and love within the fellowship. Repeatedly in the Scroll of the Rule the members are told that "they shall all be in the community of truth and virtuous humility and loving charity and scrupulous justice" (1QS 2:24; cf. 4:3; 5:3, 25). Paul is heir to these ideas, agreeing especially with the Qumran concept of humility in so far as he too holds as indispensable for unity within the community that kind of behavior that is generated by an attitude of humility. The new contribution that Paul makes to the concept is that he connects this humility to Christ Jesus, to the self-humiliating love of the one who existed in the form of God (cf. Phil 2:8; see Gnilka). Thus "humility" as Paul understands it and advocates it is not self-disparagement but an attitude inspired by the example of Christ, and is therefore specifically Christian, an attitude of mutual love within the church, the antithesis of pride, self-conceit (κενοδοξία) and selfishness (ἐριθεία).

Humility is in fact defined still more precisely by the expression which immediately follows—ἀλλήλους ἡγούμενοι ὑπερέχοντας ἑαυτῶν ("considering each other better than yourselves"). The participle ἡγούμενοι is formed from a verb (ἡγεῖσθαι) that means "to calculate," "to reckon." It implies a conscious sure judgment resting on carefully weighed facts (Vincent). Here it points to a proper evaluation of others and of one's self in light of the holiness of God, the Christian gospel and the example of Christ. The result, Paul says, will be "to set others above yourselves"—not just "the good, clever, earnest, pious" ones to whom all willingly bow, but those who lack these characteristics as well. For the word ὑπερέχοντας ("better," "superior," "above") that Paul uses here to describe one's neighbor recalls the ἐξουσίαι ὑπερέχουσαι of Rom 13:1, i.e. those who govern by virtue of their superior authority, not necessarily by virtue of their superior quality. Christians, therefore, are to consider one another "without restriction." Problems of disunity end "when we discover respect for each other, not on this ground or that, perhaps *without* any grounds, *counter* to every ground, simply because we are bidden" to do so, ordered to reckon each other better than ourselves (Barth). Naturally one does not think this way. But the divine command directed, not toward all, but to the Christian community, implies divine assistance to achieve the impossible. Such an attitude of utter respect for one another guarantees unity, and binds believers together in a mutually enriching society.

Explanation

Paul draws upon his rhetorical skills to encourage the Philippian church to strive for unity. In four successive clauses, each beginning with "if," he powerfully impresses upon his friends that they indeed are the recipients of his encouragement and love, members of an extraordinary fellowship created by the Spirit of God, and objects of God's affection and compassion. Consequently they are obliged to pay attention to God's appeal through him to strive for harmony and humility. Paul is not seeking after uniformity of opinion here. He does not ask that the Philippians all think alike. Rather he asks that they strive for an inner sentiment for each other that is full of love. He asks that they all possess a common soul, share a common affection for each other, have a common desire to live together in harmony by renouncing a party-spirit that is coupled with empty conceit and self-interest, and by adopting a humble attitude that estimates others as better than themselves. In such a climate unity thrives, the Church grows, and the individual Christian is strengthened in the faith.

3. Christ, the Supreme Example of Humility and Unselfishness (2:5–11)

Bibliography

As a supplement to this detailed bibliography, see the excellent bibliography for this section in R. P. Martin, *Carmen Christi*, 320–339; and R. B. Strimple, *WTJ* 41 (1979) 247–68, for a listing and summary of studies on Phil 2:5–11 since 1963.

Ales, D. d'. "Philip. II, 6, οὐχ ἁρπαγμὸν ἡγήσατο." *RSR* 1 (1910) 260–69. **Arvedson, T.** "Phil. 2,6 und Mt. 10,39." *ST* 5 (1951–52) 49–51. **Baarda, T.** "Jes 45,23 in het Nieuwe Testament (Rm 14:11; Flp 2, 10v)." *Gereformeerd Theologisch Tijdschrift* 71 (1971) 137–39. **Badham, E. P.** "Phillippians (*sic*) 2:6; ἁρπαγμόν." *ExpTim* 19 (1907–1908) 331–33. **Bakken, N. K.** The New Humanity: Christ and the Modern Age. A Study Centering in the Christ-Hymn: Philippians 2:6–11."*Int* 22 (1968) 71–82. **Barclay, W.** "Great Themes of the NT: Phil. 2:1–11." *ExpTim* 70 (1958–59) 4–7, 40–44. **Barnikol, E.** *Der marcionitische Ursprung des Mythos-Satzes Phil. 2,6–7.* Kiel: Muhlau, 1932. **Bartsch, H. W.** *Die konkrete Wahrheit und die Lüge der Spekulation: Untersuchung über den vorpaulinischen Christushymnus und seine gnostische Mythisierung.* Frankfurt: Lang, 1974. **Bauer, K. A.** "Der Weg der Diakonie. Predigt über Phil. 2.5–11." *EvT* 36 (1976) 280–85. **Baugher, L.** "Interpretation of Philippians 2:6–7." *LQ* 8 (1878) 119–24. **Beet, J. A.** "Harpagmos, Philippians 2:6: A Reply." *ExpTim* 6 (1894–95) 526–28. ———. "Some Difficult Passages in St. Paul's Epistles: I, Phil. 2:6." *ExpTim* 3 (1891–92) 307–308. ———. "Thought It Not Robbery to Be Equal with God." *Expositor* 3rd series 5 (1887) 115–25. **Benoit, P.** "Préexistence et incarnation." *RB* 77 (1970) 5–29. **Bindley, J. H.** "Fresh Light Upon Philippians 2:5–8." *Expositor* 8th series 26 (1923) 442–46. **Blanc, R.** "La recontre de Dieu dans l' incognito de Jésus-Christ, Phil 2,5–11." *Positions Luthériennes* 21 (1973) 49–55. **Böld, W.** "Gott-Sklave-Weltenherr. Ein Beitrage zur Christusmorphologie von Philipper 2,5–11." *Beiträg zur hermeneutischen Diskussion,* ed. W. Böld. Wuppertal: R. Brockhaus, 1968. **Boman, T.** "Fil 2,5–11." *NorTT* 53 (1952) 193–212. **Bornhäuser, K.** "Zum Verständnis von Phil. 2,5–11." *NKZ* 44 (1933) 428–34; 453–62. **Bouyer, L.** " 'ΑΡΠΑΓΜΟΣ." *RSR* 39 (1951) 281–88. **Boyer, C.** "Une étude sur le texte de l' épître aux Philippiens 2,6–11." *Doctor Communis* 32 (1979) 5–14. **Brown, S.** "The Christ-Event According to Philippians 2:6–11." *Homiletic and Pastoral Review* 73 (1973) 31–32; 55–59. **Bruppacher, H.** "Zur Redewendung 'Nicht für Raub achten' Phil. 2,6." *TZ* 3 (1947) 234. **Buchanan, B.** "The True Kenosis (Phil 2:5–11)." *ExpTim* 19 (1907–1908) 565–66. **Carmignac, J.** "L'importance de la place d'une négation οὐχ ἁρπαγμὸν ἡγήσατο (Philippiens II.6)." *NTS* 18 (1971–72) 131–66. **Cerfaux, L.** *Christ in the Theology of St Paul.* Tr. G. Webb and A. Walker. New York: Herder and Herder, 1959. ———. "L'hymne au Christ-Serviteur de Dieu (Phil 2, 6–11 = Is 52,13–53,12)." *Recueil Lucien Cerfaux, II. Etudes d'exégèse et d'histoire religieuse.* BETL 6–7. Gembloux: Duculot, 1954. **Chamberlain, J. S. F.** "The Kenosis." *ExpTim* 4 (1892–93) 189–90. **Chomondeley, F. G.** "Harpagmos, Philippians 2:6." *ExpTim* 7 (1895–96) 47–48. **Contri, A.** "Il 'Magnificat' alla luce dell'inno christologico di Filippesi 2:6–11." *Marianum* 40 (1978) 164–68. **Coppens, J.** "Phil. 2:7 et Is. 53:12." *ETL* 41 (1965) 147–50. ———. "Une nouvelle structuration de l'hymne christologique de l' épître aux Philippiens." *ETL* 43 (1967) 197–202. **Dacquino, P.** "Il testo christologico di Fil. 2.6–11." *Revista Biblica Italiana* 7 (1959) 221–29. ———. "L'umilta e l'esaltazione dell'Adamo escatologico (Fil. 2,6–11). *BeO* 17 (1975) 241–52. **Dawe, D. G.** "A Fresh look at the Kenotic Christologies." *SJT* 15 (1962) 337–49. **Deichgräber, R.** *Gotteshymnus und Christushymnus in der frühen Christenheit.* SUNT 5. Göttingen: Vandenhoeck und Ruprecht, 1967. **De Lacey, D. R.** "Image and Incarnations in Pauline Christology—a Search for Origins." *TynB* 30 (1979) 1–28. **Dibelius, M.** "ἁρπαγμός, Phil. 2,6." *TLZ* 40 (1915) 557–58. **Dodd, C. H.** *New Testament Studies.* Manchester: Manchester University Press, 1953. **Dupont, J.** "Jésus-Christ dans son abaissement et son exaltation d'après Phil. 2,6–11." *RSR* 37 (1950) 500–14. **Eckman, B.** "A Quantitative Metrical Analysis of the Philippians' Hymn." *NTS* 26 (1980) 258–66. **Ehrhardt, A.** "Ein antikes Herrscherideal." *EvT* 8 (1948–49) 101–10. ———. "Nochmals: Ein antikes Herrscherideal." *EvT* 8 (1948–49) 569–72. **Ehrhardt, A. A. T.** "Jesus Christ and Alexander the Great." *JTS* 46 (1945) 45–51. **Ernesti, H.** *Fr. Th. L.* "Noch ein Wort über Philipper 2,6." *TSK* 24 (1851) 595–630. ———. "Philipp II,6ff. aus einer Anspielung auf Genes. II. III. erläutert." *TSK* 21 (1848) 858–924. **Fairweather, E. R.** "The 'Kenotic' Christology." F. W. Beare. *A Commentary on the Epistle to the Philippians.* New York: Harper and Brothers, 1959, appended note 159–174. **Ferguson, J.** "Philippians, John and Traditions of Ephesus." *ExpTim* 83 (1971) 85–87. **Feuillet, A.** "L'hymne christologique de l'épître aux Philippiens (2.6–11)." *RB* 72 (1965) 352–80; 481–507. **Finley, M. B.** "The Spirit of Kenōsis." *Bible Today* 69 (1973) 389–94. **Foerster, W.** "Οὐχ ἁρπαγμὸν ἡγήσατο bei den griechischen Kirchenvätern." *ZNW* 29 (1930) 115–18. **Foss, O.** "Til Paul. Phil II.6." *DTT* 36 (1973) 195–96. **Fridrichsen, A.** " 'Nicht für Raub achten' Phil. 2,6." *TZ* 2 (1946) 395. ———. "Quatre conjectures sur le texte du Nouveau Testament." *RHPR* 3 (1923) 439–42. **Furness, J. M.** "The Authorship of Phil 2,6–11." *ExpTim* 70 (1958–59) 240–43. ———. "Behind the Philippians Hymn." *ExpTim* 79 (1967–68) 178–82. **Gamber, K.** "Der Christushymnus im Philipperbrief in Liturgiegeschichtlicher Sicht." *Bib* 51 (1970) 369–76. **Georgi, D.** "Der vorpaulinische Hymnus Phil. 2.6–11." *Zeit und Geschichte. Dankesgabe an R. Bultmann zum 80. Geburtstag,* ed. E. Dinkler. Tübingen: J. C. B. Mohr, 1964. **Gewiess, J.** "Zum altkirchlichen Verständnis der Kenosis-stelle (Phil 2.5–11)." *TQ* 128 (1948) 463–87. **Gibbs, J. G.** "Philippians 2:6–11." *Creation and Redemption: A Study in Pauline Theology.* Leiden: Brill, 1971. ———. "The Relation Between Creation and Redemption According to Phil II.5–11." *NovT* 12 (1970) 270–83. **Gifford, E. H.** "The Incarnation: A Study of Philippians 2:5–11." *Expositor,* 5th series 4 (1896) 161–77; 241–63. **Gilse, J. van.** "Verklaring van Philippensen II, ver 5–11." *TT* 51 (1917) 321–25. **Glasson, T. F.** "Two Notes on the Philippians Hymn (ii.6–11)." *NTS* 21 (1974) 133–39. **Grelot, P.** "Deux expressions difficiles de Philippiens 2,6–7." *Bib* 53 (1972) 495–507. ———. "Deux notes critiques sur Philippiens 2,6–11." *Bib* 54 (1973) 169–86. ———. "La Traduction et l'interprétation de Ph. 2,6–7. Quelques éléments d'enquête Patristique." *NRT* 93 (1971) 897–922, 1009–26. ———. "La valeur de ouk . . . alla . . . in Philippiens 2,6–7." *Bib* 54 (1973) 25–42. **Griffiths, D. R.** " Ἁρπαγμός and ἑαυτὸν ἐκένωσεν in Phil. 2.6–7." *ExpTim* 69 (1957–58) 237–39. **Grimm, W.** "Über die Stelle Philipp. 2,6–11." *ZWT* 16 (1873) 33–59. **Guignebert, C.** "Exégèse sur Phil 2,6–11." *RHPR* 3 (1923)

512–33. **Hain, Q.** "Ein Versuch zur endgültigen Erklärung der Elippse in Phil 2:5." *TSK* 66 (1893) 169–72. **Hamann, H. P.** "A Note on Phil. 2:6, 7a." *Lutheran Theological Journal* 12 (1978) 120–22. **Hammerich, L. L.** *An Ancient Misunderstanding* (Phil. 2.6 'robbery'), Copenhagen, 1966. **Hanssler, B.** "Der Knecht Gottes. Die Dimensionen in einer Auslegung von Phil 2,6–11." *Wort und Wahrheit* 12 (1957) 85–89. **Harvey, J.** "A New Look at the Christ-Hymn in Philippians ii.6–11." *ExpTim* 76 (1964–65) 337–39. **Helmbold, A. K.** "Redeemer Hymns—Gnostic and Christian." *New Dimensions in New Testament Study*, eds. R. N. Longenecker and M. C. Tenney. Grand Rapids: Zondervan, 1974. **Héring, J.** "Kyrios Anthropos (Phil 2,6–11)." *RHPR* 16 (1936) 196–209. **Hofius, O.** *Der Christushymnus Philipper 2,6–11.* WUNT 17. Tübingen: J. C. B. Mohr, 1976. **Holzmeister, U.** " 'Hoc enim sentite in vobis, quot et in Christo Iesu' (Phil. 2,5)." *VD* 22 (1942) 225–27. **Hooker, M. D.** "Philippians 2,6–11." *Jesus und Paulus, Festschrift für W. G. Kümmel*, eds. E. E. Ellis and E. Grässer. Göttingen: Vandenhoeck und Ruprecht, 1975. **Hoover, R. W.** "The Harpagmos Enigma: A Philological Solution." *HTR* 64 (1971) 95–119. **Horan, B. W.** "The Apostolic Kerygma in Philippians 2:6–9." *ExpTim* 62 (1950–51) 60–61. **Horne, C. M.** " 'Let This Mind be in You.' An Exposition of Phil. 2:5–11." *Grace Journal* 1 (1960) 25–33. **Howard, G.** "Phil. 2:6–11 and the Human Christ." *CBQ* 40 (1978) 368–87. **Hudson, D. F.** "A Further Note on Philippians ii.6–11." *ExpTim* 77 (1965–66) 29. **Hunzinger, C. H.** "Zur Struktur der Christushymnen in Phil 2 und 1. Petr 3." *Der Ruf Jesus und die Antwort der Gemeinde*, eds. E. Lohse, C. Burchard, B. Schaller. Göttingen: Vandenhoeck und Ruprecht, 1970. **Hurtado L.** "Jesus as Lordly Example in Phil. 2:5–11." *From Jesus to Paul. Studies in Honour of Francis Wright Beare*, eds. J. C. Hurd and G. P. Richardson, forthcoming. **Jeremias, J.** "Zur Gedankenführung in den paulinischen Briefen." *Studia Paulina in Honorem J. de Zwaan*, ed. J. N. Sevenster and W. C. van Unnik. Haarlem: E. F. Bonn, 1953. ———. "Zu Phil. 2,7: ΕΑΥΤΟΝ ΕΚΕΝΩΣΕΝ." *NovT* 6 (1963) 182–88. **Jervell, J.** *Imago Dei. Gen. i,26f im Spätjudentum in der Gnosis und in den paulinischen Briefen.* FRLANT 63. Göttingen: Vandenhoeck und Ruprecht, 1960. **Joüon, P.** "Notes philologiques sur quelques versets de l'épître aux Philippiens." *RSR* 28 (1938) 299–310. **Jülicher, A.** "Ein philologisches Gutachten über Phil. 2,6." *ZNW* 16 (1915) 1–17. **Kähler, C. N.** "Bermerkungen zu Philipper 2,5–14, besonders in Betreff des οὐχ ἁρπαγμὸν ἡγήσατο τὸ εἶναι ἴσα θεῷ." *TSK* 30 (1857) 99–112. **Kamphaus, F.** "Das Christlied des Philipperbriefs. Ermutigung zur Predigt." *Das Evangelium auf dem Weg zum Menschen*, eds. O. Knoch, F. Messerschmidt, and A. Zenner. Frankfurt: Knecht, 1973. **Käsemann, E.** "Kritische Analyse von Phil. 2,5–11." *ZTK* 47 (1960) 313–60. ET: "A Critical Analysis of Philippians 2:5–11." *God and Christ; Existence and Province.* New York: Harper and Row, 1968, 45–88. **Kattenbusch, F.** " 'ΑΡΠΑΓΜΟΝ?" ΑΠΡΑΓΜΟΝ! Phil. 2,6. Ein Beitrag zur paulinischen Christologie." *TSK* 104 (1932) 373–420. **Knox, W. L.** "The 'Divine-Hero' Christology in the New Testament." *HTR* 41 (1948) 229–49. **Kretzmann, P. E.** " 'Hielt er's nicht für einen Raub,' Phil. 2.6." *CTM* 2 (1931) 244–58. **Krinetzki, L.** "Der Einfluss von Jes 52.13–53.13 Par. auf Phil 2:6–11." *TQ* 139 (1959) 157–93; 291–336. **Labourt, J.** "Notes d' exegese sur Philip. II,5–11." *RB* 7 (1898) 402–15; 553–63. **Lewis, E.** "The Humiliated and Exalted Son (Phil. 2,5–11)." *Int* 1 (1947) 20–32. **Ligier, L.** "L'hymne christologique de Phil. 2,6–11. La liturgie eucharistique et la bénédiction synagogal 'Nishmat Kol hay'." *Stud. Paul. Congressus 1961 II.* AnBib 18. Rome, 1963, 65–74. **Lohmeyer, E.** *Kyrios Jesus: Eine Untersuchung zu Phil. 2,5–11.* Heidelberg: Winter, 1928. **Loofs, F.** "Das altkirchliche Zeugnis gegen die herrschende Aufflassung der Kenosisstelle (Phil. 2,5 bis 11)." *TSK* 100 (1927–28) 1–102. **Losie, L. A.** "A Note on the Interpretation of Phil. 2:5." *ExpTim* 90 (1978) 52–54. **Louf, A.** "Une ancienne exégèse de Phil. 2,6 dans le kᵉtaba dᵉ masqata (Livre des degrés)." *Stud. Paul. Congressus 1961 II.* AnBib 18. Rome, 1963. **Lucien, R.** "Kenotic Christology in a New Perspective." *Église et Theologie* 7 (1976) 5–39. **Magne, J.** "L'exaltation de Sabaôth dans *Hypostase des Archontes* 143, 1–31 et l'exaltation de Jésus dans Philippiens

2,6–11 ou la naissance de Jésus Christ." *Cahiers du Cercle Ernest-Renan* 21 (1973) 1–56. **Manns, F.** "Un hymne judéo-chrétien: Philippiens 2,6–11." *Euntes Docete* 29 (1976) 259–90. **Marcheselli, C. C.** "La celebrazione di Gesù Cristo Signore in Fil 2,6–11. Riflessioni letterario-storico-esegetiche sull'inno cristologico." *Ephemerides Carmeliticae* 29 (1978) 2–42. **Marshall, I. H.** "The Christ-Hymn in Philippians 2:5–11." *TynB* 19 (1968) 104–27. **Martin, R. P.** *Carmen Christi. Philippians 2:5–11 in Recent Interpretation and in the Setting of Early Christian Worship.* Cambridge: University Press, 1967. Rev. ed. Grand Rapids: Eerdmans, 1983. ———. *An Early Christian Confession. Philippians 2:5–11 in Recent Interpretation.* London: Tyndale, 1960. ———. *Worship in the Early Church.* Rev. ed. Grand Rapids: Eerdmans, 1975. ———. "The Form-Analysis of Philippians 2,5–11." *TU* 87 (1964) 611–20. ———. "*Morphē* in Philippians ii.6." *ExpTim* 70 (1959–60) 183–84. **Massie, J.** "Harpagmos, Philippians 2:6." *ExpTim* 7 (1895–96) 141. **Meinertz, M.** "Zum Verständnis des Christus-hymnus Phil. 2,5–11." *TTZ* 61 (1952) 186–92. **Michel, O.** "Zur Exegese von Phil. 2,5–11." *Theologie als Glaubenswagnis. Festschrift für K. Heim zum 80. Geburtstag.* Hamburg: Furche Verlag, 1954. **Moule, C. F. D.** "Further Reflexions on Philippians 2,5–11." *Apostolic History and the Gospel*, eds. W. W. Gasque and R. P. Martin. Grand Rapids: Eerdmans, 1970. ———. "The Manhood of Jesus in the NT." *Christ Faith and History*, eds. S. W. Sykes & J. P. Clayton. Cambridge: The University Press, 1972, 95–110. **Mowinckel, S.** "Et gammeltestamentlig analogon til ἁρπαγμός i Fil 2:6." *NorTT* 40 (1939) 208–11. **Murphy-O'Connor, J.** "Christological Anthropology in Phil. 2:6–11." *RB* 83 (1976) 25–50. **Nestle, E.** "Ἐν μορφῇ θεοῦ ὑπάρχων, Phil. 2,6." *TSK* 66 (1893) 173–74. **Neufeld, V. H.** *The Earliest Christian Confessions.* NTTS 5. Leiden: Brill, 1963. **Nisius, J. B.** "Zur Erklärung von Phil. II,5–11." *ZKT* 21 (1897) 276–306; 23 (1899) 75–113. **Ogara, F.** "Hoc sentite in vobis quod et in Christo Jesu (Phil. 2,5)." *VD* (1935) 95–109. **Petanel-Olliff, E.** "La Kénose apres la transfiguration. Etude exégétique sur Phil. 2,5–11." *RSPT* 29 (1896) 138–64. **Petersen, K.** "Ἐαυτὸν ἐκένωσεν, Phil. 2:7." *SO* 12 (1933) 96–101. **Pintard, J.** "Christologie paulinienne. Observations sur l'hymne christologique de l'Ép. aux Phil. et sur L'ensemble de la christologie paulinienne." *Esprit et Vie* 83 (1973) 328–33. **Porter, F. C.** *The Mind of Christ in Paul.* New York: 1931. **Powell, W.** "Arpagmos . . . eauton ekenōse." *ExpTim* 71 (1959–60) 88. **Prideaux, S. P. T.** " 'My Life Shall be to Thee for a Prey' (Ierem. et Phil. 2,6)." *ExpTim* 43 (1931–32) 288. **Reicke, B.** "Unité chrétienne et diaconie: Phil. 2:1–11." *Neotestamentica et Patristica: eine Freundegabe O. Cullman.* NovTSup 6. Leiden: Brill, 1962. **Reule, G.** "The Christology of Philippians 2:5–11." *Springfielder* 35 (1971) 81–85. **Richard, L.** "Kenotic Christology in a New Perspective." *Eglise et Theologie* 7 (1976) 5–39. **Robinson, D. W. B.** "Ἁρπαγμός: The Deliverance Jesus Refused?" *ExpTim* 80 (1968–69) 253–54. **Robinson, W. C. Jr.** "Christology and Christian Life: Paul's Use of the Incarnation Motif." *ANQ* 12 (1971) 108–17. **Ross, J.** "Ἁρπαγμός Phil. II. 6" *JTS* 10 (1909) 573, 574. **Salleron, L.** "Critique interne de Phil. 2,1–8." *Itinéraires* 153 (1971) 63–70. ———. "Reflexions sur la traduction de l'Ep. aux Phil (2:6–11)." *La Pensée Catholique* 132 (1971) 14–23. **Sanders, J. A.** "Dissenting Deities and Philippians 2,1–11." *JBL* 88 (1969) 278–90. **Sanders, J. T.** *New Testament Christological Hymns: Their Historical and Religious Background.* Cambridge: University Press, 1971. **Schegget, G. H. ter.** *Het lied van de Mensenzoon—Studie over de Christus-Psalm in Fil 2:6–11.* Baarn: Wereldvenster, 1975. **Scroggs, R.** *The Last Adam.* Oxford: Blackwells, 1966. **Spicq, C.** "Note sur MORPHĒ dans les papyrus et quelques inscriptions." *RB* 80 (1973) 37–45. **Stagg, F.** "The Mind in Christ Jesus: Philippians 1:27–2:18." *RevExp* 77 (1980) 337–47. **Stanley, D. M.** "The Theme of the Servant of Yahweh in Primitive Christian Soteriology and Its Transposition by St Paul." *CBQ* 16 (1954) 385–425. ———. *Christ's Resurrection in Pauline Soteriology.* AnBib, 13. Rome: Pontifical Biblical Institute, 1961. **Stein, M.** "Über Philipper 2,6." *TSK* 24 (1851) 595–630. **Stephenson, A. A.** "Christ's Self-Abasement (Phil 2,5–11)." *CBQ* 1 (1939)

296–313. **Strecker, G.** "Freiheit und Agape. Exegese und Predigt über Phil. 2,5–11." *Neues Testament und Christliche Existenz. Festschrift für H. Braun,* ed. H. D. Betz und L. Schottroff. Tübingen: Mohr, 1973. ———. "Redaction und Tradition im Christushymnus. Phil. 2,6–11." *ZNW* 55 (1964) 63–78. ———. "Zum Christushymnus in Phil. 2." *TLZ* 89 (1964) 521–22. **Streiker, L. D.** "The Christological Hymn in Phil 2." *LQ* 16 (1964) 49–58. **Strimple, R. B.** "Philippians 2:5–11 in Recent Studies: Some Exegetical Conclusions." *WJT* 41 (1979) 246–68. **Swallow, J. E.** "Philippians 2:5–8." *Theology* 30 (1935) 298–300. **Talbert, C. H.** "The Problem of Pre-existence in Phil. 2:6–11." *JBL* 86 (1967) 141–53. **Thomas, J.** "L'hymne de l'Epître aux Philippiens." *Christus* 22 (1975) 334–45. **Thomas, T. A.** "The Kenosis Question." *EvQ* 42 (1970) 142–51. **Trakatellis, D. C.** "The Preexistence of Christ in the Writings of Justin Martyr. An Exegetical Study with Reference to the Humiliation and Exaltation Christology." Ph.D. dissertation, Harvard University, 1972. **Trudinger, P.** "Ἁρπαγμός and the Christological Significance of the Ascension." *ExpTim* 79 (1967–68) 279. **Vokes, F. E.** "Ἁρπαγμός in Phil. 2,6." *TU* 87 (1964) 670–75. **Wallace, D. H.** "A Note on *Morphē.*" *TZ* 22 (1966) 19–25. **Warren, W.** "On ἑαυτόν ἐκένωσεν." *JTS* 12 (1911) 461–63. **Wetzel, L.** "Über ἁρπαγμός in der Stelle Phil. 2,6." *TSK* 60 (1897) 535–52. **Wilson, R. E.** "He Emptied Himself." *JETS* 19 (1976) 279–81. **Wilson, W. E.** "Philippians 2:7." *ExpTim* 56 (1944–45) 280.

Translation

⁵ *This* ᵃ *way of thinking must be adopted* ᵇ *by you,*
  which also was the way of thinking adopted by
  Christ Jesus.
⁶ *Precisely because he was in the form of God*
  he did not consider being equal with God
  grounds for grasping. ᶜ
⁷ *On the contrary, he rather poured himself out*
  by taking the form of a slave,
  by being born in the likeness of human beings, ᵈ
  and by being recognized as a man.
⁸ *He humbled himself,*
  by becoming obedient even to the point of
  accepting death.
  and that of all things, death on a cross.
⁹ *As a consequence, therefore, God exalted him to*
  the highest place,
  and conferred on him the ᵉ *name that is above every*
  name,
¹⁰ *in order that before the name that Jesus bears*
  every knee might bow,
  of heavenly beings,
  and of earthly beings,
  and of beings under the earth,
¹¹ *and in order that every tongue might openly*
  and thankfully acknowledge ᶠ *that Jesus Christ*
  is Lord, to the glory of God the Father.

Notes

ᵃ P⁴⁶ D F G and the majority of Greek MSS add γάρ (οὖν, 2492) after τοῦτο. This is an unnecessary attempt to link this new section (2:5-11) with the preceding verses.

ᵇ The majority text reads φρονείσθω for φρονεῖτε—"Let (this) be thought (among you)," perhaps an effort to explain more easily ἐν Χριστῷ as a parallel to ἐν ὑμῖν (see comments).

ᶜ ἀπραγμον, "pillow," has been conjectured for ἁρπαγμόν, but there is no textual evidence for this.

ᵈ P⁴⁶ reads ἀνθρώπου instead of ἀνθρώπων, as do Marcion and Cyprian, no doubt to make it parallel with the expression that follows.

ᵉ D F G and the majority of Greek MSS omit the definite article τό (τὸ ὄνομα, "a name" rather than "the name"), without noticing that *the* name is actually stated in v 10.

ᶠ A C D and many other Greek MSS have the future indicative instead of the aorist subjunctive (ἐξομολογήσεται for ἐξομολογήσηται). The change is so slight in form that it could easily be accidental. But it could also be intentional. Some early scribe may have understood v 11 eschatologically and altered it to bring out this idea, making it harmonize with the Isaiah passage from which it is taken (45:23).

Form/Structure/Setting

This section is the most important section in the letter and surely the most difficult to interpret. The number of genuine exegetical problems and the sheer mass of books and articles it has called forth leaves one wondering where to begin, despairing about adding anything new, and well-nigh stricken with mental paralysis (see Michael). It quickly becomes apparent, however, that although much has been written on these verses there is little that can be agreed upon, whether the topic discussed is the precise form of this section, its authorship, its place and purpose in the letter, the sources used in its composition, and so on.

Nevertheless, there is at least one thing that calls forth almost universal agreement. It is that vv 6–11 constitute a beautiful example of a very early hymn of the Christian church. Johannes Weiss was the first (1899) to notice the poetic, rhythmic nature of these verses (see Eckman, *NTS* 26 [1980] 258). He has been followed by many scholars, the most able of whom are E. Lohmeyer (*Kyrios Jesus*, and his commentary on Philippians), J. Jeremias (*Studia Paulina*), and R. P. Martin (*Carmen Christi*).

Agreement, however, quickly disappears when one begins to analyze the hymn structurally. Some see the hymn as composed of six strophes of three lines each, with the first three strophes proclaiming the humiliation of Christ (vv 6–8) and the last three his exaltation (vv 9–11): A. v 6; B. v 7a–b; C. vv 7c–8, but omitting the words θανάτου δὲ σταυροῦ ("even death on the cross") as not being part of the original hymn; D. v 9; E. v 10; F. v 11 (Lohmeyer; cf. Beare, Benoit, Bonnard, Héring).

Others see it as formed of a series of couplets in six pairs arranged in such a way as to lend themselves easily to a kind of antiphonal chanting: A. v 6; B. v 7a; C. v 7b; D. v 8; E. v 9; F. vv 10a and 11a (Martin, *Carmen Christi*, 36–37; see E. Norden, *Antike Kunstprosa* [Stuttgart: B. G. Teubner, 1958] 1,55–57 for a description of and evidence for this practice of chanting in the ancient world). To make the hymn fit into this kind of structure, however, it is necessary to remove the following phrases and treat them as secondary additions: θανάτου δὲ σταυροῦ ("even death on the cross"), ἐπουρανίων καὶ ἐπιγείων καὶ καταχθονίων ("of heavenly beings, and earthly beings and beings under the earth"), and εἰς δόξαν θεοῦ πατρός ("to the glory of God the Father").

Still others, after careful quantitative metrical analysis of these verses see only five strophes of varying length, and with varying length of lines within each strophe: A. vv 6–7a; B. vv 7b–8; C. vv 9–10a; D. vv 10b–11a; E. v 11b–c (Eckman, *NTS* 26 [1980] 258–66; cf. also Dibelius, Gamber, *Bib* 51 [1970] 369–76). This kind of arrangement also requires modifying the text such as deleting ὑπάρχων ("being"), altering ἐταπείνωσεν ἑαυτόν to ἐταπεινώθη, and omitting the words "of heavenly beings, and earthly beings and beings under the earth."

Others yet see the hymn as composed of four strophes, each with four lines: A. vv 6–7a; B. vv 7b–8; C. vv 9–10a; D. vv 10b–11 (Collange). This particular analysis omits no words or phrases, but does violence to the grammar of the Greek by making a verse division where no verse division would ever be expected.

Still others see in the hymn only three strophes that correspond to the three states of Jesus' existence: A. his preexistent state (vv 6–7a), his earthly life (vv 7b–8) and his exaltation (vv 9–11; Cerfaux, *Christ* 382; see Jeremias, *Studia Paulina* 152–54). Again, this kind of analysis often calls for the deletion of words and phrases from the hymn as it stands in order to have the proper balance in the strophes.

These are but some of the suggested analyses of Phil 2:6–11. There are others. Together they demonstrate beyond doubt the fact that these verses comprise an early hymn, or at least part of an early hymn that had as its subject Jesus Christ (cf. Eph 5:19; Col 3:16, and the interesting remark of Pliny the Younger, governor of Bithynia-Pontus, written to the Emperor Trajan, A.D. 112–13, that Christians were in the habit of singing hymns "to Christ as to a god," *Epistles* 10.96). And this demonstration is of great importance.

But the very great lack of agreement among scholars about the exact structure of these verses makes one question the possibility of ever knowing for certain what this hymn looked like when it was first composed, if it did not look like it does now in the texts presently available. And the necessity of omitting words and phrases, or altering expressions to make the strophes come out right according to some preconceived notion of what they should be, makes one suspicious of the whole procedure and causes one to ask whether this is not just some sort of game that scholars play.

As a consequence this commentary, while taking note of the basic hymnic nature of Phil 2:6–11, will make no attempt to specify the precise strophic structure of its composition. It (a) accepts all words and phrases as part of the original hymn and essential to its meaning, (b) recognizes from the four independent verbs in the hymn—the first two with Jesus as subject, and the last two with God as subject—that the hymn naturally falls into two parts: Jesus' humiliation by his own act, and Jesus' exaltation by the act of God, (c) allows for the possibility that such early Christian hymns as this one were not as perfectly constructed as modern scholarship might wish them to be (cf. E. Norden, *Agnostos Theos* [Stuttgart: B. G. Teubner, 1956] 257), and (*d*) refuses to accept as valid the proposition that a correct understanding of the hymn depends on a correct versification of the hymn.

The particular shape given to this hymn, and indeed the very existence of the hymn itself, may be the result of deep meditation by Paul, or by some Christian before or contemporaneous with Paul, if Paul is not the author of the hymn (so Beare; Bonnard; Gnilka; Georgi, "Der vorpaulinische Hymnus;" Käsemann, *ZTK* 47 (1960) 313–60; Martin, *Carmen Christi*, 54; but see also Dibelius, Martin, *Carmen Christi*, 60; Michaelis, Scott, Furness, *ExpTim* 70 [1958–59] 240–43), on one particular event from the life of Christ as recorded in the gospel tradition—Jesus washing his disciples' feet (John 13:3–17). Although verbal parallels between John 13:3–17 and Phil 2:6–11 are few, but nonetheless significant, the parallels in thought and in the progression of action are startling. So precise in fact are these parallels that it is difficult to consider them the result of mere coincidence. To present this parallelism more clearly the following diagram has been prepared:

John 13:3–17	*Phil 2:6–11*
1. Jesus arises from the table and lays aside (τίθησι) his outer garments (τὰ ἱμάτια) (v 4).	1. He emptied himself (ἐκένωσεν ἑαυτόν). Moffatt translates: "He laid it (his divine nature) aside" (v 7).
2. Jesus takes a towel and wraps it about himself (διέζωσεν ἑαυτόν), puts water in a basin and begins to wash his disciples feet (a menial task often assigned to slaves; 1 Sam 25:41; cf. Mark 1:7; Acts 13:25; Str-B 2.557) (v 5).	2. . . . taking the form of a slave, being born in the likeness of human beings. And being found in human form he humbled himself (ἐταπείνωσεν ἑαυτόν, v 7).
3. When Jesus finishes, he once again takes his outer garments and puts them on (ἔλαβεν τὰ ἱμάτια), and again sits down at the table (ἀνέπεσεν) from which he got up (v 12).	3. Therefore God exalted him to the highest place and gave him the name which is above every name (v 9).
4. Finally Jesus says: "You address me as teacher and Lord (κύριος) and rightly so, for that is what I am" (v 13).	4. . . . that every tongue might openly confess that Jesus Christ is Lord (κύριος, v 11).

Perhaps, then, this act and saying of Jesus became the basis for deep insights into the nature of Christ for both John and Paul. It is not necessary to say that John was dependent on Paul or Paul on John. For John and Paul could have shared a common tradition (see Ferguson, *ExpTim* 83 [1971] 86). And yet it is interesting and instructive to observe that both the Fourth Evangelist and the author of the Christ-Hymn begin what they have to say in a similar fashion. The Fourth Evangelist begins his narrative by remarking that Jesus washed his disciples' feet because he knew (εἰδώς) that the Father had given everything into his hands and that he himself had come out from God (ἀπὸ θεοῦ ἐξῆλθον) and was going back to God (πρὸς τὸν θεὸν ὑπάγε)—a remark that gives special emphasis to Jesus' act of humility (cf. C. H. Dodd, *The*

Interpretation of the Fourth Gospel [Cambridge: Cambridge University Press, 1953] 401).

Paul begins his hymn by remarking that Jesus, because he existed in the form of God, did not consider this high position as a prize to be held on to, but rather to be surrendered in order that he might serve—a remark that equally emphasizes Jesus' act of humility. (The entire hymn also preserves the descent-ascent motif that is prominent in the Johannine story.)

It is also interesting and instructive to note that the purpose of each pericope is similar. The Johannine account is an acted parable to summarize the essence of Jesus' teaching: "Whoever wants to be great among you must be your servant, and whoever wants to hold the first place among you must be everybody's slave" (Mark 10:43–44), while the Philippian text is a hymn to illustrate powerfully Paul's teaching, which at this point is identical with that of Jesus: humble, self-sacrificing service to one another done in love is a must for a Christian disciple who would live as a Christian disciple should (Phil 2:3–4).

Perhaps, then, the multitude of suggestions about sources of the hymn— whether it originated in heterodox Judaism (Lohmeyer), or in the Iranian myth of the Heavenly Redeemer (Beare), or in Hellenistic Gnosticism (Käsemann, "Critical Analysis," 62, 66, 72), or in Jewish Gnosticism (Sanders, *JBL* 88 [1969] 278–90), or in the OT servant-passages (Coppens, *ETL* 41 [1965] 147–50), or in the OT story of Adam (Bonnard), or in speculation about Hellenistic Jewish Wisdom (D. Georgi, "Der vorpaulinische Hymnus"), and so on, only serve to send one off in pursuit of a question impossible to answer. Perhaps the true answer to the origin of the hymn may be closer at hand, derived from that particular event of the life of Jesus outlined above (John 13:3–17). Yet although the form of this hymn may indeed owe its origin to the gospel tradition, and notably to this one incident from the tradition, yet very possibly the significance of that incident may have been effectually interpreted in terms of the religious language of any one of these systems of thought. These systems were everywhere present in the world of Paul, so that whoever composed the Philippian hymn would be heir to these ideas, able to draw on any or all of them to set forth the ultimate meaning of Jesus' humble act of service toward his disciples.

Comment

5. The Christ-hymn (vv 6–11) presents Jesus as the supreme example of the humble, self-sacrificing, self-denying, self-giving service that Paul has just been urging the Philippians to practice in their relations one toward another (vv 1–4). Hence, although this hymn is unquestionably a christological gem unparalleled in the NT, although it may be considered soteriological in character (Käsemann, "Critical Analysis," 45–88), and although it may have been originally composed for christological or soteriological reasons, Paul's motive in using it here is not theological but ethical. His object is not to give instruction in doctrine, but to reinforce instruction in Christian living. And he does this by appealing to the conduct of Christ. The hymn, therefore, presents Christ as the ultimate model for moral action. This is the most obvious and

natural explanation for its appearance at this point in the letter, and it is quite in keeping with Paul's practice elsewhere of using the life/death of Christ as a pattern for Christians to follow (Rom 15:1–7, especially v 5; 1 Cor 10:31–11:1; 2 Cor 8:6–9; 1 Thess 1:6; cf. also 1 Pet 2:20–21; 3:17–18. See Hendriksen, Lightfoot, Martin, *Philippians*, 1959, Moule, Müller, Plummer, Scott, Vincent; see also Bruce, *BJRL* 63 [1981] 260–84; Cerfaux, *Christ*, 375–76; Dacquino, *BeO* 17 [1975] 241–52; W. P. deBoer, *The Imitation of Paul: An Exegetical Study* [Kampen: J. H. Kok, 1962] 58–71; M. S. Enslin, *The Ethics of Paul* [New York: Abingdon, 1957] 107–19; V. P. Furnish, *Theology and Ethics in Paul* [Nashville: Abingdon, 1968] 216–23; E. Larsson, *Christus als Vorbild* [Uppsala: Almquist and Wiksells, 1962]; G. N. Stanton, *Jesus of Nazareth in New Testament Preaching* [SNTSMS 27, Cambridge: Cambridge University Press, 1974] 99–110. For contrasting views see Beare, Martin, *Carmen Christi*, 287–311 and *Philippians*, 1976, who follows Käsemann, "Critical Analysis," 45–88, but who is answered, in part at least, by Marshall, *TynB* 19 [1968] 117–19, Moule, "Further Reflexions," 264–76, and most ably by Hurtado, "Jesus as Lordly Example").

Since this is so, v 5 forms the link between the two sections. It is the transition from exhortation to illustration (notice that the verb φρονεῖν, "to hold an attitude," which dominates this verse, also appears twice in v 2, and the word ταπεινοφροσύνη, "humility," v 3, is echoed by ἐταπείνωσεν ἑαυτόν, "he humbled himself," v 8). Such an insight lessens, if it does not resolve, the exegetical difficulties found in v 5. For its meaning now is clear, even though no universally satisfying translation has as yet been provided or ever indeed can be (cf. Marshall, *TynB* 19 [1968] 118). This verse means that the hoped-for attitude outlined by Paul in vv 2–4 corresponds with that exhibited by Christ Jesus, especially in vv 6–9, and that the Philippians are bound to act in accordance with this attitude toward one another if they wish to imitate their Lord (note v 11 and cf. 1 Thess 1:6), and share with him in his exaltation and glory (2:9–11; cf. 3:11, 20–21, and see 2 Tim 2:11–13; Matt 18:4).

Thus, τοῦτο ("this"), that begins the verse, points backward to Paul's exhortation and not forward to the Christ-hymn (against Losie, *ExpTim* 90 [1978] 52–54). It stands for τοῦτο τὸ φρόνημα, "this frame of mind" that Paul just described, and it serves as the subject of the imperative, φρονείσθω (see critical notes for this form of the verb). Ἐν ὑμῖν which modifies φρονείσθω, a passive, is best understood now as expressing personal agent ("by you," cf. BDF 219,1). The clause which follows—ὃ καὶ ἐν Χριστῷ Ἰησοῦ ("which also in Christ Jesus")—is elliptic in that its verb is missing and must be supplied, probably with ἐφρονεῖτο (Lightfoot). Upon adding this verb, one discovers another of Paul's balanced sentences, the neatness of which has again been obscured through compression. When the sentence is expanded, however, it appears like this:

$$\text{τοῦτο φρονείσθω ἐν ὑμῖν}$$
$$\text{ὃ καὶ ἐφρονεῖτο ἐν Χριστῷ Ἰησοῦ.}$$

Criticism no doubt will be levelled against such a reconstruction, especially because it opts for the alleged "inferior" reading, φρονείσθω, against φρονεῖτε and argues against taking ἐν Χριστῷ Ἰησοῦ in the usual Pauline sense of "in Christ."

But the clear parallel nature of the two halves of this sentence, which demands that ἐν ὑμῖν and ἐν Χριστῷ Ἰησοῦ be treated grammatically alike—"in you"/"in Christ"; "by you"/"by Christ," etc.—pushes one inevitably to these conclusions: (1) It is impossible to maintain this grammatical parallelism here and at the same time give to ἐν Χριστῷ Ἰησοῦ the "incorporation-in-Christ" meaning so common to Paul in other contexts. For ἐν ὑμῖν cannot reach such exalted heights and must therefore be assigned a quite different meaning (NEB: "Let your bearing *towards one another* arise out of your life *in Christ Jesus*"; cf. RSV and Gnilka, 109). (2) The same impossibility of maintaining the parallelism between ἐν ὑμῖν and ἐν Χριστῷ Ἰησοῦ is true if the reading φρονεῖτε is insisted upon. For if φρονεῖτε is the preferred text then ἐν ὑμῖν must mean "among you," "towards one another," "in your mutual relations with one another." It cannot mean "in you" (i.e. "in your hearts"). For that is "at once an unlikely meaning for ὑμῖν and a redundant and unconvincing extension of φρονεῖτε (as though it were possible to think or adopt an attitude anywhere else but within oneself!)" (Moule, "Further Reflexions," 265). Thus again the parallel is destroyed as Moule so clearly and perhaps unintentionally indicates by his own translation: "Adopt *towards* one another, in your mutual relations, the same attitude which was found *in* Christ Jesus" (Moule, "Further Reflexions," 265; italics mine). A translation that is more in keeping with the clear grammatical parallelism—ἐν ὑμῖν/ἐν Χριστῷ Ἰησοῦ—and that reflects the reconstructed text suggested above is the following:

> "This way of thinking must be adopted by you,
> Which also was the way of thinking adopted by Christ Jesus."

6. The Christ-hymn proper starts here. Its initial word, the relative pronoun ὅς ("who"), recalls the way other hymnlike confessions in the NT begin (cf. Col 1:15; 1 Tim 3:16; Heb 1:3; see Norden, *Agnostos Theos*, 383–87). More importantly, however, this pronoun links and identifies the historical Jesus (v 5) with the one who existed before the incarnation. The burden of the remainder of v 6 describes Christ's preexistence and tells what took place in that earlier period.

During that period, as the hymn declares, Christ was ἐν μορφῇ θεοῦ ("in the form of God")—a difficult phrase to interpret, if for no other reason than that the word μορφή occurs only here and in v 7 in the NT. Apparently the author of the hymn did not wish to say outright that Christ was θεός ("God") as LB and Beck would lead one to believe. The verb translated "was" (ὑπάρχειν) is a widely used substitute in Hellenistic Greek for εἶναι (BDF 414), and it could easily have been followed here by a predicate noun such as θεός (cf. Gal 1:14; 2:14). But it was not.

Neither did the author mean to say by it that Christ was "the form of God," as Paul said of the husband that he was "the image and glory of God" (εἰκὼν καὶ δόξα θεοῦ ὑπάρχων, 1 Cor 11:7). For he did not write μορφὴ θεοῦ but ἐν μορφῇ θεοῦ—not "Christ was the form of God," but Christ was "*in* the form of God," as if the form of God were a sphere in which Christ existed (see Käsemann, "A Critical Analysis," 45–88) or a garment with which Christ was wrapped or clothed (cf. Luke 7:25).

Μορφή ("form"), based on its usage in Greek literature, refers primarily to that "which may be perceived by the senses" (Behm, *TDNT* 4,745–46). Yet when this word is applied to God, as here, such an understanding is quite inadequate. For God is the invisible God (Col 1:15; 1 Tim 1:17) and has not been and cannot be comprehended by the human senses.

Furthermore, when the hymn says that Christ took the "form of a slave" after his *kenōsis* (v 7), it is not likely that its author had in mind that Christ merely looked like or had the external appearance of a slave. Thus these two expressions, ἐν μορφῇ θεοῦ and μορφὴν δούλου, together demand a new and fresh meaning for μορφή (cf. E. Schweizer, *Erniedrigung und Erhöhung* [Zürich: Zwingli Verlag, 1962] 96, n. 383). And this new meaning must be one that will apply equally well to both phrases, since μορφή θεοῦ was obviously coined in antithesis to μορφὴ δούλου (Behm, *TDNT* 4,751).

Some interpreters suggest δόξα ("glory") as the new meaning for μορφή in this passage, since the equivalent of the external form of God in the OT was God's glory (Exod 16:10; 24:15; Lev 9:6, 23; Num 12:8; 14:10). If this is correct, then one can picture the preexistent Christ as clothed in the garments of divine majesty and splendor, and one can explain the words, "existing in the form of God," as exactly corresponding to the words of the incarnate Christ when he referred to the glory (δόξα) he had with his father before the world was (John 17:5; Behm, *TDNT* 4,751; Fitzmyer, *JBC* 2, 251). Attractive as this understanding of μορφή is, it seems nevertheless to founder on the fact that it cannot be applied equally to the parallel phrase μορφὴ δούλου in v 7.

Others suggest that μορφή should be understood in terms of εἰκών ("image") and the entire hymn explained in light of Gen 1:26–27 and Gen 3:1–5. These interpreters see Paul, or the writer of the hymn if not Paul, working here with the familiar first Adam–second Adam motif (cf. Rom 5:18–19; 1 Cor 15:45–47). As the first Adam was in the image and likeness of God (Gen 1:26–27), so Christ, the second Adam, existed in the image of God (Phil 2:6). Whereas the first Adam wrongly tried to become like God (Gen 3:5), the second Adam either did not strive to be equal with God, or did not regard equality with God as a thing to be held on to (cf. Caird; Houlden; O. Cullmann, *Christology of the New Testament* [Philadelphia: Westminster, 1959] 176; Héring, *Royaume de Dieu*, 162–64; Loofs, *TSK* 100 [1927–28] 28–30; Ridderbos, *Paul*, 73–77; see also Hooker, "Philippians 2,6–11," 160–64; Schweizer, *Erniedrigung*, 96, n. 383). According to this interpretation, then, the phrase, ὃς ἐν μορφῇ θεοῦ ὑπάρχων ("who being in the form of God") and the expression ὅς ἐστιν εἰκών τοῦ θεοῦ ("who is the image of God")—found in 2 Cor 4:4 and Col 1:15–are to be regarded as synonymous (but contrast Spicq, *RB* 80 [1973] 37–45; Wallace, *TZ* 22 [1966] 19–25).

Again, however, this explanation of μορφή comes to grief fundamentally on the fact that it cannot be adopted for its second occurrence—μορφὴν δούλου—in v 7 (Collange). In addition, it seems strained and unnatural to interpret μορφή by εἰκών, in order to compare and contrast Adam with Christ, unless one holds the view that this hymn refers not at all to the preexistent Christ but only to the human Jesus, his life of humility and his exaltation to an *earthly* position of glory (Howard, *CBQ* 40 [1978] 368–87; Murphy-

O'Connor, *RB* 83 [1976] 25–50; Talbert, *JBL* 86 [1967] 141–53; Dunn, *Christology*, 114–21). For only then is the comparison meaningful, only then are Adam and Christ on the same footing: both earthly and both human (cf. Cullmann, *Christology*, 177, who argues that Christ here is the preexistent heavenly Man, the pure image of God, the God-Man already in his preexistence; see also Glasson, *NTS* 21 [1974] 133–39). To argue against the view that the hymn can only refer to the earthly human Jesus is not to argue against the idea that the hymn presents Jesus as a model for Christians to follow. Although "there can be no direct duplication by mere humans of the action of a heavenly being who is seen as enjoying quasi-divine status, it is not impossible that such an action might be so described as to make it exemplary for earthly behavior, the differences notwithstanding" (Hurtado, "Jesus as Lordly Example").

"Mode of being" (*Daseinsweise*) is still another meaning suggested for μορφή. This meaning is arrived at primarily by associating the Christ-hymn with Gnostic texts (e.g. the *Corpus Hermeticum*), and understanding the hymn against the background of the Gnostic myth of the "Heavenly Man," whose rank was equal with God (see Käsemann, "Critical Analysis," 62, 66–67, 72, 78–80; R. Reitzenstein, *Die hellenistische Mysterienreligionen* [Leipzig: B. G. Teubner, 1927] 357–58). "The 'form of God' in which the pre-existent Christ existed is not mere form but the divine mode of being just as much as the 'form of a servant' is the mode of being of a servant" (R. Bultmann, *Theology of the New Testament* [New York: Scribner's, 1951] 1, 193; cf. also Collange, Dibelius, Gnilka). Although this meaning fits the context and applies equally well to μορφή θεοῦ (v 6) and μορφή δούλου (v 7), one should perhaps be slow to adopt it because of its strong dependence upon the "Heavenly Man" myth for its origin. This "Heavenly Man" myth has been severely criticized by Dieter Georgi ("Der vorpaulinische Hymnus," 263–66) and others (cf. also Sanders, *Christological Hymns*, 66–69, and Martin, *Philippians*, 1976, 94–95, who summarizes Georgi's criticisms; see also C. Colpe, *Die religionsgeschichtliche Schule* [Göttingen: Vandenhoeck & Ruprecht, 1961], M. Black, "Pauline Doctrine of the Second Adam, *SJT* 7 [1954] 177; E. Yamauchi, *Pre-Christian Gnosticism: A Survey of Proposed Evidences* (Grand Rapids: Eerdmans, 1973]).

Μορφή has also been interpreted as "condition" or "status." As such it refers "to Christ's 'original' position vis-à-vis God. He was the 'first man,' holding a unique place within the divine life and one with God. This sense of 'condition' would fit the meaning required in verse 7*b*. He who was in the beginning . . . at God's side . . . chose to identify himself with men and to accept the human condition, 'in the form of a servant' " (Martin, *Philippians*, 1976; see also Benoit, Bonnard). An objection to this interpretation, however, is the absence of such an understanding of μορφή in Greek literature (Beare, Collange, Behm, *TDNT* 4,742–49; BGD; MM).

Perhaps, then the best approach to the meaning of μορφή is (1) to admit that it is a word whose precise meaning is elusive, but (2) at the same time to recognize that from earliest Greek texts μορφή was at least used to express the way in which a thing, being what it is in itself, appears to our senses. "Μορφή always signifies a form which truly and fully expresses the being which underlies it" (MM 417). Thus, when this word is applied to God, his μορφή must refer to his deepest being, to what he is in himself, to that "which cannot be reached by our understanding or sight, precisely because God is ἀόρατος: in fact the word has meaning here only as referring to the reality of God's being" (Cerfaux, *Christ,* 305). Μορφὴ θεοῦ, then, may be correctly understood as the "essential nature and character of God" (Vincent: cf. also Lightfoot, 110 and, especially, 127–33).

To say, therefore, that Christ existed ἐν μορφῇ θεοῦ is to say that outside his human nature Christ had no other manner of existing apart from existing "in the form of God," that is, apart from being in possession of all the characteristics and qualities belonging to God. This somewhat enigmatic expression, then, appears to be a cautious, hidden way for the author to say that Christ was God, possessed of the very nature of God (GNB, NIV, Goodspeed, Knox, Moffatt, Phillips), without employing these exact words. It appears to be a statement made by one who perhaps, although reared as a strict monotheist and thus unable to bring himself to say, "Christ is God," was compelled nevertheless by the sheer force of personal encounter with the resurrected and living Christ to bear witness as best he could to the reality of Christ's divinity.

That this is the correct interpretation is corroborated by the expression τὸ εἶναι ἴσα θεῷ ("the being equal with God") which follows. The definite article in τὸ εἶναι implies that this second expression is closely connected with the first, for the function of the definite article here is to point back to something previously mentioned (BDF 399, 1). Therefore τὸ εἶναι ἴσα θεῷ should be understood thus: "the equality with God of which we have just spoken equivalently by saying ἐν μορφῇ θεοῦ ὑπάρχων" (Cerfaux, *Christ,* 387, n. 60; see also Dibelius).

The next matter of concern is the question of the meaning of ἁρπαγμόν in the sentence, "he did not consider that being equal with God was ἁρπαγμόν." Much has been written about this rare word, used only here in the NT, but no consensus has been reached as to what it means.

Some see it as referring to a thing not yet possessed but desirable, a thing to be snatched at, grasped after, as Adam or Satan, each in his own way, grasped after being equal with God (cf. Gen 3:5; Isa 14:12–13; see Michaelis). Such an understanding of ἁρπαγμός, however, implies that the preexistent Christ was not equal with God, but could have forcibly reached for and seized such equality had he chosen to do so (cf. NEB; cf. also Ehrhardt, *JTS* 46 [1945] 45–51 and Knox, *HTR* 41 [1948] 229–49).

Others see it as meaning a thing already possessed and embraced, a thing to be clutched and held on to (cf. JB). Such a meaning implies that Christ was already equal with God and that he possessed the right to hold tightly to this equality and use it to his own advantage (cf. Hoover, *HTR* 64 [1971] 95–119). Here might also be listed those other ideas suggested for ἁρπαγμός, such as "lucky find," "a piece of good fortune," "a windfall" (BGD). All these meanings suggest that Christ held a position, that of being equal with God, which opened up the possibility of future advantage for himself, of exploiting his status to selfish ends, were he to make such a choice.

Still others draw the meaning of ἁρπαγμός from its corresponding verb ἁρπάζειν, meaning, among other things, "to be caught up in a mystical rapture" (cf. 1 Thess 4:17). Paul, for example, had been caught away without his own will or power, by the Spirit, in a rapture (ἁρπαγμός) to be a short while with God (2 Cor 12:2–4). But for the Son of God "while he was in the form of God, the being with God was no *rapture,* no ἁρπαγμός; it was his nature. No spirit, no angel had brought him into this state of being with God" and nobody else could ever bring him out of it. Only he himself could do this by voluntary choice (Hammerich, reported in *ExpTim* 78 [1966–67] 193–94; Trudinger, *ExpTim* 79 [1967–68] 279).

C. F. D. Moule argues convincingly that ἁρπαγμός refers rather to the act of snatching, to acquisitiveness. "Jesus did not reckon equality with God meant snatching; on the contrary, he emptied himself." Human evaluation may assume "that God-likeness means having your own way, getting what you want, (but) Jesus saw God-likeness essentially as giving and spending oneself out" ("Manhood," 97; "Further Reflexions," 271–74). He did not consider that being equal with God was taking everything to himself, but (ἀλλά) giving everything away for the sake of others. This meaning for ἁρπαγμός best fits the context here.

Hence, in this connection the participial phrase that begins v 6—ὃς ἐν μορφῇ θεοῦ ὑπάρχων ("who *being* in the form of God"), often wrongly translated as a concessive participle—"who *though* he was in the form of God" (RSV, NASB, Beck, Confraternity, Goodspeed, Williams), is more correctly translated as a causative: "precisely *because* he was in the form of God he reckoned equality with God not as a matter of getting but of giving" (Moule, "Manhood," 97). This then makes clear that contrary to whatever anyone may think about God, his true nature is characterized not by selfish grabbing, but by an open-handed giving (see also Furness, *ExpTim* 69 [1957] 93–94; Ross, *JTS* 10 [1909] 573; Warren, *JTS* 12 [1911] 461–63).

7. This idea is clearly spelled out now in a profound statement introduced by ἀλλά ("but")—"Not this . . . *but* this!" The being equal with God does not mean filling oneself up, but on the contrary (ἀλλά) it means emptying oneself out (cf. Grelot, *Bib* 54 [1973] 25–42). Hence, the hymn states that Christ, who shared the nature of God, who was equal with God, ἑαυτὸν ἐκένωσεν ("emptied himself")! The emphatic position of ἑαυτόν ("himself") and the form of the verb strongly suggest that this act of "emptying" was voluntary on the part of the preexistent Christ.

But what did this act of self-emptying entail? Of what did Christ empty himself? Some are quick to answer: (1) he emptied himself of his glory (Plummer), (2) of his independent exercise of authority (Hendriksen), (3) of the prerogatives of deity (Lightfoot), (4) of the insignia of majesty (Lightfoot, Calvin), (5) of the "relative" attributes of deity—omniscience, omnipresence and omnipotence (the kenoticists—e.g. C. Gore, P. T. Forsyth, H. R. Mackintosh), (6) of being equal with God (Oepke, *TDNT* 3, 661), and so on. But there is no basis for any of these speculative answers in the text of the hymn, simply because it gives no clue whatsoever as to what it was that Christ emptied himself of.

A more fruitful approach to understanding this difficult phrase is to realize that the verb κενοῦν also means "to pour out" (LSJ), and ἑαυτόν can be taken as its direct object. Christ, then, who was in very nature God, but who did not reckon that this nature was characterized by acquisitiveness "effaced all thought of self and poured out his fulness to enrich others" (Jones). It is not necessary, therefore, to insist that the phrase ἑαυτὸν ἐκένωσεν demands some genitive of content be supplied from the context—e.g. "Christ emptied himself *of something.*" One need not imagine that the phrase means that Christ discarded divine substances or essences (Keck). Rather, it is a poetic, hymnlike way of saying that Christ poured out himself, putting himself totally at the disposal of people (cf. 1 John 3:16), that Christ became poor that he might make many rich (2 Cor 8:9; cf. also Eph 1:23; 4:10). Classical, Hellenistic and patristic writers furnish examples to support this meaning of κενοῦν (see Warren, *JTS* 12 [1911] 461–63; cf. τὰ ὑπάρχοντα κενοῦν—"to spend all one's property on the poor," Chrysostom, *Hom. 13 on 1 Tim,* cited by Jones), a meaning that harmonizes well with the exhortation to humility which is the motif of this entire passage—Phil 2:3–11 (Furness, *ExpTim* 69 [1957–58] 93–94). Notice the play on words in κενοδοξία ("empty opinion," "conceit," v 3) which characterized those who were demanding their rights and insisting on their own way, and κενοῦν ("to empty," v 7) which described the attitude and actions of Christ in terms of setting aside his rights and in not insisting on his own way.

The expression ἑαυτὸν ἐκένωσεν is now defined more precisely by the participial phrases that follow—"taking (λαβών) the form of a slave," "becoming (γενόμενος) in the likeness of human beings" and "being found (εὑρεθείς) in human form." These participles, although aorists, are nevertheless participles of simultaneous action (BDF 339,1) and express the means by which the action of the verb ἐκένωσεν was effected. Paradoxically, then, Christ's self-giving was accomplished by taking, his self-emptying was achieved by becoming what he was not before, his *kenōsis* not by subtracting from but by adding to.

Christ took to himself voluntarily "the form of a slave." Once again, as in v 6, the noun μορφή ("form") is used, and with the same meaning. There is no idea here that Christ possessed the external appearance of a slave, or that he disguised himself as a slave. Rather it means that he adopted the nature, "the characteristic attributes" of a slave. In other words, he became a slave.

For some interpreters this means that Christ, as a natural consequence of becoming human, accepted bondage to the *stoicheia,* "the elemental spirits of the universe," that he allowed himself to be born into a world dominated by powers of evil described as sin, death and the law (Rom 5–8), and that he subjected himself to these powers until by his death he could destroy them both for himself and for all mankind (cf. 1 Cor 2:6–8; Gal 4:3, 9; Col 2:8, 20; see Beare, Caird, Käsemann, "Critical Analysis," 45–88; Keck). But this is not an obvious meaning for the expression and it does not readily harmonize with the general thrust of Phil 2:3–11.

For others the term "slave" as applied here to Christ is to be interpreted in terms of Isaiah's Servant-passages (especially Isa 52:13–53:12). Thus the phrase, "taking the form of a slave," means "exactly playing the part" of the Servant of the Lord (Martin, *Philippians,* 1976), and the expression "he emptied himself" is equivalent to Isaiah's "he poured out his soul unto death"

(53:12; cf. J. Jeremias, *The Servant of God* [Naperville, IL: Allenson, 1957] 97). Note also that the Isaiah-poem strikes the same theme as is struck at the conclusion of the Philippian hymn—"Behold my servant . . . will be high and lifted up and greatly exalted" (Isa 52:13; cf. Phil 2:9–11). If this is the idea to be attached to δοῦλος, then "slave"/"servant" here is in reality an honorific title (see Lohmeyer)—God's specially anointed servant (cf. Isa 42). Yet the context demands that δοῦλος ("slave") be understood as a term of extreme abasement, the exact opposite of κύριος ("Lord"), a title that later is to describe the exalted Christ (see Rengstorf, *TDNT* 2, 278; Deichgräber, *Gotteshymnus*, 123–24).

If the incident from the life of Jesus, where Jesus puts himself in the place of the slave and washes his disciples' feet (John 13) played any part in shaping this hymn, if the context in which the hymn is inserted presents a call to serve one another, then δοῦλος emphasizes the fact that in the incarnation Christ entered the stream of human life as a slave, that is, as a person without advantage, with no rights or privileges of his own for the express purpose of placing himself completely at the service of all mankind (cf. Mark 10:45; Luke 22:27, and see Hurtado, "Jesus as Lordly Example"). There is no reason to ask, as does Plummer, "to whom was Christ a slave—to God or to people?" For in serving people he was serving God, and in taking the role of slave toward others, he was acting in obedience to the will of God. "The incarnation is both humiliation and mission" (Collange).

"Being born in the likeness of human beings" (ἐν ὁμοιώματι ἀνθρώπων γενόμενος) is the second participial phrase used to define more precisely the expression "he emptied himself." The participle γενόμενος, aorist, and derived from γίνεσθαι, a verb that stresses "beginning," or "becoming," stands in sharp contrast to the present participle, ὑπάρχων, in v 6. There it was claimed that Christ *always existed* (ὑπάρχων) "in the form of God." Here it is said that he *came into existence* (γενόμενος) "in the likeness of man."

But the phrase, ἐν ὁμοιώματι ("in the likeness") does not mean that Christ only appeared to be a man, or just seemed to be human. Nor can it give rise to such subtle interpretations as those which state that this phrase "suggests a mysterious appearance of one who, since he came from God, still retains a secret relationship with him, and is, to that extent, removed from men" (Martin, *Philippians*, 1976; cf. Michel, "Zur Exegese von Phil. 2.5–11," 91; Vincent). Rather ὁμοίωμα stresses "likeness," "similarity," even "identity." Christ was in all respects like other human beings (cf. Heb 4:15; see V. Vanni, U. "Homoiōma in Paolo, *Gregorianum* 58 [1977] 431–70).

This meaning of "identity" for ὁμοίωμα is reinforced now by the final phrase in the series of participial phrases that define the clause, "he emptied himself"—"being found in human form," "being discovered to be and recognized as a man" (καὶ σχήματι εὑρεθεὶς ὡς ἄνθρωπος). Although the word "form" (σχῆμα) used here denotes that "outward form or structure perceptible to the senses" (Schneider, *TDNT* 7, 954), and therefore generally refers to what is "external and changeable" over against what is "essential and permanent" (Plummer), yet in this context its meaning is not to be so restricted. Etymologies aside, σχῆμα (v 7*d*) in hymnic fashion links up with μορφή (v 7*a*) and ὁμοίωμα (v 7*c*) to form a threefold reiteration of the one fundamentally important idea, that Christ in the incarnation fully identified himself with humanity (Collange), he "truly became man, not merely in outward appearances but in thought and feeling" (Schneider, *TDNT* 7, 956), he shared man's plight in reality and was no mere " 'reasonable facsimile' of a man" (Keck). In this respect, the writer of the Philippian hymn is in full accord with other writers of the NT who insist on the genuineness and completeness of Christ's humanity (cf. Luke 2:52; John 1:14; Rom 8:3; Gal 4:4; Col 1:22; Heb 2:17; 4:15; 5:7–8; 1 John 4:2–3). It is incorrect, therefore, to single out the phrase, "in human form" (lit. "in form as a man"), relate it to Dan 7:13, and interpret it as an allusion to Daniel's heavenly Son of Man (Lohmeyer, *Kyrios Jesus,* 38–42; Michel, "Zur Exegese von Phil. 2.5–11," 90–92), thus lessening its force as the final element in an emphatically unequivocal, repetitive affirmation of the realness of Christ's humanness. This phrase, together with its two companion phrases, says in effect, "let there be no doubt—Christ was really and truly man, having to live the same kind of life as any other man had to live" (cf. Grayston, *Galatians and Philippians*).

It is this insistence on the reality of Christ's humanness and the use of the verb κενοῦν in Phil 2:7 that gave rise to and provided the name for the kenotic theory of the incarnation. This ancient theory, as recently expounded, claims that "at the incarnation Christ divested himself of the 'relative' attributes of deity, omniscience, omnipresence and omnipotence, but retained the 'essential attributes' of holiness, love and righteousness" (Collange). Such a theory, in spite of its worthy motive of attempting to do justice to the reality of Christ's humanity and his divinity, cannot be supported by the statements in Phil 2, and for the following reasons: (1) the significant statements regarding Christ's *kenōsis* are found in a hymn (2:6–11). (2) The hymn-form cautions against building a doctrine on any single statement to be found in it. For like a poem the hymn is composed not to be analyzed word by word, but to be understood in its entirety. The full impact of its meaning, therefore, is found not in the part but the whole, and the whole thrust of the hymn is alien to the issues raised by the kenoticists (Thomas, *EvQ* 42 [1970] 142–51). (3) Although the verb κενοῦν ("to empty") is used here (v 7), its meaning is too imprecise to permit one to say that Christ emptied himself of certain divine attributes. In fact, as was pointed out above, the Philippian text does not say that Christ gave up anything. Rather it says that he added to himself that which he did not have before—"the form of a servant," "the likeness of a man." Thus the implication is that at the incarnation Christ became more than God, if this is conceivable, not less than God.

It is impossible to explain such a mystery—that the one who was God undiminished could also be a human person to the fullest, a truly genuine human being possessing all the potential for physical, mental, social and spiritual growth that is proper to humanity (Luke 2:52), and be both at the same time—divine and human, God and man. Nevertheless, the Philippian hymn seems clearly to set forth just such a paradox and affirm it, but does not try to explain it. Hence, anyone coming to the text, in the hope of interpreting the text, must exercise the same kind of balance and reserve, neither tampering with anything relating to the divinity of Christ, nor calling into question any aspect of the reality of his humanity (cf. Dawe, *SJT* 15 [1962]

337–49, especially 348; see also G. F. Hawthorne, "Hebrews," in G. C. D. Howley, F. F. Bruce and H. L. Ellison [eds.] *A New Testament Commentary* [London: Pickering and Inglis, 1969] 547, and *The Significance of the Holy Spirit in the Life of Christ*, M. A. thesis, Wheaton College, 1954).

8. The writer continues now without a conjunction to say that Christ in the days of his flesh "humbled himself" (ἐταπείνωσεν ἑαυτόν). This means that as a man Christ did not strive for some pinnacle of human achievement. He did not stand where the people of Philippi apparently stood (cf. v 3)—"not where the battle was fought for honour, right and credit" (Barth). Instead, his whole life was characterized by self-surrender, self-renunciation and self-sacrifice—"he humbled himself becoming obedient unto death."

Once again a participle is used to set forth precisely the meaning of the principal verb (ἐταπείνωσεν). Christ humbled himself "by becoming (γενόμενος) obedient unto death." This concise phrase, "obedient unto death," measures the magnitude of Christ's humility and conveys the idea that he was principally "obedient to God to the full length of accepting death" (Caird). But is there not a sense, too, in which Christ was obedient to the wishes of people as well? It seems so. As a slave, he set himself not only to obey God, but also to serve humankind. Or better, he set himself to obey God by serving humankind. This service entailed a positive response to the fundamental though inarticulate demand of the human race: "Ransom us from death by your death!" To this demand Jesus' answer was not only, "I have come to do your will, O God" (cf. Heb 10:7), but also, "I have come to seek and save that which is lost (Luke 19:10), to serve and to give my life a ransom for many" (Mark 10:45). Christ's acceptance of death, therefore, was his ultimate *yes* to God and man, his ultimate act of obedience to God in his self-giving service to people.

That the death of Christ was also vicarious, i.e. a death in place of others, is not expressly stated here, but it can be correctly inferred, nonetheless, from the context: (1) Paul's appeal to the members of the Philippian church to renounce their individual rights for the benefit of the whole must get its impetus from Christ's "renunciation for the benefit of others of his own right to live." (2) It is difficult to imagine that God would require of Jesus "that he would submit not only to death but to criminal death, unless that death was in some sense vicarious," in some sense the consummation of God's redeeming purpose for mankind, and (3) there are other places in Paul's writings where he omits a point or two in his argument, simply because he is certain his audience knows enough to follow him (Rom 5:15–17). Therefore, the fact that no explicit statement exists here stating that Christ's death was vicarious does not necessarily mean it was not intended so to be understood (see Caird for these arguments; see Collange and Martin, *Philippians*, 1976 for an opposite view).

In any case, Christ's death was not a natural death. It was death on a cross (θανάτου δὲ σταυροῦ). The intensive or explicative conjunction δέ ("even") that introduces this phrase calls special attention to this most striking element in the humiliation of Christ. For crucifixion, borrowed from the Persians and perfected by the Romans, was an unusually cruel and humiliating means of capital punishment. It was generally reserved for slaves, robbers, assassins, rebellious provincials and the like. Crucifixion was abhorred by the Jew, not only because of its pain and shame, but because anyone thus hanged was considered accursed by God (Deut 21:22, 23; 1 Cor 1:23; Gal 3:13; cf. Heb 12:2; 4Qp Nah 7–8). It was no less abhorrent to the Roman. Cicero wrote: "Let the very name of the cross be far away not only from the body of a Roman citizen, but even from his thoughts, his eyes, his ears" (*Pro Rabiro*, 5.10,16; see G. F. Hawthorne, "Cross," in *Zondervan Pictorial Encyclopedia of the Bible*, ed. by M. C. Tenney [Grand Rapids: Zondervan, 1975] 1, 1038). Christ's death by crucifixion was, therefore, the ultimate in human degradation. Thus in these words the lowest point in the descent-theme that marks the first section of the hymn is reached—he who was in the form of God, was equal with God, emptied himself, humbled himself, surrendered himself to a criminal's death.

9. At this point there is a radical change in the hymn. Whereas the first half spoke of Christ as the acting subject of all the verbs, now in the last half "it is God who acts and Christ is the object of the divine action" (Beare). Whereas the first half of the hymn described Christ's self-humiliation, the last half describes his exaltation by God.

This last half opens with a strong inferential conjunction (διό) followed immediately by a second conjunction (καί) denoting that the inference is obvious. Together they may be translated, "As a consequence, therefore" (BGD; BDF 442, 12; 451, 5). They say in effect that the exaltation of Christ, soon to be mentioned, was not so much a reward for his self-abnegation (Michaelis, Moule), or a gracious gift that excludes any idea of merit on Christ's part (Collange, Gnilka, Martin, *Philippians*, 1976), as it was the natural or logical outcome of his humility. In other words, these conjunctions affirm what Jesus taught, namely that in the divine order of things self-humbling leads inevitably to exaltation. This is an inflexible law of God's kingdom that operates without variance, equally applicable for Christians at Philippi as for Christ himself.

That this interpretation is correct is confirmed by reflecting again on the prophetic act of Jesus, on the one hand (John 13:3–17), and by paying close attention to the prophetic words of Jesus, on the other: "Whoever chooses to save his life will lose it, but whoever loses his life . . . will find it . . . What will it benefit a person if he gains (κερδήσῃ) the whole world and loses (ζημιωθῇ) his own soul" (Matt 16:25–26; cf. Phil 3:7–8, where the same verbs, κερδαίνειν and ζημιοῦν, are used). Again, "Whoever will exalt (ὑψώσει) himself will be humbled (ταπεινωθήσεται) and whoever humbles himself will be exalted" (ὑψωθήσεται; Matt 23:12; cf. Luke 14:11; 18:14; note the "divine" passives and their significance). Finally, in the traditional words of Jesus it is explicitly stated that humility leads to becoming the greatest in the kingdom of heaven, i.e. to exaltation: "Whoever humbles himself as this child will be the greatest in the kingdom of heaven" (Matt 18:4).

It seems quite unnecessary, therefore, to search for the source of the themes of the Christ-hymn in places other than in the gospel tradition—for example, in the Adam story (Gen 1–3), in the Servant of the Lord passages (especially Isa 52–53), or elsewhere (see Cerfaux, *Christ*, 390–92; Contri, *Marianum* 40 [1978] 164–68; Dacquino, *BeO* 17 [1975] 241–42; Manns, *Euntes Docete* 29

[1976] 259–90; Krimetzki, *TQ* 139 [1959] 157–93; 291–336). The words and acts of Jesus are themselves a sufficient source for the principal humiliation-exaltation motif that characterizes Phil 2:6–11.

The exaltation of Christ, which is now the theme of the second half of the hymn, is not described in stages as was his humiliation-descent. Rather the hymn-writer depicts God in one dramatic act lifting Christ from the depths to the heights. The verb he chose to describe this astonishing change of events is the verb ὑπερυψοῦν, a compound word that lost none of its intended composite force through usage (Bertram, *TDNT* 8, 609). Found only here in the NT, ὑπερυψοῦν means "to super-exalt," "to raise someone to the loftiest height" (BGD).

The principal idea conveyed by this verb is not, however, comparative, i.e. that Christ is now someone greater than he was before the incarnation, or possesses a status superior to that which he had in his preexistent state (Dibelius, Cullmann, *Christology*, 174–81), but superlative, i.e. that Christ, who made himself so very lowly, was made by God very high, so high in fact, that he is placed over (ὑπέρ) all things (see Beare, Collange, G. Delling, "Zum steigernden Gebrauch von Komposita mit 'huper' bei Paulus," *NovT* 11 [1969] 127–53). Interestingly this verb, ὑπερυψοῦν, is used in the LXX OT to describe Yahweh as the one who is "exalted far above all gods" (Ps 96 [97]:9; cf. Dan 3:52, 54, 57–88).

The aorist tense is used, ὑπερύψωσεν—God "exalted" him—to refer implicitly to that moment in history marked by the resurrection-ascension of Christ. Jesus Christ, who humbled himself in obedience to God to the point of accepting death in its most horrible form, was resurrected from the dead by God, and raised to the place of supreme authority (cf. Acts 2:32, 33; 5:30, 31; Eph 1:20, 21; see Foerster, *TDNT* 3,1089). And this resurrection "was not resuscitation, not restoration to life, not an evasion of death, but death accepted and death defeated" (Synge).

The statement that God "highly exalted" Christ is accompanied by the statement that God "gave (ἐχαρίσατο) him the name (τὸ ὄνομα) that is above (ὑπέρ) every name." This second statement parallels the first, but serves both to reinforce the fact of Christ's resurrection-exaltation and at the same time to measure its extent.

In ancient thought ὄνομα ("name") was not only a means of distinguishing one individual from another, but also a means of revealing the inner being, the true nature of that individual (cf. Gen 25:26; 1 Sam 25:25), "an index of character and status" (Beare; cf. Bietenhard, *TDNT* 5,243–80). Hence, for the hymn-writer to declare that God conferred on Christ "the name that is above every name" is to declare that God not only graciously bestowed (ἐχαρίσατο) on him a designation which distinguished him from all other beings, a title which outranked all other titles, but also that he bestowed on him a nature which coincided with that title, giving substance and meaning to it. If that title (name) is κύριος ("Lord"), as the context indicates (v 11), it ultimately means then that Christ has been given the character of Lord. This is to say, not only does Christ *possess* the title "Lord," but he *is* Lord, the sovereign over the entire universe. All authority in heaven and earth is his by gift and nature (Matt 28:18; cf. Eph 1:20–21). This then is the extent of Christ's exaltation—lifted by God to the position of supreme authority in the cosmic structure of things.

10. God's purpose in thus exalting Christ and bestowing on him this all-surpassing name is twofold. The first thing that God intended by his actions is expressed in the clause: ἵνα ἐν τῷ ὀνόματι Ἰησοῦ πᾶν γόνυ κάμψη ("in order that at the name of Jesus every knee might bow"). Two matters of importance are now brought to the front: (1) One is the expression, "the name of Jesus" (τῷ ὀνόματι Ἰησοῦ). The fact that the hymn-writer mentions the name "Jesus" at this point is not because he thinks that "Jesus" and not "Lord" is the name that is above all names. For τῷ ὀνόματι Ἰησοῦ does not mean that everyone will bow "at the name Jesus" (Ἰησοῦ, dative), but that everyone will bow "at the name of Jesus" (Ἰησοῦ, genitive), i.e. "at the name belonging to or that is borne by Jesus." And that name is κύριος, "Lord" (cf. Lightfoot, Michael, Moule, Plummer). The reason he places the name of Jesus here is because by doing so he is saying that lordly power has been put into "the hands of the historical person of Jesus of Nazareth, who is not some cosmic cipher or despotic ruler but a figure to whom Christians could give a face and a name" (Martin, *Philippians*, 1976). He is saying that the one who emptied himself, who humbled himself, who became human in space and time, who became a slave, who was crucified, who died a criminal's death—this one, Jesus, whom people so ill-treated, God has made both Christ and Lord (cf. Acts 2:36). He is saying that the one "who was completely obedient must now be completely obeyed" (Bonnard).

(2) The other matter of importance is that the verb κάμπτειν ("to bow") is followed by the preposition ἐν and the dative—ἐν τῷ ὀνόματι . . . κάμψη. The significance of this lies in the fact that elsewhere, whenever this verb is used with γόνυ, meaning "to bend the knee" as a sign of religious devotion to someone, the object of this devotion is usually expressed by πρός and the accusative (cf. Eph 3:14), or by the dative alone (cf. Rom 11:4; Isa 45:23), but not by ἐν and the dative as here (BDG; cf. H. A. A. Kennedy, *Sources of New Testament Greek* [Edinburgh: T. and T. Clark, 1895]).

This fact has led some to translate the expression, "so that *in* the name of Jesus everyone should kneel" (RV, Goodspeed), and to conclude that this clause means not that homage is to be paid directly to the name of Jesus, but that *in* Jesus homage is to be paid to God. Jesus is "the mediator through whom created beings offer their worship to God," for it is to God, not Jesus, that every knee shall bow (Beare; Caird).

The context, however, is opposed to such a translation and interpretation. Jesus has just been given the name that is above every name, the name κύριος ("Lord"), the OT name for God (YHWH). In addition, Isa 45:23, which records God as saying, "Unto me every knee shall bow, every tongue shall swear allegiance," is woven here into the structure of vv 10–11 and applied to Jesus. It is significant that this quotation is taken from one of the OT passages that most strongly emphasizes the sole authority of God—"I am God and there is none else" (Isa 45:22; see Grayston, *Galatians and Philippians*). Hence, although the grammatical construction ἐν τῷ ὀνόματι κάμπτειν is unique (but cf. Ps 62[63]:5; 43[44]:10; 104[105]:3; 1 Kings 8:44; see also Moule, *Idiom-Book*, 78), and the idea astonishing, it is nonetheless necessary to understand that the writer is here asserting that homage is indeed to be paid *to* Jesus as Lord, not *through* Jesus to God (Gnilka). Therefore, the expression ἐν τῷ ὀνόματι must be translated, "at the name" (KJV, JB, NEB, NIV, RSV) or "before the name" (Knox, Moffatt), meaning that all must bring their homage to Jesus, all must fall on their knees before him to show honor to him.

The universality of this homage is now made clear by a series of three adjectives, literally translated, "pertaining to heaven, pertaining to earth and pertaining to the underworld." These adjectives are functioning as nouns and may be neuter, referring to things, animate and inanimate alike, creation in its totality (KJV, ASV, Knox; Lightfoot, Moule; cf. Rev 5:13). In antiquity people believed in a three-storied universe and universality was thus often expressed by phrases that embraced all three (cf. Hom. *Od.* 5.184–86). It is possible therefore that when Paul wished to proclaim the universality of worship due from creation to Jesus, he used the phraseology of his day (cf. Rev 5:13; Ign, *Trall.* 9.1; see E. G. Selwyn, *The First Epistle of St. Peter* [London: Macmillan, 1947] 318–19).

Or these adjective-nouns may be masculine, referring only to rational beings (GNB, JB). The context argues for the latter meaning, since only rational beings can, in the true sense of the word, acknowledge and confess something to be true (v 11). But these beings should not be limited exclusively to spirits, on the one hand (Beare), nor to humans, on the other. Rather in this series the writer describes angels, men and demons as ultimately joining together in an act of worship (cf. 1 Cor 4:9). All—all principalities and powers (cf. Col 1:16, 20; 2:15; Eph 3:10; see Foerster, *TDNT* 2,571–74) as well as all people—are to bow their knees before Jesus and do obeisance to him in adoration and awe (cf. Eph 1:10; see Moule, *Origin,* 43–44, for answers as to how this "cosmic Christology" came about).

11. The second part of God's purpose in exalting Christ and giving him the name that is above all names is now expressed. It is that "every tongue (γλῶσσα) might openly acknowledge that Jesus Christ is Lord." In these words the hymn reaches the climax anticipated from its beginning, and it at last provides the reader with the name that is above every name—"Lord."

All evidence indicates that the affirmation, "Jesus Christ is Lord," was the earliest confessional formula of the church (cf. Acts 2:36; Rom 10:9; 1 Cor 11:23; 12:3; 16:22; Kümmel, *Theology,* 157–60). And it is possible that the *Sitz im Leben* of the hymn was the liturgy of the Hellenistic church at worship celebrating the saving acts of God through Christ and recalling its baptismal pledge to Christ as Lord (Marcheselli, *Ephemerides Carmeliticae* 29 [1978] 2–42). But what is important to notice here is that this confession is not confined to the church—"*every tongue* will confess." This phrase (πᾶσα γλῶσσα) is a poetic way of saying "everyone" or "all." It especially refers to "all peoples," since γλῶσσα ("tongue") is often used as a synonym of φυλή, λαός, ἔθνος ("tribe, people, nation"—Isa 66:18; Dan 3:4, 7; Rev 5:9; 7:9; 10:11, etc.). But in the context (note especially v 10) it quite possibly refers to all rational beings, to everyone who is capable of making an intelligent acknowledgment concerning the Lordship of Jesus Christ.

What then does this mean? Does it mean that eventually every created, intelligent being will in fact admit that Jesus is Lord, either voluntarily or by compulsion? Perhaps not. One can come to such a conclusion that all will confess Jesus as Lord only by choosing ἐξομολογήσεται (future indicative) over the variant ἐξομολογήσηται (aorist subjunctive), and by breaking v 11 free from v 10, making v 11 an independent clause that asserts what will unquestionably happen in the future—"every tongue *will* confess!" But even if ἐξομολογήσεται is preferred to ἐξομολογήσηται, it can still be considered part of the subordinate ἵνα-clause of purpose begun in v 10 (ἵνα . . . κάμψῃ . . . καὶ . . . ἐξομολογήσεται), since ἵνα followed by the future indicative, though uncommon, is not unknown to the writers of the NT (Gal 2:4; Rev 22:14; see BDF 369, 2). And what is more, one should consider ἐξομολογήσεται part of this subordinate clause, since it is joined to κάμψῃ by the coordinate conjunction καί—κάμψῃ καὶ ἐξομολογήσεται ("bow and confess").

Verse 11 means, then, that the hope of God is that every intelligent being in his universe might proclaim openly and gladly (Lightfoot) that Jesus Christ alone has the right to reign. This verse together with v 10 makes clear what lay behind God's action to exalt Christ and to share with him his own name, "Lord" (κύριος, ΥΗѠΗ). It was in order that every created being in heaven, on earth and under the earth might ultimately be reconciled to himself by voluntarily and joyfully pledging allegiance to the one who chose the lowly path of self-effacement and of humble service to others (cf. Eph 1:10). Clearly then the purposes of God behind the acts of God are good and for the good of every creature. But how these purposes will be fulfilled, or when they will be fulfilled, or whether they will be fulfilled are not questions that can be answered from the statements of the hymn itself. Suffice it to say in general that not always are purposes realized or goals attained—not even divine purposes and goals (cf. Luke 7:30; Ps 32[33]:10). Hence, it is conceivable that beings, who are created with the freedom of choice, may choose never under any circumstances to submit to God or to his Christ. And it is also conceivable that these beings will never be forced to do so against their wills (cf. Rev 9:20, 21; 16:9, 11).

Finally it is to be noted that although Jesus bears the name "Lord" (κύριος), the name of God himself (κύριος translates the OT "Yahweh"), and is thus obliquely declared to be God with all the rights and privileges of God (e.g. sovereignty; cf. Foerster, *TDNT* 3,1089), yet paradoxically Jesus does not in any way displace God, or even rival God. As the hymn makes clear, the authority of Jesus Christ is a derived authority—God exalted him; God enthroned him; God conferred on him the superlative title; God purposed that created beings worship and obey him. Hence, only God the Father has ultimate authority and sovereignty. "The whole exaltation of Christ in the present and in the future is directed toward this, that God shall be all in all" (Ridderbos, *Theology*, 89–90; cf. 1 Cor 15:28; Rev 3:21; John 13:31). Therefore, whenever and by whomever the confession is made that "Jesus is Lord," God suffers no embarrassment; rather he is glorified—εἰς δόξαν θεοῦ πατρός—for he has planned that this be so. "The Lordship of Christ is therefore within the ambit of the divine glory and far from masking it actually reveals it, and this ultimate revelation is founded on the Fatherhood of God. The true glory of God is to be Father; the Father of Christ in the first place, but also through him of the entire creation. . . . From this angle again . . . the hymn shows us that history could have consisted of relationships merely of power (v 6*b:* *"harpagmos"*) whereas it culminates with the revelation of a fatherhood inspiring confidence and love" (Collange).

Explanation

Everything about this section, the way it begins, the rhythmic cadence of its words, the strophic patterning of its sentences, the uniqueness of its vocabulary, and so on, points to the fact that it was an early Christian hymn about Jesus. The source of its ideas is to be found in the words and deeds of Jesus as preserved in the gospel tradition (see especially John 13:3–17; Matt 16:25–26; 18:4; 23:12; Luke 14:11; 18:4). Hence, there is no need to look elsewhere to explain the themes of the hymn.

Who composed the hymn is a mystery. Paul may have been its author, or it may have been written by some unidentified Christian writer before Paul's time—scholars are divided on this issue. But whether or not Paul composed it is unimportant. What is important is that Paul found it compatible with his own ideas about Christ and precisely fit to illustrate what he wished to teach the Philippians, namely that the surest way up is by stepping down, the surest way to gain for oneself is by giving up oneself, the surest way to life is by death, the surest way to win the praise of God is by steadfastly serving others. The Philippians had been acting in a spirit of ambition, thinking themselves better than others, believing that they were above serving their fellows, studying how they might promote themselves and get ahead without giving adequate attention to the welfare of their neighbor. Christ of the Christ-hymn, however, challenges every one of these false values of the Philippians. He becomes, therefore, for Paul the ultimate model for moral action.

The hymn begins by describing Christ before the incarnation—he possessed the nature of God and was equal with God. But contrary to what one might expect, the true nature of God is not to grasp or get or selfishly to hold on to things for personal advantage, but to give them up for the enrichment of all. This is demonstrated by Christ, who, because he shared the nature of God, did not hold firm to the high position that was his by right, but rather stepped down from it. That is to say, he deliberately placed himself in the humblest of positions: he who was in the form of God became a man, a fully human being, a slave even, so that he might serve others. In the self-humbling act of the incarnation God became man and thus set himself wholly to seek the advantage and promote the welfare of his fellows. It was never the intent of Christ to fight for his own honor and right and credit, but through self-surrender, self-renunciation and self-sacrifice to strive for the honor, right and credit of others. To obey, as a slave must obey, was his delight. So radical was his obedience that he did not withdraw it even when he was faced with death—the most cruel of all deaths, death by crucifixion. He must somehow have known, though, that his death was not his alone, but once again an act that worked for the good of others.

As a consequence God exalted him. Thus, in the divine economy of things, by giving a person receives, by serving he is served, by losing his life he finds it, by dying he lives, by humbling himself he is exalted. The one follows the other as night follows day, but always in this order—self-sacrifice first before the self is exalted by God. This is the point Paul wishes to drive home to the Philippians, and it is made so eloquently and elegantly by the hymn that he prefers to quote it in full rather than to attempt to put it in any prose-form he could think up.

The remaining statements in the hymn are of great christological significance, but they are incidental to the one supreme lesson to be learned by Christians about how they are to live the Christian life. These statements confirm what Peter had preached (Acts 2:36), that God made Jesus, whom men crucified, Lord and Christ. He appointed him sovereign over the universe, the one to be served by all, the object of universal worship. It is possible that some beings might refuse to yield to Christ as king, might refuse to own his sovereignty over them. But whenever anyone does confess openly and gladly that Jesus Christ is Lord, God himself is pleased, the Father is glorified, for his purposes are fulfilled, his hopes for the world realized.

4. To Obedience (2:12–18)

Bibliography

Burn, J. H. "Philippians 2:12." *ExpTim* 34 (1922–23) 562. **Cook, D.** "2 Timothy iv. 6–8 and the Epistle to the Philippians." *JTS* 33 (1982) 168–71. **Denis, A. M.** "Versé en libation (Phil. 2,17)=Versé son sang? A propos d'une réference de W. Bauer." *RSR* 45 (1957) 567–70. ———. "La fonction apostolique et la liturgie nouvelle en Esprit. Etude thématique des métaphores pauliniennes du culte nouveau." *RSPT* 42 (1958) 617–56. **Finlayson, S. K.** "Lights, Stars or Beacons." *ExpTim* 77 (1965–66) 181. **Fuchs, E.** "Andacht über Philipper 2:12–18." *EvT* 7 (1947–48) 97–98. **Glombitza, O.** "Mit Furcht und Zittern, zum Verständnis von Phil. 2,12." *NovT* 3 (1959–60) 100–106. **Kühl, E.** "Über Philipper 2, 12. 13." *TSK* 71 (1898) 557–81. **Linden, J. R.** "Über Philipp. 2, 12. 13. 14, Hebr. 5, 7. 8. 9, und 2 Petri 1, 19. 20. 21." *TSK* 33 (1860) 750–62. **Michael, J. H.** "Work Out Your Own Salvation." *Expositor* 9th series, 12 (1924) 439–50. **Pedersen, S.** "Mit Furcht und Zittern (Phil. 2, 12–13)." *ST* 32 (1978) 1–31. **Pfitzner, V. C.** *The Agon Motif, Traditional Athletic Imagery in the Pauline Literature.* Leiden: E. J. Brill (1967) 99–108. **Schmidt, R.** "Über Philipper 2, 12 und 13." *TSK* 80 (1907) 344–63. **Stagg, F.** "The Mind in Christ Jesus: Philippians 1:27–2:18." *RevExp* 77 (1980) 337–47. **Thomson, P.** "Philippians 2:12." *ExpTim* 24 (1922–23) 469. **Warren, J.** "Work Out Your Own Salvation." *EvQ* 16 (1944) 125–37.

Translation

   [12] *Well then, God's dear friends and mine, just as you always obeyed, so continue to obey. Obediently work at achieving spiritual health, not only in light of* [a] *my coming to you again, but now even more in my absence from you.* [13] *For the one who effectively works among you creating both the desire and the drive to promote good will is God.* [b] [14] *Do everything without grumbling or arguing* [15] *in order that you may become* [c] *blameless, flawless, faultless* [d] *children of God surrounded by crooked and perverse people. Shine among them like lights in the sky.* [16] *Hold firm to the life-giving word, so that I may have good reason to exult in the day of Christ, knowing that I did not run the race in vain nor do my work in vain.* [17] *But if my sufferings are like a*

drink-offering poured out to complement your sacrificial service—service prompted by faith, then indeed I am glad and share my gladness with all of you. [18] *And you also be glad for the same reason and share your gladness with me.*

Notes

The variants in this section are few and of little consequence:

[a] ὡς is omitted by B 33 and a few other MSS, perhaps to ease an already difficult and cumbersome sentence.

[b] The definite article is inserted before θεός by D Ψ and the majority of witnesses in order to make "God" the probable subject of the sentence. א B and other important witnesses omit the article, thus making θεός predicate.

[c] ἦτε is read by P⁴⁶ A D* G instead of γένησθε indicating that εἶναι and γίνεσθαι were sometimes treated as interchangeable verbs.

[d] ἀμώμητα is read by D G and the majority text instead of the synonym ἄμωμα. This variant likely was influenced by μώμητα, which comes from the expression "a crooked and perverse generation" found in Deut 32:5 and also appearing here in v 15.

Form/Structure/Setting

The detailed attention just given to the Christ-hymn must not obscure the fact that vv 12–18 are part of a larger parenetic section—1:27–2:18. Exhortation is resumed again through the frequent use of the imperative mood, or through the use of participles with the force of the imperative.

At Philippi the church was being torn apart because Christians were motivated by party spirit, selfishness, conceit, pride, arrogance, etc. But hoping to heal the breach Paul begged the Philippians to live in a manner worthy of the gospel, to stand together, to work together, to think together, to serve one another, to pay attention to the concerns of one another, humbly to consider one another better than themselves. And he appealed to them to do so on the basis of Christ's own humble attitude and self-effacing action. The Christ-hymn, therefore, far from interrupting the hortatory flow, stimulates it and directs its course. Vv 12–18, while reflecting the outlook of the hymn, cannot be thought of solely as a commentary on the hymn (Lohmeyer). Nor can these verses be thought of altogether as a new beginning (*Neuansatz*, Gnilka). Inspired by the central motif of the hymn—the obedience of Christ—these verses nevertheless reach back beyond the hymn and link up with and add to the many other injunctions Paul had already given the church at Philippi for positive Christian living (1:27–2:5)—injunctions, it may be said, that the Philippians themselves were in essential agreement with (v 12) although they seem not to have been carrying them out to the extent that Paul would have desired. It is clear, too, that this section is bound to 2:1–4 and continues the plea for unselfish action already begun there. Paul makes this plea not only in words, but also by revealing his own willingness to have his life become a libation poured out in sacrifice (v 17). The apostle, then, as Christ (2:6–11), also becomes a model for Christian behavior (cf. 1 Cor 4:16; 11:1).

Comment

12. The conjunction ὥστε ("therefore," "well then") joins this new section to that which has preceded it from 1:27 onwards (cf. 2:12*b* with 1:27*b*), but

especially to the example of Christ set out in the hymn (2:6–11): "Well then, in light of the fact that Christ was obedient (ὑπήκοος, 2:8), you also must be obedient (ὑπακούειν, 2:12)." Paul, however, does not merely issue new commands unfeelingly, as an apostle with divine authority might be privileged to do. Instead he gently introduces his commands by addressing the Philippians as ἀγαπητοί ("beloved"). This is a favorite adjective of Paul's by which he means to say, "You are a people especially loved by God, but also by me" (cf. Rom 1:7; 1 Cor 15:58, etc.).

When Paul tells the Philippians that they have "always obeyed" (πάντοτε ὑπηκούσατε), he is not using hollow rhetoric as a tool to win their favor and thus force them to follow his commands (cf. Ign. *Eph.* 4.1; *Magn.* 1.1; *Trall.* 3.1, 2). Rather he is reminding them of the way in which they had in fact initially responded to the demands of God as contained in the gospel he had preached (cf. Acts 16:14, 32, 33). In light of their earlier response, therefore, Paul expects that they will now continue to heed his apostolic orders. Thus the elliptic sentence, begun with καθώς ("as") followed by the indicative, implies the correlative οὕτως ("so") and an imperative—"As you obeyed before, so continue to obey now." Past action becomes a model and a motivating force for present and future conduct. It is worth noting in passing that the verb Paul uses here for "obey" (ὑπακούειν) contains within it the twin ideas of hearing—especially the divine word as proclaimed (cf. 2 Thess 1:8)—and of submitting to that word (Kittel, *TDNT* 1,224).

Paul's next command, in fact the only explicit command in v 12, is τὴν ἑαυτῶν σωτηρίαν κατεργάζεσθε, often translated "work out your (own) salvation" (cf. KJV, RSV, NIV, NEB). Such a translation, however, is ambiguous and can lead one to a misunderstanding of what Paul actually intends to say. Paul is not here concerned with the eternal welfare of the soul *of the individual.* The individual believer is not now being called "to self-activity, to the active pursuit of the will of God . . . to a personal application of salvation" (Müller). Rather the context suggests that this command is to be understood in a corporate sense. The entire church, which had grown spiritually ill (2:3–4), is charged now with taking whatever steps are necessary to restore itself to health and wholeness. Several reasons lead to this conclusion: (1) Paul has just spoken out sharply against Christians looking out for their own individual personal interests (2:4). Hence, it is highly unlikely that he here now reverses himself by commanding them to focus on their own individual salvation. (2) The verb Paul uses, κατεργάζεσθαι, has the sense of working at something until it is brought to completion, hence "to accomplish," "to achieve," "to bring about" (BGD). Its tense is present, which heightens this idea, denoting not so much present time as continuous action. Paul in effect commands the Philippians to keep working and never let up until their "salvation" is achieved. (3) The verb κατεργάζεσθε and the reflexive pronoun ἑαυτῶν ("your own" are both plural. Once again there is here the strong indication that the exhortation is not to individual but to corporate action, to cooperative effort in the common life together as a community. (4) In the papyri σωτηρία ("salvation") is commonly used to convey the ideas of health or well-being (MM 622), ideas that are not unknown to the writers of the NT (Mark 3:4; Acts 4:9; 14:9; 27:34; cf. Phil 1:19 and the notes there). The wider context of Phil 2:12 strongly suggests that σωτηρία here is being used in this non-eschatological sense. Thus the church at Philippi is urged to work at its spiritual well-being until its well-being is complete, until its health is fully established, until every trace of spiritual disease—selfishness, dissension, and so on—is gone (Michael; see also a fuller discussion in J. H. Michael, *Expositor* 9th Series, 12 [1924] 439–50; Loh and Nida; Martin, 1976; cf. also Bonnard, Collange, Gnilka).

Two phrases modify this command to work towards spiritual health within the church at Philippi. The first, literally translated, is "not (μή) as in my presence (παρουσία) but now much more in my absence." This phrase is frequently taken with the verb ὑπηκούσατε ("you obeyed"), rather than with the verb κατεργάζεσθε ("work at"). The word "presence" is thus made to mean Paul's past presence with the Philippians—"as you always obeyed me when I was with you" (cf. GNB, JB, LB, NEB; Bonnard, Michaelis). But several things are against such an interpretation: (1) The negative introducing this phrase is μή, which is rarely used with the indicative (ὑπηκούσατε is indicative) but is regularly used with the imperative (κατεργάζεσθε is imperative; Moulton, *Grammar*, 281–82). (2) There are no verbs in this phrase, and thus no precise reference to time. If a time-period is to be insisted upon, it can as easily be future as past. (3) The word for "presence" is παρουσία, often used in the NT as a technical term for the "return" of Christ, and on occasion by Paul for his own anticipated future coming to his friends (Phil 1:26). This fact coupled with Paul's remarks in 2:23–24 indicate that παρουσία here is used to refer to the apostle's anticipated return to Philippi (Collange, Lohmeyer; see R. W. Funk, "The Apostolic 'Parousia': Form and Function," in W. R. Farmer, C. F. D. Moule and R. R. Niebuhr [eds.], *Christian History and Interpretation; Studies Presented to John Knox* [Cambridge: Cambridge University Press, 1967] 249–68). (4) The ὡς that appears in the best MSS is difficult to explain, hence its omission from some texts. Its difficulty, however, may be relieved if it is given its less frequently used meaning of "when," "in light of," or "in view of" (Collange). All of this together argues for taking the entire phrase with κατεργάζεσθε and translating, "Work at achieving spiritual health within your community, not only in light of my anticipated coming to you again, but all the more now while I am absent from you." Fear of the apostle and what he might say or do upon his return to Philippi (cf. 1 Cor 4:21) was not now to be the motivating factor for movement toward spiritual renewal (Collange). Besides, the importance of renewal was so great that it must not be delayed by waiting for Paul's expected but uncertain return.

The second phrase modifying κατεργάζεσθε ("work at") is μετὰ φόβου καὶ τρόμου, literally translated, "with fear and trembling." In light of what has been said above, however, this has no reference to the anxious concern that individual Christians might be expected to have as they face the last judgment. And thus there is no need to introduce an extra negative to relieve this tension—"work out your salvation *not* with fear and trembling" (see Glombitza, *NovT* 3 [1959] 100–106). Although φόβος can mean "fear," "alarm," "dismay" in the face of danger, it also carries the meaning of "awe" and "respect." Coupled with τρόμος, a word which means "a trembling," or "a quivering," the phrase could picture a person standing with quivering fear or trembling awe before someone or something. Yet Paul is the only NT writer to use this phrase and never does he use it to describe the attitude people are to have toward God—only the attitude they are to have toward each other or toward their leaders (1 Cor 2:3; 2 Cor 7:15; Eph 6:5). It seems, therefore, that this expression was a stock phrase that may well have meant something far less forceful than what one might expect from considering separately each word of which it is composed. The phrase comes from Jewish piety and may mean, therefore, either (1) "a nervous anxiety to do one's duty," "a fear of failure" (Plummer), or (2) an attitude within the community of "respect and reverence" toward each other (Burn, *ExpTim* 34 [1922–23] 562; Collange, Eichholz, "Bewahren und Bewähren," 103; Michael), or (3) an attitude of "obedience," or "holding oneself in weakness" toward the will of God according to the pattern of Jesus Christ (Pedersen, *ST* 32 [1978] 1–31). This last meaning excellently fits the present context. One may translate, "*Obediently* work at achieving spiritual fitness within your community." As in the life of Jesus, so in the life of the church, obedience to the Father's will must be the supreme motivating force for action.

13. But the Philippian Christians are not left to themselves to achieve such high spiritual goals. For, as the conjunction γάρ indicates, there is among them and within them an energizing force that is no less than God himself. In fact, the conjunction makes it clear that "God does not work and has not worked . . . because man has worked. . . . The contrary is true: because God works and has worked, therefore man must and can work" (Ridderbos, *Paul*, 255).

The verb here for "work" is not now κατεργάζεσθαι (v 12) but ἐνεργεῖν, the verb from which comes the English word "energy." This verb is a special Pauline word, used eighteen times by the apostle of the twenty times it is found in the NT. It carries within it the idea of working mightily, of working effectively (cf. Matt 15:2; Gal 2:8; 3:5; 5:6; Eph 2:2). The form this new verb takes is a participle used as a noun; thus it becomes another name for God. The Great Energizer, the one who is effectively at work, is God. And God is at work among the Christians (ἐν ὑμῖν) at Philippi so as to effect a change in their wills (τὸ θέλειν) and in turn a change in their conduct. Thus they will be able to achieve (τὸ ἐνεργεῖν—note this verb) the harmony and health that is so much needed. "An effective divine energy is at work in the community and if the Philippians only avail themselves of its presence, cooperate with it, and permit it to express itself in their working, the inevitable result will be not only the willing, but also the achieving, by them of the salvation of the community" (Michael). There is thus no inconsistency between Paul's command for them to bring about their own "salvation" (v 12), and this statement that "God is at work" among them creating their desire and their ability to fulfil their desire (cf. 1 Cor 9:27; 10:1–13; Gal 5:25; Col 3:3–5). "Paul never implies that God's purposes for man can be fulfilled whether man cooperates or not" (Houlden). "Divine action does not curtail human action but rather provokes a reaction which it supports" (Collange).

The phrase ὑπὲρ τῆς εὐδοκίας, which modifies the participle ὁ ἐνεργῶν ("the one who effectively works"), presents new difficulties. Εὐδοκία usually refers to the "benevolent purpose" or "good will" of God. Thus most commentators interpret εὐδοκίας here as referring to God acting in accord with his loving purpose, or in harmony with that which pleases him. But it is to be noticed (1) that there is no modifier for this word—the text does not explicitly say "God's good purpose"; (2) that the word εὐδοκία may also be used of men as well as of God, and can mean "good understanding," or "good will"; (3) that the preposition used here, ὑπέρ, hardly means "according to" or "in harmony with," but may be used to introduce that which one wants to attain (BDF 231, 2); (4) that the context is a call to harmony, selflessness and good will toward others. Hence, it seems best to interpret εὐδοκία as that good will to which Paul desires the Philippians to attain and which should be the hallmark of any Christian community (Collange, Ewald-Wohlenberg; Michael).

14. Paul continues his appeal for harmony and good will within the Philippian community by forbidding grumbling (γογγυσμός) and disputing (διαλογισμός). One should not imagine that the Christians at Philippi, like Israel in the wilderness (cf. Exod 15–17; Num 14–17; 1 Cor 10:10), were grumbling against God or doubting his promises (Beare, Caird, Gnilka, Scott). There is no hint of that kind of attitude here. Rather, as has been shown, the Philippians were doing things that generated both inward and outward feelings of unfriendliness toward one another. Γογγυσμός was one of these things. The word means "complaint" or "displeasure" expressed in murmuring or secret talk, or whisperings about someone (perhaps about their leaders)—a kind of grumbling action that promotes ill will instead of harmony and good will (cf. Acts 6:1; 1 Pet 4:9; Rengstorf, TDNT 1,736).

Διαλογισμός is still another of these divisive actions. It is a word that embraces a wide range of ideas from an evil thought to anxious reflection or doubt, to dispute or argument (Schrenk, TDNT 2,97–98). This last meaning, a meaning that is strongly supported by the papyri (MM 151), is the one that best fits the context here. The Philippians, perhaps spurred on by false teachers (cf. 3:2) were engaging in speculations (cf. Rom 1:21) that could only result in futile arguments that had the capacity to tear the community apart. These hurtful actions must go, and with them all other actions that promote disunity within the church (cf. v 3). The Christians at Philippi must not complain against one another or engage in futile arguments with one another while involved in any (πάντα—note the comprehensiveness of this word) of those activities in which their "life together" is expressed.

15. All the injunctions Paul lays upon the Philippians (2:3, 4, 12–14) are for a purpose: that (ἵνα) they might become (γένησθε) better people than they are. Characterized by assertiveness (ἐριθεία), conceit (κενοδοξία), grumbling (γογγυσμός), argumentativeness (διαλογισμός), the Philippians are promised that improvement is possible. They can become blameless (ἄμεμπτος), flawless (ἀκέραιος), faultless (ἄμωμος) children of God. But for Paul this radical transformation is possible only when there is a humble positive response of the human will to the demands of God (note the preponderance of the imperative mood here) linked together with the creative force of divine grace (cf. vv 12, 13: but contrast Barth).

The adjective ἄμεμπτος, derived as it is from the verb μέμφεσθαι ("to blame"), and prefixed with the α-negative, means that anyone so described stands above accusation or blame, either by man or God; his behavior is free from the criticism of others (cf. Phillips). Ἀκέραιος is related to the verb κεραννύναι ("to mix," "to mingle"). It was used in Paul's day to describe undiluted wine or unalloyed metal (Lightfoot). When applied to people it conveyed the idea of simplicity of character, purity, guiltlessness, or innocence (cf. Rom 16:19). Together, ἄμεμπτος and ἀκέραιος, if and when they could be applied to the Philippians, would mean that no one would be able to point to any flaw in them because none would exist. The external appearance of the Christian community would correspond exactly to what it was within, to what it was in its real nature.

One additional descriptive phrase completes Paul's aspirations for the Philippians—"faultless children of God" (τέκνα θεοῦ ἄμωμα). The word τέκνα ("children"), derived from τίκτω ("give birth to"), stresses the idea of family resemblance, of sharing in the nature of the parent, in this case, God (cf. John 1:12). Ἄμωμα, the adjective describing "children" is frequently used in the OT in connection with sacrificial animals (Num 6:14; 19:2, etc.). Only a sacrifice without blemish (ἄμωμος), one that is spotless or perfect is worthy of being offered to God (cf. Heb 9:14; 1 Pet 1:19). Hence, Paul's aim is that the Philippians would become truly "God's children—sharing his nature—without a blemish!" (Michael) thus fit to be presented to God, and to be representatives of God. These three adjectives are translated, however, "blameless," "flawless," "faultless" maintaining the same sound at the end of each word without attempting to highlight their special nuances. This is done in an effort to preserve the studied rhetoric of the apostle, who begins each of these words with the same sound by using the alpha-privative—ἄμεμπτοι, ἀκέραιοι, ἄμωμα.

The words "faultless children of God surrounded by crooked and perverse people" (v 15b) come from Deut 32:5. There, interestingly, it is Israel who is called the children (τέκνα) of God, but "blemished" (μωμητά) children, and a "crooked and perverse people" who had forsaken God. Perhaps Paul, in referring to those words from Deut here may be doing two things: (1) indicating that the church now has the privilege of replacing Israel as God's children—not as blameworthy children, however, but as blameless children, and (2) hinting that Israel, robbed of this privilege by its own lack of humility before God has nothing left to it "but to melt away into the 'perverse and straying' mass of the world's . . . humanity" (Collange). There is thus every reason for the church to divorce itself from Israel, from Judaism (cf. 3:2), and to turn away from every thing that is twisted (σκολιά) and perverted (διαστραμμένη), i.e. that is not in line with the truth in Jesus.

It is right in the middle of (μέσον) this twisted, perverse society, or of a society that has twisted the truth of God, and perverted the ways of God (cf. Matt 17:17; Acts 2:43; 13:10; 20:30) that the Philippians, having become true children of God, are commanded to shine as lights, i.e. as people who know God's truth and who live in accordance with that truth (see BDF 296 for an explanation of the form of the relative pronoun, οἷς, whose antecedent is γενεᾶς).

The verb φαίνεσθε, even though it is middle voice, does not, as Lohmeyer claims, demand the meaning, "appear." The middle form of this verb may also mean "shine" (BDG), and it is this idea that best fits here. And although φαίνεσθε is usually treated as indicative, i.e. "you are shining" (cf. KJV, JB, NEB, NIV, RSV, Goodspeed, Knox, Moffatt), it may also be correctly treated as imperative, i.e. "you must shine" (GNB, Barclay). The context favors this latter interpretation, for it is unlikely that Paul is merely reminding the Philippians of what they are already doing. There would be no purpose in that. Rather he is again appealing to them to accept their responsibility as God's children to be φωστῆρες ἐν τῷ κόσμῳ ("lights in the world").

The word φωστήρ means any light-bearing body (BGD). It was used of a torch, a lantern, even of harbor beacons (Finlayson, *ExpTim* 77 [1965–66] 181; cf. LB). Adam, Israel, the Torah, important rabbis, and so on were called "light-bearers" in the world (Str-B 1, 236–37; Conzelmann, *TDNT* 9,324, 327; see Martin, *Philippians*, 1976). The people of Qumran were known as "children of light" (1QS 1:9; 2:16; 1QM 13:5, 9). Hence, Paul may have used this expression, φωστῆρες ἐν κόσμῳ, to remind the Philippians of their heritage, and as children of light (1 Thess 5:5) they, like their illustrious forbears, are to carry the light of truth and goodness to their morally corrupt world.

But φωστήρ is used especially of heavenly bodies (BGD; cf. Gen 1:14, 16; Ecclus 43:7; Wisd Sol 13:2). It is more likely, therefore, that Paul had this meaning in mind when he made his comparison. As the sun, or moon, or stars shine in the heavens illuminating an otherwise dark sky (κόσμος, understood in a physical sense), so the Philippians, who are themselves light (cf. Matt 5:14; Eph 5:8*a*), are to let their good works—of harmony, of selflessness, of service to others, and so on—shine out so that they themselves will influence for good the people around them.

In any case, however the phrase is to be understood, one thing is clear— Paul did not intend his words to mean merely that the Philippians were "to stand out against" (Caird) the background of their society so as to show it up by way of contrast. Rather, his words came as a challenge to change that society. As light dispels darkness, so Christians are to dispel the darkness of evil and ignorance that is everywhere around them.

16. There is a break in thought at this point. Paul continues his appeal to the Philippians, to be sure, but he shifts the basis of appeal from the example of Jesus (2:3–15) to himself and to the judgment he must face at the day of Christ. Therefore, he now asks them to do something for his sake.

His words are: λόγον ζωῆς ἐπέχοντες, εἰς καύχημα ἐμοὶ εἰς ἡμέραν Χριστοῦ. The verb ἐπέχειν means either "to hold forth," or "to hold fast." The latter meaning is to be preferred as the context makes clear. The participle ἐπέχοντες is imperatival (Moulton, *Grammar*, 343; H. G. Meecham, "The Use of the Participle for the Imperative in the New Testament," *ExpTim* 58 [1947] 207–209; C. K. Barrett, "The Imperatival Participle," *ExpTim* 59 [1948] 165–67). The expression "word of life" (λόγον ζωῆς), coming first in the sentence, has the emphatic position and refers not to Christ as the Word (John 1:1, 4), but to the gospel that Paul preached, which the Philippians heard and believed and by which they had received the life of God. The construction, εἰς καύχημα ἐμοί, is a common one to indicate purpose (cf. Rom 10:1; 13:4;

1 Cor 14:22; see Moule, *Idiom-Book*, 70). The word καύχημα is a "boasting," and its cognates, καύχησις and καυχᾶσθαι, are distinctly Pauline. Of the fifty times these words occur in the NT only four of them occur outside the letters of Paul. Here καύχημα does not mean a vanity that deserves condemnation but a deep exultation or proper pride that only the Philippians can provide Paul by their obedience to God's commands (cf. Phil 4;1; 2 Cor 1:4; see G. Didier, *Le désintéressement du chrétien* [Paris: Éditions Montaigne, 1953] 152). The dative ἐμοί is a dative of possession. The expression εἰς ἡμέραν Χριστοῦ ("day of Christ") refers to that time when Paul, as all Christians, must stand before the tribunal of Christ (2 Cor 5:10; cf. Phil 1:10 and the comments there), not for the purpose of finding out his eternal destiny (cf. Rom 8:1), but to give an account of his stewardship to his Lord (1 Cor 4:1–5; see Caird). Paul's plea, therefore, is that the Philippians will hold firmly to the gospel message that he had preached—a message that not only brought them life for the future, i.e. eternal life, but a change of life in the present. Only if they hold fast to this gospel and continually obey its demands will he be able to boast about them to Christ and receive approval because of them from Christ at the day of his appearing. "Please do this for me," Paul asks the Philippians.

If they comply with his wishes he will know (looking back from that day) that he did not run or work in vain. Paul uses two metaphors to describe his apostolic ministry. One, that of running, comes from the games. It is a favorite of his (Gal 2:2; 4:11; Phil 3:12–13). With it he describes himself as an athlete who trains thoroughly, runs hard, plays by the rules, expends great physical and emotional energies—all so that he may not come to the end of the race and find himself needlessly disqualified (εἰς κένον; cf. 1 Cor 9:27).

The other metaphor, that of working hard, could easily come from Paul's own experience as a weaver of tent cloth. "We ought to place ourselves as it were within St. Paul's own class, the artisan class of the Imperial age, and then feel the force of his words. They all become much more life-like when restored to their original historical *milieu*. 'I labored more abundantly than they all'—these words, applied by St. Paul to missionary work, came originally from the joyful pride of the skilled weaver, who, working by the piece, was able to hand in the largest amount of stuff on pay day. The frequent references to 'labor in vain' are a trembling echo of the discouragement resulting from a width of cloth being rejected as badly woven and therefore not paid for" (Deissmann, *Light*, 317). Neither of these metaphors highlights honor, dignity or glory as the way of the apostle in the present struggle of life. They tell rather of toil and training, pain, striving and suffering (Pfitzner, *Agon Motif*, 99–108). Those who would run such a race must be content to train hard now and to wait for the finish for the prize. Thus Paul begs the Philippians to live in such a way that his efforts and difficulties on their behalf, which apparently were very great, may not be in vain: "May the prize be there when I finish!"

17. This verse does not begin a new paragraph (Barth, Gnilka, Jones, Lohmeyer), for it is joined to v 16 by a series of conjunctions—ἀλλὰ εἰ καί. Together, then, the thought in vv 16 and 17 runs somewhat as follows. Paul in essence is saying that as an apostle he has struggled hard to bring to the

Philippians the word of life. He asks them to hold fast to it, or all his struggles will be in vain. But (ἀλλά) lest they should think that he is too pessimistic about them, he hurries to add that he recognizes their sacrificial service to him as proof that they are indeed holding on and that his work will not be in vain. So even if (εἰ καί) he is suffering continually he is glad because his sufferings are like a libation, which, when added to their sacrifice, serves to complete it.

To make this summary statement stand it is important to notice the following things: (1) Paul turns abruptly from the language of the stadium and the weaver's loom to the language of sacrifice. But in so doing he does not turn away from the idea of struggle and striving as the marks of an apostle— the figure is different; the fact is the same.

(2) Although all sacrifices were made obsolete by the single sacrifice of Christ (Heb 9:11–14, 24–26), yet Paul often speaks metaphorically of the need for Christians continually to offer up to God legitimate and acceptable sacrifices (cf. Rom 12:1; 15:16). It is not surprising, then, to learn that Paul calls the gifts the Philippians gave him out of their poverty (2 Cor 8:2) an act of "sacrificial service" arising out of their faith in God (τῇ θυσίᾳ καὶ λειτουργίᾳ τῆς πίστεως ὑμῶν—taking θυσίᾳ and λειτουργίᾳ together by hendiadys since both nouns share one article, and taking τῆς πίστεως as a subjective genitive; see Lightfoot for the shades of meaning contained in λειτουργία).

(3) Paul speaks of what is happening to him also in sacrificial terms—"I am being poured out as a libation to God" (σπένδομαι). This is the *crux interpretum* of v 17 and is generally misunderstood. In the ancient world sacrifices, both pagan and Jewish were usually accompanied and completed by a libation of wine poured out either on top of the sacrifice or at the foot of the altar to honor the deity (2 Kings 16:13; Jer 7:18: Hos 9:4). Because this libation was at times called "the blood of the grape" (Wisd Sol 50:15), and because the use of σπένδεσθαι ("to be poured out as a libation") in 2 Tim 4:6 and Ign. *Rom.* 2.2 suggests an offering in death, interpreters see in Paul's use of σπένδεσθαι here a clear allusion to his imminent martyrdom (BGD; Barth, Bonnard, Beare, Caird, Gnilka, Lightfoot, Martin, Michael, Plummer, Synge, etc., and many translations: GNB, JB, NEB, LB). But are these interpreters and translators, for all their numbers, correct? It is not likely that they are and for the following reasons: (*a*) the note of joy—χαίρω καὶ συγχαίρω πᾶσιν ὑμῖν— would then strangely be sounded for martydom: "I am glad and glad with all of you that I am to be put to death." Ignatius may have said this, but hardly Paul. Lohmeyer attempts to relieve this difficulty somewhat by supposing the Philippians were also suffering persecution and were glad to see Paul join them in martyrdom. Gnilka, too, tries to ease the problem by attaching ἐπὶ τῇ θυσίᾳ to χαίρω and not to σπένδομαι—"I rejoice over your sacrifice," not, "I am poured out over your sacrifice." These oversubtle attempts at solution simply point up the difficulty of understanding σπένδομαι as a reference to Paul's death. (*b*) It is doubtful that σπένδομαι ever denotes a killing. True, libation accompanied most sacrifices in the Greek world and in the Jewish cultus it concluded the entire liturgy, rounding off the daily sacrifices. But "never in the Greek Bible nor in the Hellenistic world is this word used for libations of blood (='*haimassein*')" (Collange, citing the detailed study

by Denis, *RSPT* 42 [1958] 630–45; cf. also Manson, *BJRL* 23 [1939] 184–85; but see Cook, *JTS* 33 [1982] 168–71). (*c*) The tense of the verb σπένδομαι is present and is describing what is currently happening to the apostle, not what will happen. The present tense may indeed be used for the future (BDF, 323), but here there is no clue that points to future time other than that contained in one's notion of what σπένδομαι must mean. (*d*) Finally, Paul has already used two metaphors—running and working—to describe the rigors of his current apostolic activities. It seems only likely then that this third metaphor would be in keeping with the others. Therefore, when Paul uses the libation-metaphor, he does not have his death in mind—within a few sentences he will assure the Philippians with confidence that he will soon be with them again (2:24). Rather he is picturesquely referring to his sufferings as an apostle. To the degree that his sufferings are for the sake of the gospel, for the sake of the church in general, and for the sake of the church at Philippi in particular, they act as a seal on whatever sacrificial service the Philippians may make, just as a libation completes any offering made to God. And thus Paul is glad. In other words, his apostolic sufferings and the Philippians' sacrificial gifts to him because he is an apostle combine to form a perfectly complete sacrifice to God. There is therefore every reason for mutual joy and rejoicing (χαίρω καὶ συγχαίρω).

18. As Paul is happy about combining his sacrifice with that of the Philippians in order that together they may present an offering acceptable to God, so for the same reason (τὸ δὲ αὐτό) he calls upon them to share in his joy. That is to say, as he is glad to be a libation poured out to God through his sufferings, so he encourages them (χαίρετε, taken as an imperative) likewise to be glad to render service to God in their continued sharing in his work of defending and vindicating the gospel (cf. 1:7). The repetition here of words for joy (χαίρω/χαίρετε) and togetherness (συγχαίρω/συγχαίρετε)—twin themes of this letter—is striking. Χαίρειν ("to rejoice") and its cognates occur more than thirteen times in Philippians, while the preposition σύν ("with") and the long list of words compounded with it are numerous. These combine as evidence both of the apostle's own joy and of the variety of experiences, including joy, that he shared together with his friends at Philippi.

Explanation

The Christians at Philippi, torn apart by conceit, pride and selfishness, are called upon by the apostle to change their ways and in humbleness begin to serve one another (2:1–4) even as Christ humbly "emptied himself" and made his life a life of sacrificial service to others (2:5–11).

Paul continues now (2:12–18) in this same tone of exhortation, pleading with the Philippians to obey him, not only in light of his expected return to Philippi, but even now while he is away.

Further, he urges them obediently to work at bringing healing to their community and to keep at this job until it is accomplished. This is no impossible task, however. If they do what he asks, they will discover that they are merely cooperating with God, and that the saying is true, ὅταν σπεύδῃ τις αὐτός, χὠ θεὸς συνάπτεται ("whenever anyone makes an effort, God also lends a hand," Aeschylus). They will find that God is already at work among them stimulating their desires and giving them the energy to foster good will instead of ill will. In light of this Paul is bold to ask them to curb their grumbling against their leaders and to stay away from arguments that generate division.

Paul exhorts them to do all these things in order that no one, either inside the church or on the outside, will be able to find any fault or insincerity in them. He wants them to be God's children, so morally unblemished that they can affect for good the corrupt society in which they find themselves, dispelling evil and ignorance, as the lights in the sky dispel darkness. But to be this kind of people they must hold firmly to the gospel, which they have received and which is God's means to bring them life and give them direction for living.

Finally, Paul shares with the Philippians his personal hope that they will heed these exhortations of his so that when he has run out the race of life he will not have run in vain. But lest they should think that he has too many doubts about them because of this talk of "running in vain," he hastens to assure them that he considers that what they have already done is an acceptable sacrifice of service to God—one that arises out of their faith in God. And he tells them that his own current sufferings as an apostle are but the libation that is customarily poured over a sacrifice to make it complete. They have done the right thing in the past. They have generously shared what was theirs in the advancement of the gospel. He asks now that they continue as they began. Thus he and they can be glad together not in spite of self-sacrifice and whatever suffering it brings, but precisely because of it.

C. News about Timothy and Epaphroditus (2:19–30)

1. About Timothy (2:19–24)

Bibliography

Christou, P. "ΙΣΟΨΥΧΟΣ" Ph. 2.20." *JBL* 70 (1951) 293–96. **Culpepper, R. A.** "Co-workers in Suffering: Philippians 2:19–30." *RevExp* 77 (1980) 349–58. **Fridrichsen, A.** "Exegetisches zu den Paulusbriefen." *TSK* 102 (1930) 291–301. ———. "Ισόψυχος =ebenbürtig, solidarisch." *Symbolae Osloenses* 18 (1938) 42–49. **Joüon, P.** "Notes philologiques sur quelques versets de l'épître aux Philippiens." *RSR* 28 (1938) 89–93, 223–33, 299–310.

Translation

[19] *Now I hope, under the lordship* [a] *of Jesus, to send Timothy to you very soon, so that I also may be cheered up when I learn how things are going with you, as you when you hear how things are going with me.* [20] *I hope to send him, because I have no one else who equally shares my feelings and who genuinely cares about your affairs.* [21] *For all the others here are concerned about their own interests, not those of Jesus Christ.* [b] [22] *But you know* [c] *Timothy's proven worth, how that, like a child with his father, he worked hard alongside me to advance the cause of the gospel.* [23] *This one, then, is the person I hope to send to you as soon as I see about my own*

affairs. [24] *For I am confident in the Lord that I too will be coming to you very soon.*[d]

Notes

[a] For κυρίῳ a few MSS including C D* F G read Χριστῷ. This appears to be an attempt to conform κυρίῳ Ἰησοῦ to Paul's more common expression, Χριστῷ Ἰησοῦ.

[b] B and the majority text has the word order Χριστοῦ Ἰησοῦ instead of Ἰησοῦ Χριστοῦ which is read by P[46] ℵ A C D F 33 81 and others. This is a common exchange in the MSS tradition.

[c] P[46] has οἴδατε for γινώσκετε without in any way making a change in the meaning.

[d] ℵ* A C P 326 plus a few other MSS along with some OL MSS and other versions add πρὸς ὑμᾶς to ἐλεύσομαι, thereby making explicit what was deemed implicit in the text.

Form/Structure/Setting

In this section Paul focuses attention upon his co-worker, Timothy, and briefly touches on matters that concern himself. Since such things as these generally appear at the close of Paul's letters (Rom, 1 Cor, Eph, Col, Philem), many commentators conclude that Philippians is a compilation of several letters, and that this reference to Timothy, along with personal notations, signals the beginning of the end of one of these letters (Beare, Collange, Gnilka; see Introduction, xxix–xxxii).

But this conclusion is weakened by the fact that personal matters and matters concerning Paul's co-workers are not kept exclusively for the end of his letters. Sometimes they are found in the middle as well (cf. 1 Cor 4:17–19; 2 Cor 8:16–19). This is especially true when matters like these are "relevant to the problems of the church or the agenda of the letter" (Culpepper, *RevExp* 77 [1980] 350; Doty, *Letters*, 36–37, 43; White, *Body of the Letter*, 143–45). Such is the case here. Paul is troubled because the Philippians seem too much concerned with their own interests (τὰ ἑαυτῶν) and too little with the interests of others (τὰ ἑτέρων, 2:4). He combats this problem, (1) with the Christ-hymn (2:6–11), which stresses the servant-role (δοῦλος) of Christ, (2) with the example of his own life as a libation poured out for the sake of others (2:18), and (3) with the model of Timothy, who set himself to serve (ἐδούλευσεν, 2:22) and who was more genuinely concerned with the interests of the Philippians (τὰ περὶ ὑμῶν, 2:20) than he was with his own interests.

Thus in what at first appears as a simple act of informing the Philippians about the plans he has for Timothy, Paul continues to teach them from the quality of this man's life that the mission of a Christian is to serve rather than to be served. Further, it becomes clear that the theme of 2:5–11 (the Christ-hymn), illustrated immediately here in Timothy, and later in Epaphroditus, continues on through the remainder of the letter (see this illustrated by Culpepper, *RevExp* 77 [1980] 351). There is thus no good reason for seeing 2:19–24 as heralding the beginning of the end of one of several supposed letters contained now in the compass of the one Philippian letter.

Comment

19. Paul is forced by circumstances to remain away from the church at Philippi (cf. 2:12), at least temporarily. But (δέ) in the meantime he has excel-

lent contingency plans. He hopes soon to send Timothy to them (see Acts
16; Rom 16:21; 1 Cor 4:17; 16:10; 2 Cor 1:1; Phil 1:1; 1 Thess 1:1; 2 Thess
1:1; Philem 1, for information about this person).

It is striking that Paul should use the word ἐλπίζω ("I hope") when he
writes about Timothy's journey to Philippi (vv 19, 23), and πέποιθα ("I am
confident") when he writes about his own (v 24). This change in vocabulary,
which seems deliberate and more than mere rhetoric, is often obscured in
translation (KJV, JB, LB, RSV, Phillips; but see NEB, NIV). But it may be a significant change and thus should be treated accordingly. For it may be Paul's
way of subtly assuring the Philippians that his own coming to them again,
in spite of immense obstacles, is more certain than the expected arrival of
Timothy.

Yet Paul makes it clear to the Philippians that his plans for Timothy and
for himself are not made strictly on the human level without due recognition
of the fact that Jesus is Lord (cf. 2:11). Hence, his hope for Timothy and
his confidence about himself (v 24) are both ἐν κυρίῳ Ἰησοῦ ("in the Lord").
This is not a stock phrase such as "the Lord willing," tacked on unthinkingly.
Nor is it an especially self-abnegating phrase indicating that Paul was at a
loss as to what the future held and, hence, had to cast himself "upon the
Lord." That is to say, it does not indicate in any way that Paul's outlook
was "so unsettled" that he did not know what a day might bring forth and
thus could "only make his plans in the Lord Jesus" (Martin, Philippians, 1959;
cf. Lohmeyer). Rather its presence here was to remind the Philippians of
what Paul believed and practiced in good times and bad, that all his hopes
and aspirations, his plans and expectations were subject to the Lordship of
Jesus Christ (cf. Rom 14:14; 1 Cor 7:39; 1 Cor 16:7; Philem 22). Thus Paul
could be hopeful, even confident, about the days ahead, precisely because
he had already submitted himself and his future wholly to the Lord.

Paul's purpose in sending Timothy to Philippi was twofold: (1) that (ἵνα)
he himself might be cheered (εὐψυχῶ) by good news about the Philippians,
and (2) that the Philippians might also be cheered by good news about Paul.
This latter purpose is only stated implicitly in the word κἀγώ ("I also"),
but it is present in this word nonetheless: "You will be cheered and I also."

20. Apparently Paul knew that the Philippians would question his sending
Timothy. Timothy seems to have played no significant role in founding the
church at Philippi, although he was with Paul at that time. And it is conceivable
that in the eyes of the Philippians he even may have contributed negatively
to that mission. Acts is strikingly silent about Timothy at Philippi, while loudly
proclaiming the activity of Paul and Silas (Acts 16). And although Timothy
may have visited Philippi on other occasions (Acts 19:21, 22; 20:3–6) no
descriptive account is made about any of these visits. In any case, Paul felt
compelled elaborately to justify his decision: "I am sending Timothy (1) because (γάρ) I have no one like him . . . (2) because (γάρ) he, unlike the
others, is not chiefly concerned with his own interests, and (3) because (δέ)
you know what his real value is to the advancement of the gospel."

The first reason Paul gives, "I have no one like him," is expressed by a
rare adjective, ἰσόψυχον, which literally means, "of equal soul," or "feeling,"
or "mind" (BGD; cf. LXX Ps 55[54]:14—"a man my equal"). By choosing
to use this word Paul intends to make clear to the Philippians that whatever

Timothy says in his mission to Philippi and whatever decisions he makes "will be his (Paul's) as well, and no one should oppose the disciple on the grounds that his master might not think as he does" (Collange; cf. Bonnard; Christou, *JBL* 70 [1951] 293–96; Joüon, *RSR* 28 [1938] 302; Loh and Nida; Vincent; cf. also GNB, NEB, Phillips). There is little reason to say that such an interpretation as this founders on Paul's Greek construction, as though it could only mean "I have no one *like Timothy*" and not at all "I have no one *else* (besides Timothy) *like myself*" (Martin, *Philippians*, 1959, 1976; Beare, Gnilka, Jones, Michael; cf. JB, LB, NIV, RSV). Paul simply does not write as precisely as one might like. His style is often compressed (see Caird), which means that many things are taken for granted or must be inferred from the context. The context says in effect that Timothy was Paul's son in the faith, trained by him, his close companion and fellow servant in evangelism (2:22). Thus, in spite of what may be considered the roughness of Paul's Greek construction, it is clear that Timothy knows the apostle's mind better than anyone else, and for this reason Paul is sending him on the mission to Philippi.

Paul continues by saying that he is sending Timothy because Timothy genuinely cares about those things that affect the Philippians. The adverb Paul uses to express the idea of genuinely (γνησίως) is one that suggests kinship. Literally translated it would be, "legitimately born." Although it is most often rendered by words like "sincerely" (Gnilka) or "truly" (Vincent), one should not overlook its root idea. Timothy, then, is one who "legitimately" cares for the Philippians, because he is Paul's "legitimate" son (cf. 1 Tim 1:2; Titus 1:4). As a consequence, therefore, he is "the sole authorized representative of the apostle" (Collange, Lightfoot).

The verb used to describe Timothy's feelings for the Philippians, "to care about" (μεριμνᾶν), is a strong verb. Elsewhere in this letter it is used of "worry" (4:6). Without such negative connotations here, it does, nevertheless, carry with it overtones of the pressure or weight of anxiety that grows out of true concern for the welfare of others (cf. 2 Cor 11:28; see A. J. Malherbe, *The Cynic Epistles* [Missoula, MT: Scholars Press, 1977] 282, line 11).

21. The second reason Paul gives for sending Timothy is quite startling: "No one else cares! All (οἱ πάντες) are looking out for their own interests not those of Jesus Christ."

Does this statement reveal "a peevish and uncharitable tone" on Paul's part, a good example of his own personal feelings of hostility against those Christians around him in Caesarea (Synge)? Is it hyperbole, designed to enhance Timothy's worth and authority as over against any other person Paul might have chosen to send, and the Philippians might have been willing to welcome (Collange)? Could it mean that of all the Christians around him there is no one else to whom he could entrust so important a mission (Martin, *Philippians*, 1959)? Is it a general parenthetical remark regarding the world around him, one that says nothing about his fellow Christians, but is rather "his solemn reflexion when he remembers that in a world of selfishness and self-seeking (cf. Matt 6:32), it is such a rare thing to find a man like Timothy who is really anxious to promote the welfare of other people, and to give himself to a fatiguing journey and to the resolving of personal quarrels in the Philippian church" (Martin, *Philippians*, (1959)? Is it a restrictive statement where "all" does not mean all Christians in Caesarea (cf. 1:16), or in the world, but refers only to all those who were near at hand, available and in Paul's judgment able to undertake such a difficult mission but were not willing to do so (Beare, Caird, Hendriksen, Jones)? Is it an example of how Christians can differ radically in their evaluation of a particular mission within the church: For Paul the journey to Philippi was number one priority—to refuse this mission was to be seeking one's own interests and to care nothing for the cause of Christ. For others the welfare of this distant church at Philippi was not nearly so important as the welfare of their own community in Caesarea and its outreach to surrounding cities. To drop their commitments to their immediate churches and to travel to Philippi, even if an apostle did desire this, would itself be to them a seeking of their own interests and not Christ's. In the words of Vincent it is possible to speculate unceasingly about the meaning of Paul's startling statement here, but "without more information a satisfactory explanation seems impossible."

22. The third reason Paul gives to justify his decision to send Timothy comes in the form of an appeal to what the Philippians already know about him. Although apparently they needed to be reminded of who Timothy was and what he had done, yet upon reflection they would discover that they after all did know certain important things about this person: (1) They knew "his proven worth" (δοκιμήν). This noun, δοκιμή, is used only seven times in the NT and exclusively by Paul. It embraces the dual ideas of the process and the results of testing (2 Cor 8:2; Rom 5:4). Paul, therefore, is not simply saying to the Philippians that they knew "Timothy's record" (NEB), but that they knew how he had stood the test (Moffatt) and proved his worth (GNB). Thus they should realize immediately that no "mediocre substitute" was being sent to them (Beare).

(2) They knew, too, Timothy's intimate relationship with Paul. The sentence which describes this relationship is awkwardly expressed. Paul begins it as if he originally intended to say, "Timothy served *me* as a child serves a father" (Vincent). But he checked himself before this subservient idea could be expressed. Remembering that he too was a servant (δοῦλος), that Timothy and he were in fact co-workers (1:5), and that it was important to commend Timothy to the Philippians as an equal, he ultimately wrote, "he worked like a slave (ἐδούλευσεν) with me (σὺν ἐμοί)." But Paul not only says that Timothy worked side by side with him, but as a son, or more tenderly, as a child (τέκνον instead of υἱόν) works alongside his father. The picture is drawn from the world of Paul's day where it was expected that a son should learn his trade from his father (Caird). The Philippians knew, therefore, that Timothy was coming to them having learned all that Paul could teach him. He was coming to them to express exactly the apostle's mind.

(3) Finally, the Philippians knew that Timothy was Paul's colleague "in common service for a single cause, *the gospel*" (Martin, *Philippians*, 1959). Thus, if they reflect upon what they know about Timothy they should welcome him gladly and not question why Paul should be sending him to them. His distinction rests upon a desire to serve by following in the footsteps of his Master (2:7, cf. Mark 10:45) and his mentor, Paul.

23. Earlier Paul had said he would send Timothy "soon" (ταχέως), but

not immediately. Now he returns to explain his reason for this delay—ὡς ἂν ἀφίδω τὰ περὶ ἐμέ (lit. "whenever I look to the things concerning me").

There is nothing in the vocabulary Paul uses here, nor in any grammatical construction, to say that Timothy's proposed delay was caused by a lack of information about the outcome of Paul's trial, or that Timothy was required to wait until something definite could be learned about Paul's fate (JB, and the great majority of interpreters). In fact, the context points in quite a different direction. Paul was sure how his trial would turn out and was confident that he would soon travel to Philippi (v 24). Hence, he never would have delayed such an important mission as Timothy's to the Philippians just to have him present in Caesarea to hear the final verdict of acquittal handed down by the governor.

There must, therefore, be some other meaning to his words. First, note that the verb ἀφίδω (see BDF 14 for its form) has as its primary meaning "to look away from all other things to one thing only," "to exclude everything else and to concentrate on only one thing" (LSJ, BGD, MM). It is used but two times in the NT—here and in Heb 12:2—where it has this very meaning: "Look away from all else and concentrate wholly on Jesus."

Second, the phrase τὰ περὶ ἐμέ certainly does not in and of itself mean "my fate" nor "how things are going to turn out for me." Rather, this phrase belongs to a group of concise phrases involving the definite article that Paul is fond of using, but that are difficult to translate—τὰ κατ᾽ ἐμέ (1:12, "this business of mine," NEB), τὰ ἑαυτῶν, τὰ ἑτέρων (2:4, "your own interests," "the interests of others," NIV), τὰ περὶ ὑμῶν (2:20, "your welfare," RSV), τὰ Ἰησοῦ Χριστοῦ (2:21, "the cause of Jesus Christ," NEB), and so on. In light of these phrases and the variation of meanings they suggest, it is not unreasonable to understand the phrase τὰ περὶ ἐμέ of v 23 as also within this range of meanings, and to translate it, "my interests," "my cause," or "my welfare."

In other words, what Paul is telling the Philippians is that Timothy is presently indispensable to him in Caesarea, and that his stay with him for the moment is much more important than his anticipated mission to Philippi. He does not give reasons why this is so, but one can conjecture that before the apostle is able to plan his own trip to Philippi (v 24) he must first take care of personal matters—perhaps the gathering of essential data for his final defense, perhaps, more importantly, the working toward reconciling differences among local Christians that he had been responsible for creating (cf. 1:15–17). Since Paul was in prison and his own activities were curtailed, he needed Timothy to do his work for him. Hence, he writes, "When I look to my own affairs, then immediately I will send Timothy on to you."

The striking thing is that Paul expresses the need for delaying Timothy's trip in words reminiscent of those he uses to criticize the Philippians for selfishly looking out for their own interests (cf. v 23 with v 4 in the Greek text). If one should ask why Paul does this, the answer must be either that he does it to underscore his criticism with a touch of irony—"I express my legitimate needs in the vocabulary of the selfish, so you can hear how bad it sounds!" or that he does it to correct misconceptions of his criticism by showing (1) that it is not really wrong to look out for one's own interests, and (2) that it is not even wrong to look out for one's own interests *first* (the translation of the JB is incorrect here). Indeed, there are times when setting one's own house in order is prerequisite to aiding anyone else. What Paul criticizes, then, is a selfish concern for one's own affairs that excludes *any* concern for the affairs of others.

24. The apostle reaffirms what he had stated earlier in 1:25—his confidence (πέποιθα, see comments on 1:6) that he would soon come to Philippi, not in proxy but in person (cf. 1 Cor 4:17, 19). He had no sense of imminent death, nor did he suspect that his hope for immediate release would be disappointed. Nevertheless, as always, his plans for the future were subject to the wishes of his Lord and master and were made ἐν κυρίῳ ("in the Lord"). Hence, he could rest easy without worry (cf. 4:6). The problem of his future was not his to solve, but his Lord's.

Explanation

Since Paul is not himself immediately free to come to Philippi, he decides to send Timothy in his place. For some unexplained reason he feels compelled to justify his decision by elaborately describing the inner and outer qualities of this emissary, to people who should already have known him well: Timothy thinks and feels like Paul. Like Paul he genuinely cares for the Philippians. He stands out from all the rest as ready and willing to undertake a long and difficult journey to them to attempt to resolve a serious problem among them. None of the others who might have been free to travel shares Paul's same sense of urgency or his desire that they drop what they are presently doing in the church at Caesarea to take up responsibilities at the church at Philippi. Paul interprets their reluctance to go as a selfish pursuing of their own interests rather than of Christ's cause. But he judges Timothy's readiness to go as a confirmation of his tried and proven character. Already he has shown himself to the Philippians as Paul's co-laborer, having worked with Paul as a son learning his father's trade. His eagerness to assume the mission to Philippi is proof that he has learned his trade well—that of selfless service to others. Thus he is coming to the Philippians with the blessing of Paul and with apostolic authority.

Paul intends to send Timothy to Philippi soon, but not immediately. He first needs him to handle important personal affairs at Caesarea which he cannot himself take care of. When these matters are cleared up, then Timothy will be on his way immediately. And Paul is confident that he himself will follow soon after.

2. About Epaphroditus (2:25–30)

Bibliography

Beet, J. A. "Epaphroditus and the Gift from Philippi." *Expositor* 3rd series, 9 (1889) 64–75. **Buchanan, C. O.** "Epaphroditus' Sickness and the Letter to the Philippians." *EvQ* 36 (1964) 157–66. **Culpepper, R. A.** *RevExp* 77 (1980) 349–58. **Deissmann, A.** *Light,* 88. **Gnilka, J.** "La carrière du Christ, appel à l'union et à la charité (Ph. 2)."

AsSeign n.s. 57 (1971) 12–19. **Harris, R.** "Epaphroditus, Scribe and Courier." *Expositor* 8 (1898) 101–10. **Jonge, H. J. de.** "Eine Konjektur Joseph Scaligers zu Philipper II 30." *NovT* 17 (1975) 297–302. **Mackay, B. S.** *NTS* 7 (1961) 161–70. **Moffatt, J.** "Philippians II 26 and 2 Tim IV 13." *JTS* 18 (1917) 311–12.

Translation

²⁵ *In the meantime I consider it necessary to send Epaphroditus to you—my brother, my fellow worker, my fellow soldier and your envoy commissioned by you to take care of my needs.* ²⁶ *I must do this because he is very homesick for all of you*ᵃ *and greatly distressed because you heard he was sick.* ²⁷ *Indeed he was sick. He nearly died.*ᵇ *But God took pity on him. And not only on him, but on me as well, so that I might not have to suffer one grief after another.* ²⁸ *I am sending him, therefore, sooner than expected, in order that when you see him again you may be glad, and I may be relieved of anxiety.* ²⁹ *Welcome him, then, as a brother in the Lord with great gladness. Hold people like him in high esteem.* ³⁰ *For he nearly died for the cause of Christ*ᶜ *by risking*ᵈ *his life to give me the help that you yourselves were not able to give.*

Notes

ᵃ ℵ* A C C 33 81 *et al.* add ἰδεῖν here ("he longs *to see* all of you"). This looks like a reconstruction of the text to make it conform to the formula found in Rom 1:11; 1 Thess 3:6; 2 Tim 1:4.

ᵇ The majority text has the dative, θανάτῳ, after παραπλήσιον ("near to death"), while a few other MSS (B P Ψ 81) have the genitive, θανάτου. The genitive may be the original reading if for no other reason than that παραπλήσιον is usually followed by the dative and not the genitive. No difference results in translation.

ᶜ A few MSS (ℵ A P Ψ 33 81) read κυρίου for Χριστοῦ. The expression τὸ ἔργον Χριστοῦ appears nowhere else in Paul, whereas τὸ ἔργον κυρίου is found in 1 Cor 15:58 and 16:10. Κυρίου for Χριστοῦ may therefore, be taken as the result of assimilation. Lightfoot prefers the reading of C which omits both κυρίου and Χριστοῦ (cf. Acts 15:38).

ᵈ The TR reads παραβουλευσάμενος ("having no concern for") instead of παραβολευσάμενος ("to expose to danger, risk"). There is no reason to go against the weighty witness of P⁴⁶ ℵ A B D, etc., and adopt the reading of the TR when παραβολευσάμενος is a good word and makes good sense. "The nervous vigour of St. Paul's style" also argues for παραβολευσάμενος (Lightfoot).

Form/Structure/Setting

This section is totally given over to remarks concerning another of Paul's associates. Although, as noted above, one usually expects to find such matters placed at the end of a letter, this is not the case here. Paul focuses attention upon Epaphroditus at this place in his letter not only to inform the Philippians about one of their own, but to provide them with still another striking illustration of the self-sacrificing service that is demanded of all Christians and is so markedly the central theme of the letter (1:28–2:30). Thus it is connected with what has preceded not only by conjunction (δέ), but by content.

The Philippians had sent Epaphroditus as their envoy (ἀπόστολος, v 25) to bring their gift to Paul (4:18), and perhaps to stay on with him to provide him with whatever continued assistance he might need (v 25). Nothing is known about Epaphroditus beyond what Paul writes about him here—a man deserving of immense praise and respect for the service he gave to the apostle and to the work of Christ. (It is not likely that he should be identified with Epaphras, another of Paul's fellow workers, who came from Colossae: Col 1:7; 4:12; Philem 23). Epaphroditus fell ill, nearly died, recovered and is now being sent to Philippi as the bearer of this letter.

That Paul writes in such a matter-of-fact manner about the journeys of Timothy (2:19–24) and Epaphroditus to Philippi is for some scholars certain proof that Paul could not be writing from Caesarea (or Rome). Surely he would not dare send Epaphroditus, a man who had recently been so grievously ill, on such a long and arduous journey. Ephesus must therefore be the place where Paul was in prison and from where he sends his friends (see Introduction, xxxvi–xliv). Such an argument is weakened, however, by reflecting (1) on the possibility that considerable time had elapsed since Epaphroditus first became ill and that he was now fully recovered, (2) on the fact that travel within the Roman Empire at this time was relatively easy and rapid, and (3) on the impropriety of judging people of the first century in the light of modern expectations of travelling comfort (Houlden). Caesarea, as a place from which this letter came, is thus not ruled out by the details concerning Epaphroditus.

Comment

25. Paul considers it necessary (ἀναγκαῖον ἡγησάμην) to send Epaphroditus to Philippi. Although he uses the aorist tense (ἡγησάμην) to make this statement, he does not mean by it that he has already sent Epaphroditus off on his way home, so that he is no longer with him. Rather this aorist is an "epistolary" aorist, meaning that Paul, in using it, projects himself into the time-bracket of his readers for whom everything he is presently writing about Epaphroditus will belong to the past when the letter reaches them (cf. BDF, 334). It is thus more correctly translated into English by the present tense (JB, NEB, NIV) than by the past tense (KJV). Such a translation leads one to suppose that Epaphroditus himself carried Paul's letter to the church at Philippi. And the way in which the apostle begs the Philippians to give him a cordial welcome (vv 29–30) serves to confirm this supposition. In all likelihood, then, Epaphroditus was the bearer of this letter (Michael).

Paul thought it necessary to send Epaphroditus for at least four reasons: (1) Neither he himself nor Timothy were free to travel at this moment. Only Epaphroditus was immediately available to make the journey. (2) Epaphroditus was from Philippi and had become quite homesick, perhaps seriously so (ἐπιποθῶν ἦν). (3) Epaphroditus had also become gravely ill. News of this illness had reached Philippi and caused his friends to worry. The church there was most anxious to know how he was faring (vv 26–27). (4) As long as Epaphroditus was in the apostle's charge his anxiety over his welfare was immense (cf. v 28). Paul's one decision to send Epaphroditus, who had recovered, home at this critical time resolved all these problems.

Epaphroditus' name was a common name in the first century (BGD, MM). It is interesting to observe that although it embodies the name of Aphrodite, the Greek goddess of love, beauty and fertility—the personification of the sexual instinct—who was worshipped throughout almost all of the Greek world, no believer, not even the apostle Paul, demanded that this leader of the church change his pagan idolatrous name to something more Christian. One reason for such toleration may have been the awareness that a Christian is not one who merely possesses a Christian name. Rather a Christian is one who practices the Christian life. Epaphroditus was in this sense a true Christian, as Paul makes clear in a "singularly emphatic" way by the five nouns he uses to describe him.

The first of these is "brother" (ἀδελφός). This is Paul's favorite synonym for "a Christian" (von Soden, TDNT 1,145). By using it the apostle testifies to the fact that Epaphroditus is indeed one with him in the faith, a fellow member of the family of God, and a person deep in his affections (see the comments on 1:12).

The second noun, "fellow worker" (συνεργός), is a distinctly Pauline word. Paul uses it twelve of the thirteen times it appears in the NT. He does so primarily to describe associates who work together with him in his effort to get the gospel to those places where Christ's name has never been mentioned (Bertram, TDNT 7,871–76). Used here of Epaphroditus, it implies thus that he was not previously unknown to Paul (Caird). Perhaps he was associated with him in the founding of the church at Philippi.

The third noun, "fellow soldier" (συστρατιώτης), implies this same idea of extended association. Only now the focus is on the conflicts they faced together, either at Philippi in earlier days or more recently at Caesarea. It is a military term, used in general of those who fight side by side, and used specifically here by Paul of Epaphroditus and himself as men who fought together against the adversaries of the gospel (cf. 1:28, 30; Rom 16:3, 9; 2 Tim 2:3; Philem 2) or against all the powers of the enemy of God and Christ (cf. Eph 6:10–17; but see Lohmeyer and Bauernfeind, TDNT 7,710–11). This word is a reminder that the Christian shares not only in the work of the gospel but also in consequent suffering.

These three nouns are bound together grammatically with a single definite article heading up the list, and the personal pronoun, μου ("my") closing it—"My brother, my fellow worker, my fellow soldier." So arranged they serve to show the intensity of feeling that Paul had for this otherwise unknown person. His sterling character, his devotion to Paul and his dedication to the cause of Christ unfold still further in the words that follow.

The next set of nouns describing Epaphroditus begins (in the Greek text) with the personal pronoun "your" (ὑμῶν) immediately adjacent to "my" (μου) in an emphatic position that sharply contrasts what Epaphroditus was to Paul with what he was to the Philippians. He is "your envoy" (ὑμῶν ἀπόστολος). Interestingly the word "envoy" ("apostle") is the very word Paul regularly uses to assert his apostolic authority (Rom 1:1; 1 Cor 1:1; 9:1, 2; 2 Cor 1:1; 2:12, etc.), or to describe an elite group of authoritative persons, probably the Twelve, within the church (1 Cor 9:5; 12:28, 29; 2 Cor 11:5, etc.). That Paul now employs it of Epaphroditus is not adequately explained simply by saying he uses it in a "loose sense" (Collange) of "messenger" (cf. 2 Cor 8:23; Rengstorf, TDNT 1,420–24). More likely Paul, in harmony with his whole message to the Philippians, carefully chooses this word to stress again that relationships within the church must not be measured in terms of superiority or inferiority, but of equality. Epaphroditus is equally an "apostle" with Paul in that both were men commissioned and sent out with full authority to perform specific tasks of service.

The final noun describing Epaphroditus is "minister" (λειτουργός), one selected and sent by the Philippians to minister to Paul's needs. Λειτουργός originally referred to public servants of all kinds, even to those who held public office at their own expense. The LXX, however, employed the word group, to which λειτουργός belongs, to describe the priesthood and the sacrificial system (cf. Strathmann, *TDNT* 4,219–22). Thus, when Paul refers to Epaphroditus as λειτουργός ("minister") he may do so because he views Epaphroditus' mission to meet his material needs as a religious act, a priestly function, and Epaphroditus himself as performing the sacred duties of a priest. Support for this suggestion comes from observing that Paul calls the gift Epaphroditus brought him a "sacrifice," (θυσία, 4:18), and from reflecting on the fact that for Paul any practical aid given to those who strive to advance the gospel is worship that is acceptable to God (Rom 12:1, 2; Collange).

This highly valued person, then, is the person Paul decides to send to Philippi. The fact that he uses the absolute πέμψαι ("to send") and not πέμψαι modified by πάλιν or any other preposition or adverb meaning "to send *back*" (JB, NIV), implies that the Philippians had given Epaphroditus to Paul on permanent leave, so to speak, as long as he needed him. "That Paul should have it in his power to decide that Epaphroditus is to return shows" this to be true—"that the Philippians had placed their messenger at the disposal of the apostle" (Michael).

26. Two of the reasons for Paul's decision to send Epaphroditus to Philippi are discussed in this verse and in very strong words—ἐπιποθῶν ἦν and ἀδημονῶν (ἦν). The first of these words, ἐπιποθεῖν, denotes a deep "yearning" or "longing" (cf. 1:8). When the object of this yearning is one's family or friends, as here, it may describe the painful experience of homesickness (Loh and Nida, Martin, Plummer). The other of these words, ἀδημονεῖν, is the same word used of Jesus' anguish in Gethsemane (Mark 14:33). It "describes the confused, restless, half-distracted state which is produced by physical derangement or mental distress" (Lightfoot). Interestingly, this distress seems to have been caused by Epaphroditus' anxiety for the Philippians' anxiety for him upon their learning that he was sick (v 26b). For some interpreters this is strange behavior for a grown man—that he should be worried about their worry for him (Barth). But a second-century papyrus letter written by a soldier to his mother who had somehow learned he was sick, shows that this is quite a natural reaction. This soldier's words parallel the idea expressed in this verse. He writes: "Do not grieve for me. Nevertheless I was exceedingly grieved when I heard that you had heard" of my illness. Like Epaphroditus, this soldier's pain was increased by the knowledge of the pain that news of his illness had caused one who loved him (Moffatt, *JTS* 18 [1917] 311–12).

Furthermore, it needs to be pointed out that both these verbs (ἐπιποθῶν ἦν/ἀδημονῶν [ἦν]), are periphrastics. This kind of construction gives voice to a persistent continuance in something—in this case, in homesickness and in mental distress. Hence, what Epaphroditus was experiencing was not an easily satisfied yearning, on the one hand, or an easily dismissed state of the mind, on the other. Apparently only a trip home could relieve these deep-seated emotional tensions.

27. Paul now confirms in writing what the Philippians had heard by rumor: Epaphroditus had indeed (καὶ γάρ) been sick, in fact, very sick, so sick that he nearly died (παραπλήσιον θανάτῳ, lit. "a near neighbor to death," and again μέχρι θανάτου ἤγγισεν, "he came very near dying" v 30). But strangely Paul says nothing about when Epaphroditus was stricken, whether on the journey to Caesarea (cf. Mackay, NTS 7 [1960–61] 161–70), or after his arrival, nor does he say anything about the nature of his illness or the cause of it. Was it the result of a fever he contracted en route? Was it due to overexertion on his part in giving assistance to Paul and in preaching the gospel? Was it the consequence of foolhardiness? (Michael). No one can say for certain. But whatever it was Paul has no desire to mention it explicitly. He even goes out of his way, it seems, to cast it in the best light possible. All of this points to the fact that Epaphroditus' illness may have been such as to arouse criticism in the minds of the Philippian Christians. Perhaps it was an emotional instability that made him unsuitable for the work for which he was commissioned, a despondency that brought him to death's door, hinted at in the reference to his homesickness and distraught anxiety for all those at Philippi. Whatever it was, Paul is nevertheless generously ready to say that Epaphroditus had subjected himself to this condition for the work of Christ and therefore he is worthy of esteem and not disdain.

It is instructive also to note that Paul says nothing about what led to Epaphroditus' restoration to health. Apparently, however, Paul himself could not command his friend's recovery (Moule). "He mentions neither faith nor prayer nor the laying on of hands any more than he does the effect of medicines or of a doctor. It goes without saying that these various procedures are more or less taken for granted, yet what concerns the apostle is not the healing itself, but its significance. He sees it as a sovereign, merciful act of God himself" (Collange, cf. Hendriksen). Paul's words are ὁ θεὸς ἠλέησεν αὐτόν, "God pitied him, God showed him mercy." In other words, Paul views Epaphroditus' recovery as the direct merciful intervention of God which not only spared a devoted servant for the work of the gospel, but which also spared himself, Paul, the pain of bereavement added to the pain of suffering with a much loved friend during his illness. God thus delivered Paul from "wave upon wave of grief" (λύπην ἐπὶ λύπην). As a servant of Christ Paul was prepared to accept the pain of the death of a friend, recognizing the fact that believers, too, can become ill and even die (2 Kings 13:14; 20:1; John 11:1; Acts 9:37; 2 Cor 12:7–9; Gal 4:13; 1 Tim 5:23; 2 Tim 4:2). But as a normal person he was quite happy to forego this pain of losing Epaphroditus to death. Paul's naturalness and candor here are refreshing, and they serve to temper his words in 1:23. In the final analysis even for Paul death is an enemy (cf. 1 Cor 15:26), and sickness and death are bearers of pain and grief which are not at all anticipated or endured with joy.

28. Because of this illness, then (οὖν), Paul is sending (ἔπεμψα—again the "epistolary" aorist is used here) Epaphroditus home to Philippi sooner (σπουδαιοτέρως) than either he or the Philippians had expected. Σπουδαιοτέρως

is a comparative adverb from σπουδαῖος, which, although through general usage comes to mean "earnest," "serious," has as its root idea "haste" (LSJ). Σπουδαιοτέρως, therefore, while often translated "more carefully," "more eagerly," and so on, seems in context to be better translated according to its fundamental concept—"more hastily" (Meyer, Michael, von Soden, Scott, Vincent). If so, it tends to confirm the supposition that the Philippians had sent Epaphroditus not only with their material gift to Paul, but as their additional gift to him to be permanently added to his staff of co-workers (see above on v 25). Now, however, to the disappointment of all involved and contrary to previous expectations Epaphroditus must go home to Philippi immediately.

The intended result of this change of plans is two fold: (1) that upon seeing Epaphroditus again (taking πάλιν with ἰδόντες and not with χάρητε) the Philippians might be glad (ἵνα χαρῆτε) that he is alive and well rather than angry with him over the fact that he apparently failed in his mission, and (2) that he, Paul, might have less anxiety (ἵνα ἀλυπότερος ὦ) than he would have if Epaphroditus were to stay on in his company.

This reducing of anxiety could be the result either of Paul realizing that he will no longer be responsible for Epaphroditus' well-being, a thing that must have weighed heavily on his mind during the days of illness, or of his realizing that he will no longer need to be concerned about the state of the Philippian church since his valued and trusted friend is there to rally Christians and resolve their differences (Beare).

29–30. These verses combine command and explanation in such a way as to strongly indicate that Paul anticipated problems at Philippi over Epaphroditus' unexpected return. Hence, he wards off this criticism with apostolic authority and orders the Philippians to welcome (προσδέχεσθε) Epaphroditus "in the Lord" (ἐν κυρίῳ). This is to say, Paul orders them to receive Epaphroditus "in the spirit of the Lord" exhibited in the Christ-hymn (2:5–11, cf. Collange), or as the Lord himself welcomes him, or as one Christian should welcome any other Christian (cf. Rom 16:2). Furthermore, he orders them to welcome him "with all joy" (μετὰ πάσης χαρᾶς), that is, "wholeheartedly," "without ill humor" or "too facile reproaches" (Barth), and to do it with respect. Such people as Epaphroditus must be held in high esteem (ἐντίμους ἔχετε), especially because of what they have done.

In this instance Epaphroditus nearly lost his life because of the important work he did in behalf of the Philippian Christians. He left home, undertook a long and difficult journey, subjected himself to physical and emotional stresses of the severest kind, exposed himself to possible persecution—and he did all this (1) because of his desire to serve Christ (διὰ τὸ ἔργον Χριστοῦ), and (2) because of his determination to fulfill the mission of his church.

But Paul's high commendation of Epaphroditus does not come simply because of what he did, great as this may have been. It comes also because of why he did it. His was a self-renouncing motivation. He chose against himself for someone else: "He came close to losing his life," Paul writes the Philippians, "because he staked his life (παραβολευσάμενος τῇ ψυχῇ) to give me the help you were not able to give me yourselves" (cf. NEB). The vigor of Paul's

vocabulary here could not but totally overcome any remaining prejudice the
Philippians may have had against Epaphroditus. The participle παραβολευσάμενος, translated here "staked," is especially powerful and in all likelihood
Paul coined it. No lexicon cites it earlier than Phil 2:30. It seems, however,
to have been created from the verb παραβάλλεσθαι, "to throw down a stake,"
"to make a venture," or from the noun παράβολος, "gambling," "rash," "reck-
less," or from παραβολᾶνοι, "persons who risk their lives to nurse those sick
with the plague" (LSJ, Lightfoot). Deissmann notes that this hitherto unknown
word—in fact the very participial form Paul uses here—has been discovered
in an ancient (second century A.D.) inscription found at Olbia on the Black
Sea, meaning "to daringly expose oneself to danger" (Light, 84–85, 88; cf.
deJonge, NovT 17 [1975] 297–302). Thus from this word alone it is clear
that Epaphroditus was no coward, but a courageous person willing to take
enormous risks, ready to play with very high stakes in order to come to the
aid of a person in need. He did not "save" his life, but rather hazarded it
to do for Paul and for the cause of Christ what other Philippian Christians
did not or could not do. Such a word as παραβολεύεσθαι, then, "brings its
own challenge and rebuke to an easy-going Christianity which makes no stern
demands, and calls for no limits of self-denying, self-effacing sacrifice" (Martin,
Philippians, 1959).

But in coining this gambling term Paul may have been influenced by Epaphroditus' name. H. C. Lees pointed out that Aphrodite (or Venus) was
the goddess of gamblers, and whenever a Greek made the highest cast he
cried out ἐπαφρόδιτος ("epaphroditos")—"favorite of Aphrodite (Venus),"
hoping by this "invocation" to be blessed with gambler's luck in the throw
of the dice because the divine hand was behind it (cf. Plut. Vit. Sull. 34; see
LSJ). This then may be the meaning behind Epaphroditus' name. If so, Paul
may have written παραβολευσάμενος "with a smile as he did when he played on
the name Onesimus in his letter to Philemon. He says Epaphroditus gambled
with his life, but won because God was there" (Lees, ExpTim 37 [1925] 46).

The purpose behind Epaphroditus' gambling with his life is stated in the
clause introduced by ἵνα ("in order that"). It is a difficult clause to translate
into English. Literally it goes, "in order that he may fulfill your lack of service
to me." But such a literal translation leaves one with a rather bad impression
of the Philippians. There is nothing, however, in the Greek to indicate that
Paul was annoyed with those at Philippi or was censuring them for failing
to do for him what they could and should have done. Rather the opposite
is the case (cf. GNB, NEB, NIV, RSV). Paul gratefully recognizes that they had
done all they could. Thus in praising Epaphroditus he praises them, for he
sees in Epaphroditus the whole Philippian congregation engaged in a sacred
ministration (λειτουργία) to meet his needs (cf. 1 Cor 16:17). Epaphroditus
was their envoy to him, their way of telling him that they cared enough to
send their very best (cf. v 25). "He thus in this single sentence recognizes
the devotion of Epaphroditus and the good-will of the Philippians, and expresses pleasure which he himself would have had in their personal presence
and ministry" (Vincent; cf. also Beare, Gnilka, Martin, Philippians, 1976, Michael).

Explanation

Neither Paul nor Timothy are free to set off immediately for Philippi to help bring about harmony among the Christians there. Paul's solution to the problem was to let Epaphroditus go in their place. In many respects this was a happy solution: (1) Epaphroditus was from Philippi. (2) He was valued and trusted both by the Philippians and Paul (v 25). (3) Paul thus could count on him to plead for the unity he desired, and the Philippians would listen to him as a spokesman whom they respected. (4) Epaphroditus was homesick and longed to be with his Philippian friends once again. (5) The Philippians had heard of Epaphroditus' near-fatal illness and they anxiously awaited news of his condition. For Paul to send him home at this time, therefore, answered Epaphroditus' need, the Philippians questions about his health and Paul's own desire for an authoritative spokesman in his behalf in a division-troubled church.

And yet this decision to send Epaphroditus to Philippi sooner than expected carried its own peculiar risks. Apparently the Philippian church had commissioned Epaphroditus to carry their gift to Paul and to stay on with him as a permanent member of his staff. To be sent home, as it were, would very likely raise many questions: Why is he here? Why did he become sick? Could he not stand the strain? Was he unable to get along with the apostle? For these reasons, and perhaps others, Paul purposely says nothing about the nature of Epaphroditus' illness, and at the same time goes out of his way to extol him with the highest praise. It is clear, therefore, that Paul wanted no misunderstanding at Philippi about this good man. He wanted no underrating of his worth, no questioning of his character, no erosion of his authority. Epaphroditus is a man worthy of the greatest esteem, deserving to be thrust into leadership positions at Philippi, not slighted or treated with disdain. After all, had he not nearly died doing what the Philippians themselves could not do?

III. Warning against False Teachings with Paul's Experience and Life as a Model to Follow (3:1-21)

A. Warning against Circumcision and Pride in Human Achievements (3:1-3)

Bibliography

Fridrichsen, A. "Exegetisches zu den Paulusbriefen." *TSK* 102 (1930) 291–301. **Kilpatrick, G. D.** "ΒΛΕΠΕΤΕ, Philippians 3:2." *In Memoriam Paul Kahle*, ed. M. Black and G. Fohrer. BZAW 103, Berlin: A. Töpelmann, 1928, 146–48. **Köster, H.** "The Purpose of the Polemic of a Pauline Fragment (Philippians III)." *NTS* 8 (1961–62) 317–32. **Moehring, H. R.** "Some Remarks on σάρξ in Phil. 3:3ss." *TU* 102 (1968) 432–36. **Polhill, J. B.** "Twin Obstacles in the Christian Path: Philippians 3." *RevExp* 77 (1980) 359–72. **Tannehill, R. C.** *Dying and Rising with Christ. A Study in Pauline Theology.* BZNW 32. Berlin: A. Töpelmann, 1967. **Zerwick, M.** "Gaudium et pax custodia cordium (Phil. 3,1; 4,7)." *VD* 31 (1953) 101–104.

Translation

¹ *Well then, my brothers, rejoice in the Lord! To keep writing this same command is never wearisome to me and for you it is a* ᵃ *safe course to follow.* ² *Observe those dogs! Observe those evil doers! Observe those mutilators!* ³ *I call them "mutilators" for we are the circumcision—we who worship God* ᵇ *by his spirit, and who boast in Christ Jesus, and who put no confidence in ourselves.*

Notes

ᵃ A few minor MSS add the definite article τό before ἀσφαλές.

ᵇ ℵ² D* P Ψ and a few other MSS read θεῷ instead of θεοῦ. This reading should be rejected (1) because it is poorly attested, and (2) because it is an obvious attempt to ease an apparent difficulty: λατρεύειν takes the dative, not the genitive, as its object. The only dative is πνεύματι (θεοῦ). To avoid the possibility of anyone thinking that Paul meant to say, "We worship the Spirit of God," θεοῦ was changed to θεῷ and πνεύματι then could only be construed as instrument, not as object. P⁴⁶ has neither θεοῦ nor θεῷ. Neither word is necessary for in context λατρεύειν of necessity means "to worship God."

Form/Structure/Setting

This section, along with the rest of chap. 3, continues the body of the letter. Admittedly it is not always easy to outline the flow of Paul's thought, or adequately to account for the swift changes of subjects that occur without warning. But it is not necessary to resort to a theory of multiple letters in order to explain these phenomena (see Introduction, xxix–xxxii; Pollard, *NTS* 13 [1966] 57–59; Mackay, *NTS* 7 [1961] 161–63). In an informal letter like Philippians, written from prison, written at a distance from one's friends, written without full knowledge of the problems they faced, written with emotions running high, one can expect to find just such violent breaks in structure and thought as those that are present here. Paul's style "corresponds not with the desire to express a homogeneous conception, but with the requirement proper to private speech" (Dibelius, *Fresh Approach*, 166–67).

Thus it should not be surprising to discover in these verses a radical and rapid shift in Paul's tone from that of joy and affection for the Philippian Christians (v 1) to that of violent hostility against those who would undermine the spiritual vitality of his friends. Nor is this swift alteration of the apostle's mood unique to this section. It is found in other of his letters (cf. Gal 3:1; 4:21) and elsewhere in Phil (1:16–17).

That Paul's emotions are running high can be seen not only in the vivid and even abusive language he uses to describe his opponents ("dogs," "workers of evil," "mutilators"), but also in the large number of figures of speech that appear in so brief a paragraph: (1) anaphora, the repetition of the same word (βλέπετε) at the beginning of three successive clauses, (2) paronomasia, the clever play on words, similar in sound (κατατομήν/περιτομή) but set in opposition to each other so as to provide heightened antithetical force, (3) polysyndeton, the repetition of the same conjunction (καί) in close succession, (4) alliteration in -κ (κύνας . . . κακούς . . . κατατομήν), (5) short disjointed cola, sentences of approximately the same length, and (6) chiasm, where the noun-phrases alternate positions in a criss-cross fashion with the participles—all employed for rhetorical effect. Thus, Paul, who prefers not to use the clever techniques of the sophists (cf. 1 Cor 2), is nevertheless quite able to do so. In fact, it appears that his passionate reaction to those who wish to lead the Philippians astray breaks down whatever rhetorical restrictions he might normally place upon himself and allows him to give verbal vent to his feelings. But unfortunately translators either cannot preserve or are unwilling to express these figures in translation. As a consequence the vigor of the apostle's emotions is moderated so that its full force escapes the English reader.

These opponents of the gospel of grace that Paul preached appear to be visitors from abroad who were threatening to undo the work of the apostle at Philippi. Apparently they required that men be circumcised before they could acceptably worship God. According to Paul their religion was a ritual of externals that fostered pride in their own achievements instead of a boasting in Christ Jesus, and that encouraged a confidence in themselves instead of a reliance upon the Spirit.

Who were these opponents? It is not possible to say with certainty, but everything known about them points to the assumption that they were Jews—evangelistically oriented Jews who had their own missionaries (cf. Matt 23:15), who were insisting on physical signs of initiation, priding themselves on their privileges of pedigree (vv 5–6), and proclaiming a message of righteousness and perfection that was attainable *now* simply by submitting to circumcision and complying with certain food laws (see Introduction, xliv–xlvii).

Comment

1. This section begins with the words τὸ λοιπόν. Although most translators translate them as "finally," or "in conclusion" (GNB, KJV, JB, NIV, RSV), and although they may on a rare occasion be used to signal the end of a letter

(cf. 2 Cor 13:11), they also serve equally well to mark a transition to a new topic (cf. 1 Thess 4:1; 2 Thess 3:1). Since the integrity of Philippians is assumed (see Introduction, xxix–xxxii), and since there is no doubt that Paul is introducing new subject matter, it is best, therefore, to translate τὸ λοιπόν as "and now" (Goodspeed, Knox), "furthermore" (Houlden), or "well then" (Moffatt; see Moule, *Idiom-Book*, 161–62).

Χαίρετε, wrongly translated here as "good-bye" (Goodspeed) or "farewell" (NEB), is Paul's special imperative, "rejoice!" which runs like a friendly refrain throughout his letter to the Philippians (2:18; 3:1; 4:4; cf. also 1:18; 2:17, 28; 4:10). Here, however, for the first time Paul adds to this verb, "rejoice," the phrase ἐν κυρίῳ ("in the Lord"), and by doing so indicates both the true basis of Christian joy and the sphere in which it thrives (see comments on 1:4).

But to make certain the Philippians understand that he does not write this word, χαίρετε, with unthinking repetitiveness, Paul stops briefly to comment on what he is doing. He tells them in an aside (v 1*b*) that his persistence in this matter is no onerous chore that wearies him (ὀκνηρόν), but a happy task. For he sees his repeated appeals to joy (τὰ αὐτά) as a means of guaranteeing their safety (ἀσφαλές), a safeguard to their souls (Phillips). That is to say, Paul believes that if only the Philippian Christians will obey his call to rejoice, they will discover that this positive Christian attitude will save them from the ills that plague their church—murmurings, dissensions, empty conceit, and so on. For "joy of any kind is a safeguard against the utilitarian attitude which judges people and things wholly by the use that can be made of them; and Christian joy, the exaltation of spirit that flows from acceptance of the free gifts of God's grace, is the best protection" of all against such a negative and divisive outlook upon life (Caird; see also Alford, Dibelius, Ellicott, Lohmeyer, Moffatt. But in opposition to this explanation cf. Barth, Collange, Furnish, *NTS* 10 [1963] 80–83; Jones, Martin, Müller, who understand v 1*b* either as an introduction to what is to follow, or as a reference to something outside this particular letter, i.e. to warnings given orally by Paul or written to the Philippians in previous letters now lost. In reality, v 1*b* is quite enigmatic, and one cannot be absolutely certain about its meaning).

2. Three times over in quick succession Paul now uses the imperative βλέπετε followed by the accusative case—noun-phrases each with the definite article and each beginning with a *k*-sound: τοὺς κύνας . . . τοὺς κακοὺς ἐργάτας . . . τὴν κατατομήν. Thus Paul gives rhetorical expression to the very deep concern he has about the seriousness of the problem that faces his friends. (Every effort should be made clearly to articulate this concern in translation, preserving the form in which it comes as much as it is possible to do so.)

Βλέπετε here is traditionally translated "beware of," "be on your guard against." But for it to have this meaning it should be followed by an objective clause introduced by μή ("lest," Matt 8:4; 18:10; Mark 1:44; Heb 3:12; BDF 364.2; 369.2), or by the preposition ἀπό ("of," "from": καὶ σὺ βλέπε σατὸν ἀπὸ τῶν Ἰουδαίων—"you too beware of the Jews"—from a letter dated A.D. 41; see Hunt and Edgar, *Select Papyri*, 1.298). A more accurate translation, therefore, notwithstanding the threefold repetition of βλέπετε, and one more in harmony with Greek usage is: "consider," "take proper notice of," "pay attention to," or "learn your lesson from" (cf. 1 Cor 1:26; 10:18; 2 Cor 10:7; Col 4:17; see Kilpatrick, "BΛEΠETE," 146–48). Thus Paul is not so much warning the Philippians to be on guard against their opponents, as he is asking them to pay careful attention to them, to study them, so as to understand them and to avoid adopting their destructive beliefs and practices (Caird).

These opponents were not Judaizers, i.e. Jewish Christians, but Jews (see Introduction, xliv–xlvii), whom Paul in a passionate outburst calls "dogs, evildoers, mutilators."

The Jews were in the habit of referring contemptuously to Gentiles as dogs—unclean creatures with whom they would not associate if such association could be avoided (cf. Matt 15:21–28; Michel, *TDNT* 3,1101–1104; Str-B 1, 724–25; 3, 621–22). Paul now hurls this term of contempt back "on the heads of its authors" (Caird; Barth, Collange, Dibelius), for to Paul the Jews were the real pariahs that defile the holy community, the Christian church, with their erroneous teaching (Jewett, *NovT* 12 [1970] 386).

The Jews prided themselves on keeping the Law. Their sense of superiority, therefore, was due in large part to the fact that they performed accurately the works (ἔργα) demanded by God's Law (cf. Rom 3:20). They thus viewed themselves as good workers (καλοὶ ἐργάται), noble observers of the Law. But instead Paul calls them evil workers (κακοὺς ἐργάτας), "not because they do what is morally wrong, nor because they act out of malice, but . . . because their reliance on 'works' is in the end harmful both to themselves and to others" (Caird). They are harmful in that such reliance is ultimately self-reliance and tends to obscure the need for God, who alone is the source of true life and goodness. Like the Christian missionary, a worker (ἐργάτης) sent to harvest the grain (Matt 9:38), these Jews, too, were ardent propagandists sent out to preach a gospel which in Paul's understanding was no gospel (cf. Gal 1:6–9). The effects of their efforts could only be disastrous, endangering the relationship of the Christian with Christ and with God (Beare), undermining the very foundation of Paul's message, namely, that no one is justified in the eyes of God by the works of the Law, but only by faith in Christ. Hence, they are nothing less than κακοὶ ἐργάται ("evil workers").

The Jews originally understood circumcision as a symbol of the covenant relationship that existed between themselves and God. In time, however, many lost sight of its symbolic nature and made it a thing of value in itself as an external rite indispensable for establishing a correct standing before God. As a consequence the inner devotion and dedication of the heart that God required and that the prophets had long since insisted must accompany the rite (Jer 4:4; Ezek 44:7; cf. also Lev 26:41; Deut 10:16; 30:6; 1QS 5:5, 26) was neglected, if not removed altogether, by Jewish teachers who gave preeminence to the practice of the rite of circumcision. But for Paul, the Christian, this practice was done away with in Jesus. The covenant relationship once symbolized by circumcision is now perfectly realized in Christ, in his death and resurrection (cf. Matt 26:27–28). Hence, the external rite is no longer required. For just as the ancient prophets had perceived, "a man is not a Jew who is one outwardly, nor is circumcision outward and physical. No, a man is a Jew if he is one inwardly; and circumcision is circumcision of the heart by the Spirit not by the written code" (Rom 2:28–29; cf. Col 3:11). Thus, for Israel to insist on a purely physical and external rite as the means of securing salvation, now that the Christ has come, is not only benighted, it is wicked. Paul, therefore, attacks these champions of circumcision by using a pun filled with bitter irony: they are the κατατομή (katatomē, "the mutilation," "the cutters," "those who mutilate the body"; cf. 1 Kings 18:28; Gal 5:12; see also DeVries, "Paul's 'Cutting' Remarks," 115–20) instead of the περιτομή (peritomē, "the circumcision"; cf. M. E. Glasswell, "New Wine in Old Wine-Skins: VIII. Circumcision." ExpTim 85 [1973–74] 328–32; Köster, NTS 8 [1961–62] 320–31).

3. Paul now explains why he uses the term κατατομή ("mutilation") to describe ancient Israel and not περιτομή ("circumcision"). As is often the case elsewhere, Paul's explanation here is so compact that it needs expansion to be understood readily. When one does so, the apostle's argument seems to proceed as follows: Because (γάρ) Israel lost sight of the spiritual significance of circumcision, focused on the external ritual and failed to boast in the Lord alone (cf. Jer 9:23–25), it has forfeited its right to the title, "The Circumcision." The church of Jesus Christ, however (against Tillmann), is the true Israel (Gal 6:16), heir of all the rights and privileges belonging to it (Rom 9:24–26; 1 Pet 2:9–10), including the right to the title, περιτομή ("circumcision"). "We," says Paul emphatically, "are the circumcision," and not they.

He now enlarges upon this idea by means of a series of participial phrases. The first of these is οἱ πνεύματι θεοῦ λατρεύοντες ("who worship by the Spirit of God": "We are the circumcision who worship by the Spirit of God").

The participle λατρεύοντες is formed from the verb λατρεύειν which originally meant "to work for wages," then simply, "to render service," with no thought of reward or whether the one who serves is slave or free. Interestingly, this word was often employed by the LXX translators to denote the worship or service rendered to Yahweh by his chosen people, Israel (Exod 23:25; Deut 6:12; 10:12, 20; Josh 22:27, etc.; cf. Rom 9:4; Strathmann, TDNT 4,58–61). In this last fact lies the significance of its use here. The proud privilege of ancient Israel, to love and serve God from the heart (ἀγαπᾶν καὶ λατρεύειν, see Deut 10:12) has now been transferred to the New Israel. And why? The implied reason is that the Jews turned from this inner spiritual worship of God from the heart (cf. Ps 51:17) to an external religion of ritual, where human ordinances displaced divine commands and where people honored God with their lips but not with their hearts (Isa 29:13; cf. Matt 15:8–9; Mark 7:6–7).

The Christian, by contrast, whatever outward forms and ceremonies he may use in worship, is not deflected by these from worshiping God "in spirit and truth" (cf. John 4:23–24). This is to say that the Christian is one whose actions, including worship of God, is not directed by some external law that he must strive to live up to, or external ritual he can perform and about which he can boast, but by the impulse of the Spirit of God within him (for the phrase, "Spirit of God" in Paul, cf. Rom 8:9, 14; 1 Cor 7:40; 12:3; 2 Cor 3:3; see E. F. Scott, The Spirit in the New Testament [London: Hodder and Stoughton, 1923]; G. W. H. Lampe, God as Spirit [Oxford: Clarendon

Press, 1977]). The Spirit promised by the prophets (Ezek 36:25–27), dwelling within the Christian, gives to the Christian life and power and love so that he can offer to God true and acceptable worship from the heart (John 4:23–24; Rom 12:1; 1 Pet 2:5). But yet there is more involved here in Paul's words than a simple contrast between external and internal religion (Michael, Müller). The apostle's choice of the verb λατρεύειν for worship, modified as it is by πνεύματι θεοῦ, stresses the fact that the Spirit of God is the divine initiator at work in the depths of human nature, profoundly transforming a person's life so as to promote a life of love and service, so as to generate a life for others, for "such a life is the only worship [λατρεύειν] acceptable to God" (Collange).

The second participial phrase Paul uses to explain further why Christians and not Jews are the circumcision is καυχώμενοι ἐν Χριστῷ Ἰησοῦ. The verb καυχᾶσθαι, used only this once in Philippians, is a favorite of Paul. He uses it at least thirty times in his letters, and other writers only use it twice. Translated here "rejoice in" (KJV), or "glory in" (LB, NIV, RSV), it is only proper to give to it in this context "its noblest meaning" (Michael; cf. Betz, *Galatians, passim*), namely, "to boast in," "to pride oneself in" (BGD; NEB, Phillips). For here Christians are rightfully described as possessing a triumphant, exultant, boastful attitude, not in themselves, however, nor in their accomplishments, or personal goodness (cf. Gal 6:13), but in Christ Jesus. Theirs is no hollow confidence in an external rite or "heritage of law or privilege of race" (Beare). Rather, their basis of pride, their reason for boasting, their grounds for full and exultant confidence is God himself, who acted in grace and mercy toward all people in Christ Jesus (Gal 6:14; cf. Jer 9:23–24; 1 Cor 1:31). Christians are the circumcision precisely because they take no pride in what they might do by themselves to earn God's favor, but only in what God in his favor has already done for them in Christ Jesus. The Christian's boasting begins where knowledge of the Law and the corresponding ceremonial and moral righteousness cease, namely, "at the point where . . . man lays down his arms, [and] where God *entirely* alone begins to speak, utters his *Word of grace* which man can do *no more* than believe" (Barth).

The final participial phrase is, οὐκ ἐν σαρκὶ πεποιθότες (lit. "who have no confidence in the flesh"), a phrase which negatively restates the immediately preceding claim that the Christian does have grounds for confidence, but not ἐν σαρκί.

The word σάρξ ("flesh") is in itself an ambiguous word embracing a whole range of meanings from physical flesh (Luke 24:39), to human nature (John 1:14), to fallen human nature (Rom 7:5; 8:9, 19), and so on (see Schweizer, *TDNT* 7,125–51). By using it here Paul seems to cast at least a passing glance at the rite of circumcision, an operation performed on the body—in the flesh— as the sign and seal of membership within the covenant community of God (cf. W. D. Davies, *Christian Origins and Judaism*, [Philadelphia: Westminster Press, 1962] 145–77). It is more likely, however, that Paul is using σάρξ in his customary way to denote "'man's lower' unredeemed nature, not inherently bad but the target of sin's attack and the occasion of his becoming a victim under sin's dominion" (Martin, *Philippians*, 1976). Here, then, σάρξ really pictures man at his highest and best, striving to achieve an adequate status before God, but without dependence upon God. It pictures him counting on his privilege and position and ability to fulfil the Law of God and to attain to the righteousness that God requires, without realizing that such righteousness can be attained only by abandoning self and throwing oneself wholly on the mercy and grace of God. "It is this self-reliance, this confidence in his own capacity to please God and earn a favorable verdict from the Judge, which vitiates the religion of the Jew even when he follows it with the utmost devoted zeal for God and the most sincere striving to fulfil his law" (Beare; cf. Rom 10:3). Therefore, Christians and not the Jews are the circumcision because they do not make such a fatal error. Instead of arrogantly relying on themselves (ἐν σαρκὶ πεποιθότες), they humbly submit to God and accept the gracious gift of righteousness offered them in Christ Jesus. They thus become "the seed of Abraham" (Gal 3:29), the "sons of Abraham" (Gal 3:7) through faith in Christ Jesus (cf. Jer 4:4; Gal 6:14–15; Col 2:11–13; see Fitzmyer; Moehring, *TU* 102 [1968] 32–36; Ridderbos, *Paul* 138).

B. *Paul's Life, Past and Present: An Answer to Judaism (3:4–11)*

Bibliography

Ahern, B. M. "The Fellowship of His Sufferings (Phil. 3, 10)." *CBQ* 22 (1960) 1–32. **Baeck, L.** *Paulus, die Pharisäer und das Neue Testament.* Frankfurt am Main: Ner-Tamid Verlag, 1961. **Conzelmann, H.** "Current Problems in Pauline Research, IV: The Righteousness of God." *Int* 22 (1968) 178–82. **Dupont, J.** *Gnosis: La connaissance religieuse dans les épîtres de saint Paul.* Bruges: Desclée, de Brouwer, 1949. **Ferrar, W. J.** "A Study on Paul." *Expositor,* 8th series 23 (1922) 353–59. **Fitzmyer, J. A.** "To Know Him and the Power of His Resurrection; Phil. 3:10." *Mélanges B. Rigaux,* ed. A. Descamps and A. de Halleux. Gembloux: Duculot, 1970. **Forestell, J. T.** "Christian Perfection and Gnosis in Phil. 3, 7–16." *CBQ* 18 (1956) 123–36. **Gärtner, B.** "The Pauline and Johannine Idea 'To Know God' Against the Hellenistic Background." *NTS* 14 (1967–68) 209–31. **Goguel, M.** "Κατὰ δικαιοσύνην τὴν ἐν νόμῳ γενόμενος ἄμεμπτος (Phil. 3, 6). Remarques sur un aspect de la conversion de Paul." *JBL* 53 (1934) 257–67. **Gremmels, C.** "Selbstreflexive Interpretation konfligierender Identifikationen am Beispiel des Apostels Paulus (Phil. 3, 7–9)." *Theologische Existenz heute* 182 (1974) 44–57. **Käsemann, E.** " 'The Righteousness of God' in Paul." *New Testament Questions of Today.* Philadelphia: Fortress Press, 1969. **Kuhn, H. B.** "Phil. 3, 10–12: Issues in Discussion." *Asbury Seminarian* 29 (1974) 32–38. **Léon-Dufour, X.** "Quand parle un témoin. Dans l'épître aux Philippiens." *Resurrection de Jésus et message pascal.* Paris: Editions du Seuil, 1971. **Moule, C. F. D.** "Once More, Who Were the Hellenists?" *ExpTim* 70 (1958–59) 100–102. **Müller, C.** *Gottes Gerechtigkeit und Gottes Volk.* Göttingen: Vandenhoeck und Ruprecht, 1964. **Owen, J. J.** "Examination of Philip. 3:11 and Rev. 20:4." *BSac* 21 (1864) 362–83. **Polhill, J. B.** *RevExp* 77 (1980) 359–72. **Reicke, B.** "Paul's Understanding of Righteousness." *Soli Deo Gloria,* ed. J. M. Richards. Richmond, VA: John Knox Press, 1968. **Roach, S. N.** "The Power of His Resurrection." *RevExp* 24 (1927) 45–55, 297–304; 25 (1928) 29–38, 176–94. **Siber, P.** *Mit Christus Leben. Eine Studie zur paulinischen Auferstehungshoffnung.* Zürich: Theologischer Verlag, 1971. **Stanley, D. M.** " 'Become Imitators of me.' The Pauline Conception of Apostolic Tradition." *Bib* 40 (1959) 857–77. **Stuhlmacher, P.** *Gerechtigkeit Gottes bei Paulus.* Göttingen: Vandenhoeck und Ruprecht, 1965. **Tannehill, R. C.** *Dying and Rising with Christ.* BZNW 32. Berlin: Töpelmann, 1967. **Unnik, W. C. van.** *Tarsus or Jerusalem? The City of Paul's*

Youth. Tr. G. Ogg. London: Epworth Press, 1962. **Ziesler, J. A.** *The Meaning of Righteousness in Paul.* Cambridge: Cambridge University Press, 1972.

Translation

⁴ *Although I have good reasons for putting confidence in myself, I will not do so. But if any other person thinks that he has reasons for confidence in himself I have more reasons than he:* ⁵ *I was circumcised on the eighth day of my life. I am an Israelite by birth. I belong to the tribe of Benjamin. I am a Hebrew born of Hebrew parents. With regard to the Jewish Law I was a Pharisee.* ⁶ *With regard to zeal* ª *I was a persecutor of the church.* ᵇ *With regard to a righteousness based on the Law I was a blameless person.* ⁷ *But* ᶜ *what things were then gain to me, I now count as loss because of Christ.* ⁸ *And what is more,* ᵈ *I continue to count everything as loss because of the one supreme value, namely, a personal knowledge of Christ* ᵉ *Jesus my Lord. For him I did in fact lose everything. But I consider it all as unspeakable filth for the goal of gaining Christ* ⁹ *and of being found in him, not with my own righteousness, earned by keeping the Law, but with God's righteousness given through faith in Christ—the righteousness that is given by God and is obtained through faith.* ¹⁰ *Yes, I consider everything as unspeakable filth for the goal of knowing Christ in the power of his resurrection, and in the* ᵍ *fellowship of his sufferings,* ᵍ *continually conforming myself to his death* ¹¹ *in the hope of attaining the resurrection from among the dead.* ʰ

Notes

ª The majority text reads ζῆλον (masculine) for ζῆλος (neuter). There is no difference in meaning but the masculine form is the more common form in the NT.

ᵇ F G and a few other MSS add θεοῦ after ἐκκλησίαν—an attempt, perhaps, to harmonize this text with 1 Cor 10:32; 11:16, 22; 15:9; 2 Cor 1:1; Gal 1:13; 1 Thess 2:14; 2 Thess 1:4; see also 1 Tim 3:5, 15.

ᶜ p⁴⁶ ℵ G 33 and other MSS omit ἀλλά, while B D Ψ and the majority text include it. Ἀλλά seems to be the *lectio facilior*, and therefore secondary.

ᵈ p⁴⁶ (apparently) ℵ* 33 and other MSS omit the καί, possibly because of the superfluity of conjunctions at the beginning of this verse.

ᵉ p⁴⁶ p⁶¹ and B add the definite article τοῦ before Χριστοῦ Ἰησοῦ.

ᶠ A Ψ and the majority text add εἶναι after ἡγοῦμαι σκύβαλα, but this addition of the infinitive in indirect discourse is quite unnecessary.

ᵍ p⁴⁶ ℵ* B omit the articles τὴν (κοινωνίαν) and τῶν (παθημάτων), while ℵ² D F G Ψ and the majority text include them. It appears that scribes, understanding κοινωνίαν as a totally separate entity exactly parallel with δύναμιν, added the article τὴν to make this distinction and parallelism clear. Hence, the τὴν should be considered secondary.

ʰ τῶν νεκρῶν (majority text) is read instead of τὴν ἐκ νεκρῶν (p¹⁶, ⁴⁶ ℵ A B D P Ψ 33 81 and Latin and Sahidic versions). The mild τῶν νέκρων, though more the common phrase, eliminates the striking emphasis of ἐξανάστασις ἐκ. It must be considered secondary.

Form/Structure/Setting

In this section, linked as it is to the previous one by the cognate noun πεποίθησιν (πεποιθότες [v 3] . . . πεποίθησιν [v 4]), Paul begins to explain to his friends why he has spoken so harshly against the Jews. Using himself, "an authentic Jew" (Benoit), as an example, he draws back the curtain on his past religious life so as to permit the Philippians to understand, not abstractly but concretely, what it means to consider oneself no longer religious except through the Spirit, no longer able to boast except in Christ Jesus, and no longer able to rely on human privilege or achievement to gain favor with God (see Barth). One is not surprised, therefore, to note the preponderance of the first person singular pronoun running throughout this section. Such a phenomenon not only accords well with the highly personal character of Philippians, but it accentuates the intensely personal nature of Paul's own religious experience. Nowhere else in his letters does Paul make so clear, and with such feeling, how vitally important the person of Christ is to him, and how tremendous was the impact of the resurrected Christ upon his life and outlook as he does here in these verses. Here is "one of the most remarkable personal confessions which antiquity has bequeathed to us" (Bonnard, as quoted by Martin, *Philippians*, 1959).

But as a preface to this humble confession of reliance upon Christ, Paul, in what seems to be a rather surprising way, first presents his own pedigree, listing his heritage and achievements as bases for personal boasting (καύχημα; cf. v 3) or as grounds for showing that he is "somebody" (cf. H. D. Betz, "On Self-praise," in H. D. Betz [ed.], *Plutarch's Ethical Writings and Early Christian Literature* [Leiden: E. J. Brill, 1978] 367–78; on the whole subject of "boasting," see Bultmann, *TDNT* 3,645–54). Paul may be doing this to "put down" his adversaries, since the form he uses is somewhat reminiscent of epideictic oratory—a speech-form designed to praise or blame. Topics for such oratory on which praise was founded—descent, education, wealth, kinds of power, titles to fame, citizenship, and so on—could also serve as bases for blame (see Cicero, *Ad Herennium* [LCL 403 Cambridge: Harvard University Press, 1954] 173–75; Plato, *Grg.* 477C; *Phlb.* 48E; *Leg.* 697B, 727A–C; Aristotle, *Rh. Al.* 1440b 13; *Eth. Nic.* 1. 8, 1098b). Hence, Paul in praising himself may simply be attempting to diminish the status of his opponents by implicitly faulting them for not being his equal. Notice that Paul uses the ancient technique of comparison (ἐγὼ μᾶλλον—"I more than they," v 4) in his favor and to the disadvantage of those with whom he compares himself (see Betz, *Galatians* 303).

Whether this can be satisfactorily demonstrated may not be certain. But one thing can be said with assurance: Paul recounts matters of his descent, rights and privileges, titles to distinction, and so on at this crucial point in his letter not really to exalt himself (boasting about himself is distasteful to the apostle—2 Cor 11:16–29; 12:1–10), but to make clear to all that, when he proceeds to disparage personal assets which can make one proud and self-reliant, he does so not because he is a "have-not," a frustrated person lashing out in envy due to his own lack of resources or achievements, but because he is one who, although having everything, learned he had nothing, not having Christ.

There are themes and words in this section which link it with earlier parts of Philippians, and which argue still more strongly for its integrity (see Pollard, *NTS* 13 [1966] 57–59; Mackay, *NTS* 7 (1961) 161–63). For example, the expression, "being found in human form" (2:8) is echoed in the words, "that

I may be found in him" (3:9). The purpose of God in exalting Jesus—that every person should openly and gladly acknowledge him as Lord (2:11)—is answered by Paul's confession, "Christ Jesus *my Lord*" (3:8). The rare word κέρδος is found both in 1:21 and 3:7. "More broadly, it is certainly the case that the themes of humility and obedience are common to both parts of the epistle. 2:1–11 and 3:8 make the parallel between Christ's self-abasement and Paul's own personal surrender of what was dearest to him on the worldly plane" (Houlden). There is thus no good reason for separating this section from the rest of Philippians, or for failing to consider it as part of the main body of the letter.

The strong emotions so apparent in vv 1–3 continue on in vv 7–11. Once again Paul expresses his feelings most powerfully in a rhetorical fashion that is almost poetic—short verb-less phrases, rhythmic expressions successively introduced with κατά ("according to"), chiasm, polysyndeton, hapaxlegomena (words used only once in the NT), a piling up of conjunctions, the careful choice of tense, the extended fuguelike playing with the themes of profit (κέρδος, κερδαίνω) and loss (ζημία, ζημιόω), and so on. Thus, with all his considerable skill with words Paul shares with the Philippians the all-surpassing worth of Christ Jesus his Lord. Once again he employs the tools of the rhetorical schools to serve him in powerfully expressing his conviction that no person profits who does not surrender to Christ, and no person loses who surrenders everything for Christ.

Comment

4. Paul has said (v 3) that Christians, those who alone can rightly lay claim to the title, "the Circumcision," are those who, among other things, do not rely on themselves to earn the favor of God. Their "confidence" for this lies not at all within themselves (οὐκ ἐν σαρκὶ πεποιθότες). And yet, surprisingly, having just made this important statement, he proceeds to write, "although I certainly have good reasons for putting confidence in myself" (καίπερ ἐγὼ ἔχων πεποίθησιν καὶ ἐν σαρκί: πεποίθησις can mean "ground of confidence" as well as "confidence," BGD; Vincent). It is not proper to weaken this remark by translating it, "though I might have confidence," or "I could have confidence," and so on (cf. GNB, JB, KJV), for the construction indicates that Paul fully intends to say that he does indeed (καί) have whatever it takes to boast in or rely upon himself. But his sentence is elliptical—a subordinate participial phrase without a main verb upon which it can depend. And the ellipse must be supplied from the context before it becomes clear what Paul is driving at, e.g. οὐ δ' ἔσομαι πεποιθὼς ἐν σαρκί ("but I will not do this"). The apostle for a moment "places himself on the same standing ground" with the Jews (Lightfoot) "to show that he is fully on a par with the best of them. But he immediately removes himself from that place, refusing to trust in himself. Why? Because he has discovered through his encounter with the living Christ that nothing he received by way of heritage, or did by way of human achievement can be the means of life nor the grounds of his righteousness before God—only the redeeming significance of Christ's death and resurrection can

become these for him or anyone (see Ridderbos, *Paul*, 138). Thus, although as an authentic Jew he has every reason to rely upon himself (ἐν σαρκί), he will not do this!

Paul's refusal to rely upon himself to establish the righteousness demanded by God is not because he thinks that he is inferior to anyone else, or lacks a proper pedigree, or is devoid of significant accomplishments, if that is what it takes. Without hesitation the apostle proceeds to say that he possesses personal advantages greater than (ἐγὼ μᾶλλον) any other authentic Jew who considers (δοκεῖ) that he has grounds for boasting in himself.

5. Paul now begins to list these advantages, the first of which is contained in the terse verbless expression, περιτομῇ ὀκταήμερος (lit. "with respect to circumcision an eighth-day-er"). Περιτομῇ, a noun with passive force in the dative case, a dative of reference (BDF 197), is coupled with ὀκταήμερος, an adjective not found elsewhere in the NT but used substantivally here to mean "an eighth-day person" (cf. John 11:39). Together they describe one who was circumcised on the eighth day of his life. With only two words, then, the apostle has made for himself the proudest claim any Jew could make, namely, that in strict conformity with the Law he was circumcised on precisely the right day (Gen 17:12; Lev 12:3; cf. Luke 1:59; 2:21). Unlike Ishmael, who was circumcised when he was thirteen years old (Gen 17:25; contrast Gen 21:4), as were his descendants (cf. Joseph. *Ant.* 1.12.2), and unlike heathen proselytes to Judaism who were circumcised as adults, Paul was circumcised on the eighth day by parents who were meticulous in fulfilling the prescriptions of the Law. He was a true Jew, a Jew by birth.

Next, Paul proudly affirms that he descended from the nation of Israel (ἐκ γένους Ἰσραήλ). He means by this that he possesses all the rights and privileges of God's chosen people because he belongs to them by birth, not by conversion. Ἰσραήλ ("of Israel"), a genitive of apposition, refers here to the race (γένος) and not to the patriarch. It was the sacred name for the Jews, as the nation of the theocracy, the people in covenant relation with God (J. B. Lightfoot, *Epistle to the Galatians* [London: Macmillan, 1881] 224; Rom 9:4; 11:1; 2 Cor 11:22). The name "Israel" calls to mind the glorious history of an illustrious nation (see von Rad, Kuhn, Gutbrod, *TDNT* 3,356–91), and was of such continuing significance that apparently Hellenistic Jews used it prominently in their propaganda efforts (Georgi, *Gegner*, 60–63; Collange, Martin, *Philippians*, 1976).

Further, Paul says that he belongs to the tribe of Benjamin (φυλῆς Βενιαμείν). Again there is a note of pride expressed as the apostle writes these words, for the tribe of Benjamin, though small (Ps 68:27), was nevertheless highly esteemed: (1) Its progenitor was the younger of the two sons born to Rachael, Jacob's favorite wife (Gen 30:23, 24; 35:16–18). (2) Of all the sons of Jacob only Benjamin was born in the Promised Land (Gen 35:9–19; see Str-B 3, 622). (3) From this tribe came Israel's first lawful king (whose name the apostle carried: Beare, Moule; cf. 1 Sam 9:1, 2). (4) The holy city of Jerusalem and the temple were within the borders of the territory assigned to Benjamin (Judg 1:21). (5) The tribe of Benjamin remained loyal to the house of David at the time of the break-up of the monarchy (1 Kings 12:21). (6) After the exile, Benjamin and Judah formed the core of the new colony in Palestine

(Vincent; cf. Ezra 4:1). (7) The tribe of Benjamin always held the post of honor in the army, a fact that gave rise to the battle cry, "Behind you, O Benjamin!" (Judg 5:14; Hos 5:8). (8) The famous Mordecai, responsible for that great national deliverance commemorated in the feast of Purim, was a Benjamite (Esth 2:5). (9) Benjamin resisted the inroads that pagan culture made among the other tribes and remained "pure" (Gnilka). (10) It is possible that respect for Benjamin can be traced further back to an even earlier period than that indicated in the references cited above (see A. Parrot, *Abraham et son temps* [Neuchâtel: Delachaux et Niestlé, 1962] 42–51; see Collange). Paul, then, seems to revel in the fact that he is a Benjamite. He seems also to have inherited the good qualities of strength and courage and purity and loyalty that characterized his tribe.

In addition Paul can say that he is a "Hebrew of Hebrews" ('Εβραῖος ἐξ 'Εβραίων). He may have meant by this that he was a "Hebrew born of Hebrew parents" (JB; note the force of the preposition ἐκ, "from," "out of"), i.e. that there was no heathen blood in his veins. Or he may have meant that, like his parents and grandparents before him, he was brought up to speak the Hebrew language (Moule, *ExpTim* 70 [1958–59] 100–102; Str-B 3, 622; but see also Gutbrod, *TDNT* 3,389–90), and carefully to observe the Jewish national way of life. He may, then, in effect be contrasting himself with the Hellenists who were Jews who usually spoke Greek and who allowed their style of life to be affected by Gentile customs and culture (Acts 6:1; 22:2; cf. 2 Cor 11:22).

Although Paul himself was born outside of Palestine (in Tarsus), and therefore could rightly be labeled a Hellenist, he in essence rejects this label, because not only was he the son of Pharisees (Acts 23:6), who saw to it that he was educated precisely in the ways of the Jewish Law in Jerusalem under a Hebrew teacher (Acts 22:3), but he himself gladly adopted the Hebrew language as his own language (Acts 21:40; 22:2), and accepted the customs and manner of life of his forefathers (Acts 26:4–5). Paul claims, therefore, to be a Hebrew of Hebrews, one belonging to the elite of his race, tracing his ancestry beyond Tarsus to Palestine (see van Unnik, *Tarsus or Jerusalem*, 46–47), a person safeguarded against the influences of Hellenization by the protective walls of Jewish tradition (Dibelius).

Paul turns now from the things that he enjoyed as a result of his birth and upbringing to describe those advantages he possessed by virtue of his own choice and diligence. He does this with a series of three terse phrases, none of which has a verb and each of which begins with the preposition κατά ("according to," "in relation to," "concerning," "as far as it concerns," "in respect to," and so on). The first of these is κατὰ νόμον Φαρισαῖος (lit. "according to Law, a Pharisee," meaning "with regard to the Jewish Law I was a Pharisee"). Although the word "Pharisee" is used ninety-nine times in the NT this is its only occurrence outside the Gospels and Acts. The Pharisees were a "small" religious party in Paul's day (Joseph. *Ant.* 17.2.4; 18.1.3), but it was the strictest of the Jewish sects (Acts 26:5) as far as adherence to the Law was concerned. Not content merely to obey the Law of Moses, the Pharisees bound themselves also to observe every one of the myriad of commandments contained in the oral Law, the interpretive traditions of the

Scribes. The most ardent of the Pharisees scrupulously avoided even accidental violations of the Law and did more than they were commanded to do
(Caird; Jeremias, *Jerusalem*, 246–67; Moore, *Judaism*, 1, 66). Paul, a son of
Pharisees (Acts 23:6), and a disciple of the great Pharisee, Gamaliel (Acts
5:34; 22:3), chose to be a Pharisee himself and set himself to be the most
earnest of the earnest observers of the Jewish Law (Gal 1:14). "Pharisee"
for Paul was not a term of reproach, but a title of honor, a claim to "the
highest degree of faithfulness and sincerity in the fulfilment of duty to God
as prescribed by the divine Torah" (Beare).

6. But Paul was not satisfied with merely keeping the Law. His zeal as a
Pharisee drove him to persecute the church, κατὰ ζῆλος διώκων τὴν ἐκκλησίαν
(lit. "according to zeal, a persecutor of the church"). Ζῆλος, "zeal for God,"
for the purity of his covenant-community, for his Law, marked the true servant
of God (cf. Num 25:1–18; Ps 106:30, 31; Ecclus 45:23; 4 Macc 18:12; cf.
also 1 Kings 19:10, 14; Ps 69:9), and it was a "well-known characteristic of
the Pharisees, who in part traced their line to the Maccabees" (Martin, *Philippians*, 1976; cf. 1 Macc 2:24–29; *T. Asher* 4:5; 1QH 14:14). Hence, not because
Paul was evil, but precisely because he was "good," an ardent Pharisee, zealous
for God, inflamed with zeal for the Law and committed to keeping the community of God pure that he did what he later came to lament, namely, persecute
the church (1 Cor 15:9; cf. Acts 22:2, 5; 26:9–11; 1 Tim 1:13).

The verb "to persecute" (διώκειν) has as its basic idea "to cause something
to run," "to pursue or chase." It pictures an army pursuing its enemy and
setting it to flight, or a hunter tracking down his quarry and putting it on
the run. In much the same way Paul harried the church, only he did so, on
his own confession, with a maniacal (ἐμμαινόμενος) zealousness that brought
prison and death to innocent men and women of the Way as people who
belonged to the church of Jesus Christ (Acts 22:4, 5; 26:9–11).

The word for "church" that Paul uses here is ἐκκλησία. It is interesting
and instructive to note that on occasion it is used in the OT (LXX) for the
people of Israel (1 Kings 17:47; 3 Kgs 8:14, 55; 1 Chron 13:2; Ps 21[22]:23;
Mic 2:5; Joel 2:16), and what is more, it is used for the people of Israel
gathered to conclude the covenant at Sinai (Deut 9:10; 1:4; 23:2–4), the people
of Yahweh bound to him by the rules he has given them to keep. Thus, the
word ἐκκλησία, perhaps more than any other, reveals the irony with which
Paul writes this section. He seems to be saying that while he, an ardent young
Pharisee, a new Phineas (cf. Numb 25:1–18), attempted to preserve the purity
of the church (i.e. the ancient Israel of God, the holy community), he ended
up persecuting the church (i.e. the new Israel, the true heir and successor
of God's Chosen People).

The third achievement Paul could point to with pride as a result of his
diligence was his ability to say, "With regard to a righteousness rooted in
the law, I became a blameless person" (κατὰ δικαιοσύνην τὴν ἐν νόμῳ γενόμενος
ἄμεμπτος). Like the rich young ruler in the gospel story (Luke 18:21) Paul
had kept all the commandments from his youth up. He had met the standards
necessary for achieving a righteousness which is rooted in the Law. Here
Paul is using "righteousness" (δικαιοσύνη) in the sense of conformity to external rules that are considered to be the requirements of God (on the meaning

of this difficult word in Paul see D. Hill, *Greek Words and Hebrew Meanings*. [SNTSMS 5. Cambridge: Cambridge University Press, 1967] 139–62). Since he had worked to achieve complete conformity to these rules, leaving nothing undone, no outsider could blame him, nor did he blame himself (γενόμενος ἄμεμπτος—ἄμεμπτος is related to the verb μέμφεσθαι, "to blame someone" for sins of omission [Lightfoot]). In this sense, then, of omitting nothing that was required of him Paul could claim without presumption that he had become faultless (cf. Grundmann, *TDNT* 4,573; Goguel, *JBL* 53 [1934] 257–67). This statement by Paul leaves no place for the modern view, deduced from Rom 7, "that before his conversion Paul was a Jew who had an uneasy conscience over the stoning of Stephen and a growing dissatisfaction with his own religion" (Keck; see also Mitton, *ExpTim* 65 [1953–54] 78–81, 99–103, 132–35; Ridderbos, *Paul*, 129, n. 3; Stauffer, *Theology* 93; against A. Deissmann, *Paul, A Study in Social and Religious History* [New York: G. Doran, 1926] 93–95). In every way he considered himself to be a model Jew, quite satisfied with himself until he met the living Christ.

7. Whether or not the conjunction ἀλλά ("but") belongs to the original text (see Notes), there is, nevertheless, a marked transition at this point. Suddenly all those "good" things Paul enjoyed, all those advantages he possessed from his parents and from his own efforts that made him proud and self-reliant are considered now not as assets but as liabilities. Of a sudden there is set before the Philippians a startling *Umwertung der Werte* ("a re-evaluation of values," Gnilka) on Paul's part, and any conjunction, however strong, may serve only to weaken the radicalness of this change in his outlook.

There are several things worth noting here: (1) Paul stresses the importance of human decision and judgment in any radical change of outlook on life such as he has experienced. The verb ἡγεῖσθαι means "to think, consider, regard" (BGD), and the perfect tense that Paul uses here, ἥγημαι, implies that he has come to a final decision only after considering matters "with deliberate judgment" (Vincent). "It is still true that divine grace far from annihilating the faculties of man stimulates them rather and recreates them in freedom" (Collange). (2) Paul describes this change in outlook on his part in business terms, using the familiar motifs of profit (κέρδος) and loss (ζημία; see MM 273, 341)—motifs also used by the Rabbis (Str-B 3, 622) and by Jesus (Matt 16:26). The metaphor is the familiar one of the balance sheet with its columns marked "assets" and "liabilities." (3) Paul admits that there were certain things in his past that were in fact gains for him, or things that he did in fact consider as gains (ἅτινα ἦν μοι κέρδη). They were not merely potential or supposed gains (cf. GNB)—the verb ἦν is indicative, and μοι ("for me") is dative of advantage. Pedigree, covenant-connection, zeal, and the like, Paul actually valued. They did contribute to his well-being on the human plane. (4) Nevertheless Paul now bundles up these many gains (κέρδη, plural) and treats them all as a single loss (ζημία). One might have expected him to say, in light of what he said before, that his previous personal advantages, although still good, are being left behind because he has found something better. But no! In Paul's thinking, the decision he made was not the decision to go from good to better, nor was it the surrender of a valued possession. It was an abandoning of ζημία ("a loss"). In the process of reevaluation he perceived with horror that the things he had hitherto viewed as benefiting him had in reality been working to destroy him because they were blinding him to his need for the real righteousness which God required that he himself could in no way achieve by his own efforts however earnest they may be (cf. Acts 1:2–3; Gnilka, Schlier, *TDNT* 3,672). (5) This radical transvaluation of values took place within the apostle διὰ τὸν Χριστόν ("because of the Christ"). But what precisely does Paul mean by this prepositional phrase? He does not mean that he made this reassessment "for Christ" (KJV) or "for Christ's sake" (GNB, NIV, RSV), as though somehow Christ would in any way benefit by his decision. Rather, he means that his own outlook on life was radically altered "because of the *fact* of Christ." That is to say, Paul, encountering the risen Jesus on the Damascus road, understanding there that he was *the* Christ, the Messiah whom he had longed for and worked for totally unawares, gladly gave up all his former advantages to gain this one person of supreme worth. The impact of Christ upon Paul thus was life-altering. And "from that moment on the Damascus road he never wavered in his fidelity to the decision then made" (Michael).

A parenthetical cautionary note may be helpful at this point. Paul's conversion experience, including the sudden and dramatic renunciation of his heritage and achievements, is not offered here as a model to be emulated. One need not feel less Christian than Paul if, unlike Paul, the course and conduct of his life, his occupation and aspirations are not radically different from what they were before encountering the living Christ. If, however, one's observance of religious ritual, one's status due to birth, one's outstanding accomplishments due to innate intelligence or sustained effort, and so on, should ever make that person proud or self-reliant, unaware of his need of God and of the righteousness that only Christ can provide, then, upon being made aware of this danger, he should jettison these privileges and achievements as one would jettison a valuable cargo to save a ship that would otherwise sink in a storm. Paul *had* to abandon his past advantages precisely because they were the very things that kept him from coming to God. They kept him from surrendering to Christ, who is the only way to God.

8. Now in a long and involved sentence extending through v 11 Paul enlarges on this theme of the "loss" of his "gains" because of the fact of Christ. It begins with an extraordinary accumulation of particles—ἀλλὰ μὲν οὖν γε καί, which are impossible to translate but which in Greek, nevertheless, powerfully emphasize the shift in tense from the perfect tense, ἥγημαι (*"I have counted"* all my advantages as loss) to the present tense, ἡγοῦμαι (And what is more *"I continue to count"* them as loss), and from the particular (ἅτινα) to the universal (πάντα—"all things;" see BDF 448, 6; M. E. Thrall, *Greek Particles in the New Testament* [Leiden: E. J. Brill, 1962] 11–16).

This change from the perfect tense to the present tense of the same verb (ἥγημαι to ἡγοῦμαι), then, is deliberate. In it Paul is saying that the settled decision he made in the past as the result of careful reflection is not enough. It must be reinforced daily by continuous conscious moral choices against depending upon himself—who he is, the things he possesses, what he has accomplished—for gaining favor with God. Further, Paul expands on his statement in v 7 by saying that those things he listed as "gains" in vv 5 and 6 are not the only things that he now considers as "loss." Rather, he considers all things (πάντα) as loss, whatever they may be that might compete with Christ for his allegiance, or might be thought of as meritorious and claimed as acceptable to God by the "religious" person (Martin, *Philippians*, 1959; see also Bonnard, Collange, Dibelius, Michael; but contrast Vincent).

Paul's extraordinary evaluation of things that are normally considered "gains"—privilege, family, religious heritage, comfort, position, wealth, power, and so on—as one gigantic loss is not made without good reason. Paul now states his reason in a single prepositional phrase—διὰ τὸ ὑπερέχον τῆς γνώσεως Χριστοῦ Ἰησοῦ τοῦ κυρίου μου—but one so compact that it is necessary to analyze its parts fully to get at what Paul is saying:

(1) The preposition διά followed here by the accusative case should be translated "for" or "because of." It simply and clearly introduces the reason for Paul's decision, nothing more, and therefore should not be translated "for the sake of" (GNB), "compared to" or "compared with" (LB, NIV, Goodspeed, Knox, Moffatt, Phillips).

(2) Τὸ ὑπερέχον, the neuter singular participle of the verb ὑπερέχειν ("to surpass, excel") is functioning as an abstract noun that serves more graphically than can its cognate noun, ὑπεροχή ("superiority") to accentuate the worth of that for which Paul abandoned everything else (see BDF 263,2). It is the object of the preposition διά. Τὸ ὑπερέχον, "the surpassing greatness" (BGD), "the supreme advantage" (Goodspeed, JB), "the ultimate value," then, is that for which Paul gave up all those things the world holds on to for dear life.

(3) This ultimate value is immediately qualified by the genitive, τῆς γνώσεως ("of the knowledge"), which in turn is qualified by the genitive, Χριστοῦ Ἰησοῦ ("of Christ Jesus"), which in turn is qualified by the genitives, τοῦ κυρίου μου ("my Lord"). All three of these genitives need explanation.

(*a*) The first of these, τῆς γνώσεως, is a genitive of apposition, which means that τὸ ὑπερέχον and τῆς γνώσεως are the same thing, i.e. "ultimate value" is "knowledge."

(*b*) The second genitive, Χριστοῦ Ἰησοῦ, is more difficult to explain because of its potential ambiguity. It could be a subjective genitive, meaning, then, that for Paul "ultimate value" is "to be known by Christ Jesus" (cf. 1 Cor 13:12; see P. Valloton, *Le Christ et la foi* [Geneva: Labor et Fides, 1960] 86–87), a divine knowledge which in turn is answered by the human "knowledge" of v 10. But Χριστοῦ Ἰησοῦ could also be, and most likely is, an objective genitive, meaning that Christ Jesus, in this instance, is not the one who knows, but the one who is known. Thus the surpassing worth Paul is thinking of is to know Christ—Christ Jesus is the ultimate object of his quest. (Although this latter interpretation of the genitive best fits the context, perhaps in choosing such an ambiguous construction Paul intends to include both ideas—to know Christ as well as to be known by Christ [cf. Gal 4:9].)

(*c*) The third set of genitives, τοῦ κυρίου μου, is merely appositive to Χριστοῦ Ἰησοῦ, and not in any sense predicate. In other words, it is not the mere objective intellectual awareness *that* Christ Jesus *is* Lord that Paul has in mind here. Rather, it is the personal knowledge or intimate acquaintance of Christ as "my" Lord (the only place in Paul's writings where this intimate expression occurs) that for him makes all other "values" appear worthless.

(4) The noun translated "knowledge" (γνῶσις) had such a wide range of meanings in Paul's day that it is difficult to sort out exactly what he meant when he used it. Among the contemporary pagan religions γνῶσις ("knowledge") was one of their key words referring to a kind of mystical knowledge of or communion with the god—"a revelation of the god in which the vision (granted in the mystery cults) leads to a transformation of the beholder" (Dibelius; Beare; cf. 2 Cor 3:18; 4:6). It apparently also was used by Gnostic Jewish Christians of some "higher" salvific knowledge accessible only to themselves and to their initiates (cf. 1 Cor 8:1–11; 13:2, 8; 14:6; cf. also Gal 4:9; Schmithals, *Paul*, 90–92). Γνῶσις ("knowledge") has been understood by some to have been used in a peculiar if not unique way to refer to the experience of the martyrs (Lohmeyer). It is possible, therefore, that γνῶσις may have been chosen by Paul precisely because it embraced a combination of ideas, rather than a single one, and would have had significant meaning to a wide range of people (Gnilka; see also Gärtner, *NTS* 14 [1967–68] 209–31; Forestell, *CBQ* 18 [1956] 123–36; Tannehill, *Dying and Rising*, 114–23).

Much more probable is the view that Paul's meaning for γνῶσις here was controlled exclusively by his understanding of the OT concept of knowledge—both God's knowledge of his people "in election and grace" (Exod 33:12, 17; Amos 3:2) and his people's knowledge of him "in love and obedience" to his self-revelation (Martin, *Philippians*, 1959; cf. Jer 31:34; Hos 6:3; and see also Davies, *Christian Origins*, 141; Dupont, *Gnosis*, 34–36). Such knowledge involves more than an acquisition of facts. It also involves "loyalty, repentance, love and service" (Beare)—the "Yes" of the soul to the address of God. Knowledge, then, is not primarily intellectual but experiential. Thus, in the context of Phil 3, "the knowledge of Christ is personal and intimate, as the expression 'my Lord' shows, certainly more than an intellectual apprehension of truth about Christ. Rather, it is a personal appropriation of and communion with Christ himself. 'The knowledge of Christ' no doubt does involve one's thoughts, but in its distinctive biblical usage it may be said to involve primarily one's heart" (Loh and Nida).

The reason Paul gives for considering his former "gains" as loss can now be stated with clarity. It is because of the one thing that now has ultimate value, namely a personal knowledge of Christ Jesus—an experiential encounter with the Savior—that the apostle is led to respond to him in loyalty, love and obedience as Lord of his life, and to set himself to serve him with all his heart.

But this glad acceptance of Christ Jesus as Lord had its price to pay. Paul not only *considered* all things as "loss" because of Christ, he actually experienced the loss of all things. His words are τὰ πάντα ἐζημιώθην. By placing the definite article τά before πάντα ("all things") and both words before the verb Paul gives emphasis to the fact that he lost everything. Furthermore, the verb he uses ζημιοῦν ("to lose," a play on the noun ζημία, vv 7, 8) is an aorist passive which may point to a particular time when this loss occurred, and hint at the possibility that he was stripped of all his advantages by the Jewish authorities. Since, however, ζημιοῦν is found only in a passive form in the NT with a somewhat shifted meaning (i.e. not, "to be mulcted," but, "to lose"; BDF 159,2), it is more likely that Paul is thinking of those things such as his high status within Judaism and the like, that he himself *voluntarily* renounced (cf. 2:6–7). In any case, his loss was a real loss, and Paul's claim to consider everything as "loss" was therefore no empty boast nor a purely academic exercise.

Paul did not lament this loss. For him it was a welcomed relief. In fact it was the freeing of himself from something that he unwaveringly continued to consider (ἡγοῦμαι) σκύβαλα. The derivation of this word, σκύβαλον (used only here in the NT), has never been cleared up. Although traced to the expression τὸ τοῖς κυσὶ βαλλόμενον ("that which is thrown to the dogs"), it seems to have meant by usage either (1) "dung," "muck" both as excrement and as food gone bad, (2) "scraps," i.e. "what is left after a meal," and (3) "refuse." It is also used to describe a pitiful and horrible thing like a half-eaten corpse, or "filth" such as lumps of manure. Thus when Paul uses it here as the final object of his studied threefold use of ἡγεῖσθαι ("to consider"), it provides the climax of a crescendo that has been building up. "The perfect ἥγημαι (v 7) relates to conversion; since this Paul has learned to regard all his former κέρδη ['gains'] as ζημίαν ['loss'] for Christ's sake. The present ἡγοῦμαι (v 8a) confirms that this is his judgment now. The second present ἡγοῦμαι (v 8c) strengthens this by substituting σκύβαλα for ζημία. The intensification lies in the element of resolute turning aside from something worthless and abhorrent with which one will have nothing more to do. The choice of the vulgar term stresses the force and totality of this renunciation" (Lang, *TDNT* 7,445–47; against Lightfoot, Michael). Therefore, Paul's deliberate choice of the word σκύβαλα over ζημία shows the utter revulsion he now feels toward those "advantages" he surrendered. It is quite improper to weaken its meaning in any way by translation or by interpretation (cf. Martin, *Philippians,* 1959 with Martin, *Philippians,* 1976; see also Vincent who draws attention to how some of the patristic writers, embarrassed by this passage, attempted to modify the meaning of σκύβαλα).

Finally now, Paul states his motives for counting everything as loss (vv 8c–10): They are (1) that he might "gain Christ," (2) "that he might be found in Christ," and (3) "that he might know Christ and the power of his resurrection."

The first of these, ἵνα Χριστὸν κερδήσω ("in order that I might gain Christ"), is a strange expression that must be understood in light of the imagery Paul uses throughout this section of a profit and loss system and the balancing of accounts. The verb κερδαίνειν ("to gain") is a play on the noun κέρδη ("gains," v 7). Paul has given up all other forms of "gain" (κέρδη), in order that he might get the true "gain" (κερδήσω) which is Christ, that is, Christ himself, not merely the favor of Christ. Or in other words, were Paul to place the whole world with its wealth and power and advantages, its prestige and accolades and rewards in one scalepan of the balance and Christ in the other, Christ alone would overwhelmingly outweigh everything else in terms of real worth. Hence, from the standpoint of simple logic Paul cannot afford to gain the whole world if it means losing Christ (cf. the words of Jesus in Mark 8:36=Matt 16:26=Luke 9:25).

Although Paul, somewhat caught in the web of his rhetoric, does speak of "gaining" Christ, he does not intend to convey solely the idea of a personal profiting from Christ. "To gain Christ" must also have involved for Paul the concept of bowing before Christ in humble repentance, of recognizing him as the only Savior from sin, of claiming him as the only basis for a right standing before God, and at the same time of being accepted by him. It must also have embraced the idea of communion with Christ in an ever deepening relationship that will continue until it reaches its consummation at the Parousia. And yet, there is in these words of Paul the unmistakable idea that to know Christ in the intimacy of personal trust and surrender is indeed to benefit personally from him (so Melanchthon, as cited by Martin, *Philippians*, 1959).

One thing more. The construction Paul uses to express this goal—ἵνα with the subjunctive (ἵνα Χριστὸν κερδήσω, "that I might gain Christ")—implies more than that Paul surrendered all *to gain Christ*, and that he has therefore *fully gained Christ*. There is also in this construction the idea of the future, the sense that Paul has both gained Christ and is yet to gain Christ. "Christ, who has already given himself in many ways is still to be 'gained.'. . . Experience of his Lordship is therefore essentially a dynamic experience which sets one on the road. That road, from self to Christ, is a long one" (Collange).

9. That the future element attends Paul's expression, "that I may gain Christ" (v 8), is corroborated now by the coordinate expression καὶ εὑρεθῶ ἐν αὐτῷ ("and that I may be found in him"), εὑρεθῶ meaning "to be found when surprised by death" (cf. 2 Cor 5:3 and see J. Moffatt, "Found in Him," *ExpTim* 24 [1912–13] 46). Here the apostle's mind seems to focus on the coming day of judgment when he must stand before God who is the Judge of all the earth. But as a result of his conversion and the enlightening experience stemming from his encounter at that time with the living Christ, it is obvious that Paul fears now to stand before God ἐν σαρκί, i.e. by himself. He desires (and fully intends) to be found ἐν Χριστῷ, "in Christ," incorporate in him (see comments on 1:1), and thus to stand before the Judge not presenting himself and his merits, but, because he is in Christ, presenting Christ and the all-prevailing merits of Christ. He no longer has aspirations to be a self-reliant person who has (ἔχων) only his own goodness (δικαιοσύνην) to offer to God. He understands now that his is an inadequate goodness that can in no way commend him to God.

Thus it is that Paul is led back to a favorite topic of his—δικαιοσύνη ("righteousness"), but one he does not develop at this point. Unquestionably Paul had thoroughly instructed the Philippians in what it means to be righteous before God. But for others to understand the meaning of δικαιοσύνη ("righteousness") here in Phil.3:9 they must attend carefully to Romans and Galatians which provide the necessary commentaries on this important concept.

Often, both in Hebrew and Greek, the words "righteous" (δίκαιος; צַדִּיק), "righteousness" (δικαιοσύνη; צְדָקָה) and the related verb "to justify" (δικαιοῦν; צָדַק) were used as legal terms. In a court of law the judge, who had to decide between two parties, was forced "to justify" the one and "to condemn" the other. That is to say, he had to decide in favor of the one and against the other. Thus "to justify" often meant "to give a person his rights," "to vindicate or exonerate" him, or "to declare him in the right." What is important to observe is that this decision did not necessarily depend on the moral character of the person involved.

Now when these terms are employed in a religious context, the question naturally arises: "What must a man do if God is to declare that he is in the right and so give judgment in his favor?" (Caird). For the Jew the answer was: "I must obey the Law of Moses!" Paul's answer, stemming from his new understanding of the OT (cf. Pss 14:1–3; 53:1–3; 143:2), developed now in the light of his Damascus road experience, is that human beings are too sinful ever to be able to do enough good to be declared good by God. What is more, God does not ask for good works, but for faith (cf. Gen 15:6). The trouble with a righteousness based on what a person can do is that it is always self-righteousness (cf. Rom 10:1–3), providing a basis for self-boasting. Paul's argument runs thus: "If I try to earn God's favorable verdict by my own goodness, I am aiming at a righteousness of my own [ἐμὴν δικαιοσύνην], one which is my own achievement and which will give me a claim on God's recognition. But as long as I am doing this, I disqualify myself from the true righteousness, which is not based on merit [cf. Isa 61:10]. For *faith* is not an alternative way of earning God's favor; *faith* is the opposite of merit, an admission that I cannot earn God's approval, but can only accept his free offer of forgiveness, grace and love. And since the offer is made in the life and above all in the death of Christ, true righteousness, the condition of being truly right with God, must come through faith in Christ."

Faith, therefore, in its strictest sense is not intellectual assent to a series of propositions about Christ, but the act of personal trust in and self-surrender to Christ. It is the movement of one's whole soul in confidence out toward Christ. It is the " 'yes' of the whole personality to the fact of Christ." (For this, and for similar additional ideas, see Caird, Beare, Michael; A. Richardson, *An Introduction to the Theology of the New Testament* [New York: Harper, 1958] 23–25; Bultmann, *Theology*, 1, 270–84; Conzelmann, *Int* 22 [1968] 178–82; C. E. B. Cranfield, *A Critical and Exegetical Commentary on the Epistle to the Romans* [Edinburgh: T. and T. Clark, 1975] 1,91–102; *passim*; but for other perspectives on the Righteousness of God see also Käsemann, *New Testament Questions*, 168–82; *Commentary on Romans* [Grand Rapids: Eerdmans, 1980] 91–129; K. Kertelege, *"Rechtfertigung" bei Paulus* [Münster: Aschendorff, 1967]; E. P. Sanders, *Paul and Palestinian Judaism* [Philadelphia: Fortress Press, 1977] 474–523; M. T. Brauch, "Perspectives on 'God's Righteousness' in Recent German Discussion," in Sanders, *Paul and Palestinian Judaism*, 523–35; Stuhlmacher, *Gerechtigkeit Gottes;* Synge.)

Hence, when Paul writes of the righteousness which is διὰ πίστεως Χριστοῦ (lit. "through faith of Christ") one must take the genitive Χριστοῦ as an objective genitive (cf. Mark 11:22; Acts 3:16; Gal 2:20 for similar constructions). Paul does not have in mind here a righteousness that is based on the faithfulness, loyalty or fidelity of Christ to the Father (Vallotton, *Le Christ*, 88, 89; R. N. Longenecker, "The Obedience of Christ in the Theology of the Early Church," in R. Banks [ed.], *Reconciliation and Hope* [Grand Rapids: Eerdmans, 1975] 142–52; D. W. B. Robinson, " 'Faith of Jesus Christ—a New Testament Debate," *Reformed Theological Review* 29 [1970] 71–81). Rather, he has in mind a righteousness that has its origin in God (ἐκ θεοῦ) and that is humbly appropriated by a person through faith *in* Christ (διὰ πίστεως Χριστοῦ). It is useless to reject this interpretation of διὰ πίστεως Χριστοῦ ("through faith *in* Christ") here in v 9 simply by claiming that if so interpreted Paul creates a tautology when he then adds the phrase τὴν ἐκ θεοῦ δικαιοσύνην ἐπὶ τῇ πίστει ("the righteousness of God based on faith")—twice calling attention to the human response without once stating the objective grounds for God's justifying action (Martin, *Philippians*, 1976). Such a rejection hangs by too thin a thread, because the phrase, "the righteousness of God based on faith" in v 9c is simply added for clarification and emphasis without any concern for being tautological, and because just such emphatic redundancy is in keeping with Paul's style of writing. In Gal 2:16 he does exactly what he does here, though in a much more awkard fashion. There he repeats three times over the phrase "faith in Christ Jesus"—διὰ πίστεως Ἰησοῦ Χριστοῦ . . . εἰς Χριστὸν Ἰησοῦν ἐπιστεύσαμεν . . . ἐκ πίστεως Χριστοῦ—referring each time to the human reaction to God's gift without once specifying the objective ground of God's action (see Betz's translation, *Galatians*, 113).

In this one verse, then, Paul distils his great fundamental doctrine of justification by faith: (1) All human beings are alienated from God. (2) No one can possibly reestablish the necessary right relationship with God by his own efforts (ἐμὴν δικαιοσύνην τὴν ἐκ νόμου—"my righteousness which comes from my keeping the Law," is for Paul an impossible feat). (3) God must take the initiative to restore this right relationship; the source of true righteousness is the redemptive action of God himself (τὴν ἐκ θεοῦ δικαιοσύνην). (4) God has indeed taken this initiative in Christ, in his life, death and resurrection. (5) God's initiative must be met with human response. Right relationship with God is established by one's faith in Christ (διὰ πίστεως Χριστοῦ), that is to say, by one's continual confession of total dependence upon Christ for the necessary true righteousness, by one's personal trust in and surrender to Christ. (6) Faith in Christ, then, is another way of stating what it means to be found in Christ (εὑρεθῶ ἐν αὐτῷ), incorporated in him, and united with him to such a degree that all that Christ is and has done is received by the person who trusts in Christ.

10. Finally, Paul considers all his personal advantages and everything else, for that matter, as unspeakable filth for the goal "of knowing Christ and the power of his resurrection and the fellowship of his sufferings."

This final goal is expressed differently from the previous two (vv 8, 9), which were introduced by ἵνα and the subjunctive—ἵνα Χριστὸν κερδήσω ("that I may gain Christ") and ἵνα εὑρεθῶ ἐν αὐτῷ ("that I may be found in him"). It is expressed by an infinitive with the genitive definite article, τοῦ γνῶναι αὐτόν (lit. "to know him"). For this reason several commentators understand τοῦ γνῶναι as an explanatory infinitive more precisely defining the nature and power of faith (v 9)—πίστει, τοῦ γνῶναι αὐτόν ("faith, which is to know him"; see Collange, Hendriksen, Keck, Martin, *Philippians*, 1976). There is certainly a sense in which faith and knowledge are close in idea, and the meaning of the one is strengthened by sharing in the meaning of the other. And it is true that the infinitive may be used to explain or define more precisely another word (Moule, *Idiom Book*, 129). But it is not likely that this is the case here: (1) Nowhere else in the NT is the noun πίστις ("faith") followed by an explanatory articular infinitive. (2) On the other hand, the infinitive with the genitive definite article, as here, is often used to express purpose in the NT, especially in Luke and Paul (Luke 24:29; 1 Cor 10:13; cf. BDF 400, 5). (3) Furthermore, to change constructions in the same sentence from ἵνα and the subjunctive to an infinitive in order to show purpose is not an uncommon change in Paul's writings (Rom 6:6; Col 1:9, 10). (4) By taking τοῦ γνῶναι as an infinitive of design, parallel in idea to ἵνα Χριστὸν κερδήσω and ἵνα εὑρεθῶ ἐν αὐτῷ, one sees immediately in this expression a fitting climax to Paul's passionate willingness to treat everything as trash that would prevent him from achieving his objectives which is "to gain Christ," "to be found in Christ," and "to know Christ." "To know Christ," therefore, is the ultimate goal toward which the apostle sets the course of his life.

The tense of the infinitive τοῦ γνῶναι is aorist, and very likely an ingressive aorist, i.e. an aorist that sums up the action of the verb at the point at which it commences (but see Beare). This suggests, therefore, a crisis of knowledge. It suggests that for Paul just the *coming* to know Christ outweighs all other values, that for him the significance of Christ, "in whom are hid all the treasures of wisdom and knowledge" (Col 2:3), is so vast that even to *begin* to know him is more important than anything else in all the world. The crisis, however, implies a process. The coming to know Christ results in a growing knowledge of Christ, as Paul makes clear here and elsewhere (Moule).

Once again it should be noted that the verb γινώσκειν/γνῶναι ("to know") and its cognates (cf. v 8) often focus attention upon the ideas of understanding, experience and intimacy, even the intimacy of the sexual relationship in marriage (cf. Matt 1:25). Hence, when Paul speaks of his desire to know Christ he does not have in mind a mere intellectual knowledge about Christ (Paul had that when he was persecuting the church). Rather, he is thinking about a personal encounter with Christ that inaugurates a special intimacy with Christ that is life-changing and on-going (cf. John 17:3; 1 Cor 2:8; 1 John 2:3, 4; 4:8; 5:20).

That this knowledge of Christ is personal and relational is now made clear by the phrases that follow, the first of which is καὶ τὴν δύναμιν τῆς ἀναστάσεως αὐτοῦ (lit. "and the power of his resurrection"). Here the καί is more than a simple conjunction, however. It serves to link the words that follow together with αὐτόν ("him") in such a way as to define and more fully explain what is meant by αὐτόν (cf. BGD, καί, 3). It is not that Paul is saying, "I want to know him *and* the power of his resurrection," as though "him" and "power" were equally worthy objects of his knowing. Rather, he is saying, "I want to know him *in* the power of his resurrection" (Goodspeed, Moffatt). That is to say, Paul is not content merely to know Christ as a fact of history, but to know him personally as the resurrected ever-living Lord of his life. And the power (δύναμις) he wishes to know is not something separable from him, but the power with which the risen Christ is endowed. He wishes to know Christ "by experiencing the power he wields in virtue of his resurrection" (Michael). He wishes to know him alive and creatively at work to save him from himself, to transform him from bad to good, to propel him forward toward a life of service to others, to inaugurate "newness of life," life in

the Spirit, in a word, to resurrect him from death in sin to life in God, to
quicken and stimulate his whole moral and spiritual being (cf. Rom 6:4-11;
Dibelius, Gnilka, Lightfoot, Michael).

The second phrase, καὶ κοινωνίαν παθημάτων αὐτοῦ (lit. "and the fellowship
of his sufferings"), is to be taken closely with the first phrase, not only because
it is linked with the connective καί ("and"), but especially because the word
"fellowship" (κοινωνίαν) shares the same definite article with the word "power"
(δύναμιν): τὴν δύναμιν . . . καὶ κοινωνίαν. This suggests that the power of the
resurrected Christ and the fellowship of his sufferings are not to be thought
of as two totally separate experiences, but as alternate aspects of the same
experience.

Now if the first phrase is interpreted to mean that Paul wishes to know
the power of the resurrected Christ at work within him, and if the second
phrase is as closely related to the first as the sentence structure seems to
suggest, then it is not plausible to interpret the one of an inner subjective
experience and the other of an external objective happening. Paul is not
now thinking of his own physical sufferings as in any way completing the
full tale of Christ's afflictions (Col 1:24), nor does he here have in mind
the principle he enunciates elsewhere—"to suffer with Christ is to be glorified
with him" (Rom 8:17-18; cf. 2 Cor 4:7-11). Rather, this phrase in its context
of being found in Christ, clothed with his righteousness, is highly reminiscent
of Rom 6:4-11. Thus, just as knowing Christ in the power of his resurrection
is an inward experience that can be expressed in terms of being resurrected
with Christ (cf. Rom 6:4), so knowing Christ in the fellowship of his sufferings
is equally an inward experience that can be described in terms of having
died with Christ (cf. Rom 6:8 and see Gal 2:19-20).

This becomes especially clear when one remembers (1) that the Greek
word κοινωνία ("fellowship"), followed by the genitive case as here, also carries
with it the idea of "participation or sharing in" something (BGD), and (2)
that a favorite theme of Paul is that of Christ as the Last Adam. As such
Christ embodies the whole of humankind. He identifies himself so completely
with human beings in their state of sin and helplessness that as a result
they might be equally identified with him in his resurrected new life of goodness (cf. Rom 5:12-18; 8:3; 2 Cor 5:21; Phil 2:7; 1 Cor 15:22, 49). In Christ's
suffering and death the old humanity came to an end. In his resurrection
the new humanity began (2 Cor 5:14-17). Therefore, for Paul to say that
he wishes to know Christ and the fellowship of his sufferings is not to say
that he seeks to know Christ and to experience physical sufferings of martyrdom (cf. RSV: "that I may share his sufferings"), but to know Christ who
suffered and died for him (cf. 1 Pet 3:18; 4:1), to know that he therefore
has suffered and died in Christ, only to be resurrected in him to a new and
superlative kind of life (Caird, Jones, Loh and Nida, Michael; see also Barrett,
First Adam to Last; Jervell, *Imago Dei,* 206-208; 261-75; R. Scroggs, *The Last
Adam* [Oxford: Blackwells, 1966]; Seesemann, KOINΩNIA; but see Collange;
Jewett, *NovT* 12 [1970] 198-212; Martin, *Philippians,* 1976; Siber, *Mit Christus,*
111 for a different view that interprets these phrases polemically as Paul's
rebuttal to the wrong-headed teaching of a group or groups of religious
leaders who oppose him).

That the phrase, "the fellowship of his sufferings," has been correctly interpreted is corroborated now by the participial expression which immediately follows: συμμορφιζόμενος τῷ θανάτῳ αὐτοῦ ("conforming myself to his death"). To understand this there are several things to take note of: (1) In a criss-cross chiastic structure Paul equates Christ's "sufferings" with Christ's death:

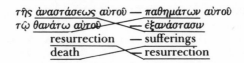

τῆς ἀναστάσεως αὐτοῦ — παθημάτων αὐτοῦ
τῷ θανάτω αὐτοῦ — ἐξανάστασιν
resurrection   — sufferings
death   — resurrection

(2) Συμμορφίζεσθαι, "to conform onself, to make oneself like," is a hapax legomenon, a word occurring only here in the NT. Nevertheless, in spite of its uniqueness, it immediately brings to mind the vocabulary of Rom 6: "For if we have become united (σύμφυτοι, lit. "growing together") with him in the likeness (ὁμοιώματι) of his death, we shall also be in the likeness of his resurrection" (v 5). "If we died with (σύν) Christ, we believe that we will also live with (συζήσομεν) him" (v 8). (3) Therefore, by coining this word and using it here Paul is not colorfully claiming that he is looking to suffer physically as Christ suffered, or to die as he died (JB, Phillips, Weymouth; see also Lohmeyer, Meyer, Plummer). Rather, captivated by the staggering idea that he and all believers are caught up into Christ and are indissolubly linked together with him to share with him in all the events of his life, including his death and resurrection, and loving to express this great fundamental concept by words compounded with σύν ("with"), such as συσταυροῦν, "to crucify together with" (Rom 6:6); συνθάπτω, "to bury together with" (Rom 6:4); συζωοποιεῖν, "to make alive together with" (Eph 2:5), and so on (see Grundmann, *TDNT* 7,786–87 for a complete listing of these compounds; see also Moule, *Christology*, 124), Paul creates a new word capable not only of stating that he has died with Christ (cf. Rom 6:10) as a fact of the past, but also of stating his conscious glad choice to identify himself with that death and to conform his life to the implications of that death now in the present.

Συμμορφιζόμενος is a participle, middle in voice and present in tense. As such it says that Paul, already dead to sin by virtue of Christ's death, nevertheless strives to make the effects of that death an ever-present reality within himself by his own constant choice to consider himself in fact dead to sin and alive to God (cf. Rom 6:11), to conform his practice in the world to his position in Christ, to renounce his own selfish desires and say "yes" to Christ who calls him to take up his cross daily and follow him as a servant of God for the good of mankind (cf. Phil 2:6–8 where μορφὴ δούλου is recalled by συμμορφιζόμενος).

This interpretation does not totally rule out the thought of physical sufferings or death playing out their transforming role in the Christian's life. In fact, the mystical union with Christ in his sufferings and death as outlined above is but strengthened and deepened by any physical pain that may be experienced because of one's faith in Christ. The hazards that Paul faced in his apostolic work, the batterings he was subjected to as a Christian had the potential for being "the concrete external means" by which he could be conformed to Christ's death (Beare). Thus, the expression, "conforming oneself to his death," can be enlarged to include "costly discipleship," the kind of suffering expressed so poignantly by the apostle in his letter to the Corinthians: "Always carrying about in the body the dying of Jesus, that the life of Jesus also may be manifested in our body. For we who live are constantly being delivered over to death for Jesus' sake, that the life of Jesus also may be manifested in our mortal flesh" (2 Cor 4:7–12, especially vv 10–11).

11. If by reading v 10 one should begin to think that Paul has shifted from a futuristic eschatology (cf. 1 Thess 4:13–17) to a "realized" eschatology, where the Christian's resurrection has already taken place, and completely so, in Christ's resurrection (cf. Gal 2:20), that person is soon made to understand that this is not the case. The apostle does assert that the Christian died and rose with Christ and is now living in the power of Christ's resurrected life (Collange, Dibelius, Gnilka). But this conviction does not cause him to surrender the hope of a future resurrection when all conflicts will be resolved, all ills be healed, all human frailties, both moral and physical, be eliminated, and all wrongs forever set right (cf. 3:21).

Paul expresses this hope of a future resurrection in an unusual way. He begins with the words εἰ πως καταντήσω (lit. "if somehow I might attain"). These words seem to convey an element of doubt or uncertainty, however slight. But if there is any doubt in Paul's mind it is not about the realness of the resurrection to come (cf. 2 Cor 5:1–8; Phil 3:20–21), nor about the trustworthiness of God (Rom 8:38–39), nor about the way in which he will attain the resurrection, i.e. by martyrdom or by some other way (Martin, *Philippians*, 1976), nor about himself (Collange, Michael, Vincent) as to whether he might be rejected for his own defects (1 Cor 9:27; but see Phil 3:9; Rom 5:17, 18, 21). Rather, it would appear that Paul uses such an unexpected hypothetical construction simply because of humility on his part, a humility that recognizes that salvation is the gift of God from start to finish and that as a consequence he dare not presume on this divine mercy (Caird). A translation such as Goodspeed's, "in the hope of attaining" adequately and accurately expresses Paul's feeling of awe and wonder as he wrote the phrase εἰ πως καταντήσω (cf. Acts 27:12; Rom 1:10; 11:14 for similar expressions of expectation: BDF 375). Such an attitude of humility is not in any way weakened by the active voice of the verb καταντήσω ("*I* might attain") as though Paul were thinking that by himself and his own efforts he could attain the resurrection. His expression as it stands implies the following modification: "If by the grace and goodness of God I might be privileged to participate in the resurrection. . . .'"

The expression Paul uses here for the resurrection, ἐξανάστασις, does not appear in the LXX, nor is it found elsewhere in the NT. Paul coined it, perhaps, compounding the preposition ἐκ ("out of") with the usual word for "resurrection" (ἀνάστασις) so that by using this strengthened form along with the repeated ἐκ—ἐκ νεκρῶν—he might stress in a striking way that it is precisely the rising from among the dead he has in mind here, not the mystical rising with Christ which is the present experience of all believers. That future resurrection which will be in incorruption, glory and power (1 Cor 15:42–44) now has the focus of his attention, and only this resurrection is in view.

Explanation

In this section, Paul makes it clear that human advantages, such as birth, religion, position in society, and so on, and human accomplishments, however arduously achieved, ultimately are things without value. He says this not because of pique due to a personal lack of distinction, nor because of failure in his occupational pursuits or religious endeavors. By human standards he was the best of the best, the most religious of the religious, with every right to boast in himself and to believe in his own goodness. Rather, he says this in light of what occurred to him on the Damascus road and the life-altering happening that took place there. Of a sudden he encountered the very Christ whose followers he had been harassing. As a result his life was never the same again.

Immediately he experienced a radical transvaluation of values. At once he realized that those "good" things he had cherished and striven for were not "gains" at all. They were losses that had bankrupted him. They were "evil" things bent on destroying him because they made him self-reliant, self-satisfied, content to offer to God his own goodness. They acted as an opiate dulling his awareness of his need for the real righteousness that God requires and that only God could supply.

The blinding light of the Christ-encounter (Acts 9:3–5) paradoxically opened Paul's eyes to see everything clearly and in proper perspective. As a result he came to realize that to know Christ Jesus as *his* Lord was the one thing in life of ultimate worth—everything else that would compete for his allegiance was not only "loss" but "filth" by comparison, things to be abhorred and abandoned. And the actual loss of all those things he once lived for in no way altered his thinking. He continued with happy resolve to value only Christ. He considered himself a person who profited to the extreme by having gained Christ, by having become incorporate in him. Now there was no longer any doubt in his mind about whether his own goodness based on keeping the Law was good enough for God: it was not. Instead, Paul came to see that by faith, that is, by his "yes" to the address of Christ, he stood now before God in Christ, and in his goodness. He came to understand that the ultimate goodness that God demanded has been provided by God himself, but only in Christ. Thus, he came to understand that to have gained everything, and lost Christ, would have been to profit not at all. Whereas to have lost everything and yet gained Christ was to have become the richest of the rich.

Hence Paul desired to come to know Christ more fully, not as a theological topic to be discussed, much as he used to discuss different points of the Jewish Law, but as a person to be enjoyed. He desires to experience in practice what he knew to be true in theory, i.e. that when Christ died he died, when Christ was resurrected he, too, was resurrected. He desired to sense within himself the power of the resurrected living Christ. He desired to realize in personal experience the fact that Christ's suffering for sin had indeed put to the death his own sin. To this end Paul, although indeed dead to sin by virtue of Christ's death for him, nevertheless, by his own continuous, conscious choice was prepared to take this fact seriously, to take sides with Christ against himself, to bring his practice in the world in line with his position in Christ, to renounce his own selfish desires, and say "yes" to Christ who was calling him to conform himself to his death by daily taking up his cross in self-sacrificing service to others.

Thus it is, in a deep sense of humility and trust, of expectation and hope, that Paul looks forward to the future and to his own bodily resurrection from among the dead.

C. *Warning against Perfection Now (3:12-16)*

Bibliography

Bröse, E. "Paulus durch Virgil kommentiert, zu Phil. 3,12-14." *TSK* 93 (1920-21) **Fernández, E. L.** "En torno a Fil 3,12." *Estudios Bíblicos* 34 (1975) 121-23. **Forestell, J. T.** *CBQ* 18 (1956) 123-36. **Fridrichsen, A.** "EN ΔΕ, zu Phil. 3,13." *ConNT* (1944) 31-32. **Pfitzner, V. C.** *The Agon Motif.* **Polhill, J. B.** *RevExp* 77 (1980) 359-72. **Turner, G. A.** "Paul's Central Concern: Exegesis of Phil. 3,10-15." *Asbury Seminarian* 29 (1975) 9-14.

Translation

12 *I do not say that I have at this time grasped* a *the meaning of Christ, or that I have already become perfect in my knowledge of him. But I keep pressing on to see whether* b *I might apprehend Christ Jesus,* c *inasmuch as I was indeed apprehended by him.* 13 *Brothers, I do not* d *reckon that I have fully apprehended him yet. But I focus on one thing only: while forgetting what is behind me, and stretching out to what lies before me,* 14 *I keep running towards the goal-marker, straight for the prize to which God calls me up,* e *the prize that is contained in Christ Jesus.* f 15 *So, this is the attitude all of us who are "perfect" must* g *have. But since you have a somewhat different attitude, God will surely reveal to you the truth even about this.* 16 *In any case, let us live up to whatever truth we have already attained.* h

Notes

a P46 D and a few other witnesses add ἢ ἤδη δεδικαίωμαι ("or have already been justified"), perhaps influenced by 1 Cor 4:4, or perhaps compensating for the lack of any objects for the verbs in this verse. If this phrase is an omission it can be explained as an error due to homoioteleuton. Its inclusion would provide a good example of paronomasia with διώκω (see Fernández, *Estudios Bíblicos* 34 [1975] 121-23).

b Many MSS add καί ("and," "indeed") at this point. א* D* F G and a few other witnesses omit it.

c B F G 33 and a few other witnesses omit Ἰησοῦς. As is often the case, this name, "Christ Jesus," generates variant readings. P46, 61א A Ψ and the majority text read Χριστοῦ Ἰησοῦ.

d א A D* P 33 81 and apparently P16 and P61 read οὔπω ("not yet") for οὐ ("not") which is supported by P46 B F G and the majority text. οὔπω is the easier of the two readings and should be rejected as secondary.

e The margin of 1739 and Tertullian have ἀνεγκλησίας ("irreproachability") instead of ἄνω κλήσεως ("upward call"), perhaps an early emendation of the text to make sense out of an otherwise difficult expression (cf. 1:10; 2:15; 3:6 to see that the idea of "irreproachableness" is a concern of Paul).

ᶠ Some few MSS add κυρίῳ ("Lord") to the phrase ἐν Χριστῷ Ἰησοῦ—ἐν κυρίῳ Ἰησοῦ Χριστῷ ("in the Lord Jesus Christ").

ᵍ ℵ L and a few other witnesses read φρονοῦμεν (indicative) instead of φρονῶμεν (hortatory subjunctive). This kind of variant appears elsewhere (cf. Rom 5:1), perhaps as a result of confusion in sound or sight.

ʰ Some witnesses read τῷ αὐτῷ στοιχεῖν κανόνι, αὐτὸ φρονεῖν or τὸ αὐτὸ φρονεῖν αὐτῷ κανόνι στοιχεῖν ("to walk by the same rule, to think the same thing"), or other various combinations of these same words. The shorter reading, adopted for this translation, is supported by the oldest MSS: P¹⁶ P⁴⁶ ℵ* A B 33 and others.

Form/ Structure/ Setting

Paul's Greek at this point is difficult. Hence, it is not possible to see precisely how it relates to what has gone before. True, the new section does begin with a conjunction—ὅτι, but the ambiguous nature of this conjunction (="that," or "because") does not permit one to speak with any assurance. This ambiguity of meaning, and the fact that the several verbs in v 12 are without objects, compound the problem of relationship. One can only hope, therefore, to make an intelligent guess as to how vv 12–16 fit with vv 4–11.

The dominant theme in the previous section (vv 4–11) was the superlative significance of Christ. Although Paul does recite his own personal worthy attributes as well, he does so simply to accentuate the values of Christ—for he considers these attributes of his to be worse than nothing when compared with Christ. They can be easily set aside, abandoned even, if this is necessary to gain Christ. Paul is obsessed with Christ. Nothing else matters but Christ. He can afford to lose all, but not Christ. For him to gain the world but not Christ is to have lost everything. Whereas to gain Christ and lose everything is to possess all. Hence, the apostle's desire is to gain Christ, to be found in Christ. In a word, the total focus of his life is to know Christ intimately. Paul closes this section by giving expression to his hope of attaining the resurrection from the dead. But this mention of the resurrection is made more like an aside than anything else. Certainly it is not the burden of vv 4–11. Christ is the chief theme. Any hope for resurrection and any hope of standing before God in a goodness acceptable to God are based wholly upon Christ.

Hence vv 12–16 may be viewed as relating to the previous section in this way: they provide a caution about past experiences, and a plan of action for the future. Paul has just said that his supreme desire is to know Christ (and this is a worthy goal for any Christian). But lest some should assume that he, Paul (or anyone else for that matter), had already attained complete knowledge of Christ, he immediately proceeds to disabuse them of such an assumption. Christ is too great to be grasped in a single lifetime. And yet this fact does not discourage Paul or dampen his ardor. Rather, it drives him on to know more. The more he knows about Christ, the more he wishes to know. Hence, he views his future as a race course stretching out before a runner who is pressing on to reach the goal and win the prize. Thus, the incomprehensible majesty of Christ is no deterrent to Paul's quest, but a spur urging him to press on to a still greater knowledge of Christ until it is finally complete when he is called up to receive the prize.

At the same time that Paul continues to bare his soul and disclose the motive that drives him, he may also intend his words to be a warning against any claim that "perfection" is possible in the present. Those same Jewish teachers, whom he attacked so vehemently in vv 2–3, were known to state repeatedly that a person who has been circumcised and is true to the Law can reach perfection (Rigaux, *NTS* 4 [1957–58] 237–62). Hence, if they were teaching this in Philippi, Paul, the Christian, who now knows that "perfection" cannot be attained in this way, surely would wish to remind his friends that "perfection" comes only through Jesus Christ and at the resurrection at the last day (cf. 3:21). There is no need, then, to suppose that in addition to such Jewish propagandists the Philippian Christians were beset by still another opponent—Gnostics, who also believed and taught that perfection could be attained on earth now without waiting for, or without any need for the resurrection (Friedrich, NTS 8 [1962] 120). This is not to say there was no Gnostic influence present in Philippi, or that Paul did not know and use Gnostic key words and phrases in his teaching. But there seems little need here to ferret out a new opponent for Paul to attack, in addition to the Jews, in order to justify the statements he makes.

Rather, the elegance of Paul's rhetoric, the depth of feeling he emotes, the unique intimate revelation of his own consuming desire to know Christ and to follow on to know him better—all breathe more the spirit of parenetic rather than polemic. Paul seems more like a pastor who gladly risks being ridiculed or misunderstood in order to care properly for his flock, than a warrior fending off an enemy. He seems more concerned to win converts to Christ, than to win an argument from his opponents. For his style of writing appears designed powerfully to affect his readers, to move them to change, to create within them the same appreciation for and pursuit of Christ that he himself experiences, rather than to put down any enemies one can imagine. Christ is so real to him and so ultimately significant that he wants the Philippians and the whole world, for that matter, to know what he knows and feels.

Comment

12. Paul continues his passionate writing, beginning his new sentence abruptly with οὐχ ὅτι ("not that")—a distinctively NT formula meaning, "I do not say that," or "I do not claim that" (cf. John 6:46; 7:42; 2 Cor 1:24; 3:5; 2 Thess 3:9).

But what is it that Paul here so emphatically disclaims? To answer this question is not an easy matter. First, it is difficult because the verb of the subordinate clause introduced by ὅτι is ἔλαβον, a verb with a wide range of meanings: "to take hold of," "to receive or accept," "to get or obtain," "to make one's own," "to apprehend or comprehend" mentally or spiritually. And second, it is difficult because this verb has no direct object to say what it was that Paul obtained or apprehended. As a consequence many answers to the question have been suggested.

Some say that Paul disclaims having already attained to the resurrection of the dead (cf. v 11; W. Lütgert, *Die Vollkommenen im Philipperbrief und die Enthusiasten in Thessalonich* [BFCT 13, 6. Gütersloh: C. Bertelsmann, 1909]). Others say that he denies having fully achieved righteousness (Klijn, *NovT* 7 [1964–65] 281; Pfitzner, *The Agon Motif*, 142–53, supported by the variant reading of P⁴⁶ and D which add ἢ ἤδη δεδικαίωμαι—"or am already justified"), or moral and spiritual perfection (Müller, Vincent), or the prize at the end of the race (Beare, Bonnard, Moule, Synge). Still others say that Paul deliberately left the object of the verb unexpressed to counter the arrogance of the Gnostics who claimed to know everything, to have attained everything, to have reached the goal, to have become perfect (Collange, Ewald, Gnilka, Haupt, Schmithals, *Paul and the Gnostics*, 97).

None of these interpretations of Paul's concise statement, οὐχ ὅτι ἤδη ἔλαβον, does justice to its vocabulary nor to its context. Hence, one more suggestion may be permitted: Paul means to say that he does not lay claim to having fully grasped the meaning of Christ at this point in time. Christ, then, and the full significance of this person, is the missing object of the verb ἔλαβον.

In justification of this interpretation note the following factors: (1) The verb λαμβάνειν can indeed mean, among other things, "to comprehend mentally or spiritually" (BGD). (2) The strengthened form of λαμβάνειν (καταλαμβάνειν) that appears twice over in immediately succeeding clauses (καταλάβω . . . κατελήμφθην) also carries the idea of "to grasp" in the sense of "to comprehend" (cf. John 1:5; Acts 4:13; 10:34; Eph 3:18; Plato, *Phdr.* 250d; Polyb. 8.4.6; Dion. Hal. 5.46; Joseph. *Vit.* 56; see also the helpful remarks in R. Bultmann, *The Gospel of John*, tr. G. R. Beasley-Murray [Philadelphia: Westminster Press, 1971] 47–48; J. A. Dyer, "The Unappreciated Light," *JBL* 79 [1960] 170–71). (3) The aorist tense of λαμβάνειν (ἔλαβον) that is used here, is a constative aorist collecting Paul's past experiences up to the time of the present and viewing them as a single whole. This is confirmed by the temporal adjunct, ἤδη ("at this time"), that accompanies it (BDF 332,1). (4) The past experiences that are especially envisaged are those described in vv 8–11, but especially the experiences involving Christ—gaining Christ, being found in Christ and coming to know Christ. Paul's encounter with the resurrected and living Christ not only created within him a consuming desire to know Christ intimately and fully, but also an awareness that this is something that cannot be achieved in a moment. To know the incomprehensible greatness of Christ demands a lifetime of arduous inquiry.

It is in just such a context of thought that the next verb, τετελείωμαι, must also be interpreted. With it Paul carries further and underscores his disclaimer by saying, "Nor am I already perfect," i.e. "perfect" in my knowledge and understanding of Christ. (Cf. ἤδη τέλειος ["already perfect"], which seems to have been a catch-phrase of the Gnostics who considered themselves the only ones to have been fully instructed and so to have reached the proper level of illumination, knowledge or understanding: see W. Schmithals, *Paul and the Gnostics*, 99; idem, *Gnosticism in Corinth*, tr. J. E. Steely [Nashville: Abingdon, 1971] 30; cf. also Lightfoot on Col 1:28.) The apostle is keenly aware that his knowledge of Christ is partial, and that he must wait for a future day, the eschatological day (?), when the partial will give way to the perfect (τὸ τέλειον in 1 Cor 13:9–10).

The realization that there is too much to know about Christ for one's knowledge of him ever to be complete this side of the resurrection incites Paul to keep pressing on to see how much understanding he can achieve: διώκω δὲ εἰ καταλάβω. The adversative conjunction δέ ("but") emphasizes this determination. The immensity of the task might indeed paralyze some, *but* not Paul. Διώκειν ("to keep pressing on") belongs to the world of the hunter rather than that of the athlete. It does not properly mean "to run," but "to pursue," "to chase," "to hunt down." Nevertheless, because Paul uses διώκειν in v 14 of an athlete running a race, it is quite likely that he already had this metaphor in mind in v 12 (Beare, Caird). In any case this verb gives expression to the greatness of the effort required, whether it is to make a catch or to win a race, or, in this instance, to know Christ.

Διώκω ("to press on") is followed by εἰ καταλάβω, an example of the subjunctive employed in a dependent construction to express a deliberative question (BDF 368). Εἰ, therefore, is to be translated "whether." Καταλάβω, which is the truly difficult word, may mean "to seize, win, attain," as a runner in a race might run to win the prize (1 Cor 9:24). But it can also have the very different meaning, even in its active form, of "to grasp an idea with one's mind," hence, "to understand" (BGD; J. Dupont, *Gnosis* [Bruges: Des-clée, de Brouwer, 1949] 501–21). It is this latter meaning that makes the most sense here. Paul's one desire is to know Christ. But he is keenly aware that he has not yet grasped (οὐκ ἔλαβον) the full import of the significance of Christ. As a consequence, he sets out, very much like a runner, to see whether he might at last be able to comprehend (καταλάβω) him fully.

The reason Paul gives for this lifetime quest is stated in the clause ἐφ᾽ ᾧ καὶ κατελήμφθην ὑπὸ Χριστοῦ Ἰησου ("inasmuch as I was indeed grasped by Christ Jesus"; for ἐφ᾽ ᾧ as an idiom meaning "because" see BDF 235,2). Once again Paul's rhetorical skill becomes obvious as he plays with two forms of the same verb: καταλάβω . . . κατελήμφθην. First Paul states his goal: it is to grasp Christ Jesus for good and all, but to grasp (καταλάβω) him with his mind and heart and to comprehend him with the full comprehension of faith (cf. Bultmann, *Gospel of John*, 48). But second, in giving a motive for this driving force within him, Paul states that it was because he himself had been grasped (κατελήμφθην) by Christ. Now the meaning of this verb shifts slightly. As Paul uses it here he may intend it to retain still overtones of grasping with the mind, hence, of being known by Christ, i.e. of being chosen by Christ for a specific task (Gal 1:15–16; 4:9; cf. Amos 3:2). But Paul seems now to be using it primarily to refer to that Christ-encounter he experienced on the Damascus road at which time Christ laid violent hands on him, so to speak, forcefully arresting him and setting him off in a new lifelong direction (1 Cor 15:8–10; Michael). Perhaps, then, the English verb "to apprehend" is the one best suited· to express the idea involved in Paul's καταλαμβάνειν. For "to apprehend" can mean both "to lay hold of with the understanding," as well as "to arrest or seize."

13. Once again, with repetitive emphasis, Paul makes it clear to his fellow Christian family members (ἀδελφοί) at Philippi (some of whom may have claimed that they had reached perfection) that even after a further careful weighing of the evidence (λογίζομαι, a verb meaning "to calculate precisely") he must reaffirm his former conclusion that he has not completely grasped

the full significance of Christ (οὐ . . . κατειληφέναι). And if this is true for Paul, it is equally true for all others. What then is to be done? There is only one thing (ἕν; but see Fridrichsen, *ConNT* 9 [1944] 31–32) that can be done. Having come to know Christ partially, one must press on to know Christ perfectly.

Paul expresses this idea in a highly rhetorical, emotion-filled, passionate way. Even the form and structure of his sentence radiate the depth of his feelings. It begins with two concise participial phrases that are perfectly balanced:

$$\begin{array}{llll} τὰ & μὲν & ὀπίσω & ἐπιλανθανόμενος \\ τοῖς & δὲ & ἔμπροσθεν & ἐπεκτεινόμενος \end{array}$$

The μέν ("on the one hand") in the first phrase is answered by the δέ ("on the other hand") in the second; the article and the adverb, τὰ ὀπίσω ("the things behind") in the one, by the article and the adverb, τοῖς ἔμπροσθεν ("the things in front") in the other, and ἐπιλανθανόμενος ("forgetting") by ἐπεκτεινόμενος ("stretching out"). One can easily imagine that Paul took special pains in selecting the double prepositional compound, ἐπ-εκ-τεινόμενος, a word found nowhere else in the Greek Bible. (Ἐκτείνειν, however, is often found in the Gospels: Matt 8:3; 12:13, 49, etc.) With it he carefully matches the corresponding participle, ἐπιλανθανόμενος, and uses it to express precisely what he intends the future course of his life to be.

What is it then that Paul wishes to express so powerfully by such carefully chosen phrases? (1) He wishes to express the importance of completely forgetting (ἐπιλανθανόμενος—note the present tense) the past. Forget those wrongs done, e.g. the persecution of the church (v 6), and so on, whose memory could paralyze one with guilt and despair. Forget, too, those attainments so far achieved as a Christian, the recollection of which might cause one to put life into neutral and to say, "I have arrived." Forget in such a way that the past, good or bad, will have no negative bearing on one's present spiritual growth or conduct. (2) He wishes also to express the importance of continuous concentration on the things that are in front, i.e. on the goal of the full and complete knowledge of Christ Jesus. Live full out now (ἐπεκτεινόμενος—note again the present tense); unceasingly reach out toward something other than oneself (Collange). The participle ἐπεκτεινόμενος is a graphic word, chosen from the arena (Pfitzner, *The Agon Motif,* 139–56) and pictures the Christian as a runner with his body bent over, his hand outstretched, his head fixed forward never giving a backward glance, and his eye fastened on the goal (Vincent, Michael, Moule). It powerfully describes the need for concentration and effort in the Christian life if one is to advance in the knowledge of Christ. It pictures the ceaseless personal exertion, the intensity of the desire of the Christian participant in the contest if he is to achieve the hoped for goal, namely the full and complete understanding of the Savior.

14. The participles in v 13 are circumstantial participles of manner. With them Paul tells *how* he has determined to run the race by not looking back over his shoulder, but straining forward, stretching every nerve and muscle. Now he describes the actual race itself by the verb διώκω. The fundamental

idea underlying διώκειν (cf. v 12), "to pursue," and the present tense in which
this verb now appears underscore once again the incompleteness of Paul's
present situation (W. A. Beardslee, *Human Achievement and Divine Vocation in
the Message of Paul*, SBT 31 [London: SCM Press, 1961] 68). They remind
the reader of the constant alternation back and forth between the "already"
and the "not yet." Διώκω stresses the "not yet" of this dialectical tension
of the life of faith (Bultmann, *Theology* 1, 322). It focuses on the necessity
of constantly striving for the goal. It represents the necessity of constantly
pursuing the end of the course with resolute determination. Διώκω, then,
characterizes one very important aspect of Paul's (and the Christian's) life,
that of progressively discovering what it means to know Christ and so of
pressing forward to reach the "not yet": διώκω ("I keep on running").

But Paul's running is not aimless. It is directed toward the goal—κατὰ
σκοπόν. To be precise, however, the word σκοπός, found only here in the
NT, is not the goal, but the goal-marker. It is that post at the end of the
race upon which the runner fixes his attention (cf. σκοπεῖν, "to keep one's
eyes on"). Unfortunately, Paul in his intensity and desire to make full use
of the stadium-imagery, fails to say what this "goal-marker" corresponds to
in his or the Christian's life. But since it originally was intended to give
direction to the runner and incentive to his flagging energies, one might
guess, then, that Paul meant by σκοπός anything or anyone that kept the
believer from straying from the course of the Christian life, or from slackening
in his moral strivings.

While keeping the goal-marker in view, taking full advantage of its benefits,
Paul races for the prize: τὸ βραβεῖον. This word is qualified by the genitive
phrase, τῆς ἄνω κλήσεως τοῦ θεοῦ (lit. "of the upward call of God"). But what
is intended by this striking expression? Does it refer to God's invitation to
enter the kingdom (1 Thess 2:12) which is perpetually offered and is ἄνω
("upward") in its action and result (RSV; Hendriksen, Plummer)? Does it refer
to "an invitation to a life which is to be lived above, i.e. in God's own eternal
presence," "our heavenward calling" (Caird, Gnilka, Lightfoot; NEB; cf. Philo,
Plant. 6; Heb 3:1)? Does it refer to the high vocation to which God called
Paul and calls all Christians (Beare)? Apparently all these explanations view
the genitive, τῆς ἄνω κλήσεως ("of the upward call") as appositional, meaning
that the "prize" is identical with God's "call."

In keeping with the vivid imagery drawn from the Greek games that pervades this section there is still another explanation of the "upward call" that
seems the most reasonable explanation of all. It sees in the expression τῆς
ἄνω κλήσεως an allusion to the fact that the Olympian games, which included
foot-races, were organized and presided over by agonothetes, highly respected
officers called *Hellenodikai*. "After each event they had a herald announce
the name of the victor, his father's name and his country, and the athlete
or charioteer would come and receive a palm branch at their hands" (G.
Glotz, "Hellenodikai," in C. Daremberg and E. Saglio [eds.], *Dictionnaire des
antiqués grecques et romaines* [Paris: Hachette, 1900–1963] 3,1,60–64). This is
the call to which Paul is now alluding (Collange). Such an explanation as
this has the virtue of *not* identifying the "upward call" with the "prize," and
allows the force of the context to determine what Paul had in mind when

he spoke of that prize. For him it was to be found in Christ (ἐν Χριστῷ), i.e. Christ was his prize. To know Christ fully and completely was the prize for which he had been striving ever since his encounter with Christ on the Damascus road. Hence, the entire verbless expression (v 14*b*) can be paraphrased as follows: "The prize that God, the Agonothete, will give me when he calls me up and announces my name, the prize that is contained in Christ Jesus."

15. "Therefore" (οὖν) with a touch of irony coupled with gentleness Paul exhorts his friends to remember that to be apprehended by Christ does not put the human will out of action, but rather raises it to its highest power, that as the power of Christ's will grows, the effort of the Christian's will does not decrease but grows accordingly (Stauffer, *Theology*, 184). This is the meaning of the imperative-idea with which the apostle now directly addresses the Philippians.

Paul's gentleness is expressed by the hortatory subjunctive, φρονῶμεν. He does not say, "You must" (φρονεῖτε), but more delicately, "we must" (φρονῶμεν). He includes himself along with those to whom he is writing: he and they together stand equally under the same ethical demand of not holding an attitude (φρονεῖν) that assumes such a level of spiritual attainment that further striving becomes unnecessary (see comments at 1:7 for the meaning of φρονεῖν). It is this gentle tone of exhortation that argues against viewing this section (vv 12–16) as a polemic written to oppose either Jewish Christian Gnostics (Schmithals, *Paul and the Gnostics*, 99–104), or legalistic Jews who asserted that they only have perfectly kept the Law and are thus perfect (Klijn, *NovT* 7 [1964–65] 282), or Judaizers who boasted in circumcision as an indication of their being "complete" Christians (Gnilka, Köster, *NTS* 8 [1961–62] 322–23), or martyrs whose death for the faith made them "perfect" (Lohmeyer; cf. Ign. *Rom.* 1.2; 2.1). It seems more reasonable to suppose that what Paul wrote here he wrote because some of his friends at Philippi misunderstood his teaching about justification by faith alone, and as a consequence believed that they had "arrived" and had ceased from that moral striving so characteristic of and essential to the Christian life. He wishes to set the record straight and prompt them to exert themselves once again.

Paul's irony is expressed by his use of τέλειοι ("perfect"). Only a few sentences earlier he had stated unconditionally that as for himself he had not yet reached "perfection" (οὐκ ἤδη τετελείωμαι—v 12). But now he includes himself among the τέλειοι, "the perfect." How can this be?

Some suggest that it is because in v 12 Paul was speaking of *absolute* perfection, the ultimate level of understanding he could only deny having already attained, whereas in v 15 he is speaking of *relative* perfection, i.e. "maturity" as over against a childish immaturity in spiritual matters—a level of understanding he could justly claim both for himself and other Christians (cf. 1 Cor 2:6; 15:20; Heb 5:14; note also Matt 5:48; James 1:4; 3:2 and see Vincent, Hendriksen; GNB, JB, LB, NEB, NIV, RSV).

Others, slightly modifying this interpretation, see the "perfection" of v 12 as ethical perfection, and that of v 15 as perfection in principle (cf. Paul's use of the word ἅγιος, "holy"). "Just as a little child is a perfect human being, but is still far from perfect in his development as man, so the true child of God is also perfect in all parts, although not yet perfect in all stages of his development in faith. In verse 12 Paul confessed that he was not yet perfect in all stages, but here he confesses his perfection in all parts, as child of God" (Müller).

It is best, however, to see in Paul's use of τέλειοι ("perfect") a touch of reproachful, though loving, almost whimsical, irony (Lightfoot, Jones, Moule), for the following reasons: (1) There is no indication whatsoever that the apostle is using the terms, τελείοω/τέλειος, in two different senses within such a short span of words, and thus there is no reason to translate one "perfect" and the other "mature." (2) It seems certain that there were those at Philippi, who, for whatever reasons, believed that they had reached the very kind of "perfection" which Paul denied was attainable this side of the resurrection. Hence, the meaning "perfect" in both places is necessary fully to understand what he is saying. (3) Irony is a favorite technique of the apostle by which he prods his readers on to still greater moral action (Rom 15:1; 1 Cor 8:1; Gal 6:1). He means to say, therefore, that as many of us "as suppose we have reached perfection" (cf. JB) must nevertheless take the following view of things: we must forget the past and continuously push forward toward the goal. He is saying, "Christian perfection really consists only in this constant striving for perfection" (Weiss), that "it is the mark of the perfect man, not to reckon himself perfect" (Chrysostom), that "the nature of a Christian does not lie in what he has become but in what he is becoming" (Luther; see Beare for the last two quotations).

Paul continues once again in words and phrases that are difficult to understand: καὶ εἴ τι ἑτέρως φρονεῖτε. To try to grasp what he means it is necessary to look carefully at each part of this clause: (1) The καί is most likely an adversative conjunction, emphasizing a fact that is surprising, but nevertheless true (BGD). It should be translated "but" rather than "and"—"All of us who are perfect must have a certain attitude, but . . ." (2) The conjunction εἰ ("if") followed by the indicative (φρονεῖτε) can introduce a condition of reality, in which case the if-clause is assumed to be true (BDF 372). Εἰ, therefore, is more accurately translated "since" (cf. Matt 4:6; 6:30; Luke 11:19, 20; 1 Cor 9:11; Phil 2:1, etc.): "but *since* something is so." (3) The "something which is so" is that the Philippians actually *did have* a somewhat different attitude about perfection from the attitude Paul demanded of those who claimed to be "perfect." (τι is used adverbially, meaning "somewhat" [BDF 137, 2] and is coupled with ἑτέρως, a word used only here in the NT, meaning "differently," or "wrongly" [BGD; Lightfoot]). (4) Φρονεῖτε, which answers to φρονῶμεν in v 15*a* is a key word in this letter to the Philippians (1:7; 2:2, 5; 3:19; 4:2, 10)—a word that primarily envisions attitudes rather than specific thoughts about points of doctrine. In adding up all these details one arrives at the conclusion that Paul is saying, "All of us who claim to be perfect must have the attitude that Christian perfection is in reality a constant striving for perfection. *But since you have a somewhat different attitude about this matter. . . .*"

This sentence, whose beginning sounds discouraging, finishes with a note of confidence: καὶ τοῦτο ὁ θεὸς ὑμῖν ἀποκαλύψει ("God will reveal even this to you"). By this clause the apostle says, in effect, to the Philippians: (1) I know what the correct attitude toward "perfection" is which must be held by all who would be "perfect." (2) I know, too, that you hold a different attitude from mine. (3) I know I cannot convince you to change your attitude by logical arguments or apostolic commands. (4) But I know that God can, for he is at work within you. By his gracious activity of unveiling he will reveal (ἀποκαλύψει) even this (καὶ τοῦτο) to you as he did to me, namely, what the truth about perfection really is. The verb ἀποκαλύπτειν has a rather special sense here (cf. Oepke, *TDNT* 4,582–87), meaning that "the revelation of divine truth is not conveyed solely through the apostolate, nor indeed can it be made effective by virtue of external authority of any kind; it requires also the [divine] enlightening of 'the eyes of the heart' (Eph 1:18)" (Beare).

16. The final sentence in this section is the most difficult of all, and its difficulty has been the cause of numerous alterations of the Greek text (see notes above). This sentence begins with the particle πλήν, a word that is used here to break off the discussion in order to emphasize what is truly important (BGD; BDF 449,2) and is translated, "in any case."

The main verb of the sentence is really an infinitive, στοιχεῖν, used with the force of an emphatic imperative (for this use of the infinitive see BDF 389). It is derived from a verb that originally meant "to be drawn up in a line," but which came to be used metaphorically in the sense of "to be in line with," "to follow in someone else's steps," "to hold to" or "to agree with" (BGD; cf. Gal 6:16). In choosing this verb Paul once again stresses the importance of harmony and mutual cooperation in spite of whatever divergence of opinion may exist.

The remaining words, εἰς ὃ ἐφθάσαμεν, τῷ αὐτῷ (lit. "toward that which we have attained, by the same"), although certainly awkward are nevertheless fairly understandable. Εἰς with the accusative indicates the direction of the Christian's moral movement. The relative pronoun ὅ ("that which") has no clear and certain antecedent, but based upon the context one may correctly infer that it points back to whatever knowledge God will reveal and to whatever level of knowledge has already been attained (ἐφθάσαμεν). Τῷ αὐτῷ ("by the same") is a pronoun that refers to the preceding clause: εἰς ὃ ἐφθάσαμεν ("to that which we have attained"), and the dative case is the dative of the norm or standard (cf. Acts 15:1; Gal 5:16, 25; 6:16; Vincent). Together these words constitute Paul's appeal to the Philippians to fall in step with him and together with him begin to live up to whatever level of knowledge they have already acquired by revelation. Granted there may be differences of opinion, different levels of understanding, different degrees of apprehension of truth: and granted there may be need for further revelations, yet these differences must not be allowed to create dissension, nor generate criticism of one another. They must not cause Christians to fall back from high spiritual attainment. What Christians are and claim to be (i.e. men and women of the Spirit, as in Gal 5:25), must govern how they live (Martin, *Philippians*, 1976). The conduct of Christians must be consistent with the level of truth they have already reached (cf. NEB).

Explanation

After having expressed to the Philippians his all-consuming desire to know Christ, Paul proceeds now to disclaim that he has reached that goal. Intense as his desire may be he has not yet grasped the full significance of Christ, nor has he come to a perfect knowledge of him. He emphatically refuses to place himself among any who might claim such perfection. But this falling short of a complete knowledge of Christ in no way dampens his ardor. Rather, it causes him to set out on a course, much like a runner in a race, to see whether he might indeed fully comprehend the meaning of this majestic person. He is spurred on in his endeavor by the fact that not only is he fully known by Christ, but also by the fact that he was forcefully taken hold of by Christ, saved from ruining his life and set off in a new direction of useful service to God and people.

Thus, although he again disclaims having achieved perfect knowledge of Christ, even after a careful evaluation of his successful life as Christ's apostle, he also reaffirms the one course of action open before him: to forget the past with all its failures and successes—all those things that could paralyze him with guilt, or impede him with pride, and to stretch out to the future. Like an athlete with every nerve and muscle taut, with body thrust forward, with eyes firmly fixed on the goal, so Paul pictures his own ceaseless exertion, his own intensity of desire to reach the end of life and gain the prize. Every part of his existence is thrust wholly into the contest to win. Just as the victor in the Olympian games was called up to the judges' stand to receive the crown at the hands of the Agonothete, so Paul hoped to be called up to receive from God the award he coveted: full knowledge of Christ Jesus. Such perfection, he had come to realize, could only be achieved beyond this life, at the end of the race.

As a consequence he urges all who claim already to be perfect to realize that for the time being true Christian perfection "consists only in striving for perfection." He fears that "the perfect" will cease their moral striving, falsely believing that they have achieved their goal, whereas Paul knows that the goal is at the end of the course, at the end of life. Consequently, he knows that the mark of the perfect person is not to reckon oneself perfect, but to realize that he still has a long way to go, and much good still to do.

But since there were those at Philippi who had a different attitude about perfection from that which Paul championed, and since they could not be convinced by logical argument or won over by apostolic demands, Paul lovingly commends them to God who alone can reveal the truth to them by enlightening their minds. The apostle is certain that God will do this for them. In the meantime he asks only that together and in harmony they march forward into the future, living up to the level of understanding they have already reached.

D. Paul's Life: A Model to Imitate (3:17)

Bibliography

Betz, H. D. *Nachfolge und Nachahmung Jesu Christi im Neuen Testament.* Tübingen: J. C. B. Mohr, 1967. **Boer, W. P. de.** *The Imitation of Paul: An Exegetical Study.* Kampen: J. H. Kok, 1962. **McMichael, W. F.** "Be Ye Followers Together of Me: Συμμιμηταί μου γίνεσθε—Phil. III.17." *ExpTim* 5 (1893–94) 287. **Schulz, A.** *Nachfolgen und Nachahmen.* München: Kösel-Verlag, 1962. **Wulf, F.** "Seid meine Nachahmer, Brüder! (Phil 3,17)." *Geist und Leben* 34 (1961) 241–47.

Translation

¹⁷ *Continue to join with one another in imitating me, my brothers. Keep your eyes constantly on those who live according to the pattern I gave you.*

Form/Structure/Setting

In accordance with the form of instruction established within the letter, namely warnings followed by encouragement through example, Paul again encourages his Philippian friends (ἀδελφοί) by giving them a model, or models, to follow as they set about organizing their lives within a pagan world where values differed radically from Judeo-Christian values. Against ambition, conceit, pride and a self-serving attitude, Paul holds before the eyes of the Philippians the humility, self-emptying, self-giving conduct of Christ whose whole life was dedicated to obeying God and serving others (2:3–8). Against the cry of "perfection now" (3:12–16) Paul shows by the striking and authoritative example of his own personal experience that this is a false cry, harmful to progress, and an impediment to the life of constant moral struggle that must characterize the Christian's entire existence.

This one verse, then, stands as a warning by example against two wrong emphases originating from the same group of people, the Jews (cf. v 2). It is a warning against the belief that one can be perfect now (vv 12–16), and against the belief that external rituals can be a means of grace (vv 18–19). Paul, an apostle of Jesus Christ, not having yet attained perfection, is thereby driven on to still greater moral endeavors. Follow his example. Leave off claiming perfection and get busy living the Christian life. Paul, a Jew par excellence (vv 5–6), having seen the all-sufficiency of Christ is thereby forced to surrender confidence in the effectiveness of the observance of food laws, or rites of circumcision (v 19), to establish a right relationship between himself and God. Follow his example and leave off thinking only of things that belong to this world. Leave off putting confidence solely in human accomplishments (πεποιθότες ἐν σαρκί). This verse stands as a transition point between these two errors. It forms the conclusion to the one and the introduction to the other.

Comment

17. For the third time now in chap. 3 Paul addresses the Philippians as "brothers" (cf. vv 1, 13), reminding them that they with him belong to the same spiritual family in which equality is the hallmark. This reminder is important to prevent any irritation at or misunderstanding of what the apostle is now about to say, namely, "Imitate me!" In this statement Paul does not intend to say that he is better than anyone else. In calling for imitation, it is not for people to emulate his privileges, achievements or advantages, but rather his self-denying, self-giving acts (1 Cor 11:1), his willingness to suffer for the sake of others (1 Thess 1:6; 2:14; cf. 2 Thess 3:7–9), his losing all for Christ, his imitation of Christ (1 Cor 11:1; 1 Thess 1:6; cf. Eph 5:1; Phil 2:6–11), his seeking for a goodness not in himself but in God, his admis-

sion that perfection is not yet his, but is eagerly pursued by him, and so on (cf. 1 Cor 4:16–17).

In calling for imitation Paul uses an ambiguous expression that is open to more than one interpretation: συμμιμηταί μου γίνεσθε (lit. either "become fellow imitators of me," or "become fellow imitators with me"). The noun συμμιμητής is found only here in all of Greek literature, hence the ambiguity. Some have pursued its meaning by studying each of the nouns in the NT that are similarly compounded with the preposition σύν ("with"). They conclude from their study that Paul means, "Become imitators along with me of something or someone," i.e. Christ (cf. 1 Cor 11:1, and see McMichael, *ExpTim* [1893–94] 287).

Others suggest that the συμ- in συμμιμητής has no meaningful value whatsoever. Συμμιμηταί, therefore, is equivalent to μιμηταί ("imitators"), on the analogy of ἕπομαι and συνέπομαι both of which mean, "to follow along with." Paul, then, is saying nothing more than he has said elsewhere, simply, "Become *imitators* of me" (1 Cor 4:16, and see Michaelis, *TDNT* 4,667, n. 13).

More likely, however, the noun συμμιμητής was coined by Paul from the verb συμμιμεῖσθαι ("to join in imitating"; see LSJ) to stress his desire that there be a community effort in following his example: "Imitate me, one and all of you together!" (Betz, *Nachfolge*, 145–53; see also de Boer, *Imitation*, 169–88; Schulz, *Nachfolgen, passim*). Such an interpretation (1) best accounts for the origin and meaning of the compound word, συμμιμητής, (2) does justice to the genitive, μου, by taking it as the object of the action implied in the noun it modifies: συμμιμητής, (3) takes into consideration the fact that there is nothing in the context to indicate that Paul wishes the Philippians to imitate him *as he imitates Christ,* and (4) reinforces Paul's emphasis on the importance of the Christians' corporate life, of doing things together and in harmony.

Paul, however, recognizes that it may be difficult for some to imitate one who is absent from them. Hence, he continues by urging the Philippians to fix their eyes on those nearer at hand, on those, perhaps, within their own community, like Epaphroditus (2:25–30), whose lives conform to his teaching.

The verb Paul uses here, σκοπεῖν, picks up on the theme introduced by σκοπός ("the goal-marker," that upon which the runner fixes his eyes) in v 14. It conveys the idea of close observation, of fixed attention. Sometimes it means, "Mark" and stay away from (Rom 16:17). Here, however, it means, "Mark" and follow (Lightfoot). Paul's concern is that his friends will notice and follow people who consistently walk (τοὺς περιπατοῦντας, a present participle), i.e. who continuously behave in such a way (οὕτως) that their daily conduct embodies the essence of the Christian faith as he, Paul, has experienced it and modeled (τύπον) it. The apostle asks them to "look at men they know and see the proof of his teaching in their lives" (Martin, *Philippians,* 1976).

The Greek at this point, however, raises a question. Literally it says, "as you have us (ἡμᾶς) for a pattern (τύπον)." Does the ἡμᾶς here mean Paul *and others,* or simply Paul by himself? Should it be translated "us" (as most translations), or "me" (cf. LB, Moffatt)? Several factors point to "me" as the correct translation: (1) The word τύπος, originally meaning an "impression left by a blow" (cf. John 20:25), comes through usage to mean an "archetype," "pattern" or "model" (BGD). In Paul's letters it refers to "the determinative 'example,'" "the model which makes an impress because it is moulded by God" (Goppelt, *TDNT* 8,248–49). (2) τύπον is singular and ἡμᾶς is plural. If ἡμᾶς is a real plural one might have expected τύπους (plural) to match it: "us as examples." (3) The order and choice of words in this sentence imply that Paul differentiates between himself as model and others and considers himself to be the supreme model (τύπος), on a plane above other worthy models. His words are: "Be *imitators* of me" (συμμιμηταί μου), on the one hand, but "*Mark and follow* those who walk in a certain way" (σκοπεῖτε τοὺς οὕτω περιπατοῦντας), on the other. (4) The Philippians are to follow "those who walk in this certain way" *only* because their teaching and life style accords with the pattern laid down by someone other than themselves. The Philippians have a standard by which they can judge any so-called leader: καθὼς ἔχετε τύπον ἡμᾶς. (5) If the "us" in this phrase is pressed, one is immediately at a loss to know who it is that Paul elevates along with himself to this high place of "determinative example." He gives no hint in the immediate context as to who these might be. (6) The literary plural, i.e. the use of "we" instead of "I," was a widespread tendency among Greek authors (BDF 280). (7) Paul himself sometimes uses "we/us" when he really means "I/me" (Rom 1:5; 2 Cor 11:6 [φανερώσαντες]; 1 Thess 2:18; 3:1–5, especially vv 3 and 5; see Moule, *Idiom Book,* 118–19). As a consequence it is not always possible to determine when he is referring to his own life and personal experiences and when he is identifying himself with some or all of the group he mentions (but see W. F. Lofthouse, "Singular and Plural in St. Paul's Letters," *ExpTim* 58 [1947] 179–82). (8) It has been suggested that the context indicates that Paul intends by his remarks here in v 17 to assert his apostolic authority in order to counter conflicting ideas and practices at Philippi (cf. vv 16, 18–19). "Imitate me" means, then, not only, "Walk as I do, but . . . also . . . (and primarily): Recognize my authority, be obedient" (Michaelis, *TDNT* 4,668, against de Boer, *Imitation,* 184–87). When all these elements are put together it appears that Paul is here using the plural pronoun, ἡμᾶς, but has in mind the singular, ἐμέ. He uses the literary "us" to mean "me."

Explanation

Paul's instruction, "Join together in imitating me," appears on the surface to be an expression of intolerable conceit. But it is not. The apostle is fully aware of his potential to fail (1 Cor 9:27), of his lack of "perfection," of his struggle to attain (vv 12–14). Nevertheless, confident that his own manner of life, characterized by self-renunciation, humility, and service to others, and his own presuppositions, namely, that God is, that Christ is the only way to approach God, and that the Holy Spirit provides the power to live acceptably before God, and so on, are so thoroughly right and true, he is unafraid to present himself, in whom these characteristics and beliefs are embodied, as a model for others to follow. Like an experienced craftsman who shows an apprentice how to do a difficult job (Grayston), or like a scout, who knows the way and leads a caravan through perilous terrain, he is in no way ashamed to say, "Follow me!" nor is he arrogant in doing so.

But if the Philippians find it difficult to imitate Paul because he is many miles removed from them, he urges them to seek out others whose conduct is wholly in accord with the pattern he himself has established.

All of this shows the importance of models for the early church. Those first Christians, coming as they did from a pagan society with values often totally antithetic to Christian values, needed not only to hear what was right, but to see it done. It was inadequate for them to have Christian truth presented in a code of precepts and maxims. They needed to observe it embodied in the lives of Christ's ministers. Hence, Paul was keenly conscious of his own responsibility to give the Philippians tangible proof of the truth of the gospel as truth made tangible, quantifiable, measurable in a human life, in his life and the lives of those who followed his example.

E. Warning against Imitating Other Teachers (3:18, 19)

Bibliography

Gnilka, J. *BZ* 9 (1965) 258–76. **Gunther, J. J.** *St. Paul's Opponents.* **Holladay, C. R.** *Restoration Quarterly* 3 (1969) 77–90. **Jewett, R.** *NTS* 17 (1970–71) 198–212. **Klijn, A. F. J.** *NovT* 7 (1964–65) 278–84. **Köster, H.** *NTS* 8 (1961–62) 317–32. **Schmithals, W.** *Paul and the Gnostics.*

Translation

[18] *For many are living* [a] *as enemies of the cross of Christ. I told you about them many times before, and I tell you about them again weeping as I do so.* [19] *Their end is destruction. Their observance of food laws and their glorying in circumcision has become their god. They are people whose minds are set on earthly things.*

Notes

[a] p[46] inserts βλέπετε before τοὺς ἐχθρούς, perhaps in an unnecessary attempt to explain the accusative, τοὺς ἐχθρούς, or perhaps to make βλέπετε τοὺς ἐχθροὺς analogous to βλέπετε τοὺς κύνας, κ.τ.λ., in 3:2.

Form/Structure/Setting

This section relates to the preceding section as cause to effect. Why does Paul press the Philippians to join together in imitating him (v 17)? Why is he concerned that they mark and follow those who "walk" according to the pattern he has cut out (v 17)? Because (γάρ) there are many would-be leaders, teachers, models, and so on, who "walk" contrary to this pattern. They are people who teach wrong doctrine and model wrong behavior, and who, if followed, would carry with them to destruction all who pay heed to them.

Once again, as in v 2, the apostle breaks out into the harshest kind of language to describe these persons, these "enemies of the cross of Christ": "their end is destruction; their god is their belly; their glory is in their shame; their mind-set is fixed on this world." Once again his passionate feelings against them are registered in his rhetoric. Its features are short, verbless sentences; constructions that are broken off without proper completion; clipped phrases whose meaning defies precise explanation; strong words, whose force lies not in lexical definitions, but in the sound and suddenness with which they come. Once again he writes furiously about people whom he does not name.

Because Paul does not name these "enemies" no one today can be certain of their identity. This fact, however, does not stop speculation about who they were, nor should it. One's understanding of who Paul is talking about, determines to a large extent the meaning of the words he uses to describe them. Therefore, any attempt to identify them can only be met with appreciation.

Some interpreters see these as Jewish Christians (Judaizers) who opposed the gospel of free grace as Paul preached it, refused to believe that the death of Christ on the cross was sufficiently meritorious in itself to secure the favor of God, and required, therefore, the keeping of the Law as a necessary supplement for salvation (Müller). Others understand them to be heathen who opposed the Christian gospel because it disturbed their life of shameful lust (Weiss). Others believe that they were antinomian Christians, people who had distorted Paul's doctrine of grace and interpreted Christian liberty as license to gratify the lusts of the flesh (Michael; Beare, Betz, *Nachfolge*, 151; Jones, Scott), or Christians with gnostic tendencies, people who had reached such a degree of spiritual perfection that what they did on the physical plane was inconsequential (cf. Köster, *NTS* 8 [1962] 328). Others think that Paul had in mind those who were willing to deny Christ in the time of persecution and the threat of martyrdom (Lohmeyer). Others view these as Christians who refused to recognize the decisive eschatological nature of the event of the Cross and Resurrection of Christ which inaugurated a radically new order of things and which stamped this new way of life as a life of self-sacrifice and service (Collange). Others are certain that Paul had in mind here the same group of people he addressed at the beginning of chap 3 and to whom he alludes again in vv 12–16. They are not Jewish Christians, but Jews who were ardent propagandists seeking to win converts to their religion in every part of the world (Houlden). This last view of who these "enemies" were is the one adopted here, and it is in light of such a view that vv 18–19 will be interpreted in the comments that follow (see Introduction, xliv–xlvii).

Comment

18. If one should inquire as to why Paul so urgently asked his Philippian friends to imitate him and closely to follow other worthy leaders like himself, the answer is quickly given. The conjunction γάρ ("for"), with which this new section begins, states the reason: It was because, in contrast to the few who conducted themselves (τοὺς περιπατοῦντας) in accordance with the pattern of teaching and living set forth by the apostle, there were many (πολλοί) who conducted themselves (περιπατοῦσι) in a very different way that was not only wrong-headed, but evil (κακῶς: although this word is not in the text, it may correctly be inferred from the context; see Vincent). This statement

is not necessarily a comment on their moral performance, however. These people may have been, and probably were, very religious, honest, law-abiding citizens. But for Paul, if their "goodness" and the religious acts that they faithfully performed in any way tended to keep them from casting themselves wholly upon God and asking for the righteousness that he supplies only through Jesus Christ, if their beliefs and practices set them in opposition to the gospel of salvation by Christ alone, if their doing the Law threatened the exclusiveness of the forgiveness of sins by faith in Christ, then their conduct was indeed "evil" because it brought ultimate harm both to themselves and to others (see comments on v 2; Richardson, *Israel*, 114; see also Sanders, *Paul and Palestinian Judaism*, 426–28, 550). And even if these Jewish missionaries had not yet reached Philippi with their teaching, Paul nevertheless considered it necessary to warn against them simply because he knew of their numbers (πολλοί) and the zeal with which they propagated their religion (cf. A. Harnack, *The Mission and Expansion of Christianity in the First Three Centuries*, tr. J. Moffatt [New York: G. P. Putnam's Sons, 1908] 1,1–10; Moore, *Judaism* 1, 93–121; E. Schürer, *The History of the Jewish People in the Age of Jesus Christ* [New York: Scribners, 1891] 2.2, 220–25).

So numerous were these missionaries, and so persuasive their message that Paul had often warned the Philippians about them (οὓς πολλάκις ἔλεγον ὑμῖν) believing that repetition was an excellent preventative. He used to warn them (note the imperfect, ἔλεγον) in speech when he was present with them in Philippi, and in letters (cf. Pol. *Phil.* 3.2) when he was absent. He warns them again now (νῦν). And he does so with tears. Actually the word translated "with tears" is a participle called a circumstantial participle of manner (κλαίων), formed from the verb κλαίειν. This verb implies not tears only "but lamentation, audible grief" (Moule; BGD; Matt 2:18). It was chosen by Paul to express the depth of his emotion at this point as he reflects on these people.

Now what is interesting to note is that Paul does not say that he weeps *for* anyone (cf. Matt 2:18; Rev 18:9 t.r.). This may indeed have been the case, that is, that he wept for his enemies, for Paul witnesses elsewhere to the deep grief he has for the Jews, the ceaseless pain he has in his heart for them expressing the wish that he himself might be accursed could this effect the salvation of his brothers, the Israelites (Rom 9:1–5). It is easy, therefore, to imagine his pain here spilling over once again into lamentation for these about whom he writes (cf. Acts 20:31; 2 Cor 2:4 to see the tenderness which characterized Paul's dealing with people). But the verb κλαίειν in fact is used here without any object, indicating, perhaps, that his tears were tears not of compassion for the Jews, but of frustration at their obduracy. His experience with them presently in Jerusalem and in Caesarea showed to him more clearly than ever how closed off they were to the gospel, and how vigorously they opposed—to the point of persecution—anyone who dared to proclaim it (Acts 23:1–3, 12–15; 24:1–9; 28:25–29).

Thus in frustration and anguish Paul labels them not merely "enemies of the cross of Christ," but "*the* enemies (τοὺς ἐχθρούς) of the cross." And why does he so label them? Because the message of the cross, which is nothing other than the gospel, indeed an exhaustive statement of the content of the gospel—namely, that Christ must be crucified, that the Messiah had to die in order for sinners to be forgiven by God—was the very thing that scandalized the Jews (1 Cor 1:23). The gospel was an "offense" to them and "foolishness," because in the cross God did precisely the opposite of what they expected him to do (cf. C. K. Barrett, *The First Epistle to the Corinthians* [New York: Harper and Row, 1968] 51, 55; H. Conzelmann, *1 Corinthians* [Philadelphia: Fortress Press, 1975] 41, 47). They, therefore, could not accept the message of the cross, nor could they tolerate its dissemination. Paul himself had experienced their hostility. He knew first hand their opposition to the gospel and their determination to stamp out that message which struck at the very heart of their religion (cf. Acts 17:5, 13; 18:6; 19:9). In those earliest days of the history of the church the Jews could thus rightly be termed "*the* enemies of the cross of Christ."

19. If "the cross of Christ," i.e. "Christ's death on the cross," is the one essential thing for salvation, and if the Jews, or anyone else for that matter, reject this as absurd and scandalous, then they, by the nature of things, have turned away from salvation to its opposite. Paul says of them, not with any sense of delight but rather of pain, that their "end" (τὸ τέλος) as the natural result, the inevitable consequences of their sustained decision, is "destruction" (ἀπωλεία; cf. 1 Cor 1:18).

᾿Απωλεία originally was used in the sense of "loss." Later it came to mean "waste" (Mark 14:4), or "destruction," "annihilation," "ruin." Especially it was used of eternal destruction as punishment for the wicked (Matt 7:13; Rev 17:8, 11; 2 Pet 3:7). Paul seems to be using it here in this last sense since he couples it with τὸ τέλος ("the end," "the goal"). Even so the precise meaning of ἀπωλεία is difficult to pin down. Hence, as often is the case it is best explained in terms of its opposites: σωτηρία ("salvation," Phil 1:28); περιποίησις ψυχῆς ("the preserving of one's soul," Heb 10:39); ζωὴ αἰώνιος ("eternal life," John 3:16). For Paul, then, to reject the crucified Christ as the sole means of salvation is in effect to reject salvation. It is to lose one's soul and thus forfeit life. Elsewhere he says of such people, τὸ τέλος ἐκείνων θάνατος ("their end is death," Rom 6:21), a condition in which the destiny of life outside of Christ is turned to its opposite, i.e. corruption (Gal 6:8) or destruction (Rom 9:22) in the active sense of the word (Oepke, *TDNT* 1,396–97), "the absolute antithesis of the life intended by God and saved by Christ" (Ridderbos, *Paul,* 112–13).

Paul continues his description of these "enemies" with words that are ambiguous in nature, and with a sentence structure capable of mistranslation: ὧν ὁ θεὸς ἡ κοιλία καὶ ἡ δόξα ἐν τῇ αἰσχύνῃ αὐτῶν.

The key words in this clause are κοιλία ("belly") and αἰσχύνη ("shame"). On the surface they seem to say that these people are licentious individuals who "conceive of no higher good than the satisfaction of their bodily appetites" (Scott), who take delight in sexual sins (see Schmithals, *Paul,* 110–11; cf. also Beare, Jones, Michael, Weiss). But if the exegesis of this passage is correct thus far then κοιλία and αἰσχύνη must mean something very different from gross self-indulgence.

In Rom 16:18 κοιλία is used "for that sphere of things which is opposed by Christ and which is passing away" (Houlden; Behm, *TDNT* 3,788), things which, in Paul's mind, could and did include devotion to the Law. Early Christian commentators, such as Theodore of Mopsuestia, Ambrosiaster, and Pelagius took κοιλία as a reference to Jewish laws about food (see Behm, *TDNT* 3,788, n. 14). The NT does not elsewhere describe a licentious person in terms of one who "serves his belly." On the other hand it does make clear that the Jews were people very much concerned about laws relating to food and drink, about what they could and could not eat, about how they were to eat, etc. (Col 2:16, 20–21, 23; cf. Heb 9:10). The NT indicates, too, that the Jews on occasion had elevated traditions having to do with "the belly" to such an exalted place that they took precedence over the laws of God (cf. Mark 7:1–16). In this sense, then, it could be said that their god, i.e. that which they devoted themselves to, was their belly. Their scrupulous observance of food laws became their belly-god (see Barth, Behm, *TDNT* 3,788, Ewald, P. Feine, "Die Abfassung des Phil. in Ephesus," *BFCT* 20 [1914] 26–28, Müller, who understand κοιλία indeed as a reference to food laws, but see the persons involved as Judaizers rather than Jews).

Furthermore, if, as is argued here, Paul is alluding to punctilious, Law-keeping Jews rather than to libertines, then αἰσχύνη ("shame") is more likely to be a reference to "nakedness," one's private parts meaning those parts of the body that are unpresentable (cf. 1 Cor 12:23) than it is to shameful lusts. Αἰσχύνη, therefore, becomes Paul's way of pouring bitter scorn on the rite of circumcision (cf. 3:2), when in his judgment circumcision becomes that in which a person boasts (cf. Gal 6:13) and upon which one depends for salvation. (Barth: " 'Their god the belly and their glory in their shame!'— a further allusion to circumcision, which for concreteness leaves nothing to be desired.")

One further observation about the structure of the sentence is needed. The conjunction καί ("and") links ἡ κοιλία ("the belly") and ἡ δόξα ("the glory") together as a single subject with ὁ θεός ("the god") as the predicate. The entire clause (ὧν ὁ θεὸς ἡ κοιλία καὶ ἡ δόξα ἐν τῇ αἰσχύνῃ αὐτῶν) literally translated should be as follows: "whose god is the belly *and* the glory in their shame." When interpreted this concise expression means not "god is their stomach, and their glory is in their shame" (cf. GNB, JB, NEB, NIV, RSV), but "they have made their stomach *and* their glory in their shame their god." This is to say that these people have permitted food laws and the rite of circumcision to become god to them. They have become so preoccupied with scrupulous observance of ritual detail, so obsessed with the supreme importance (δόξα) of circumcision and with seeing that it was carried out and carried out correctly, that they had no thought for anything or anyone higher. God became obscured by religion. The true God was replaced by a false god to whom devotion was duly paid.

It is no wonder then that Paul sums up his attack on these "enemies of the cross of Christ" with his most stinging criticism, presented in a nominative participial phrase that, without any grammatical connection, expresses his strongest feelings of amazement (Lightfoot) (οἱ τὰ ἐπίγεια φρονοῦντες, "these are people whose minds are fixed on earthly things"). Again, it must be pointed out "this is not a comment on their moral performance; it simply states that for Paul 'they are concerned with values which pass away, having neither divine origin or eternal quality' " (Houlden; Köster, *NTS* 8 [1962] 328; see also Klijn, *NovT* 7 [1965] 278–80). What stands as a judgment against the Jews becomes a warning to everyone. There exists always the tragic possibility of exchanging the glorious immortal God for some lesser deity. Strangely, this potentiality has the greatest chance of becoming reality in the realm of the religious, where doctrine and ritual so easily become that to which people wholly devote themselves and to which they commit themselves completely (cf. Rom 1:21–23).

Explanation

In this section Paul explains why he asks the Philippians to imitate him and to follow closely those leaders who adhere to his teaching and practice. It is because there are many other leaders who go off in a very different and wrong-headed direction, and who would gladly take them along with them. The apostle has often spoken to his friends about these teachers. He does so once again with tears of frustration as he realizes finally that they will not change and their hostility toward him will never abate.

They are enemies. Not Paul's enemies only, but more accurately enemies of the cross of Christ, i.e. of the fact that the Messiah died on a cross. They are Jews who have set themselves against Paul's gospel which says that salvation is exclusively through the crucified and resurrected Christ. They are enemy "Number One" of the cross, *the* enemy, to whom the message of the cross is a *skandalon,* a cause of utter revulsion, a reason for anger and opposition. They will have nothing to do with it, and they will try to do everything they can against it. Thus, because these Jews reject out of hand the only one who can save them, preserve their souls, and give them life, there is nothing left but for them to experience the opposite—loss, destruction, death—the utter ruin of their lives.

Destruction will most surely be their end if they persist in their rejection of the crucified Christ, even though they are scrupulously precise in keeping the Law. The care with which they observed every last precept concerning food and drink and their glorying in the ancient covenantal rite of circumcision did not solve their problem, but rather exacerbated it. Why? Because these who faithfully performed such religious practices made them their god. They overlooked the true God by paying too much attention to ritual. Their minds became set on earthly things and they lost any ability to look up (cf. Col 3:2).

What makes this section so poignant is that Paul takes the most exalted religious and ethical austerity of those he would warn against and describes it in terms which, if found in any other context, would have to be understood as a description of the basest of bodily sins. But this is *intentional.* That is precisely how Jewish piety "really does look, seen from the standpoint of the preaching of the cross. . . . Of course Paul is speaking of depravity, but the fact that he brands as depraved those who, bypassing the cross of Christ and bypassing faith and its righteousness, call for *holiness* and *cleanness—*

that he drags their *glory* in the mire (he may well and truly do it, after having done exactly the same with his own glory in vv 7–9)—*that* is the bitter point of vv [18–19]" (Barth).

F. Paul's Life: Hope in the Future and Unseen (3:20, 21)

Bibliography

Becker, J. "Erwägungen zu Phil 3,20–21." *TZ* 27 (1971) 16–29. **Böttger, P. C.** "Die eschatologische Existenz der Christen. Erwägungen zu Philipper 3:20." *ZNW* 60 (1969) 244–63. 1938. **Bornhäuser, K.** *Jesus Imperator Mundi.* Gütersloh: C. Bertelsmann, 1938. **Cox, S.** "The Heavenly Citizenship." *Expositor,* 2nd series, 3 (1882) 303–13. **Flanagan, N.** "A Note on Philippians 3:20–21." *CBQ* 18 (1956) 8–9. **Güttgemanns, E.** "Die Problematik von Phil 3,20f." *Der leidende Apostel und sein Herr.* Göttingen: Vandenhoeck und Ruprecht, 1966. **Levie, J.** "Le chrétien citoyen du ciel (Phil 3,20)." *Studiorum Paulinorum Congressus Internationalis Catholicus, 1961,* vol 2. AnBib 18 (1963) 81–88. **Schneider, N.** *Die rhetorische Eigenart der paulinischen Antithese.* Tübingen: J. C. B. Mohr, 1970. **Siber, P.** *Mit Christus Leben.* **Stanley, D. M.** *Christ's Resurrection in Pauline Soteriology.* Rome: Pontificio Instituto Biblico, 1960. **Strecker, G.** "Redaktion und Tradition in Christus-Hymnus." *ZNW* 55 (1964) 75–78. **Volz, P.** *Die Eschatologie der jüdischen Gemeinde.* Tübingen: J. C. B. Mohr, 1934. **Zwaan, J. de.** "Philippenzen 3:20 en de κοινή." *Theologische Studiën* 31 (1913) 289–300.

Translation

20 For our citizenship is in heaven,
    and from heaven we eagerly wait for a Savior,
    The Lord Jesus Christ.
21 He will transform our lowly bodies
    so that they might become [a] like his glorious
    body.
    And he will achieve this goal by the out-working
    of his ability to subject everything to himself.[b]

Notes

[a] D² ℵ and the majority text add εἰς τὸ γένεσθαι αὐτό before σύμμορφον. ℵ A B D and several other witnesses omit these words. The addition apparently is secondary in that it serves to smooth out and make clear an otherwise awkward but understandable construction.

[b] ℵ² L Ψ and other MSS read ἑαυτῷ ("to himself") for αὐτῷ. This change simply makes precise the ambiguity contained in αὐτῷ.

Form/Structure/Setting

This section seems not to fit easily with the context in which it is placed. Its apocalyptic theme of the church as a colony of heaven, eagerly expecting a savior to come from above to set everything right, to deliver it from its present mortal weakness, and to transfigure it from lowliness to glory, is unexpected to say the least. Nothing that has immediately preceded these verses has prepared the reader for this kind of happy outburst. There has been no recounting of suffering, no tale of woe, no despairing of life as things that would naturally give rise to such an affirmation of hopeful confidence of deliverance in the future (cf. 2 Cor 1:8–10; 4:7–14).

In addition, conjunctions are particles designed to connect sentences or groups of sentences logically to each other. But the conjunction that connects this section with the section before it (vv 18–19) hardly seems capable of doing so. It is the conjunction γάρ ("for") whose normal function is to introduce the reason or cause for that which has just been mentioned. Paul has just finished saying that the enemies of the cross of Christ are people whose minds are fixed on earthly things. Now he continues with γάρ: *"For* our citizenship is in heaven. . . ."* This presents such a difficulty that the earliest quotations of this passage by Greek authors substitute δέ ("but") for γάρ (Lightfoot), and modern versions translate γάρ as "but."

Furthermore, a careful examination of the language and style of writing found in this section and a study of its unusual words and rhythmic patterns, and so on, suggest that it is another christological hymn, perhaps composed early in the church's existence, found and used by Paul because it precisely expressed his own ideas. If he used it in its entirety, quoting it exactly, then the conjunction γάρ with which it begins is inconsequential and should be ignored as not originally being intended to do what translators must now try to make it do (see Becker, *TZ* 27 [1917] 16–29; Flanagan, *CBQ* 18 [1956] 8–9; Güttgemanns, *Leidende Apostel,* 240–47; Lohmeyer; Strecker, *ZNW* 55 [1964] 75–78). Like the Christ-hymn (2:6–11) this hymn, too, has a cosmic sweep to it, seeing Jesus Christ as sovereign Lord with everything subject to him and everything under his control. But now for the first time the title σωτήρ ("savior") is added to his name (Becker, *TZ* 27 [1971] 16–29). Even the vocabulary of this new hymn, its words and phrases, its essential ideas, parallel those of the earlier hymn (cf. Martin, *Philippians,* 1976; Flanagan, *CBQ* 18 [1956] 8–9; Güttgemanns, *Leidende Apostel,* 214):

σύμμορφον ("conform," 3:21)	μορφή ("form," 2:6, 7)
ὑπάρχει ("is," 3:20)	ὑπάρχων ("being," 2:6)
μετασχηματίσει ("change the likeness," 3:21)	σχῆμα ("likeness," 2:7)
ταπεινώσεως ("humble station," 3:21)	ἐταπείνωσεν ("humbled," 2:8)
δύνασθαι . . . ὑποτάξαι τὰ πάντα ("able to subdue all things," 3:21)	πᾶν γόνυ κάμψῃ ("every knee shall bow," 2:10)
κύριον Ἰησοῦν Χριστόν ("the Lord Jesus Christ," 3:20)	κύριος Ἰησοῦς Χριστός ("Jesus Christ is Lord," 2:11)
δόξης ("glory," 3:21)	δόξαν ("glory," 2:11)

Thus, when translating, one is fully justified in setting this section forth in poetic form to call attention to its hymnlike characteristics.

Although, as has been pointed out, this section does not fit easily into its context, and although it may originally have been part of a very different context with a very different train of thought, it is here nevertheless, and one is compelled to ask why Paul puts it here. Paul does so because it provides the final answer to his verbal contest with the Jews: Their πολίτευμα ("colony") is here in this world; the Christians' πολίτευμα is in heaven. Jews are people whose minds are earth-bound since the earth is the limit of their mental horizon; Christians have their minds fixed on heaven from where they eagerly expect the Savior to come. Jews expect perfection now by keeping the Law; Christians yearn for the future at which time perfection will be achieved. Jews stand as enemies of the crucified Christ; Christians own Christ as Lord and see him as sovereign over the universe. Jews will find their end to be destruction, however ecstatic and glorious their present may be; Christians may be straining now, morally struggling to attain. But their goal will be so full of richness that nothing can compare with it. Their weak mortal bodies will be transformed and made like Christ's resplendent body. This section, thus, is a capstone to Paul's teaching: In Christ the Christian has been brought into a new ethically controlled relationship to God. This new relationship "commits the believer to a life-style in which suffering and hardship are his present lot in anticipation of the day when he will be set free. The Pauline disciple is like a runner in a race, or an athlete at the games. He struggles and exerts himself now, by God's assistance, in the hope that he one day will reach the winning post and gain the prize. He is thus faced with a paradox: already 'saved' and with the race begun, he awaits and strains forward to attain his resurrection, which will be the completion of his salvation under God . . . (1:6; 2:16; 3:11–14)" (Martin, *Philippians*, 1976).

Comment

20. "Our citizenship is in heaven," ἡμῶν γὰρ τὸ πολίτευμα ἐν οὐρανοῖς ὑπάρχει. The pronoun ἡμῶν ("our") stands first in this new section. It has the emphatic position (as in v 3) in order again to draw sharp contrast between "them" and "us," between Jews and Christians. Their citizenship is on earth (v 19); *ours* is in heaven.

The word translated "citizenship" (πολίτευμα), found only here in the NT, is more accurately translated "commonwealth" or "state." Often πολίτευμα was used to designate a colony of foreigners or relocated veterans (BGD) whose purpose was to secure the conquered country for the conquering country by spreading abroad that country's way of doing things, its customs, its culture, its laws, and so on. When Paul wrote his letters, Rome was the conqueror and its empire spread over the Mediterranean world. Macedonia was under its domination. But the Macedonian city of Philippi had been designated a Roman colony and had been awarded the *ius italicum*, the highest legal privilege obtainable by any provincial municipality (Lemerle, *Philippe*, 7–10). Its citizens, therefore, were also citizens of Rome with all of the rights and privileges awarded to any Roman born in the imperial city. In writing this word, πολίτευμα, to the Philippian church, Paul was thus using a word that would appeal to them and to which they could easily relate. With it he "pictures the world as an empire over which Christ rules de jure, though not yet de facto. Each local church is a colony of heaven, its members enjoying full citizenship of the heavenly city (cf. Gal 4:26; Eph 2:19), but charged with the responsibility of bringing the world to acknowledge the sovereignty of

Christ. Neither the Roman colonist nor the Christian depended for the mean-ing, character and purpose of his life on the ethos of his alien environment, nor did he allow that environment to determine the quality of his behavior" (Caird; see also Dibelius, Zwaan, *Theologische Studiën* 31 [1913] 298–300; M. Engers, "Πολίτευμα," *Mnemosyne* 54 [1926] 154–61; but see Sherwin-White, *Roman Society*, 184–85; Strathmann, *TDNT* 6,535; Volz, *Die Eschatologie*, 114–16). Note Dibelius' paraphrase of v 20a: "Our home is in heaven, and here on earth we are a colony of heavenly citizens" (BGD).

Paul also may have chosen this word, πολίτευμα, conscious still of his contest with the Jews. He knew that they were a favored people, treated in a special manner by the Romans. He knew that they were allowed to live a more or less independent existence as small colonies surrounded by ethnologically different populations. He knew that the Jews made up their own πολιτεύματα wherever they settled and that they were permitted to live according to their own laws and follow their own religious practices (Klijn, *Introduction*, 110; L. Fuchs, *Die Juden in Ägypten* [Wien: M. Rath, 1924] 89). But Paul believed that these Jews, irrespective of what they themselves might have speculated about themselves, belonged only to colonies that were linked to Palestinian Jerusalem, earthbound, time-bound colonies without any enduring quality. By contrast, he says that Christians are a colony of heaven, living here on earth, to be sure, but belonging to a heavenly city that is enduring. Therefore, they enjoy all the rights and privileges of that city, including the right to eternal life.

Then with language that is characteristic of apocalyptic literature Paul pro-ceeds to say that Christians are eagerly anticipating a savior to come from heaven. (The relative pronoun οὗ—ἐξ οὗ, "from which"—formally agrees with πολίτευμα, but by sense it agrees with οὐρανοῖς, "heaven." For this kind of *constructio ad sensum* see BDF 134 and 296; cf. also Gnilka, Michaelis).

The verb that expresses the church's eager anticipation, ἀπεκδεχόμεθα, is used six times by Paul of the eight times it appears in the NT (Rom 8:19, 23, 25; 1 Cor 1:7; Gal 5:5; Phil 3:20). It is his special word, the one that for him best describes the Christian's persistent yearning for, his happy expec-tation of, and his earnest desire for the second coming of Christ, when this travailing creation will be freed from its "thraldom to decay" (Moffatt) and restored to its pristine wholeness once again (cf. Rom 8:19–25).

Thus the church's expectation focuses on a person who is Savior (σωτήρ). The absence of the definite article before "Savior" does not mean "a savior," as though any savior would do. Rather, its absence is to be understood in a qualitative sense, where a *single* individual represents an entire class (BDF 252,2). That single individual is Jesus Christ who is confessed by the church as Lord: κύριον Ἰησοῦν Χριστόν (cf. 2:11). It is he who will bring about the final stage of God's saving work that was also begun by him, namely the "decisive laying aside of the coming wrath (Rom 5:9; 1 Cor 3:15; 5:5; 1 Thess 5:19) or, as here, the ultimate acquisition of Glory" (Collange; see also Foerster, *TDNT* 7,993, 1015–18). Σωτήρ ("Savior") is a term that also reaches back into and gains substance from the OT. There it is used of God himself who is described as Vindicator of his people, the one who will ultimately deliver them from all their adversaries (cf. Isa 35:4).

Surprisingly the word σωτήρ is found only here and in Eph 5:23 in the earlier letters of Paul: it does, however, have a special place in the Pastorals and 2 Pet. Why Paul uses it so sparingly as a title for Jesus and why he uses it here are questions difficult to answer. Perhaps its rarity can be explained (1) by noting that σωτήρ was a word frequently used by the masses to refer to their pagan gods, or to designate the emperor (V. Taylor, *The Names of Jesus* [London: Macmillan, 1953] 109; see Martin, *Philippians*, 1976). Paul may then have been reluctant to use such a common term of someone so unique as Christ (cf. Collange). Or the rarity of σωτήρ may also be explained (2) by observing that for Paul the word "salvation" is not generally used of that state in which the believer now finds himself in this life. Rather, salvation is that state into which he will be brought at the return of Christ. The Christian has been "justified" but not yet "saved." He is "being saved" (1 Cor 1:18), but salvation is a process that will not be completed until the Parousia. Hence, Paul prefers "justification" to describe what has already been done in the Christian by God's action in Christ, while he reserves "salvation" for what yet remains to be done (Beare; cf. Rom 5:9–10).

On the other hand, the presence of the word σωτήρ here may be explained variously: It may be explained (1) by noting the fact that it is fittingly placed within the context of the end times. Or it may be explained (2) by recalling that this section may be an early Christian hymn not composed by Paul, and hence σωτήρ is really not his choice of title. Or it may be explained (3) by noting that the imagery of this section inevitably sets up a contrast with the Roman emperor. Paul, therefore, opposes the head of imperial Rome with the true Emperor-Savior, the Lord Jesus Christ (Martin, *Philippians*, 1959; cf. Bornhäuser, *Jesus Imperator Mundi*).

21. In any case, the Savior will perform his saving work upon "our lowly bodies," more literally, "the body of our humiliation" (τὸ σῶμα τῆς ταπεινώσεως ἡμῶν). This expression, of all expressions, describes the fallenness, the weakness, the corruptibility, the mortality of everyone, including all Christians. Τὸ σῶμα ("the body") for Paul was not some sort of outer husk covering the human spirit that he hopes will some day be discarded, nor some prison-house of the soul that might better be done without. Rather, for Paul a person's body *is* that person (see R. H. Gundry, *Soma in Biblical Theology* [Cambridge: Cambridge University Press, 1976]). And that person, every person, this side of the Parousia, is marked by frailty, suffering, sorrow, vanity, death and corruption. His body can only be described by ταπείνωσις.

But when Christ returns, described here as when the Savior comes from heaven, *the* thing he will do for Christians which gets singled out for special attention is that he will transform (μετασχηματίσει) their bodies of humiliation and make them like his own body of glory. (Again, it must be noted that the blessed state is never described by Paul as a separation of the soul from the body. Salvation for him is *not* the survival of the soul alone, but the preservation and restoration of a person in his wholeness—spirit, soul and body [1 Thess 5:23].)

Paul believed that when Christ was resurrected, his physical body was transformed into a spiritual body. But he did not mean by this that Christ no longer had any part in the corporeal. Rather, he was freed from the weakness and limitations and humiliation of the flesh, so that his new mode of existence could be identified with that of the Spirit (2 Cor 3:17; 1 Cor 15:45).

Paul also believed that just such a radical transformation would be effected in the bodies of Christians by the Lord Jesus Christ at his return. The exact nature of these transformed bodies Paul does not here describe, except to say that they will be like (σύμμορφον) Christ's body of glory, i.e. they too will be spiritual bodies—not bodies consisting of spirit merely, but bodies with a new determining or motivating force. They will be bodies brought forth and determined by divine, heavenly power. As a consequence, it will be possible to say of these bodies—these transformed people, rather—that they are imperishable and immortal, models of glory and power (cf. 1 Cor 15:42, 43, 48, 53; see Ridderbos, *Paul*, 538–39, 544–45).

Thus this section closes with a liturgical confession ascribing all power to Jesus Christ as Lord (cf. Norden, *Agnostos Theos*, 240–42; Martin, *Philippians*, 1976). He who will raise the dead and transform their bodies of humiliation into incorruptible glorious bodies will do so by means of divine "power" (ἐνέργεια). Ἐνέργεια, most frequently translated "power," is more dynamic than such a translation might lead one to believe. In classical Greek it was used of physiological "function" (Gal 6.21), or of the "activity" of drugs (Galen, 6.467). Diodorus Siculus used it of the "driving force" of an engine (LSJ). Hence, ἐνέργεια is not merely "power" but "power in action," "power in operation," "power working" (cf. KJV). It is not simply supernatural "power" that Paul has in mind here, but supernatural "action." The resurrection and transformation of the body is but the "out-working" of Christ's ability (τοῦ δύνασθαι αὐτόν) even to subject (ὑποτάξαι) the entire universe (τὰ πάντα) to himself. The genitive infinitive (τοῦ δύνασθαι) with its accusative of reference (αὐτόν) is descriptive of this divine "out-working" (ἐνέργειαν), while the infinitive, ὑποτάξαι, is complementary to δύνασθαι: "the out-working of his ability." The resurrection of the body, then, is not to be viewed as an isolated event, "but as the last act in the drama of cosmic redemption" (Caird; cf. Rom 8:19–25; Eph 1:7–10, 22).

Explanation

Paul concludes his polemic against the Jews with what might have been one of the earliest hymns of the church (vv 20–21). It begins with the triumphant but challenging claim that Christians are a colony of heaven on earth. As such they enjoy full citizenship rights in the City of God, but they are also responsible for spreading abroad in this "conquered" world the customs, culture, manner of life and laws of their heavenly home.

As a colony of heaven Christians stand in contrast with the Jews. Often the Jews were allowed by the Roman government to form little enclaves, colonies of Jerusalem, so to speak, to keep their own traditions and obey their own laws. But for Paul their colonies were strictly earthbound and time-bound, because they were made up of people whose minds were entirely fixed on earthly matters. Fastening upon the present, living for the now, they looked for nothing beyond today.

But Christians live in eager expectation of the future. They have a persistent yearning, a joyful anticipation of a coming day when the crucified Christ, whom the Jews reject, will return as Savior and Lord. When that day comes, when the Savior arrives, his special saving act will be utterly to transform their bodies. From bodies of humiliation, i.e. from bodies marked by limitation, frustration, feebleness, mortality and corruption, Christ will transfigure them into bodies like his own glorious resurrected body, that is, bodies infused with a new determining force of the Spirit that is heavenly and divine, bodies that are imperishable and immortal, models of glory and power.

But this Christ is not merely the Savior of Christians. He is also *Imperator Mundi*. The energy by which he transfigures mortal bodies is the energy by which he subdues the universe and subjects all things to his authority. The resurrection of the dead and the transformation of broken persons is but one part, the most significant part, to be sure, of the great drama of cosmic redemption.

IV. Exhortations to Harmony, Joy and Mental Soundness (4:1-9)

Bibliography

Beet, J. A. "Did Euodia and Syntyche Quarrel?" *ExpTim* 5 (1893–94) 179–80. **Bigaré, C.** "La paix de Dieu dans le Christ Jésus. Priér et mettre in pratique. Ph. 4, 6–9." *AsSeign* 58 (1974) 11–15. **Chambers, T. W.** "'Ο κύριος ἐγγύς, Philip. iv.5." *JBL* 6 (1886) 108–10. **Ellis, E. E.** "Paul and his Co-Workers." *NTS* (1970–71) 437–52. **Ezell, D.** "The Sufficiency of Christ. Philippians 4." *RevExp* 77 (1980) 373–87. **Hájek, M.** "Comments on Philippians 4:3—Who was 'Gnésios Sygygos'?" *Communio Viatorum* 7 (1964) 261–62. **Harris, J. R.** "St. Paul and Aeschylus (Phil 4:4)." *ExpTim* 35 (1923–24) 151–53. **Holzmeister, U.** " 'Gaudete in Domino semper' (Phil. 4,4–9)." *VD* 4 (1924) 358–62. **Moffatt, J.** "The History of Joy; a Brief Exposition of Phil. 4:4–7 (R.V.)." *ExpTim* 9 (1897–98) 334–36. **Ogara, F.** " 'Dominus propre est' (Phil 4,4–7)." *VD* 17 (1937) 353–59. **Rhijn, C. H. van.** "Euodia en Syntyche." *Theologische Studiën* 21 (1903) 300–309. **Sevenster, J. N.** *Paul and Seneca.* Leiden: Brill, 1961. **Stewart, J. S.** "Philippians 4:6–7 (Moffatt)." *ExpTim* 49 (1937–38) 269–71. **Thomas, W. D.** "The Place of Women in the Church at Philippi." *ExpTim* 83 (1971–72) 117–20. **Watts, J. C.** "The Alleged Quarrel of Euodia and Syntyche." *ExpTim* 5 (1893–94) 286–87. **Weeda, W. H.** "Filippenzen 4 vs 6 en 7. Over Bezorgdheid." *Theologische Studiën* 34 (1916) 326–35. **Wiles, G. P.** *Paul's Intercessory Prayers.* Cambridge: Cambridge University Press, 1974.

Translation

[1] *Well then, my Christian friends, you whom I love and long for, my joy and my crown—this, my Christian friends,[a] is how you must stand firm in the Lord:* [2] *First, I beg Euodia and I beg Syntyche to agree with each other in the Lord.* [3] *Yes, and I ask you, my loyal yoke-fellows,[b] to help them because they are women who fought at my side in the spread of the gospel along with Clement and the rest of my coworkers.[c] All their names are in the book of life.* [4] *Second, rejoice in the Lord at all times. Once again I will say it, rejoice!* [5] *Next, let your magnanimity be known to everybody. The Lord is near!* [6] *Do not worry about anything, but in every situation make your requests known to God by prayer and petition with thanksgiving.* [7] *As a result God's[d] peace which excels all human planning will stand guard over your thoughts[e] and feelings in Christ[f] Jesus.* [8] *And last of all, my Christian friends, since there is moral excellence, and since there are things worthy of praise,[g] focus your minds on these things—on whatever is truthful, whatever is majestic and awe-inspiring, whatever is just, whatever is pure, whatever calls forth love, whatever is winsome.* [9] *And keep putting into practice the lessons that you learned from me and the traditions that I passed on to you, and the things that you heard about me, and the things that you saw in me. If you do, the God of peace will be with you.*

Notes

[a] B 33 add μου after this second ἀγαπητοί at the end of the verse. Its presence is not needed to preserve the possessive idea. D* and a few other witnesses omit this second ἀγαπητοί and the μου, perhaps as useless redundancy.

ᵇ Some commentators take σύζυγε as Σύζυγε, a proper name. See comments below.

ᶜ ℵ* and apparently P⁴⁶ because of scribal inadvertence have a slightly longer text: τῶν συνεργῶν μου καὶ τῶν λοιπῶν for τῶν λοιπῶν συνεργῶν μου—"Clement, and 'my fellow-workers and the rest' whose names . . ." for "Clement and 'the rest of my fellow-workers.' "

ᵈ A and some early versions have Χριστοῦ for θεοῦ. There is no substantial reason to consider seriously this reading.

ᵉ For νοήματα ("thoughts") F G read σώματα ("bodies") and apparently P¹⁶ reads νοήματα καὶ σώματα. Again there is no good reason for adopting these changes in spite of the fact that Lohmeyer considers them favorable to his thesis about martyrdom.

ᶠ P⁴⁶ has κυρίῳ ('Lord') for Χριστῷ ("Christ"). Titles for Jesus as usual are extremely susceptible to variation.

ᵍ Whereas most MSS read εἰ τις ἔπαινος (lit. "if there is any praise"), D* F G, apparently uncomfortable with leaving ἔπαινος without an object, add ἐπιστήμης after it: "If there is any praise of understanding."

Form/Structure/Setting

Upon the assumption that Philippians is a single letter and not a compilation of letters that Paul wrote to the church at Philippi (see Introduction), one can easily view 4:1 as a transition verse. The apostle now shifts from theological or polemical matters to concluding remarks, i.e. exhortations, expressions of gratitude, words of farewell, and so on. Thus he brings his letter to a close in a rather protracted way.

In this first section (4:1–9) familiar motifs are reechoed: ἀγαπητοί ("beloved," 2:12), ἐπιπόθητοι ("longed for," cf. 1:8; 2:26), χαρά ("joy," 1:4, 25; 2:2, 29), στήκετε ("stand firm," 1:27), τὸ αὐτὸ φρονεῖν ("to agree," cf. 1:7; 2:2, 5; 3:15, 19), ἐν τῷ εὐαγγελίῳ συναθλεῖν ("struggling together in the gospel," 1:27), τὸ εὐαγγέλιον ("the gospel," 1:5, 7, 12, 16, 22; 2:22), and so on. They serve to bind the whole of the letter together, and at the same time show how unstructured it is and how difficult a task it is to outline any logical flow of the apostle's thought from first to last. Once again there is here a sharp reminder of the very personal nature of this letter, not only in the affectionate language Paul uses in addressing his friends, but also in his frequent use of the first person pronoun that appears again and again: "my brothers," "my crown," "I beg," "I ask," "I will say," "with me," etc.

Paul customarily brings his letters to a close with a section dealing with practical and personal matters, and greetings. So here in Philippians. However, the contrast between the theoretical and the practical, the didactic and the personal application, so prominent in other Pauline letters, is not nearly so pronounced in Philippians (1) because it is such a personal letter in all its parts, and (2) because practical matters have been dealt with throughout. Nevertheless, this final chapter is more pronounced in its practical application and in its attention to personal notices than those that have preceded it. In this it shows itself to be in harmony with the Pauline style and pattern of writing. Thus, as is to be expected, the imperative mood is the predominant mood. And as is usual, too, the exhortations given here are given to the entire Christian community. If individual Christians are singled out for special instruction, it is always with the understanding that they are part of the church and that behind them to support, encourage, guide and to be responsible for them is the church, which with them is equally the recipient of the apostolic commands.

There have been indications throughout the letter that all was not well at Philippi. Hints have been given of selfishness, self-interest, conceit, pride, and so on existing with harmful effects within the Christian community. Now one of these problems surfaces: that of intense disagreement, along with the names of those party to the quarrel. Two women could not agree and the church may have been in danger of taking sides and dividing. What was equally troubling to Paul was that the spiritual leaders within the congregation were not taking the problem seriously enough to become involved in solving it. He was forced to ask them specifically to do what they should already have been doing.

In the rapid-fire commands that Paul now flings out in all directions one gets the impression that there were many other spiritual irritants present at Philippi, such as depression, harshness of spirit, anxiety, the failure to take prayer seriously, troubled minds, minds filled with all the wrong kinds of things, and so on. Paul is confident that there are solutions to the problems at Philippi, and thus he encourages them to change not only their actions, but more fundamentally their attitude.

Comment

1. This verse is a transitional verse. The ὥστε ("well then") is a conjunction designed to ask the readers to look back and to take action in light of what has just been said: in light of the fact that Christians are a colony of heaven, that they eagerly expect the Lord Jesus Christ to come as Savior, that their hope is in him for a complete transformation of their bodies from frailty to glory they must, "therefore," stand firm. But in what way are they to stand firm? Οὕτως ("thus," "in this way") is Paul's answer. And with this word the apostle points them in the opposite direction (cf. BGD)—not backward now, but forward and onward to undertake immediately those things he is about to introduce with a flurry of imperatives. Hence, this verse is no more linked with what precedes (Barth, Bonnard, Collange, Friedrich, Haupt, Martin) than it is with what follows. For vv 2–9 state precisely how Christians are to stand firm (cf. Lohmeyer).

But before the apostle begins his commands, he first commends. He does so with an extraordinary long series of appellatives designed to express powerfully to the Philippians his feeling of closeness to them and his great affection for them: (1) Ἀδελφοί (lit. "brothers," cf. also 1:12; 3:1, 13, 17; 4:8, 21) reminds them that they and he belong to the same divine family and hold equal status in relation to God as Father (see notes on 1:12). (2) Ἀγαπητοί (lit. "beloved") is a verbal adjective with passive force (BDF 112), and, appearing in this context twice over, it focuses attention on the Philippians as the object of *Paul's* love. It is his humble way of saying, "I love you," but it is not less powerful for being so humbly expressed. (3) Ἐπιπόθητοι (lit. "longed for"), like ἀγαπητοί, is also a verbal adjective with passive force, but unlike ἀγαπητοί, this word occurs nowhere else in the NT. Its rarity perhaps adds intensity to the emotion of "homesick tenderness," especially to the pain of separation that Paul feels and expresses here (cf. 1:8 where Paul uses the cognate verb ἐπιποθεῖν, and see the comments there; cf. also 2:26). (4) χαρά ("joy") is a word that belongs to the special vocabulary of Philippians (1:4, 25; 2:2; cf. also 1:18; 2:17, 18, 28; 3:7; 4:4, 10), and gives expression to a fundamental Christian emotion. But what is worth noting here is that the Philippians *are* Paul's joy, which is a striking way of saying that they are his source or cause of joy. People, not things—these friends, his children in the faith, even with all their failings—are what stimulate within him this great gladness. (5) Στέφανος ("crown"), as Paul uses it here, is not to be thought of as the diadem worn by a king (διάδημα; cf. Rev 19:12 and see Deissmann, *Light,* 315) or as the martyr's crown (Lohmeyer), but either as the garland placed on the head of a guest at a banquet (Ar. *Ach.* 636; Plato *Symp.* 212; see Vincent) or as a victor's wreath presented by the judges to the winner in the Olympian games (Pfitzner, *Agon Motif,* 104–106), or both at the same time. With this single word, then, Paul may be reinforcing the idea that the Philippians are a cause for his festal-like joy, on the one hand, and informing them that they are also a source of great honor for him, on the other. There is no need to push this idea of "crowning" exclusively into the eschatological period as though the continued fidelity of the Philippian church would only then result in a reward, a crown, being given Paul for the success of his pastoral work (Collange; Martin, *Philippians,* 1976; Grundmann, *TDNT* 7,615–36). The Philippians already *are* a cause of Paul's boasting, merriment and honor. They *are* his crown.

Now, after so powerfully expressing his affection for them, Paul asks the Philippians to stand firm (στήκετε). By this word, στήκετε, he describes them as soldiers who are to stand at their post irrespective of the pressures to abandon it (cf. 1:16), or as runners who must adhere without deviation to the course marked out by the gospel. With it he calls upon them to live thoroughly Christian lives (cf. 1:27). But how are they to "stand firm"? What will this thoroughly Christian life look like? Paul's answer: "Stand firm thus" (οὕτως). Then in a series of imperatives he puts meaning into the word οὕτως. The course marked out by the gospel will look like this:

2. First—and this word is added to the text to make clear the connection between v 1 and v 2—unity among believers is an essential element in a truly Christian way of living. Paul appeals to Euodia and Syntyche "to reach agreement in the Lord." The earnestness of his appeal is seen (1) in the verb he uses to make it, παρακαλεῖν ("to urge, exhort, appeal to," "to implore or beg"), and (2) in the fact that Paul uses it twice so as to heighten its effect by repetition, and to emphasize the idea that his apostolic exhortation is made to both parties equally. This exhortation is to live harmoniously together a way of life that is fit and proper for all who claim to have placed themselves under the Lordship of Christ (τὸ αὐτὸ φρονεῖν ἐν κυρίῳ). Once again the important Pauline word φρονεῖν appears (1:27; 2:3, 5; 3:15, 19; 4:2, 10). And the richness of meaning in the phrase τὸ αὐτὸ φρονεῖν exceeds any single translation such as "to agree," for it embraces not only the idea of possessing "a common mind" but also of having identical feelings and attitudes toward each other, a total harmony of life (see comments on 1:27).

The principal parties involved in this quarrel, Euodia and Syntyche, were women. Their names appear quite frequently in inscriptions, always in the feminine form (BGD), and Paul refers back to them in v 3 with feminine forms of the pronouns, αὐταῖς and αἵτινες. There is thus no grounds for taking one or both of these names as names of men as did Theodore of Mopsuestia (*ca.* A.D. 350–428). He claimed to have heard that Syntyche should be spelled Syntyches, a man's name, and that Syntyches was in fact the Philippian jailer of Acts 16, the husband of Euodia. But this is an admitted rumor and is totally without support in fact (Michael, Vincent). Nor is there any support for the fanciful view of the Tübingen school that saw Eudoia and Syntyche not as two individuals, but as symbols for the Jewish Christians on the one hand, and the Gentile Christians on the other, and the σύζυγος of v 3 (Synzygos=the Unifier) as the apostle Peter who was charged with mediating between these two factions within the church and with bringing them together (cf. Barth).

Nothing is known about these two women or the nature of their quarrel. Just possibly one of them could have been the Lydia of Acts 16 (cf. vv 14, 40)—Lydia being an adjective meaning "the Lydian," i.e. the woman from Lydia of Asia Minor, with either "Euodia" or "Syntyche" being her proper name. Lydia's prominent role in the founding of the church at Philippi lends a certain credibility to this conjecture.

In any case, these two women appear to have been important persons within the church, among its most active workers, perhaps deaconesses; perhaps within each of their homes a separate congregation met for worship. Certainly it is clear from the Acts account that women played a noteworthy role in the founding and establishing of the Macedonian churches (Acts 16:14, 40; 17:4, 12; see Thomas, *ExpTim* 83 [1971–72] 117–20). Thus the fact that these people in particular were quarreling as two influential women who had the potential for upsetting the harmony of the larger community caused Paul to beg each, face to face as it were, to make up their differences. Their differences may have had to do with church leadership, and with which of the two women was to have the greater say within the church at Philippi. Paul's plea here for them to be of the same mind (τὸ αὐτὸ φρονεῖν) recalls 2:1–5, where the general problems that plagued the Philippians, i.e. self-serving, self-seeking attitudes, were set over against (τοῦτο φρονεῖτε) the self-sacrificing, self-giving attitude of Christ who was in the form of God but who poured himself out unselfishly for the good of others.

3. Paul was a realist. He understood how difficult it would be for Euodia and Syntyche to reach agreement on their own. Hence, he solicits the help of a third party, whom he addresses simply as γνήσιε σύζυγε ("true yoke-fellow," RSV). But who was this mysterious person and why did Paul suddenly address a single individual in a letter otherwise addressed to a whole church (1:1)?. These questions have given rise to almost endless and sometimes absurd answers: (1) Paul's wife (Clement of Alexandria) who, Renan conjectured, was Lydia; (2) The husband or brother of Euodia or Syntyche (Chrysostom); (3) Epaphroditus (Lightfoot); (4) Timothy, of whom it was said that he "legitimately" (γνησίως, 2:20) cared for the Philippians (Collange); (5) Silas (Delling, *TDNT* 7,749–50); (6) Luke (Manson, *BJRL* 23 [1939] 199;

Hájek, *Communio Viatorum* 7 [1964] 261–62); (7) The chief bishop at Philippi (Ellicott); (8) Christ, with the ναί ("yea") introducing a prayer to the one who joins people together (Wiesler); (9) A person named Σύζυγος (Michael, Müller; cf. JB: "I ask you, Sygygus, to be truly a 'companion' "). But the simplest and perhaps the best answer is to say that Paul sees the entire Philippian church as a unit, as a single individual, who shares with him the burden of his apostolic work, and he so addresses them. He sees the Philippian church yoked together with him as two oxen teamed up to accomplish an important task (Houlden). Notice Paul's subtle, though nonetheless powerful, stress on the importance of community effort in that he uses five words compounded with the preposition σύν ("with") within the space of two verses (vv 2–3). Thus he asks (ἐρωτᾶν) them to cooperate with him now by resisting division and by effectively working to restore harmony.

Together, then, the Philippians are to help these women reconcile their differences. Even the verb Paul chooses for "help" (συλλαμβάνειν, used sixteen times in the NT but only one time by the apostle, i.e. here) implies this unity of effort. Although through usage it has simply come to mean "to aid or assist," yet, compounded as it is with σύν (συλ-, "with"), there lingers still about this word the idea of "taking hold *along with* someone" in order to provide needed assistance. And the construction of ἐρωτῶ ("I ask") followed by a finite verb, an imperative (συλλαμβάνου) where the infinitive or ὅτι *recitativum* would have been expected, intensifies the sense of urgency: "Help them! You must! It is an order, even though I ask (ἐρωτῶ) you!"

One very important reason for thus helping Euodia and Syntyche is now introduced by the relative pronoun αἵτινες ("who": relative pronouns can introduce subordinate causal clauses; see H. E. Dana and J. R. Mantey, *A Manual Grammar of the Greek New Testament* [London: Macmillan, 1927] 275; cf. Acts 10:41, 47; Rom 6:2; Phil 2:20). It is because they had fought together side by side with Paul in the struggle to preach the gospel (αἵτινες ἐν τῷ εὐαγγελίῳ συνήθλησάν μοι). Συναθλεῖν ("to fight together side by side with") is a metaphorical word drawn from the games or the gladiatorial arena. It appears in the NT only here and in 1:27 (where see comments). It implies a united struggle in preaching the gospel, on the one hand, and a sharing in the suffering that results from the struggle, on the other (Pfitzner, *Agon Motif,* 116). There is also contained in the choice of this verb more than a hint of cooperation on the same level. By using it Paul wishes to say that these women are not in any way to be degraded for their disagreements, but to be respected highly for their energetic cooperation with him, working at his side as esteemed members of his team. There is no justification whatsoever for making the limiting comment that "these two must have been among those [women] who, having believed, labored *among their own sex* for" the spread of the gospel (Alford, italics mine). They were rather Paul's coworkers (συνεργοί), equal in importance to Clement and the rest (οἱ λοιποί) of Paul's fellow laborers. The phrase, "with Clement and the rest of my fellow workers," should be connected with the statement, "they fought side by side with me" and not as Lightfoot suggests with "help these women." The structure of the sentence argues for this as does the fact that the σέ ("you"), though singular, probably refers to the church as a whole which would then already have included Clement and the rest.

Who was this Clement? It is impossible to answer this question, other than to say that in all likelihood he was a Philippian Christian. Evidently he was so well known within the church that Paul did not need to identify him, and he did not think to do so for strangers who might chance to read his letter. Clement was a common Roman name. Hence, to say that he was the Clement who later became the third bishop of Rome (cf. Euseb. *H.E.* 3.4; 5.6) is simply to be making a guess. Such identification rests solely on agreement in name, not at all on historical evidence.

Who were these other coworkers (λοιποὶ συνεργοί) of Paul? Again it is a question impossible to answer. They too must have been Philippians, but too numerous to mention by name (cf. Ellis, *NTS* 17 [1970–71] 437–52). Yet they did have names, and although time and space did not permit Paul to list them, God listed them all in the "Book of Life." Just as Philippi, and other cities like it, must have had a civic register that included all the names of its citizens, so the heavenly commonwealth (cf. 3:20) has its own roll where God inscribes the names of those to whom he promises life. Thus it is not important that succeeding generations know the names of Paul's coworkers; it is important that "God *knows* them and knows they belong to him" (Barth). The expression "Book of Life," often found in late apocalyptic literature (cf. Rev 3:5, 20; 15:21, 27) and at Qumran (1QM 12:3), is drawn from Exod 32:32; Pss 69:28; 139:16 where in the figurative language of the OT it refers to the register of God's covenant people (Martin, *Philippians*, 1976; Lightfoot).

In discussing the pronoun ὧν ("whose") one could argue that it relates the clause that follows it only to συνεργῶν ("fellow workers *whose* names are in the Book of Life"), since, like συνεργῶν, ὧν too is masculine and plural. But this interpretation is too restrictive and unnecessary, for ὧν can be the generic use of the masculine, intended to refer not only to the remaining fellow workers, but also to Clement and to Euodia and Syntyche. The names of all these are inscribed in the Book of Life: all are God's children. Nor is there anything about the expression, "whose names are in the Book of Life," to indicate that those people so designated had already died in the faith (cf. Luke 10:20), although many interpreters assume this to be a fact (cf. Beare, Michael, Müller).

4. Second, Paul once again tells the Philippians to rejoice in the Lord on all occasions (πάντοτε, not ἀεί). And with emphatic determination he insists on repeating this injunction. Χαίρειν, the verb translated, "rejoice," seems also to have been used as a formula of farewell (cf. E. J. Goodspeed, *Problems of New Testament Translation* [Chicago: University of Chicago Press, 1945] 174–75; cf. NEB). Hence, it is possible that at this juncture in the letter the imperative, χαίρετε, "combines a parting benediction with an exhortation to cheerfulness. It is neither 'farewell' alone, nor 'rejoice' alone" (Lightfoot). Nevertheless, whatever appeal there is here to joy, it is made with the realization that a Christian's faith "in the Lord" (ἐν κυρίῳ) is what makes such an appeal meaningful, especially when that one is faced with situations which are conducive not to merriment but to sorrow and situations marked by difficulties,

hurts and trials (see the fuller treatment of "joy" in the comments on 1:4).

5. The Christian life, furthermore, is to be characterized by τὸ ἐπιεικές, "magnaminity." This quality is such an important one that the apostle demands that it become evident among the Philippian Christians to such a degree that it will be seen and recognized (γνωσθήτω) by everybody (πᾶσιν ἀνθρώποις), not just by their fellow believers (cf. John 13:35). Τὸ ἐπιεικές, a neuter adjective used as an abstract noun, is one of the truly great Greek words that is almost untranslatable (cf. MM). Related as it is to εἰκός ("reasonable") it radiates the positive ideas of magnanimity or "sweet reasonableness." Aristotle contrasted it with ἀκριβοδίκαιος ("strict justice"). For him it meant a generous treatment of others which, while demanding equity, does not insist on the letter of the law. Willing to admit limitations it is prepared to make allowances so that justice does not injure. It is a quality, therefore, that keeps one from insisting on his full rights, "where rigidity would be harsh" (Plummer; cf. Aristotle, Eth. Nic. 5.10.3), or from making a rigorous and obstinate stand for what is justly due him (Vincent). In the NT ἐπιεικής keeps company with such words as ἄμαχος ("peaceable," 1 Tim 3:3; Titus 3:2), ἀγαθός ("good," 1 Pet 2:18), ἁγνή ("pure"), εἰρηνική ("peace-loving"), εὐπειθής ("open to reason") and μεστὴ ἐλέους ("rich in mercy," James 3:17). Thus τὸ ἐπιεικές "is that considerate courtesy and respect for the integrity of others which prompts a [person] not to be forever standing on his rights; and it is pre-eminently the character of Jesus (2 Cor 10:1)" (Caird; cf. Preisker, TDNT 2,588–90).

Then, without warning and without any conjunctions to join it either with what precedes or with what follows, Paul suddenly interjects the phrase ὁ κύριος ἐγγύς ("the Lord is near"). The meaning of this phrase is rendered elusive by the ambiguity contained in ἐγγύς. Ἐγγύς can refer both to space and time. Thus, "the Lord is near" may mean that the Lord is close to you, present with you, hence aware of your conduct, concerned about your attitude, available to come to your aid, at hand to assist, and so on (cf. Pss 33[34]:18; 118[119]:151; 144[145]:18; see Caird, Michaelis, and especially note 1 Clem 21.3). Or these words may mean that the return of the Lord Jesus Christ is imminent. There would thus be good reason to rejoice, good reason to magnanimously put up with the harassment of pagans, good reason to live worry-free, and so on. It is that the Lord is coming soon to reward the faithful, to punish the evil-doers, to heal all ills and to right all wrongs (cf. 1 Cor 16:22; Heb 10:24–25; James 5:8; Rev 1:7; 3:11; 22:20; cf. 2 Thess 1:7–8; Barn. 21.3). Thus the shortness of time and the nearness of salvation heightens the earnestness of the exhortations (Beare, Bonnard, Dibelius, Gnilka, Haupt, Houlden, Martin, Ridderbos, Paul, 490). It may be wrong, however, to choose between these two interpretations and to remove all ambiguity by translation (cf. GNB, LB, Goodspeed). Just possibly Paul deliberately chose this particular word, ἐγγύς, with all its ambiguity precisely to include both ideas of time and space together: the Lord who will soon return is the Lord who once came so close to humanity (2:6–8) as actually to share the human lot and who though absent now in body is still near at hand in his Spirit to guide, instruct, encourage, infuse with strength, assist, transform, renew, etc. (cf. John 14:12, 16–18, 26; 16:12–13; Rom 8:9–11; 2 Cor 3:17–18; see Collange).

6. Paul continues his exhortation by adding still another imperative without any conjunction. The figure of speech called "asyndeton" runs throughout this section, where commands are given in rapid-fire fashion without any connecting words to link one command to the other. Now the order is, "Do not worry about anything" (μηδὲν μεριμνᾶτε), or more accurately, "stop worrying. . . ." Once again Paul echoes the teaching of Jesus, and reveals his familiarity with the gospel tradition (cf. Matt 6:25–34 and see A. M. Hunter, *Paul and His Predecessors* [Philadelphia: Westminster Press, 1961] 52–61; Davies, *Paul and Rabbinic Judaism*, 136–41; D. L. Dungan, *The Sayings of Jesus in the Churches of Paul* [Philadelphia: Fortress Press, 1971]).

The verb translated here as "worry" (μεριμνᾶν) is the same verb that was used in 2:20 where it had the positive sense of "to be solicitously concerned for" the welfare of others. Now, however, it has the negative connotation of "anxious harassing care," of attempting "to carry the burden of the future oneself," of "unreasonable anxiety," especially about things over which one has no control (Caird, Lightfoot, Plummer). Paul and the Philippians had ample reason for anxiety since the one was in prison and the others were threatened with persecution (cf. 1:28). So he is not speaking of imaginary troubles or phantom anxieties. Hence, when he tells them to stop worrying, to be overly anxious for nothing, leaving them no exceptions (μηδέν; cf. 1 Cor 7:32), it is not because he makes light of the troubles which they face, but because he knows that God is greater than all their troubles (Beare; cf. Ps 54[55]:22; 1 Pet 5:7; 1 Cor 7:32).

What then is the alternative to worry? How does one gain and keep his equilibrium in a world heaving with anxiety-creating situations? Paul's answer: by prayer. Believing that God is, that he is greater than the greatest problem and that he is the rewarder of those who earnestly seek him (cf. Heb 11:6), Paul, with the use of three synonyms strung together in a row—προσευχή, δέησις and αἰτήματα ("prayer," "petition" and "requests"; see comments on 1:4, 9)—emphatically urges the Philippians to find release from anxiety in prayer and more prayer. From personal experience he had learned that "the way to be anxious about nothing was to be prayerful about everything" (R. Rainy, "Philippians," in *The Expositor's Bible*, quoted by Michael). "Let God know what is troubling you" (τὰ αἰτήματα ὑμῶν γνωριζέσθω πρὸς τὸν θεόν)—as though God needed to be informed (cf. Matt 6:8)—is but the apostle's quaint way of expressing the very personal nature of prayer. He is saying, in effect, that prayer is a conversation with, a plea directed to, a request made of, information given to a person, in this case the supreme Person of the universe (πρὸς τὸν θεόν) who can hear, know, understand, care about and respond to the concerns that otherwise would sink you in despair.

It may be, however, that the real accent of this sentence is not on the fact that the Philippians are to pray, but on the fact that they are to do this with thanksgiving (μετὰ εὐχαριστίας; cf. Rom 1:21 to see how all-important this matter of thankfulness is to Paul). Such God-directed gratitude accords with the tenor of 1:12–18 and 2:17–18. "To begin by praising God for the fact that in *this* situation, as it is, he is so mightily God—such a beginning is the *end* of anxiety. To be anxious means that we ourselves suffer, ourselves groan, ourselves seek to see ahead. Thanksgiving means giving God the glory in everything, making room for him, casting our care on him, letting it be his care. The troubles that exercise us then cease to be hidden and bottled up. They are, so to speak, laid open to God, spread out before him" (Barth).

7. As a result (καί here is consecutive) "the peace of God" (ἡ εἰρήνη τοῦ θεοῦ) will ensue. This expression, "the peace of God," is found nowhere else in the NT. With it Paul is not now referring to the peace *with* God (τοῦ θεοῦ viewed as an objective genitive) that the Philippians had as a result of their being justified by faith in Jesus Christ: such peace is presupposed. Nor is he exclusively referring to that "inward peace of soul which comes *from* God" (τοῦ θεοῦ viewed as subjective genitive), a peace that "is grounded in God's presence and promise," the result of believing prayer (Vincent; cf. Rom 14:17; 15:13; Col 3:15). Paul seems here to be referring to the tranquillity of God's own eternal being (Caird), the peace which God himself has (Barth), the calm serenity that characterizes his very nature (τοῦ θεοῦ viewed as a descriptive genitive; cf. 4:9; *Sipre* 42 on Num 6:26: Gnilka) and which grateful, trusting Christians are welcome to share (cf. Foerster, *TDNT* 2,411–17). If they do, then not only will inner strife resulting from worry cease, but external strife resulting from disagreements among Christians has the potential of coming to an end as well.

Paul now describes this peace by a participial phrase, ἡ ὑπερέχουσα πάντα νοῦν (lit. "which rises above every mind"). This phrase is open to more than one interpretation: (1) It may mean that the peace of God "surpasses all human understanding" (cf. GNB, NIV, RSV, Moffatt, Phillips), i.e. it is so marvelously vast that no human mind can ever fully comprehend its significance. Or (2) it may mean that God's peace is able to produce exceedingly better results than human planning or that it is far superior to any person's schemes for security or that it is more effective for removing anxiety than any intellectual effort or power of reasoning (Plummer). Any of these interpretations is possible, although the latter one fits better the context in which this phrase appears. The context certainly argues against the attempt to see in these words a subtle rebuke to Paul's enemies who claimed superior knowledge, or to those Philippians who were jockeying for position by wanting to surpass or to outstrip their fellow Christians. The fact that the verb ὑπερέχειν ("to go beyond"), from which the participle ὑπερέχουσα is derived, appears three times in this letter out of the total of four times Paul uses it in all of his letters (2:3; 3:8; 4:7; Rom 13:1), although striking, cannot override the context, however, and allow one to say that the expression, "the peace of God which passes all understanding" means that "the 'understanding' ('*nous*') which the Philippians put into their dissensions ought in the end to be subjected to the peace which God gives" (Collange; cf. Bonnard, Martin, *Philippians*, 1976). This expression is found in a section where the apostle seeks to help his friends to cope with anxiety through prayer and thanksgiving and to begin to share in the profundity of God's peace, rather than to rebuke them for their self-centeredness. He has done that elsewhere.

And so God's peace will protect (φρουρήσει) their hearts and minds. The verb φρουρεῖν is a military term picturing God's peace as a detachment of soldiers "standing guard over" (cf. 2 Cor 11:32) a city so as to protect it from attack. Philippi in Paul's time housed a Roman garrison. Thus the metaphor would have been easily understood and appreciated by the Philippian Christians who read it: God's peace, like a garrison of soldiers, will keep guard over our thoughts and feelings so that they will be as safe against the assaults of worry and fear as any fortress.

Καρδία ("heart") in the NT never means the physical organ that pumps the blood. Nor is it used solely to refer to the center of one's emotions (Rom 9:2; 10:1; 2 Cor 2:4; 6:11; Phil 1:7). It is sometimes used to describe the source of thought (Rom 1:21; Eph 1:21) and moral choice (1 Cor 7:37; 2 Cor 9:7)—that which "gives impulse and character to action" (Vincent; Behm, *TDNT* 3,611–13). But here, where Paul places καρδία alongside νόημα grammatically in such a way as to distinguish the one from the other—τὰς καρδίας ὑμῶν καὶ τὰ νοήματα ὑμῶν (note the definite articles with both nouns as also the pronoun ὑμῶν)—καρδία very likely has its meaning narrowed simply to that of designating the seat of one's emotions or deepest feelings, or simply to the emotions and feelings themselves. Τὰ νοήματα, however, are the products of the νοῦς, the mind, hence, "thoughts" (2 Cor 2:11; cf. JB, NEB; but see Behm, *TDNT* 4,960–61). Together these words refer to the entire inner being of the Christian, his emotions, affections, thoughts and moral choices. This inner part of a person, then, so vulnerable to attack by the enemy, is that which God's peace is set, like battle-ready soldiers, to protect.

But this peace which acts as guard to one's emotions and thoughts, Paul says, is reserved for, or available only to, those who are in Christ Jesus (ἐν Χριστῷ Ἰησοῦ; see comments on this phrase at 1:1). That is to say, only in union with Christ, "in obedience to his authority and submission to his will" can anyone have the secure assurance that he is indeed the object of the protection of God's peace (Martin, *Philippians*, 1976). But this assurance, arising as it does from the great work of God's redeeming love which is based upon the historic fact of Christ's death and resurrection, was not only for the Philippians; it is still continuing today, available to all who gladly submit to the lordship of Jesus Christ.

8–9. These verses constitute a single sentence in Greek that is marvelous for its rhetorical expression and for the loftiness of the moral standards it sets forth. It begins with τὸ λοιπόν ("finally"), which does not signal the end of the letter (against LB), or even its near end, but rather the last of the imperatives in a parenetic section that states in detail how one is to "stand firm as a Christian" (v 1).

This sentence is a conditional sentence. Its protasis ("if" clause) is constructed in such a way that, at least for the sake of argument, what is said in it must be assumed to be true (BDF 372,1): εἴ τις ἀρετὴ καὶ εἴ τις ἔπαινος: "if there is any excellence, if there is any praise," means, then, that "there *is* excellence, and there *are* things worthy of praise."

Based on this assumption, namely that excellence and praise do exist, Paul proceeds to declare that there are two matters binding upon Christians as a result. They fairly well sum up what is involved in standing firm in the Lord: (1) λογίζεσθε ("you must think"), and (2) πράσσετε ("you must act"). He then spells out in a highly rhetorical fashion precisely how a Christian should think and act, making use of several figures of speech—anaphora, asyndeton, polysyndeton and homoioteleuton—in order to make his point with emphasis. The main part of the sentence is diagrammed as follows so that these figures may be seen clearly:

(v 8) λογίζεσθε ταῦτα
         ὅσα ἐστὶν ἀληθῆ
         ὅσα σεμνά
         ὅσα δίκαια
         ὅσα ἁγνά
         ὅσα προσφιλῆ
         ὅσα εὔφημα
(v 9) πράσσετε ταῦτα
         ἃ καὶ ἐμάθετε
           καὶ παρελάβετε
           καὶ ἠκούσατε
           καὶ εἴδετε
             ἐν ἐμοί

Returning now to discuss first the subordinate ("if") clause of this sentence, one is immediately struck with the two nouns that Paul uses to set the stage for what is to follow: ἀρετή and ἔπαινος. They are comprehensive qualities that the apostle says must characterize a Christian's attitude and actions. The first of these words, ἀρετή, is rarely used in the NT (1 Pet 2:9; 2 Pet 1:3), and only here by Paul. It is variously translated: "virtue," "excellence" and "goodness." Among classical writers it was an all-inclusive term to describe excellence of any kind, whether that of a person, an animal, or a thing. (Perhaps it was this "very width of significance" that kept NT writers from using it to any great degree: it did not have "precision enough for large use in Christian language," MM 75.) In the LXX it had the restricted meaning of "glory" or "praise" (Hab 3:3), while to the Stoic philosophers ἀρετή meant the highest good of man, "the only end to which a man should devote himself" (Beare). Very likely Paul, in using this word, had in mind the Stoic sense of "moral excellence or goodness" in spite of the fact that for the Stoic ἀρετή tended to focus attention on the excellence, merits and achievement of mankind rather than upon God's deeds (Sevenster, *Paul and Seneca*, 152).

The other word, ἔπαινος, means both "praise" and "something worthy of praise" (BGD). Often Paul used it of things which merit the praise of God (Rom 2:29; 1 Cor 4:5). But here in this particular context where he puts it in the company of ἀρετή, a word from the vocabulary of the Stoic moralists, and where he discusses the acknowledged good in pagan culture, he seems rather to have in view for ἔπαινος those things that merit the praise of men. Such was its meaning in contemporary public life where it was used of conduct that called down universal human approval (cf. Preisker, *TDNT* 2,586–88).

Thus Paul seems to be drawing upon the cultural background of the Philippians and is saying to them: "If there is such a thing as moral excellence, and you believe there is. If there is a kind of behavior that elicits universal approval, and you believe there is," then continue to strive for this goodness and to attain to this level of behavior that will command the praise of men and of God. You must not fail to live up to the ideals of your fellow men, which were also your ideals, before you were converted (cf. Sevenster, *Paul and Seneca,* 156). Thus, in all probability the apostle is here acknowledging that there was much good in pagan life and morality, and urges his friends (notice that once again he addresses the Philippians as ἀδελφοί) not to be blind to this fact, nor to repudiate it. He asks rather that they recognize and incorporate all that is good in natural morality into their own lives, to pay heed to quite simple but solid truths, even if they first learned them from pagan sources. For as Justin Martyr put it a century later, "The truth which men in all lands have rightly spoken belong to us" (*Apol.* 2.13).

And so Paul continues his sentence by coming now to its first main verb and object: "Think on these things" (ταῦτα λογίζεσθε). Λογίζεσθαι is a strong word, and a favorite of the apostle, used by him thirty-four of the forty times it appears in the NT. It means "to reckon, calculate, take into account," and as a result "to evaluate" a person, thing, quality or event (cf. BGD; MM). It includes also within the range of its meaning the ideas of "to ponder or let one's mind dwell on" something. Perhaps Paul employs it here to imply that the Philippians must ever be critical towards heathen culture and evaluate carefully its standards of morality. But certainly he does not intend by its use any encouragement to reflection without action. Rather he intends to say that the Philippian Christians must carefully consider certain things and evaluate them thoughtfully for the ultimate purpose of letting these things guide them into good deeds (cf. Heidland, *TDNT* 4,289).

"These things" (ταῦτα) that the Christians at Philippi are asked to evaluate and put into practice are now expressed in beautiful fashion, full of fervor and eloquence. Paul lists each "virtue" separately and thus gives each one individual attention by the constant repetition of the relative pronoun ὅσα ("whatever things"). (These clauses that enumerate the virtues and are introduced by ὅσα actually come first in the sentence for emphasis, but grammatically they are subordinate to ταῦτα ["these things"], which comes at the end of the sentence: "reflect on these things, namely the things *which* are true," etc.)

The apostle does this listing in much the same way that the moral philosophers of his day taught by reciting catalogues of virtues and vices. This fact, added to the fact that many of the words in Paul's list are not elsewhere used by him, or at least not by him in the same sense as here, seems to confirm the suggestion made above that Paul probably at this point has taken over these qualities, these "virtues," from popular moral philosophy familiar to his contemporaries in order to show that there was much in heathen views that might and ought to be valued and retained by Christians (Sevenster, *Paul and Seneca,* 154; Beare, Dibelius, Michael, Plummer; cf. A. Vögtle, *Die Tugend- und Lasterkataloge im Neuen Testament* [Münster: W. Aschendorff, 1936]; S. Wibbing, *Die Tugend- und Lasterkataloge im Neuen Testament* [Berlin: A Töpelmann, 1959] 80, 83–84; 101–103; 118–19; but see Lohmeyer and Michaelis who attempt rather to show the influence of the Greek Bible on the choice of words found in v 8; cf. Martin, *Philippians,* 1976).

The list of virtues, then, includes in order the following: (1) Ἀληθῆ. Since the whole series refers to ethical qualities, ἀληθῆ must mean "true" in the sense of "truthful," and "truthful" in every aspect of life including thought, speech and act.

(2) Σεμνά, found only here and in the Pastorals (1 Tim 3:8, 11; Titus 2:2), has such a richness about it that it is impossible to equate it with any one English word: "honest," "honorable," "noble," "worthy," "venerable," "that which wins respect or commands reverence," "esteemed" (Malherbe, *Cynic Epistles*, 180.23) are some of the suggested translations. Since it was often associated with gods and temples and holy things (cf. BGD; LSJ), it of necessity includes ideas of majesty, dignity and awe. Hence, although it may not be possible to translate σεμνά with a single word, its basic idea is clear. It refers to lofty things, majestic things, things that lift the mind from the cheap and tawdry to that which is noble and good and of moral worth.

(3) Δίκαια means "just," but again, "just" in the widest sense possible, not only in the relation of one person to another, but also in the relation of that person to God (cf. Acts 10:22; Rom 5:7). It concerns giving to God and men their due. It involves duty and responsibility. It entails satisfying all obligations.

(4) Ἁγνά means "pure." But this meaning is not to be restricted to the idea of "chaste" in the sense of freedom from bodily sins. It may also refer to ceremonial cleanness which fits someone or something for God, for his presence and service. And certainly it embraces the idea of purity in motives and actions including pure in every part of life (cf. 2 Cor 11:2; 1 Tim 5:22; James 3:17; 1 John 3:3).

(5) Προσφιλῆ is used only here in the NT and is not found at all in the lists of virtues that were current in the ancient world (see Wibbing, *Tugend- und Lasterkataloge*). It has as its fundamental meaning "that which calls forth love," hence, "lovely," "amiable," "attractive," "winsome." "Make yourself attractive (προσφιλῆ) to the congregation" is the advice of the sage to his child (Ecclus 4:7), something a wise person can do, for example, by his gracious speech (Ecclus 20:13). Thus the Christian's mind is to be set on things that elicit from others not bitterness and hostility, but admiration and affection.

(6) Εὔφημα, again, is a word found only here in the NT, and variously translated as "of good report," "of good repute," "admirable," "gracious," "gracious in the telling," "honorable," "kindly," "high-toned," "auspicious" (Malherbe, *Cynic Epistles*, 150.17). Apparently, however, this word never seems to be used elsewhere with a passive meaning, e.g. "well-spoken of, well-reputed" as some of the translations listed above might indicate, but only in an active sense of "well-speaking," hence, "winning, attractive" (Lightfoot). It is used, therefore, of "expressing what is kind and likely to win people, and avoiding what is likely to give offence" (Plummer).

These then are the excellent qualities that belonged to the culture of Paul's day, not at all unique to Christianity, which the apostle availed himself of and commended to his friends at Philippi. He asked them continuously to focus their minds (λογίζεσθε) on these things, to give full critical attention to them, and so to reflect carefully upon them with an action-provoking kind of meditation. It was not his desire to ask them merely to think about such noble matters without putting them into practice in their lives.

Yet "what may be gathered from the fact that [these virtues are] followed immediately by verse 9 is that obedience to 'what you have learned and re-

ceived and heard and seen in me' is what is ultimately of most importance
for the church." This means that for Paul, excellent as natural morality may
be, those qualities mentioned in v 8 must always be viewed in the light of v
9. That is to say, that for a Christian, "life and fellowship, as it is here formulated with the aid of terms taken from Greek moral philosophy, entails obedience to God's commandments, an obedience which . . . proceeds from belonging to Christ and from the possession of the Spirit which is at work in
the church. And so it is that there is something rather provisional about
verse 8: in appealing to the Philippians Paul takes into account their environment in order to obtain every possible support and understanding for what
he wishes to say in verse 9" (Sevenster, *Paul and Seneca*, 155–56). The last
word, therefore, lies with distinctively Christian teachings.

9. Thus Paul insists that the Philippians continuously put into practice,
that is to say, he insists that they loyally stand by, hold unswervingly to,
allow their lives to be controlled and altered by (1) the things that they learned
(ἐμάθετε) from him. Notice now that this new series is introduced by ἅ, the
definite relative pronoun ("those things which"), not by ὅσα ("whatever things
which"). General matters are not now in view, but rather those particular
things that Paul himself had taught and which the Philippians had learned
from him. This teaching is not spelled out here, but one can imagine that
what the apostle told the Ephesian elders would be applicable to the Philippian
elders as well: "I never shrank from letting you know anything that was for
your good, or from teaching you alike in public and from house to house,
bearing my testimony, both to Jews and Greeks, of repentance before God
and faith in our Lord Jesus Christ" (Acts 20:20–21).

(2) They must also put into practice the things which they "received"
from him (RSV). The verb translated "received" is παρελάβετε, and in meaning
it is not merely a repetition of ἐμάθετε ("learned") for rhetorical effect. Rather,
παραλαμβάνειν in this context is a technical term for the receiving of a tradition
for the purpose of handing it on intact to others (see Norden, *Agnostos Theos*,
288–89; O. Cullmann, *The Early Church*, A. J. B. Higgins [ed.] [London; SCM
Press, 1956] 55–99; Davies, *Paul and Rabbinic Judaism*, 248–49; cf. 'Abot 1.1:
"Moses received the Torah from Sinai and transmitted it to Joshua, Joshua
to the elders . . .' etc. [Str-B 3,444]). With this word, παραλαμβάνειν, Paul
in effect is saying that he passed on to the Philippians not only the things
that had come to him by revelation, but also those established elements of
the Christian message that had first been carefully passed on to him by others,
e.g. "that Christ died for our sins . . . was buried . . . was raised from the
dead . . . and appeared to Cephas," and so on (cf. 1 Cor 15:1–5). Paul classifies
himself, then, as a link in the chain of tradition (Conzelmann, *1 Corinthians*,
195–96), and his word, παρελάβετε, implies that the obligation of the Philippians was not only to receive it, believe it, act upon it, but also themselves to
pass it carefully on to others.

(3) They are also to act on what they heard (ἠκούσατε). This is a cryptic
remark that may mean either, "what you heard me preach"—but then it simply
repeats what has already been said, or "what you heard me saying when I
was present with you, not through my preaching, but informally through

my many conversations with you"—but this is improbable, or it may mean, "what you heard of as being characteristic of me, the kind of person I am, the things I do, how I face trials," and so on. This last-named is the most probable meaning because it goes hand in hand with the next thing in this series.

(4) They are also to do what they have seen in Paul—(εἴδετε ἐν ἐμοί). Thus the command to do all this that the Philippians have learned and received, and so on, is not given apart from a pattern that shows how it can be done. Paul believed that those who tell others to become Christians are obliged to show them what it is to be a Christian. Hence, because there always existed such a close connection between the word Paul preached and the life he lived (Gnilka), he could say without embarrassment or arrogance—"Look to me! Follow my example! Imitate me!" (1 Cor 11:1; Phil 3:17); "What you have seen in me (ἐν ἐμοί) do!" Although the ἐν ἐμοί ("in me") strictly relates to εἴδετε ("you saw"), and although one may wish to add "from me" after the other clauses, "what you learned and received and heard *from me,*" in order to gain smoothness in translation, it should at least be suggested that Paul may have deliberately placed the ἐν ἐμοί ("in me") at the end of the list, not only for rhetorical effect, but to say as forcefully as possible that everything he knew and believed and taught was embodied in himself, so that those who learn, receive and hear could see what doctrine looked like in living form. It appears that he was of the conviction that the truths of the Christian gospel must never be abstracted from action and put into high-toned words and phrases, but always expressed in the life of the teacher.

Paul's wish is that the Philippians might enjoy productive, worry-free lives (μηδὲν μεριμνᾶτε, 4:6) with their thoughts and feelings guarded by the peace of God. He told them that they might attain this goal with the aid of prayer and thanksgiving. But that is not all that is required. In vv 8 and 9 he adds still other important steps. He says that fear, worry, anxiety, depression— all the countless concerns that bombard the Philippian Christians' minds— can be kept at bay, if they will continuously reckon up, think over, estimate aright, fill their minds with all things good and true, and then rise up and put into practice the demands of the Christian gospel. "Then indeed" (καί, again as in v 7, is consecutive), Paul says, "the God of peace will be with you." This expression, "the God of peace" (ὁ θεὸς τῆς εἰρήνης) means either that God is the source and origin of peace, or is himself characterized by peace, or both at once. It is an advance in thought over the promise provided in v 7. There it was said that God's peace would be with them; now it is said that God himself, who gives peace, or who is himself peace, will be with them (cf. Bigaré, *AsSeign* 58 [1974] 11–15). To think of God as "the God of peace" was a most refreshing and encouraging exercise for Paul who lived constantly in the center of turmoil and trouble (cf. 2 Cor 11:23–33). As a consequence he often found himself writing this very phrase to his friends who also were experiencing difficulties of various kinds. It became for him a prayer of benediction: "The God of peace will be with you!" (cf. Rom 15:33; 16:20; 2 Cor 13:11; 1 Thess 5:23; cf. 1 Cor 14:33; 2 Thess 3:16; Heb 13:20).

Explanation

In light of the fact that the Philippians are in reality a colony of heaven and that they eagerly anticipate the return of Christ, who will transform their frail, mortal bodies into glorious bodies, they must take their stand as Christians, not only holding firmly to the truth of the gospel but behaving in a manner consonant with that truth.

Everywhere within this brief letter Paul's affection for the Philippians is obvious. But nowhere is it more obvious than here. He not only addresses them as "brothers," but also as people whom he loves, whom he is homesick to see, the source of his joy and honor. It is his deep affection for the Philippian Christians that prompts him to describe in detail how they are to stand firm, how they are to live consonant with the truth of the gospel.

"Standing firm" means living in harmony with each other. Hence, he begs Euodia and Syntyche, two sparring women, quickly to settle their dispute. What little is known about these women indicates that they were prominent people within the Christian community at Philippi. They may even have held important positions of leadership in the church. Once they had been united in working together side by side with Paul in the arduous task of spreading the gospel as his coworkers. Now, however, some unknown thing had set them at odds with each other, and the quarrel between two people threatened to destroy the unity of the whole. The apostle appeals, therefore, not only to Euodia and Syntyche, but beyond them to a third party, whom he simply addresses as his "true yoke-fellow." He asks "him" to come to their aid and to help them find a solution to their problem. Who was this mysterious person? Many different answers have been offered, but the best of these is the suggestion that perhaps the single individual was in reality the entire Philippian church viewed by Paul as one person yoked together with him to pull hard together to resist every inroad of division and to strive to restore harmony.

Again, "standing firm" means that the Philippians must rejoice on all occasions, even when those occasions are not occasions for merriment but mourning. But the thing that keeps such an appeal from being ridiculous is the fact of the Christian's faith. It is a faith in Jesus Christ as Lord, who as Lord has the power to subdue all things to his authority (cf. 3:21). It is a faith in Jesus Christ as Lord, who permitted *this* situation as it is to occur. It is a faith in Jesus Christ as Lord that causes the Christian willingly to submit and say, "Yes!"

In addition, "standing firm" includes the development of an extraordinary quality which must be so much a part of the Christian's life that it will be obvious to everyone, Christian and non-Christian alike. It is the quality of "sweet reasonableness" which enables one to be just without being harsh. It is the spirit of magnanimity that was so characteristic of Jesus Christ himself (2 Cor 10:1).

Then right in the middle of everything, Paul interjects the exclamation, "The Lord is near!" But what did he mean by this? Did he mean that the Lord is close by, present to aid and give assistance, thus providing further reason for joy and gentleness? Or did he mean that the return of Christ is imminent, thus heightening the earnestness of his commands by calling attention to the shortness of time? Most likely Paul was intentionally vague, so that both ideas might be fused into one sharp sentence: the Lord who will come again is presently very near in his Spirit.

Finally, "standing firm" means not giving way to anxiety, but allowing the peace of God to stand guard over one's thoughts and feelings, so protecting them against attack as a garrison of soldiers protects a city against its enemies. The cure for worry, therefore, is (1) in prayer and thanksgiving, giving to God every care, every unreasonable anxiety, every harassing burden and trusting him to take care of these worrisome matters, (2) in deliberately filling one's mind constantly with good thoughts that are praise-worthy, true, majestic and awe-inspiring, just, pure, attractive, high-toned, and (3) in putting into practice the supreme teachings of the gospel that one has learned both from having heard them spoken and having seen them lived.

If the Philippians, or any other Christian, will be careful to observe and follow these three things, then they will encounter peace through the presence of the God of peace.

V. Gratitude Expressed for the Philippians' Generosity (4:10-20)

Bibliography

Baumert, N. "Ist Ph. 4:10 richtig übersetzt?" *BZ* 13 (1969) 256–62. **Beet, J. A.** "The Christian Secret." *Expositor*, 3rd series, 10 (1889) 174–89. **Buchanan, C. O.** *EvQ* 36 (1964) 157–66. **Drummond, R. J.** "A Note on Philippians 4:10–19." *ExpTim* 11 (1899–1900) 284, 381. **Glombitza, O.** "Der Dank des Apostels. Zum Verständnis von Phil. 4:10–20." *NovT* 7 (1964–65) 135–41. **Kennedy, H. A. A.** "The Financial Colouring of Philippians 4:15–18." *ExpTim* 12 (1900–1901) 43–44. **Lambert, J. C.** "Note on Philippians 4:10–19." *ExpTim* 11 (1899–1900) 333–34. **Levy, J. P.** "Une Société de fait dans l'Église apostolique (Phil. 4:10–22)." *Mélanges Philippe Meylan*. Lausanne: Université de Lausanne, 1963, 2, 41–59. **Morris, L.** "Καὶ ἅπαξ καὶ δίς." *NovT* 1 (1956) 205–208. **Pratscher, W.** "Der Verzicht des Paulus auf finanziellen Unterhalt durch seine Gemeinde: ein Aspekt seiner Missionsweise." *NTS* 25 (1979) 284–98. **Rolland, B.** "Saint Paul et la pauvreté: Ph. 4:12–14, 19–20." *AsSeign* 59 (1974) 10–15.

Translation

[10] *O yes, and I rejoice in the Lord greatly because now at last your thoughtful care of me*[a] *has blossomed once again. Indeed, you have always cared about me, but you have not always had the opportunity to show it.* [11] *I am not saying this because of any need I had, for I have learned to be self-sufficient in every situation in which I find myself.* [12] *Hence, I know how to be humbled and I know how to abound. In every and all circumstances I have learned the secret of being well-fed and of going hungry, of having more than enough and of having too little.* [13] *I have the power to face all such situations in union with the One who continuously infuses me with strength.*[b] [14] *And yet it was good of you to become partners with me in my hardships.* [15] *Now*[c] *you Philippians know as well as I that when the gospel was in its beginning, when I set out from Macedonia, no other church entered into a partnership with me in an accounting of expenditures and receipts except you alone.* [16] *You know as well as I that when I was in Thessalonica you sent money to meet my needs*[d] *more than once.* [17] *I do not say this meaning that I have my heart set on your giving. But I certainly do have my heart set on interest increasing that may accrue to your account.* [18] *Here, then, is my receipt for everything you have given me. I have more than enough. I am fully supplied*[e] *now that I have received from Epaphroditus the gifts you sent me. They are a fragrant odor, a sacrifice that God accepts and that pleases him.* [19] *In return, I pray that God may meet*[f] *every need you have in accordance with his marvelous wealth in Christ Jesus.* [20] *Now surely the glory belongs to God our Father forever and ever. Amen!*

Notes

[a] F G use the genitive definite article τοῦ for τό—τοῦ ὑπὲρ ἐμοῦ φρονεῖν for τὸ ὑπὲρ ἐμοῦ φρονεῖν.

[b] ℵ² D² and the majority text add Χριστῷ ("Christ") to make clear who it is who strengthens Paul. If "Christ" had been part of the original text there would have been no reason to omit it except by accident.

ᶜ p⁴⁶ D* and a few other witnesses omit δέ ("but," "and"), perhaps seeing it as superfluous along with καί ("and," "indeed").

ᵈ ℵ B F G Ψ and the majority of witnesses read εἰς τὴν χρείαν μοι ("to me for my need"). p⁴⁶ A 81 read τὴν χρείαν μοι ("what I needed") omitting the preposition εἰς by accident after δίς (ΔΙΣΕΙΣ), or on purpose so as to provide a direct object for the verb. D has τὴν χρείαν μου ("my need") and D² L P have εἰς τὴν χρείαν μου ("for my need"), both replacing the less usual, but better attested μοι with the genitive μου.

ᵉ p⁴⁶ adds δέ ("but") after the verb πεπλήρωμαι ("I am fully supplied").

ᶠ p⁴⁶ ℵ A B D² and the majority text read πληρώσει future indicative ("will take care of"), whereas D* F G 6 33 81 104 326 365 and other witnesses read πληρῶσαι, aorist optative ("may [God] take care of"). Although less well attested than πληρώσει, there are nevertheless good witnesses in support of πληρῶσαι, a reading which better reflects the apostle's own reverent attitude. He does not say categorically what God *will do* for his friends, but he prayerfully asks God to come to their aid (see comments).

Form/ Structure/ Setting

This part of the letter is Paul's response to the gift sent to him by the Philippian church through the good offices of their own emissary, Epaphroditus (v 18). In a sense it is the apostle's formal receipt (note the use of the technical term, ἀπέχω, v 18) acknowledging that the things had arrived intact and had been duly received by him. He alluded to their kindness earlier in the letter (1:5) and at that point had thanked God for them and for their generosity (cf. 1:3, 5). But not until now does he discuss the gift of the Philippians in any detail. The reason for this delay has been variously interpreted: (1) These verses constitute a separate letter of thanks sent to the Philippian Christians months earlier than the letter in which it now appears. Only at a much later time, when some unidentified scribe wished to collect all of Paul's correspondence to the church at Philippi and weave it all into a single epistle, was it by chance placed in this unexpected spot. (This suggestion has been noted and rejected in the Introduction.) (2) Paul, in the custom of his day, dictated the early part of his letter, but picked up the pen to sign it in his own hand, and in doing so wrote his own personal "thank you" quite naturally at the end (cf. Bahr, *JBL* 87 [1968] 27–41). This explanation accounts for the particle, δέ ("but") with which this section begins. For it appears to arrest "a subject which is in danger of escaping." Its presence here "is as if the apostle said 'I must not forget to thank you for your gift' " (Lightfoot). (3) A more likely reason is that which suggests that the whole matter of giving and receiving was a touchy subject with Paul. And reading between the lines here, and listening to what was said and for what was not said, one might easily infer that there was something about the Philippians' gift that was troubling to the apostle. He, therefore, delays discussion of it until the end of his letter, as one naturally tends to put off bringing up sensitive issues by leaving them to the very last moment possible.

It is known from elsewhere that, although Paul championed the right of an apostle to be supported financially by those to whom he preached the gospel, and although he never renounced that right, he preferred to support himself and his mission by manual labor, and jealously insisted on doing so: (1) in order that he might offer the gospel of God's free grace without charge, (2) in order that no opponent of his could ever accuse him of using his mission as a pretext for greed, and (3) in order that he might set the proper example for others to follow (see 1 Cor 4:8–13, especially v 12; 8:1–18; 2 Cor 11:7–10; 1 Thess 2:5–12, especially v 9; 2 Thess 3:7–12, especially vv 8–9; cf. Pratscher, *NTS* 25 [1979] 284–98). Paul had no hesitation about asking money from his churches to aid others, e.g. the needy Christians in Jerusalem (1 Cor 16:1–3; 2 Cor 8–9), but he refused to do so for himself. And yet the Macedonian Christians, which surely would have included the Christians at Philippi, not only made a generous contribution out of their own deep poverty to the needy saints' fund (2 Cor 8:1–5), but they also more than once (Phil 4:16) made generous contributions to Paul's own personal fund (2 Cor 11:8–9). It may be suggested, therefore, that this violation of one of Paul's strict principles, entailing giving of a personal gift to him which was not only unsolicited, but which the Macedonian churches knew from personal experience he opposed (1 Thess 2:9; 2 Thess 3:8–9), was the very thing which prompted him to leave this matter of the gift until the last, and caused him to write a careful reply that combined cautious gratitude with a gentle but firm demand that they not henceforth infringe on his own self-reliance. Nowhere else in all of Paul's letters nor in all of the letters of antiquity that have survived until the present is there any other acknowledgment of a gift that can compare with this one in terms of such a tactful treatment of so sensitive a matter (von Soden; see Plummer, Michael).

The very structure of this section makes clear what has just been said. It exhibits a nervous alternation back and forth between Paul's appreciation on the one hand (vv 10, 14–16, 18–20), and his insistence on his own independence and self-sufficiency on the other (vv 11–13, 17). It is of utmost importance to him that this matter of personal independence not be compromised in any way. Thus he cannot write as one who is wholly free to express his thanks without reservations or qualifications (Michael). It fact, it is remarkable that in this so-called "thank you" section, Paul does not use the verb εὐχαριστεῖν ("to thank" someone for something; cf. Rom 16:4). Thus, in a sense Paul pens to his friends in Philippi a "thankless thanks" (Dibelius, Gnilka), masterfully written, constructed in such a way as neither to offend those who gave their gift out of love, nor to encourage their continued violation of his strict instructions not to send him assistance (cf. Buchanan, *EvQ* 36 [1964] 161–63). He admits that he is very glad *in the Lord* that they once again were able to show their concern for him, but he never praises them directly for the tangible form this concern took. He readily acknowledges that these Philippians alone of all the churches he founded became partners with him in the matter of giving, but he tempers this potentially laudatory remark by reminding them that he never asked for their gift. He feels free to boast about the generosity of the Philippians to other churches (2 Cor 11:8–9), but he is restrained when he addresses the Philippians directly about this matter. He informs them that what they did for him is accepted by God as a beautiful sacrifice, but he weakens this praise by the businesslike tone in which he personally responds to this very same act: "Here is my receipt for what you gave me. I have more than enough as a result, too much! I am full up!"—words which imply that he wants no more of their assistance (but see Glombitza, *NovT* [1964–65] 135–41).

Comment

10. Paul begins this section with ἐχάρην δὲ ἐν κυρίῳ ("I rejoice in the Lord": ἐχάρην is an epistolary aorist). And once again he strikes the keynote of the epistle, "joy." The particle, δέ, often ignored and passed over by the translators, is really an important word here. As we saw, it "arrests a subject which is in danger of escaping" (Lightfoot). It indicates that something has just occurred to the writer which, if let go any longer, might be forgotten altogether. Yet, very likely Paul used it for rhetorical effect. He could never really forget what the Philippians had done for him, nor could he even come close to sending his letter off without these important remarks. But he approaches the whole matter of thanking them for their gift as if it were possible for him to do so. The assistance provided him by the Philippians and the problems it created for him were subjects very much in his mind, even matters he could not possibly forget, but he waits until the last moment to broach them, and then he does so in what appears to be an off-hand way. The δέ might be paraphrased: "O yes, and I must not forget . . ." (cf. 1 Cor 16:1; Gal 4:20).

There are now several things worth noting: (1) Paul says that his joy is immense. Although the idea of "great joy" is consonant with the Christian gospel and often associated with it (Matt 2:10; Luke 2:10; 24:52; Acts 8:8; 15:3), this is the only place where the apostle quantifies his own experience of joy. The adverb he uses, μεγάλως ("greatly, immensely"), is found nowhere else in the NT, and its very uniqueness intensifies what he is saying about the depth of his feelings at this point.

(2) Furthermore, Paul says that his joy is *in the Lord.* If one expected him to say instead that his joy was in the generosity of the Philippians, he is going to be surprised. Paul never says this. He never thanks them directly for anything they gave him. Yet, by saying that his joy was "in the Lord" he was saying that it was thoroughly Christian, flowing out of his union with Christ and therefore totally free from ingratitude or resentment (cf. Michael).

(3) Even though for Paul the final, the ultimate, cause of his joy was "the Lord," there was also a more immediate cause as well. This is stated now by the apostle in a clause introduced by ὅτι ("because"). But again it is remarkable that Paul does not say that this immediate cause of his joy was the Philippians' *gift*. It was rather what that gift pointed to, namely, the care and concern (φρονεῖν) of the Philippians for him and their determination to see to his welfare. What gave him joy was not things, but people and how they behaved. If a gift of money troubled him because it was against his principle to take such a gift for himself from any of his churches, yet the loving thoughfulness that prompted his friends to override his wishes and give sacrificially (cf. 2 Cor 8:1–3) pleased him greatly.

The verb Paul uses to express this "thoughtful love" is φρονεῖν, the key verb of this letter (1:7; 2:2, 5; 3:15, 19; 4:2, 10). Fundamental to its meaning is the idea of "thinking." Paul, therefore, was never out of the thoughts of the Philippians. But φρονεῖν means more than merely "thinking" about someone. It also describes an active interest in that person's affairs. Thus, because φρονεῖν characterized the relationship of the Philippian Christians to Paul, it meant that they of necessity would be personally involved in promoting the welfare of the apostle by whatever means they had at their disposal.

For some unknown reason the Philippians for an extended period of time were cut off from Paul and he from them. As a consequence doubts may have arisen, as would only be natural, about the genuineness of their concern for him. Hence, it was with a great sense of relief that this silence of uncertainty was broken with the arrival of Epaphroditus from Philippi (v 18). "At long last" (ἤδη ποτέ; cf. BGD), Paul writes his friends, "you have renewed your concern for me" (ἀνεθάλετε τὸ ὑπέρ ἐμοῦ φρονεῖν). The verb translated "renewed" (ἀναθάλλειν) is a highly metaphorical word, filled with poetic boldness, beautiful in its idea, chosen no doubt to convey affectionate understanding. This is its only occurrence in the NT, but it is used elsewhere to describe trees and flowers "bursting into bloom again" in the springtime, or plants "sprouting afresh" from the ground (cf. BGD). To translate it as "renew," or "revive," or "show" (GNB, JB, NIV, RSV, Phillips) is almost to mistranslate it. Paul is not here complaining but marvelling. Like a person rejoicing over the signs of spring after a hard winter, so Paul rejoiced to see again the signs of personal concern from Philippi after a long interval of silence. His carefully chosen word expresses his delight: "Your care for me has now blossomed afresh!" (NEB). (Whether this verb is considered intransitive [Gnilka, Haupt; Baumert, BZ 13 (1969) 256–62; LXX Ps 27:7; Wisd Sol 4:4] or transitive [Beare, Bonnard, Dibelius, Scott, GNB, JB, NIV, RSV; Ecclus 1:18; 11:22; 50:10] makes little difference: Paul is most happy because of this "blossoming.")

That the words, "Now at last your care for me has blossomed once again," were not in the least intended as a criticism Paul makes clear by giving powerful expression to a fresh reason for joy. He introduces it with the phrase ἐφ᾽ ᾧ ("because, for"; cf. BDF 235,2; Rom 5:12; 2 Cor 5:4; Phil 3:12; but see Baumert, BZ 13 [1969] 256–62), and follows it with a studiedly balanced chiastic (crisscross) sentence that ends in an unusual fashion, with the conjunction δέ: καὶ ἐφρονεῖτε, ἠκαιρεῖσθε δέ ("surely you were all the while thinking how you might aid me; you were all the while lacking opportunity to do so, however"). The conjunctions at the beginning and end bracketing these words, the short, abrupt, precise clauses, the imperfect tenses highlighting the continuous uninterrupted flow of the thought and action described here, the chiastic structure of the sentence—all combine to state afresh and with force this new reason for joy. It was this: Paul had come to realize that the Philippians were not to blame for the slow arrival of help, but rather the circumstances were beyond their control. The verb, ἀκαιρεῖσθαι, a late and rare word, found only here in the NT, means that the Philippians were "without opportunity" (καιρός) to exhibit their willingness and readiness to send aid. It alludes to those unfavorable circumstances, namely the lack of the right person to send on the long and difficult journey to Caesarea, a lack of funds (cf. 2 Cor 8:2), a lack of suitable weather for travel, whatever it may have been, that robbed the Philippians of doing for Paul what they wished to do.

11. But having praised the Philippians to this extent Paul immediately begins a disclaimer: "my gratitude is not a beggar's thanks for charity" (Beet's translation of οὐχ ὅτι καθ᾽ ὑστέρησιν λέγω, quoted by Jones).

Οὐχ ὅτι, "I do not say that," with which this sentence begins, is a distinctively

NT expression. It usually appears without a verb of "saying" which must be supplied by the reader (cf. John 6:46; 7:22; 2 Cor 1:24; 3:5; 2 Thess 3:9), but Paul chooses to include it here (λέγω; cf. BDF 480,5). The prepositional phrase καθ' ὑστέρησιν (lit. "in accordance with need") merges the idea of norm or standard with that of reason (cf. Rom 2:7; 8:28; 11:5; 16:26; Eph 1:11; 3:3; 1 Tim 1:1; Titus 1:3), and thus is more properly to be translated, "because I need anything" (BGD, κατά, II, 5δ). The noun, ὑστέρησις, is another of those rare words that show up regularly in this carefully phrased section. Used only here and in Mark 12:44, it denotes "need, lack or poverty." Thus, Paul is making very clear that his joy at the gift from the Philippians was not because he was in dire straits at the time it arrived with himself in poverty—apparently he either did not need or did not want their money—but because he saw in this act of generosity a truly Christian deed of sacrificial self-giving love (cf. 2 Cor 8:5). He says in effect, "I am glad that you assisted me, yes, but I do not say this because I lacked anything or needed your help."

How is it that Paul was able to say this? Was it because he had fallen heir to family property which enabled him to pay all his expenses, including those involved in a costly appeal to Caesar, and thus had no need for outside assistance (cf. W. M. Ramsay, *St. Paul the Traveller and the Roman Citizen* [London: Hodder and Stoughton, 1905] 310–13)? Possibly, but that is not the answer that he himself gives. He claims to be able to say this because of what he had learned: ἐγὼ γὰρ ἔμαθον. The pronoun, ἐγώ ("I"), is used emphatically: "whether or not others have learned, I have." The aorist tense (ἔμαθον) is a constative aorist used here for linear actions which having been completed are regarded as a whole (BDF 332,1). It implies that Paul's whole experience, especially as a Christian, up to the present has been a sort of schooling from which he has not failed to master its lessons.

The primary lesson he learned from the school of experience (cf. 2 Cor 11:23–29) was to be self-sufficient (αὐτάρκης) in all the circumstances of the moment (ἐν οἷς εἰμί). The adjective αὐτάρκης, usually translated "content" or "satisfied" (GNB, KJV, NIV, RSV, Goodspeed, Knox, Moffatt, Phillips), along with its corresponding noun, αὐτάρκεια, was used to describe the person who through discipline had become independent of external circumstances, and who discovered within himself resources that were more than adequate for any situation that might arise. It was a favorite word in the vocabularies of the Stoic and Cynic philosophers to refer to that independent spirit and that free outlook on life that characterized the wise man (cf. Malherbe, *Cynic Epistles*, 124.25; 176.12; 244.4). It expressed the doctrine "that man should be sufficient unto himself for all things, and able, by the power of his own will, to resist the force of circumstances" (Vincent; cf. Plato, *Tim.* 33D). Paul, familiar with the vocabulary of the Stoics, and himself in harmony with many of their ideals (see comments on v 8), appears also to have borrowed αὐτάρκης from them—this is the only place it appears in the NT—to declare that he too has acquired the virtue of a spirit free from worry, untroubled by the vicissitudes of external events, independent of people and things. And Paul cherishes this self-sufficiency.

But the difference between Paul, the self-sufficient Christian and the self-sufficient Stoic, is vast: "The self-sufficiency of the Christian is relative: an independence of the world through dependence upon God. The Stoic self-sufficiency pretends to be absolute. One is the contentment of faith, the other of pride. Cato and Paul both stand erect and fearless before a persecuting world: one with a look of rigid, defiant scorn, the other with a face now lighted up with unutterable joy in God. . . . The Christian martyr and the Stoic suicide are the final examples of these two memorable and contemporaneous protests against the evils of the world" (G. G. Findlay, *Christian Doctrine and Morals* [London: Chas. H. Kelly, 1894], quoted by Jones; cf. 2 Cor 9:8; 1 Tim 6:6; see also A. Bonhoeffer, *Epiktet und das Neue Testament* [Giessen: Töpelmann, 1911] 109–110, 291, 335–36; Glombitza, *NovT* 7 [1964–65] 135–41; Kittel, *TDNT* 1,466–67; Sevenster, *Paul and Seneca*, 113–14).

12–13. Paul now begins to explain in detail what he means when he says, "I have learned to be self-sufficient in every situation." This explanation, some interpreters claim, is stated in a poetic fashion that makes use of two three-lined strophes (Friedrich, Gnilka, Lohmeyer, followed by Martin, *Philippians*, 1976). Although the passage is indeed rhythmical in form, a poetic verse-structure is not obvious (Collange). Hence, the passage can best be interpreted by taking the first three finite verbs, οἶδα . . . οἶδα . . . μεμύημαι ("I know . . . I know . . . I know the secret"), as exactly parallel to each other, developing the idea already expressed by ἔμαθον ("I have learned," v 11), and the last verb, ἰσχύω ("I am able"), as a summary statement qualifying what Paul means by his idea of self-sufficiency.

With rhetorical repetitiveness Paul twice over uses the verb οἶδα giving it here the meaning of "I know how," or "I am able" (BGD), and showing by its use what it was he had learned: "I have learned; therefore I know: I know how to cope." The things he learned to cope with are now expressed by infinitives, one, either middle or passive in voice, the other, active: ταπεινοῦ-σθαι/περισσεύειν.

The verb ταπεινοῦν literally means "to lower," as one would lower the level of water behind a dam, or the height of a mountain or hill (cf. Luke 3:5; see BGD). Figuratively it means "to humble," both in a good sense and in a bad sense (cf. Matt 18:4; 2 Cor 12:21). Here Paul uses the infinitive, ταπεινοῦσθαι, with οἶδα to mean either that he knows how "to discipline himself," "to humble himself," e.g. by fasting (cf. Isa 58:5; see Deissmann, *Light*, 419), or that he knows how "to be humbled, to be brought low" by want or poverty. In any case it denotes a going down into deprivation whether self-imposed or imposed by external forces, and Paul is saying, "I know how to cope with this, I am able for this." There is also in this choice of ταπεινοῦσθαι an echo of the self-humbling of Christ (ἐταπείνωσεν ἑαυτόν, "he humbled himself") already so poignantly described by the apostle (2:8) and with which he proudly associates himself (cf. Rolland, *AsSeign* 59 [1974] 10–15; on the meaning of the whole word see Grundmann, *TDNT* 9,16–18; Schweizer, *Erniedrigung und Erhöhung*).

The very antithesis of this deprivation is expressed now by περισσεύειν, although one might have expected ὑψοῦν ("to exalt"). By contrast to ταπεινοῦσθαι it means "to abound, to overflow, to have more than enough, to be extremely rich." And by linking this infinitive with οἶδα Paul says, "I also know how to cope with abundance." Not all of Paul's life was marked by a cramping and oppressive want of resources. He also experienced great prosperity. But in the same way that privations could do him no harm, so "he was equally immune from harm when fortune smiled" (Michael). He knew that grace was needed to handle prosperity properly as well as penury. But there is no indication that he favored the one state over the other. One should also note in passing that there is in the use of περισσεύειν an echo of the overflowing abundance that Paul envisions as characteristic of the new age inaugurated by Christ's coming (1:9, 26). It is a distinctively Pauline word, used by the apostle twenty-six of the thirty-nine times it appears in the NT.

Still a third thing that Paul knew as a result of his learning experience is expressed now by a verb found nowhere else in the NT: μεμύημαι. It is formed from μυεῖν ("to initiate"), a technical term referring to those initiatory rites required of any person who wished to enter into the secrets and privileges of the ancient mystery religions (BGD). Once again Paul appears to borrow from the vocabulary of his pagan environment just the right word that would be readily understood by his readers to express the precise idea he wished to impart. He does not mean to say that he automatically knew the secret of a contented life, but that he came to know this secret (μεμύημαι: note the perfect tense) through a difficult process that could be described as an initiation: "I have been very thoroughly initiated into the human lot with all of its ups and downs" (NEB). Thus, the ἐν παντὶ καὶ ἐν πᾶσιν ("in every and all circumstances") with which this new sentence begins should be connected adverbially with μεμύημαι.

Now these inclusive and varied circumstances are described in part by two sets of paired infinitives: καὶ χορτάζεσθαι καὶ πεινᾶν/καὶ περισσεύειν καὶ ὑστερεῖσθαι. Χορτάζεσθαι ("to be full") was used of force-feeding animals for the purpose of fattening them, of birds gorging themselves on their prey (Rev 19:21), of satisfying the needs of a hungry crowd (Matt 14:20). Above all it denotes amplitude, and Paul uses it to refer to his having plenty to eat without any overtones of brutishness (cf. Plummer). Πεινᾶν is the direct opposite of this first verb. Instead of portraying plenty of food it pictures the absence of food and the hunger that results (cf. Matt 4:2; 12:1). More than once Paul experienced the grim literal reality of this word as he engaged himself in the work of carrying out the Christian mission (1 Cor 4:11; 2 Cor 11:27).

To drive home further his point on the alternating nature of human life Paul repeats himself in the next pair of infinitives. He had earlier written ὑστέρησις (v 11) and περισσεύειν (v 12); now he writes περισσεύειν ("to have more than enough") and ὑστερεῖσθαι ("to have too little, to be in need").

It is as if Paul were saying, "I have been initiated into all the mysteries of life. I know the secrets of everyday reality. God has taught me through good times and bad how to cope not only with hunger and privation, but with plenty to eat and an abundance of wealth." It is as if he were saying that "the vicissitudes of his life were the rites of admission to a secret society" (Beare).

13. Paul now both reaffirms his self-sufficiency and qualifies it in these his most famous words: πάντα ἰσχύω ἐν τῷ ἐνδυναμοῦντί με. Those translations which give the impression that Paul meant he could do anything and that

nothing was beyond his powers (ASV, KJV, NASB, NEB, NIV, RSV, Goodspeed, Knox, Moffatt) are misleading to the point of being false. Πάντα does literally mean "all things." But the real meaning of this or any word is determined by its context. Thus, irrespective of whether Paul wrote πάντα or τὰ πάντα the context does not permit one to say that he has moved without warning from the particular to the general, from "all *these* things," to "all things" (but cf. Alford, Vincent). Πάντα as used here can only refer to "all those situations," both good and bad, that have just been described—"all the prosperous and adverse circumstances" which one must encounter in the course of everyday living.

All these things, Paul says, he has the power to cope with or is competent and able to handle (ἰσχύω). This verb, ἰσχύειν ("to have power") is not a favorite of the apostle, used by him only two of the twenty-eight times it occurs in the NT, i.e. here and in Gal 5:6. Nevertheless, by using this word Paul reaffirms his own sufficiency: "*I* have the power to face all conditions of life (cf. GNB), humiliation or exaltation, plenty to eat or not enough, wealth or poverty, as well as all other external circumstances like these. *I* can endure all these things (cf. Gnilka). *I* have the resources in myself to master them. *I* am strong to face them down. *I* can prevail over and be absolute master of all the vicissitudes of life." This indeed is the force of the active voice of the verb, ἰσχύω.

But then Paul adds a most important qualifying phrase: ἐν τῷ ἐνδυναμοῦντί με ("in union with the one who infuses me with strength"). And thus is established the grand paradox. The secret of Paul's independence was his dependence upon Another. His self-sufficiency in reality came from being in vital union with One who is all-sufficient. Who is this Other, this all-sufficient One? Paul does not say. He simply identifies him by means of a present active participle used as a noun: "the One who continually infuses power." The verb, ἐνδυναμοῦν, however, is used elsewhere to denote the powerful activity of the Lord Jesus Christ (cf. Eph 6:10; 1 Tim 1:12; 2 Tim 2:1; 4:17). Thus those later scribes who added Χριστῷ ("Christ") to the text properly understood Paul's intent. He whose life was seized by Christ; he who gladly gave up all for Christ; he who paradoxically gained all by losing all for Christ; he who longed to know Christ and the *power* of his resurrection (3:7–10), and so on, could only envision Christ as his true source of inner strength. So, although he had carefully disciplined himself and had discovered within himself untapped resources of power that, when drawn upon, made him independent of outward circumstances, he could never bring himself to deny his need of Christ and of his reliance upon the strength which Christ supplies. The truth of the matter is that in himself Paul did not perceive a strong, totally independent soul. But united with Christ, the source of ultimate power, he was able to face life forcefully. Note 2 Cor 12:9–10 in this connection where he speaks of his weaknesses as advantages because they made him all the more receptive of Christ's strength, which is made perfect in weakness. "Most gladly, then," writes Paul, "will I rather glory in my weaknesses, that the power of Christ may rest upon me. Therefore I am content with weaknesses . . . and hardships for the sake of Christ; for when I am weak, then am I strong" (cf. Beare). Paul, thus, never allowed his weaknesses or perceived weaknesses to be an excuse for inactivity, or for a failure to attempt the impossible task. They in a sense became his greatest assets, and surrendering them to Christ he discovered that they were transformed for his own enrichment and for the enrichment of others. "L'entreprise est grand; mais le secours est égal au travail. Dieu, qui vous appele si haut, vous tend la main; son Fils, qui lui est égal, descend à vous pour vous porter" (Bousset, quoted by Plummer).

14. With the word πλήν ("but," "yet," "even so," "nevertheless," "all the same," "notwithstanding") Paul does two things—(1) he underscores for the Philippians the fact that he could just as well have done without their contributions, and (2) returns to the task of affirming them for the personal care and concern they showed him by these contributions. Paul sees it as very important that his desire for and insistence upon independence not be interpreted by the Philippians as indifference to the love they displayed for him in their giving. And so he says in effect, "Although I did not need what you sent, yet you did the right, even the beautifully right (καλῶς), thing in sharing with me in my troubles." Thus in this idiomatic expression, καλῶς ἐποιήσατε (Acts 10:32; 2 Pet 1:19; 3 John 6), Paul comes as close to saying "Thank you" as ever he does in this letter (Martin, *Philippians*, 1976).

The expression "sharing in" is an aorist participle (συγκοινωνήσαντες) referring exclusively to this most recent gesture of love, and used circumstantially to denote manner. In what way did the Philippians do the right thing? Precisely in that they became partners (συγκοινωνεῖν) with Paul. And in this instance, they became his partners in trouble (θλίψει). The word "trouble" (θλίψις), although on occasion used of the disaster that is to come on the world at the end of the age (Matt 24:29; Mark 13:19; 2 Thess 1:6), is used here in a nontechnical sense of severe hardships, afflictions, burdens, and so on, which is the most frequent sense in which Paul uses this word (cf. 1:17; 2 Cor 1:4, 8; 2:4; 4:17; 1 Thess 1:6). Thus it seems strained to argue that the apostle, in praising the Philippians, may have chosen this word in order to commend them for their support of him "as 'eschatological apostle,' destined to promote God's purposes in the spread of the gospel to the Gentiles and so prepare the way for the dénouement of history" (so Martin, *Philippians*, 1976, citing A. Fridrichsen, *The Apostle and His Message* [Uppsala: Lundequistska Bokhandeln, 1947]; J. Munck, *Paul and the Salvation of Mankind* [London: SCM Press, 1959] chap. 2). Rather, by the practical sympathy of the Philippians in providing material help for Paul and in sending Epaphroditus to him, they had indeed become partners with him in his imprisonment and sufferings, although they were many miles removed from him. They had taken some of his burden upon themselves in their genuine and deep sense of concern that expressed itself in constructive action on behalf of the apostle, and therefore on behalf of the gospel (1:12–17; see Collange, Glombitza, *NovT* 7 [1964–65] 135–41; Seesemann, *Der Begriff* KOINΩNIA, 33–34). And it was exactly this sympathy and companionship that the apostle valued far more than any financial relief that came to him as a result (cf. Lightfoot).

15–16. These verses comprise one long sentence in Greek. It is simple in its construction and basic idea, having one main verb, οἴδατε ("you know"), with two direct objects, each introduced by ὅτι: "You know *that* no other church was a partner with me except you, and *that* you sent me gifts even in Thessalonica." Yet within this simple structure there are difficulties that need explanation.

If the text is correct, the sentence begins with two particles, δέ and καί (see Notes). The first of these, δέ, is often used to set up a contrast between two clauses and is then translated "but." Here, however, it is a simple connective, a transitional particle that moves the reader on (BGD) to the mention of previous acts of kindness done by the Philippians. It cannot be translated at all, or at best by the word "now." The second particle, καί, compares the Philippians, not with other witnesses to the Philippians' generosity, whom Paul might mention, but with himself—"You know *as well as I,*" not "You know *as well as others*" (cf. Vincent).

The very fact that Paul feels compelled to say this—"You know as well as I"—reinforces the idea that he sensed the possibility of the Philippians interpreting his faint praise as a rebuke, which to some extent it was. As has already been pointed out, but needs repeating, the apostle deliberately restrained himself in extending his thanks, because he wished to maintain his independence. But at the same time he had no desire to offend by what might be conceived of as ingratitude on his part for what was an obvious act of love on their part. He therefore looked for a middle course between effusiveness on the one hand, and rebuke on the other. Hence, without a straightforward "thank you," he nevertheless tells them that they did the right thing in sharing with him (v 14), and reminds them also that they know and he knows what good things they did in the past, which in his judgment were quite sufficient to prove their love for him (cf. Gnilka), to which nothing further need be added.

One must note now that this is the first and only time Paul directly addresses his friends with the vocative form, Φιλιππήσιοι, "Philippians." Rarely does he ever do this, that is, address the readers of his letters by name. In fact, the only times he does so are in letters where he rebukes them and then softens the rebuke by addressing them as "Corinthians" (2 Cor 6:11) or "Galatians" (Gal 3:1). In each case this manner of direct address seems to strike a note of exasperation tempered by obvious earnestness and great affection. His address here to the Philippians by name appears to be extended in the same vein.

The form, Φιλιππήσιοι, that Paul uses, which is not one of the regular Greek forms for "Philippians"—Φιλιππεῖς or Φιλιππηνοί—certainly indicates that if he intended any rebuke, he intended it to be a gentle and loving one. For Φιλιππήσιοι is a Greek transcription of the Latin, *Philippenses,* the name by which Roman citizens living in the colony, Augusta Julia Victrix Philippensium, designated themselves. Thus Paul in using this word, which is a *monstrum* in Greek, was nevertheless courteously respecting a feeling of justifiable pride on the part of the Philippians by acknowledging the Latin character of their city and the dignity that was theirs as Roman citizens (see Collart, *Philippes,* 212–13; W. M. Ramsay, "On the Greek Form of the Name Philippians," *JTS* 1 [1900] 116; Beare). He does everything possible to praise them without encouraging them to do more for him than they have already done.

Paul tells the Philippians that they were uniquely his partners in his missionary endeavors ἐν ἀρχῇ τοῦ εὐαγγελίου, ὅτε ἐξῆλθον ἀπὸ Μακεδονίας (lit. "in the beginning of the gospel, when I went out from Macedonia"). But what can he mean when he writes that the gospel had its "beginning" when he went out from Macedonia? Had he not already been preaching the gospel for many years, at least for fourteen years, in Syria and Cilicia (Gal 1:18–2:1), in Cyprus and Galatia (Acts 13–14), before ever he came over into Macedonia? Several answers have been suggested: (1) Paul, contrary to what is generally supposed, actually began his ministry of preaching the gospel in Macedonia in the 40s (M. J. Suggs, "Concerning the Date of Paul's Macedonian Ministry," *NovT* 4 [1960] 60–68). (2) Paul in fact had preached the gospel elsewhere for many years before he came to Macedonia, but by comparison with his work now he considered his earlier mission of no consequence; it could be set aside and forgotten as though it had never occurred (Glombitza, *NovT* [1964–65] 140). (3) Paul was thinking of "the beginning of the gospel" from the standpoint of the Philippians, i.e. "the beginning of the gospel *in their vicinity*" (cf. the NIV: "In the early days of your acquaintance with the gospel"; see Dibelius, Scott). (4) Paul for the first time became entirely responsible for the mission of the gospel only when he came into Macedonia and moved out from there (Gnilka). In his earlier activities he took second place behind Barnabas (Acts 13–14). Now that he is fully in charge "it is possible that he may have regarded Europe as the mission field which fell particularly to his lot and the true starting point of his 'Gospel' " (Collange). Although none of these suggestions is completely satisfactory, the last of them is perhaps the best, if for no other reason than that Paul's move to Macedonia is described in Acts as a "decisive turning-point" for the gospel (E. Meyer, *Ursprung und Anfänge des Christentums* [Berlin: J. G. Cotta, 1921–23] 3,80, cited by Gnilka). Thereafter Macedonia remains in the foreground of Paul's mission strategy and is mentioned by him in his letters some thirteen times (Martin, *Philippians*, 1976).

Once again there is evidence that Paul deliberately tempers his thanks to the Philippians in the fact that he employs so many financial terms when he refers here to the assistance that they gave him (cf. Kennedy, *ExpTim* 12 [1900] 43–44). It is almost as though he viewed the entire matter as a strictly business affair: the Philippians had entered into a partnership (ἐκοινώνησεν) with him (cf. Seesemann, *Der Begriff* ΚΟΙΝΩΝΙΑ, 33). And this partnership involved a strict accounting (εἰς λόγον) of all transactions between them (see Lightfoot for references to this meaning of λόγος). All expenditures and receipts (δόσις καὶ λήμψις) were carefully recorded. Δόσις καὶ λήμψις (lit. "giving and receiving") are words that belong to the commercial vocabulary of the ancient world, and refer to the debit and credit sides of the ledger. They invariably refer to financial transactions (see MM, and the examples from the papyri texts collected by Lohmeyer; but cf. also Str-B 3,624). So it is unlikely that Chrysostom and those many commentators who follow him can be right in saying that this expression means that the Philippians gave (δόσις) material goods and in turn received (λήμψις) spiritual goods from Paul (cf. 1 Cor 9:11; Rom 15:27; Martin, *Philippians*, 1976), because this mixes two different things, material and spiritual, and thus alters the normal meaning of δόσις καὶ λήμψις. More likely, then, these words refer to the financial gift of the Philippians, on the one hand, and the receipt they received back from the apostle acknowledging its safe arrival on the other hand. (Note in this connection the word ἀπέχειν in v 18, a technical term meaning to receive a sum in full and give a receipt for it: BGD.) Paul will use still more of these commercial terms as he continues.

16. Now, however, he reminds them that they know and he knows as well that (ὅτι) they had sent things to meet his needs when he was in Thessalonica. This is an amazing fact, and it shows the immense concern the Philippians had for Paul, their loyalty to him, and their commitment to the advancement of the gospel he preached. For when Paul, upon having founded the church in Philippi, left there, he went immediately to Thessalonica, a city only a short distance away, to carry on his mission (Acts 17:1–9). Even (καί) there, and so soon after their own beginning as a church, the Philippians began their pattern of giving by sending help to relieve the pressure of his needs (εἰς τὴν χρείαν: εἰς with the accusative to denote purpose).

It is possible that Paul was in Thessalonica for a longer period of time than one might imagine from reading the Acts account (Collange, Gnilka; cf. E. Haenchen, *The Acts of the Apostles* [Philadelphia: Westminster Press, 1971] 511–12). Paul's reference to the labor and hardship he experienced in Thessalonica, working day and night so as not to be a burden to anyone, paying all his own expenses by working at his trade by day and preaching the gospel by night (cf. 1 Thess 2:9; 2 Thess 3:8), implies that his mission there was an extended one. This then gave the Philippians opportunity to learn of the apostle's strenuous schedule of activities and a chance to make it lighter. They did so by sending gifts, welcomed or not, to meet his needs. Paul acknowledges that they sent gifts to him καὶ ἅπαξ καὶ δίς, a phrase that may be understood in the restricted sense of "once or twice" (Bonnard, Lohmeyer, Vincent), probably meaning "twice" (cf. Job 5:19; Eccl 11:2; Amos 1:3, 6, 9, 11, 13, etc.), or more generally as "more than once" (Gnilka, Lightfoot; see B. Rigaux, *Les épîtres aux Thessaloniciens* [Paris: J. Gabalda, 1956] 461, and the study by Morris, *NovT* 1 [1956] 205–208). Perhaps the more restricted meaning is the intended meaning for this phrase, because from Paul's remarks written to the Thessalonian church (1 Thess 2:9; 2 Thess 3:8), one might readily infer that the aid which came from the Philippians fell far short of meeting all his needs (cf. Collange).

17. Once again Paul intermingles his unswerving determination to be free from the gifts of anyone with his desire to show his appreciation for the affection that obviously lies behind the giving. Hence, because his acknowledgment of the past generosity of the Philippians must not be interpreted as an eager desire on his part for more, he quickly moves now to deny that he ever was anxious for (ἐπιζητῶ) the gift. He introduces this disclaimer with the idiomatic formula οὐχ ὅτι, "I am not saying that . . ." "I do not mean to say that . . ." (see comments on v 11; BDF 480,5) and follows it with the verb ἐπιζητῶ. The preposition, ἐπί, here compounded with the verb ζητεῖν ("to seek") is in part intensive ("to seek *eagerly*") and in part directional especially marking the direction of the action ("to seek *for* eagerly"): "I do not mean to say that I have set my heart on the gift" (cf. NEB). Then by way of emphasis he repeats this same verb, ἐπιζητῶ: "I *do not* have my heart

set on the gift. But I *do* have my heart set on things quite different from this." The real object of his intense desire Paul now expresses in a phrase filled once more with commercial terms: ἐπιζητῶ τὸν καρπὸν τὸν πλεονάζοντα εἰς λόγον ὑμῶν. The first of these is καρπόν—"I really have my heart set on καρπόν." Literally this word means "fruit" (cf. KJV, RSV), in the sense of the "produce" of the land generally. But in light of the meaning of its cognates, καρπεία and καρπίζεσθαι, and the present context in which it appears, καρπός must be understood in the sense of "profit" or "credit" (see MM 321). And the participle which modifies it, πλεονάζοντα (lit. "increasing"), although it does not appear elsewhere as a technical word belonging to the vocabulary of commerce (against Martin, *Philippians*, 1976, who says that it is "a regular banking term for financial growth"), nevertheless appears to have a commercial meaning thrust upon it by the business words and phrases that surround it. The prepositional phrase, εἰς λόγον ὑμῶν, that immediately follows is one of these, meaning, "to your account." Paul therefore views this gift to him as a spiritual *investment* entered as a *credit* to the *account* of the Philippians, an investment which will *increasingly* pay them rich dividends (Hendriksen). This then is what Paul really had his heart set on. And although he could do without the gift, and would prefer to do so, he is nevertheless jealous for the welfare of his friends at Philippi. For this reason he accepts their generosity, namely because he knows that such an attitude of liberality pays great dividends in the lives of those who give (cf. 2 Cor 9:8–11).

18. Paul was not at all eager for this most recent gift that came to him from the Philippians. But he did accept it. Now he sends back with Epaphroditus his receipt saying it has been duly received. Everything still is done in a very businesslike manner. Ἀπέχω πάντα, often translated quite literally, "I have all" (KJV; cf. also JB, LB, Phillips), really means, "Here then is my receipt for everything" (GNB). Ἀπέχειν, as has been shown by Deissmann from examples from the papyri and ostraca, was a technical expression used in drawing up a receipt, meaning "paid in full," and regularly appeared at the bottom of the receipt (*Light*, 110–12; BGD; MM; see also Bonnard, Gnilka, Lohmeyer). The two verbs that immediately follow, περισσεύω ("I have more than enough") and πεπλήρωμαι ("I am filled"), which repeats and intensifies the idea expressed in περισσεύω, seem to imply a pleading for no more gifts. He has all that he needs and more, and could not possibly ask anything further from the Philippians. The bearer of this final gift (τὰ παρ᾽ ὑμῶν, lit. "the things from you") was Epaphroditus, whom Paul earlier had described as a messenger sent by the church at Philippi to provide for him the things that were lacking (2:25; cf. 2:30).

Then suddenly Paul turns from the vocabulary of banking to the language of religion in order to finish his description of this gift from the Philippians. Of first importance is Paul's remark that although he himself was the immediate recipient of their generosity, the ultimate recipient was God: δεκτὴν . . . τῷ θεῷ ("acceptable to God"). With this statement he lifts their gift from the level of mere mutual courtesy and compassion and looks upon it in its relation to God (Jones), and at the same time he enunciates an important principle, namely, that whatever is done for the servant is in reality done for the Master; that whatever is given to a child of God is given to God himself (cf. Matt 10:40–42; 25:31–40; Acts 9:3–5).

Paul now with sacrificial language describes "the things sent from you" (τὰ παρ' ὑμῶν) as ὀσμὴν εὐωδίας (lit. "an odor of fragrance"; "a fragrant odor") and θυσίαν ("sacrifice"). The first of these is a common expression taken over from the OT. It pictures God as literally taking pleasure in the smell of the sacrifices offered by his people (cf. Gen 8:21). Symbolically it refers to the quality an offering must possess in order for it to be pleasing and acceptable to God (Exod 29:18, 25, 41; Lev 1:9, 13; Ezek 20:41; cf. Eph 5:2). Thus in describing their gift as ὀσμὴν εὐωδίας Paul makes clear to the Philippians that it is of the first rank, of the highest quality.

The second of these terms, θυσία ("sacrifice"), again is a common OT word to refer literally to the multitude of animal sacrifices offered to God (cf. Lev 1:2–13, etc.), the sacrifices of birds (Lev 1:13–17), of grain (Lev 2:1–10), of the first fruits of the harvest (Lev 2:12–13), and so on. Yet even within the OT itself this word began to be spiritualized so that "a crushed and humbled spirit" (LXX Ps 50:18–19) could be viewed as an equally valid sacrifice acceptable to God, in fact, the kind of sacrifice that God preferred. Such a spiritualizing of the Levitical sacrifices continued and was broadened in meaning as time went on to include prayer and praise (1QS 8:7–9; 9:3–5; 10:6), doing good and sharing (Heb 13:16). Thus it was but natural for Paul to interpret the assistance provided him by the Philippians at great cost to themselves (cf. 2 Cor 8:1–2) as the proper sacrifice that would be pleasing and acceptable to God (cf. Rom 12:1). Here again both the terminology and the thought of 2:17 recur: "The apostle's activity and the financial help of the Philippians which supports it form a unity the 'judge' of which is God" (Collange).

19. This verse is closely and carefully linked with what has just been said, not only by the conjunction, δέ, ("and," "now," "in return"), but also by the deliberate repetition of two highly important words from the immediate context: πληροῦν and χρεία: πεπλήρωμαι, "I have been filled up" (v 18)/πληρώσει, God "will fill up" (v 19); χρείαν μοι, "my need" (v 16)/χρείαν ὑμῶν, "your need" (v 19). Thus in v 19 Paul has in mind exactly the same kind of needs that he was talking about in v 16, namely, present material needs that can only be met right now by material resources. He has not suddenly shifted to discuss spiritual needs or to promise his Philippian friends that God will fill up their needs, but only ἐν δόξῃ, i.e. when he places them in glory (Lightfoot). He has no intention here of telling the Philippians that they will receive full satisfaction, but only ἐν δόξῃ, i.e. in the glorious age to come (Lohmeyer, Michaelis). Hence, it becomes clear that the phrase must not be taken with the verb πληρώσει in such a way as to point to the future kingdom—"God will fill up your need *in glory,*" but only as reflecting a Hebrew adverbial construction, "God will fill up your need *in a glorious manner.*" Or it may be taken, not at all with the verb πληρώσει, but as an adjective modifying the noun πλοῦτος ("wealth"). Πλοῦτος ἐν δόξῃ, then, would mean his "glorious or marvelous riches." Once more, let it be said, the needs that are under consideration here are similar to those kinds of needs that Paul himself had

experienced due to hardships, suffering, deprivations, afflictions (θλίψεις, v 14), and so on, that could be alleviated only by earthly goods and services and by human associates.

Now the question is did Paul say ὁ θεός μου πληρώσει πᾶσαν χρείαν ὑμῶν ("my God will fill your every need"), or did he say ὁ θεός μου πληρώσαι . . . ("may my God fill . . .")? The future indicative (πληρώσει) states a fact informing the Philippians what God will do. The aorist optative (πληρώσαι), not the aorist infinitive as Collange (148) mistakenly calls it, expresses a wish, offers a prayer to God, makes a request of him. If one were to depend solely upon manuscript evidence for the answer, he would most likely opt for πληρώσει ("he will fill"), even though there are some excellent witnesses in support of πληρώσαι ("may he fill"; see Notes). But (1) the fact that material, physical needs are exclusively under discussion here, (2) the fact that Paul elsewhere, in a similar context, refuses to say what God *will do* in meeting such material needs, although he confidently says what God *can do* (2 Cor 9:8), (3) the fact that, although the optative mood is dying out in Koine Greek, Paul nevertheless is familiar with its genius (he uses it thirty-one times: BDF 65,2) and is quite capable of using it correctly, (4) the fact that Paul occasionally comes near the close of his letters with a prayer asking God to do something favorable for his friends and using precisely the same formula that appears here in 4:19: δέ (postpositive) + ὁ θεός/ὁ κύριος + optative (Rom 15:5; 1 Thess 5:23; 2 Thess 3:16), (5) the fact that Paul's final benediction—ὁ δὲ θεός . . . μετὰ ὑμῶν, etc. (Rom 15:33; 1 Cor 16:23; 2 Cor 13:13; Gal 6:18; Eph 6:24) asking that God's presence might be with his readers, his grace upon them, and so on, implies the optative εἴη ("may it be"), even though the optative is not present—suggests that πληρώσαι is the preferred reading here in v 19. If, however, πληρώσει is insisted upon, then it is necessary to point out that the very form of the verse is such that the future indicative itself must be translated so as to express a wish-prayer, not a simple statement of fact (cf. Wiles, *Intercessory Prayers*, 101–107): "In return for your meeting my needs (δέ), I pray that my God may meet all your needs" (cf. Confraternity, Knox). Such an interpretation (1) does not have Paul saying what God will or will not do, (2) allows God the freedom to be God, to fulfill needs or not as he sees best, even the needs of the Philippians, (3) wards off disappointment or disillusionment when material, physical needs are not met, and (4) keeps one from having to make excuses for God, from drawing fine lines of distinction between needs and wants, and from pushing off the fulfillment of needs until the eschatological day to avoid any embarrassment.

God's ability to meet the Philippians' need, Paul now says, is κατὰ τὸ πλοῦτος αὐτοῦ ἐν δόξῃ (lit. "according to his wealth in glory"). Κατά with the accusative means that "the rewarding will not be merely *from* his wealth, but also in a manner that befits his wealth—on a scale worthy of His wealth" (Michael). Since God's wealth is limitless, it is therefore impossible to exhaust it by all needs combined. Paul thus cannot ask too much from God as he prays for the needs of his friends.

As has already been argued these needs are present material needs, needs that the Philippians have here and now (cf. 2 Cor 8:2). Hence, ἐν δόξῃ should not be given any futuristic meaning, but should be curtailed and limited here to a description of God's wealth: it is magnificent, eye-catching, splendid, renowned (cf. BGD).

The prepositional phrase, ἐν Χριστῷ ("in Christ") is in the emphatic position at the end of the sentence. But it is to be taken with the verb πληρώσαι because the treasures of God are unlocked and made available in Christ. God makes his wealth known and fulfills needs only because of and in Christ (cf. Col 2:9–10: ἐστὲ ἐν αὐτῷ πεπληρωμένοι, "you are filled up in him," i.e. Christ; and 1 Cor 1:5: ἐν παντὶ ἐπλουτίσθητε ἐν αὐτῷ, "you have been made rich by God in him," i.e. Christ).

20. In v 19 Paul used a rare expression: ὁ θεός μου ("*my* God," only here and in 1:3), so as to distinguish himself and his needs from the Philippians and their needs. But now as he breaks out into a doxology he addresses the doxology to "*our* God and Father" (τῷ θεῷ καὶ πατρὶ ἡμῶν), uniting himself once again with his converts in a song of praise to the one who provides for the needs of all his people.

In the doxologies of the NT δόξα usually has the definite article as here: ἡ δόξα (Rom 11:36; 16:27; Gal 1:5; Eph 3:21; 2 Tim 4:18; Heb 13:21; 1 Pet 4:11; 2 Pet 3:18; but also Luke 2:14; 19:38). The definite article signals to the reader that it is "*that* glory," "*that* honor," "*that* splendor" which properly belongs to God and is rightly ascribed to him, that is in focus.

Δόξα "glory," as it is used in the Bible (OT and NT), is an elusive word with meanings ranging from "divine honor," "divine splendor," "divine power," "visible divine radiance," to the "divine mode of being." Thus, when one gives glory to God (διδόναι δόξαν τῷ θεῷ; cf. Jer 13:16; Pss 18:1; 28:1–2; 113:9; Rev 4:9; 5:13; 7:12, etc.), or bursts out in a doxological refrain as here, he is not adding to God something not already present, but is actively acknowledging or extolling God for what he already is (cf. Isa 42:8 with 41:12; see also Luke 2:14; 19:38; Rom 11:36, etc.; cf. Kittel, *TDNT* 2,244–48). Therefore this doxology, as all doxologies, presupposes that the verb "to be," which is missing and must be supplied, is indicative, ἐστίν ("is," "belongs"), rather than optative, εἴη ("may it be," "be"; cf. 1 Pet 4:11).

The doxology is presented as follows: τῷ θεῷ καὶ πατρὶ ἡμῶν. Very likely the definite article (τῷ) is used only with the noun "God" (θεῷ): "to *the* God, *the* one supreme God of the universe, belongs all the praise, honor glory," and so on, that living beings are capable of ascribing to him. But by adding πατρὶ ἡμῶν ("our Father"), Paul reminds the Philippians that this God, so magnificent and splendid, is "*our* Father," a tender phrase picked up from the prayer Jesus taught his first disciples (cf. Matt 6:9; Luke 11:2) and cherished by his church ever since.

This praise to God is εἰς τοὺς αἰῶνας τῶν αἰώνων (lit. "unto the ages of the ages"). The idea expressed by the Greek, "is of cycles consisting of, embracing, other cycles, *ad infinitum;* the ever-developing 'ages' of heavenly life" (Moule). This phrase, unique to the NT, represents a long, indefinite period. Praise to God, therefore, is not restricted to "this age" but belongs appropriately to "the age to come" as well—and to ages upon ages yet to follow, to "an incalculable vastness of duration" (Plummer).

And to this is added the ἀμήν ("amen"), that spontaneous and joyful endorsement of all that has been said. It is the "yes" of the worshiping church to God, and acknowledgment and acceptance of the promises he has made in Jesus Christ (cf. 2 Cor 1:20; see Schlier, *TDNT* 1,336–38).

Explanation

Some commentators consider that this section (4:10–20) was originally a separate letter of thanks written by Paul long before he ever wrote the main part of his epistle to the Philippians. The arguments for this view, however, are not completely convincing (see Introduction), and thus the exegesis here proceeds on the assumption that vv 10–20 are an integral part of the whole letter.

If we are asked why then did Paul leave his "thank you" to the last, several answers are forthcoming: (1) The fact of the matter is that he did not do this: right at the beginning of his letter he thanks God, and them, for their generous partnership with him in the spread of the gospel (1:3, 5). (2) If Paul dictated this letter, as was his custom, and if as usual he took up the pen to sign it, it would be most appropriate for him to express more fully his appreciation in his own handwriting at the end of the letter. (3) But most likely, Paul left it to the last because the whole matter of receiving gifts from the churches he founded was a very sensitive issue with him. And like one who hesitates to bring up a delicate matter so the apostle waits until he can wait no longer. Thus in a carefully worded statement he thanks the Philippians for their kindness to him without ever really thanking them. One senses in this section a nervous alternation back and forth between acknowledging his indebtedness to the Philippians, on the one hand, and asserting his independence from them, on the other.

Paul begins by telling the Philippians that he is glad that their concern for him has blossomed again. For some unstated reason the Philippians were unable to make contact with Paul for an extended period of time. No message of any kind came through to let the apostle know how his friends at Philippi fared, or if they cared at all for him or for the gospel he preached. Doubts arose. Then all of a sudden there came a breakthrough. Epaphroditus arrived sent by the church to be his coworker and fellow soldier, not only carrying instructions to do whatever Paul needed to have done (cf. 2:25), but also bringing an abundance of material goods, or financial resources (4:19), so as to free him from whatever sufferings or hardships that poverty might have inflicted upon him. This overwhelming generosity made him very happy, but only because it showed that all during the silent period the Philippians had never stopped thinking of him and planning how they might help him. "He values their gift principally as an expression of the spirit of Christ in them, and as an evidence of their Christian proficiency" (Vincent).

But this gift caused him problems. It violated his principle of paying his own way by working with his hands, so that he might himself be free of depending on others, and so as to make the gospel free of charge to everybody. Consequently he swings suddenly from praising the Philippians to informing them that he did not need their gift, that he had learned self-sufficiency, that he knew how to cope with all the ups and downs of life, that he had been initiated into the vicissitudes of existence—hunger and fullness, too much and too little, privation and plenty—and was able to accept and survive either without preference. He affirms, almost too emphatically, it seems, that he has the power to face all such situations on his own without help from anyone. But then he catches himself, stops and gladly acknowledges that in reality his independence comes only from his dependence upon Christ. It is he who continuously infuses him with strength.

Then Paul turns back to affirming them not only for what they had just given to him, but also for what they had given to him on previous occasions as well. But even as he praises them, his praise seems checked, reined in somewhat by the businesslike way in which he discusses what they have done. They alone of all the churches he founded entered into a partnership with him. Between them and him there was a strict accounting of expenditures and receipts. They were generous in their giving but he never asked for their gifts. The only thing he looked for and sought after was that the Philippians might follow the principle that the generous will be treated generously, that those who sow bountifully will reap bountifully, that they might get a good return on their investment and that interest might increase and be credited to their account. He speaks in banking terms of sending them a receipt for the gifts they sent him through Epaphroditus duly marked by him, "paid in full."

One final time, it seems, he pleads for his independence and implicitly begs that they send no more. His words are, "I have more than enough. I am full up!"

But then Paul's greatest praise for their gifts comes now when he likens them to the fragrant odor that arose from proper sacrifices properly prepared and properly offered so as to measure up to the quality standards required of them to be pleasing and acceptable to God. Furthermore, he says, the things that had come from them to him actually had come from them *to God,* and were accepted by God. By this statement he was saying that their gifts were of the very highest quality.

So in return for supplying his needs out of their poverty (cf. 2 Cor 8:2), he asks God to meet all their needs out of his riches, in accordance with his vast assets, "on a scale worthy of his wealth."

And as he reflects then on the limitless resources that exist in God, he cannot refrain from breaking out in a joyous doxology: "The glory belongs to the supreme God who is also our Father. Amen!"

Conclusion (4:21–23)

Bibliography

Brooke, D. *Private Letters*. **Doty, W. G.** *Letters in Primitive Christianity*. **Roller, O.** *Das Formular de paulinischen Briefe*.

Translation

[21] Give my greetings to every one of the saints in Christ Jesus. The brothers who are with me here send you their greetings, [22] as do all the saints, especially those of the imperial household. [23] May the grace of the Lord Jesus Christ be with you each one.[a] Amen.[b,c]

Notes

[a] Instead of τοῦ πνεύματος ("spirit") א² Ψ and the majority text read πάντων ("all"). The change may have been because there was discontent over the anthropology expressed here: why would "grace" be ascribed only to the "spirit" when human beings are both body and spirit? Or the change may have been accidental due to similarity in appearance.

[b] Most MSS add a *subscriptio*: either (1) Πρὸς Φιλιππησίους ("To Philippians")—א A B* Ψ 33, or (2) Πρὸς Φιλιππησίους ἐγράφη ἀπὸ Ῥώμης (ἐξ Ἀθηνῶν, 945) διὰ Ἐπαφροδίτου ("To Philippians was written from Rome [from Athens] through Epaphroditus"). P⁴⁶ and a few other Greek MSS have no subscript.

[c] Ἀμήν, although omitted by the Nestle-Aland edition, following the MSS B F G, is nevertheless strongly attested to by P⁴⁶ א A D Ψ and the majority text.

Form/Structure/Setting

Paul now concludes his letter. It is time to say "Good-bye." And although he does this essentially in accordance with the pattern of ancient letter-writing, he does not here, nor in any of his letters, use the standard "farewell" (ἔρρωσο) or "good luck" (εὐτύχει) that one is accustomed to find at the end of pagan or even Christian letters (cf. Hunt and Edgar, *Select Papyri*, 1, 269–395; Acts 15:29; 23:30; Ign. *Eph.* 21.2; *Magn.* 15; *Rom.* 10.3, etc.). Instead, his favorite word is some form of the verb ἀσπάζεσθαι by which he not only signs off, but sends personal greetings from himself, his associates and other Christians around him to his dear friends who will read what he has written (cf. Rom 16; 1 Cor 16:19–20; 2 Cor 13:12; Phil 4:21–22; Col 4:10–15; 1 Thess 5:26; Philem 23; cf. 1 Tim 4:19, 21; Titus 3:15).

Paul's letters not only accord with the pattern of ancient letter-writing but they radically differ from that pattern as well. The Epistle to the Philippians, as a model, shows this to be true. The stark ἔρρωσο/ἔρρωσθε ("farewell") with which other contemporary letters were brought to a close is amplified by Paul in such a way as to bring out into the open the warmth of Christian relations, the marvel of Christian ideas and ideals and the One who motivates and gives meaning to all (cf. Collange). Note that in this simple farewell appear such profoundly important words as "saints," "brothers," "grace," "Christ Jesus" and "Lord." .

The doxology in v 20, which has the appearance of a proper ending to a letter, confirms in the minds of some that vv 10–20 constitute a separate letter of thanks to the Philippian church. Verses 21–23, therefore, are out of order and belong as a conclusion to one of the other letters contained in Philippians, perhaps to that letter made up of chaps. 1–2. This suggestion has already been rejected in favor of seeing each part of Philippians as integral to the whole. And in this connection it is worth noting that a considerable number of NT epistles end much like Philippians in a four-part structure made up of (1) personal information and instructions (vv 10–19), (2) a formal benediction or doxology (v 20), (3) brief personal counsel, expressed less formally (vv 21–22) and (4) a simple benediction as a final greeting (v 23; cf. F. V. Filson, *Yesterday*, SBT 4 [London: SCM Press, 1967] 22–24; see 1 and 2 Cor, Gal, 2 Tim, Heb). "This structure seems almost as stereotyped as the opening pattern of greeting followed by thanksgiving. It arises from the dual purpose of nearly all the NT letters; they were both general communications to a congregation or group of congregations and also personal letters to friends. The first two sections of the fourfold pattern spring from the first purpose, the last two from the second" (Houlden).

The letter to the Philippians is the most intimate of all Paul's letters. Here the personal pronouns, "I" and "you," abound. The generosity of the church at Philippi exceeded that of all the churches Paul founded or was associated with (4:15), and this generosity reflected the deep affection the Philippians had for Paul. Obviously the feeling was mutual. Thus, it is surprising to discover in a section reserved for greetings that not one person is greeted by name (contrast Rom 16). One could wish it had been otherwise, i.e. that instead of a comprehensive general greeting, some of the Christians there had been singled out and identified by what they had done. Had this happened, those living at a distance from Philippi in space and time, unfamiliar with the believers there, would have had a better chance of understanding people and events associated with this famous church. Paul's reason for greeting no one in particular no doubt stemmed from his wish that all his readers might feel they were each one equally dear to him (Scott).

Comments

21. This letter of Paul was addressed "to the saints (ἁγίοις) with the overseers who serve" (1:1). It is this address that makes the final greeting striking: ἀσπάσασθε πάντα ἅγιον ("give my greetings to every one of the saints"). For now Paul is not writing directions to the Philippian church as a whole as he did at the beginning, but to certain individuals within the church, who in turn are to pass along his greetings to "each and every saint" (πάντα ἅγιον) belonging to that church. The verb ἀσπάσασθε ("give my greetings") is second person plural: "you all give them my greetings." But who are these individuals to whom Paul gives these final instructions? It is impossible to give a definitive answer to this question, and "a trifle such as this makes us realize how little

we know about the organization in these early churches" (Beare). But to remark that "the best guess is that the Philippians are to greet one another, and so cement cordial relations as they are brought together by Paul's letter" (Martin, *Philippians*, 1976) is unsatisfactory. It is especially so since Paul not only had the linguistic tools available to him to say, "greet one another," if that is what he intended to say, but on more than one occasion he actually used these tools: ἀσπάσασθε ἀλλήλους ("greet *one another*": 1 Cor 16:20; 2 Cor 13:12). Much more likely, then, Paul calls upon the leaders, the overseers of the church, to pass along his greetings to the Christian fellowship. Surely, in spite of the wording of the opening address (1:1), this letter would not have been handed over by Epaphroditus to the church as a whole, but to the responsible officials of the church who would then read it aloud to the assembled congregation.

These officials were to give Paul's greetings to "every saint" (πάντα ἅγιον). His wording here, although surprising, is nonetheless precise. The phrase, πάντα ἅγιον, is singular and its uniqueness must not be lost by translating it as "all the saints" (NIV; cf. GNB). For with the singular Paul conveys his love and affection to each individual Christian alike (Alford). None is to be treated differently from any other. In a church troubled by disunity the apostle will not take sides; each and every believer is, as it were, the sole object of his greeting. Perhaps then as has been suggested, this is why Paul, contrary to his usual custom, mentions no one by name in these final greetings (Collange).

The final phrase in the initial greeting is the familiar Pauline phrase, ἐν Χριστῷ Ἰησοῦ ("in Christ Jesus"); for its meaning see the comments on 1:1). It is variously taken with the verb ἀσπάσασθε: "Give my greetings in the fellowship of Christ Jesus . . ." (cf. NEB, and see Alford, Dibelius, Jones, Lightfoot, Plummer), or with the noun phrase, πάντα ἅγιον—"every saint in Christ Jesus" (RSV, and see Hendriksen, Martin, *Philippians*, 1976, Moule). Although the matter is indeed unimportant (Vincent), yet for the sake of precision it may be observed that the phrase "in Christ Jesus" is taken with "saints" in 1:1; that since it stands in closest proximity to "every saint" here; and that since to be a "saint" in the Pauline sense of the word means to be one of God's special people by virtue of being united to Christ, of being "in union with Christ," it is better to link the phrase "in Christ" with the phrase "every saint" than with the verb "greet."

Paul continues by saying, "the brothers who are with me greet you." Thus, he is not alone in sending greetings to the Philippians; he belongs to a brotherhood which joins him in saluting the congregation at Philippi. How large this group was or who all was in it is information which is not provided and which cannot be recovered. Certainly the group must be restricted to such people as Timothy (2:19) and Luke (cf. Acts 27:1), close personal associates of the apostle, as distinguished from the Christians who lived in Caesarea and were not so intimately identified with the apostle and his work. These latter will be referred to in the next verse (cf. also 1:15–17; 2:20–21).

22. Greetings come to Philippi from Paul, from his close companions and now from all the Christians (πάντες οἱ ἅγιοι) in Caesarea. But there is a group here that is singled out as sending its special greetings: οἱ ἐκ τῆς Καίσαρος

οἰκίας, "those of the imperial household." The expression, οἰκία Καίσαρος, "household of Caesar," is used in the literature to refer both to the highest officials in the Roman government and to the lowest servants in the emperor's employ (Lightfoot, especially the detached note on 171–78). Since there is no evidence that members of the royal family had converted to Christianity as early as this letter of Paul, nor any high public officials attached to the praetorium (cf. 1:13), it is likely that Paul is speaking now of Roman soldiers stationed in the barracks, or slaves or freedmen handling the domestic affairs of the emperor, or both. The reason these are singled out may be to show that the gospel was beginning to penetrate even these loftier circles, or to indicate that there was a link "between the Christian members of the imperial staff on government service at the place of Paul's imprisonment and the citizens of Philippi which was a Roman colony" (Martin, *Philippians*, 1976; Michaelis, Scott).

23. Paul begins his letter with "grace" (χάρις); he now concludes it with that same rich word: ἡ χάρις τοῦ κυρίου Ἰησοῦ Χριστοῦ μετὰ τοῦ πνεύματος ὑμῶν ("the grace of the Lord Jesus Christ be with your spirit"). With few exceptions Paul speaks of this grace as being "the grace of God our Father and of the Lord Jesus Christ" whenever he begins his letters (but see Col 1:2: 1 Thess 1:1). With equally few exceptions in the benediction at the close of these same letters he only speaks of this grace as being the grace of the Lord Jesus Christ (but see Eph 6:23 and cf. 1 Tim 6:21; 2 Tim 4:22; Titus 3:15). Observing this fact one quickly comes to understand that for Paul Christ has the right to perform the divine role with full authority. He is the source of grace, the fountainhead of free beneficent saving love (χάρις). He is the one who bestows this grace freely on his church. He is the one through whom undeserving mankind comes to know the mercy, love and favor of God. He is the Lord whom the church confesses (cf. 2:11 and comments there).

Paul's final benediction, then, is that this grace of Jesus Christ as Lord may be μετὰ τοῦ πνεύματος ὑμῶν (lit. "with your spirit"). This expression, τοῦ πνεύματος ὑμῶν ("your spirit"), sounds strange to modern ears. Thus several things should be noted: (1) Simply from the fact that "spirit" (πνεύματος) is singular and "your" (ὑμῶν) is plural there is no reason to conclude that Paul uses the singular noun to stress "the unity of the body of believers in which one spirit is to be found" (Martin, *Philippians*, 1976). The distributive singular, seen in "you (plural) have a hardened heart (πεπωρωμένην ἔχετε τὴν καρδίαν ὑμῶν [Mark 8:17])" meaning, "each of you has his own hardened heart," is a common enough phenomenon in both classical and NT Greek (Smyth, *Grammar*, 269.998; BDF 140). Hence, the singular here has no significant meaning beyond the fact that Paul's prayer is for Christ's grace to rest and abide upon the spirit of *each one* of his readers. (2) The word πνεῦμα ("spirit") is frequently used in the NT of the whole person, but especially of the mental and spiritual aspects belonging to personality (cf. Schweizer, *TDNT* 6,435). (3) The phrase "with your spirit" is not unique to Philippians (against Beare); it appears also in Gal 6:18; Philem 25 (cf. 2 Tim 4:22). It stands in the same position in the several benedictions as—and replaces the more usual—μεθ' ὑμῶν ("with you"). (4) Hence, in all likelihood Paul means to say nothing more profound by the expression "with your spirit" than to say "with you." It should thus be translated accordingly.

If the ἀμήν ("amen") is part of the original, and the evidence for it is strong (see Notes), it reflects either Paul's own response to the benediction, authenticating what has just been pronounced: "Amen!"–"It is true!" (cf. Rom 16:22; 1 Cor 16:21; Gal 6:11; Col 4:18; 2 Thess 3:17; see Collange), or the affirmative response of the congregation to the divine promise on which the hoped-for blessing rests—"Amen!"–"Yes, let it be so!" (cf. Rev 1:7; 2 Cor 1:20; see Schlier, *TDNT* 1,336–38).

Explanation

In a style characteristic of all his letters Paul brings this one addressed to the Philippians to a close with a greeting and benediction. He asks the leaders of the church to convey his personal greetings to each and every Christian at Philippi, irrespective of who he may be or what he may have done or failed to do. So important is it that none be excluded from this greeting that Paul refuses to name anyone lest he offend any by an accidental omission of his name. What is more, his close associates such as Timothy and Luke, those persons intimately involved with him in his apostolic work, send their greetings along with his. There is a bond of brotherhood there that strengthens the good wishes that come from Paul.

Finally Paul wants the Philippians to know that not only he and his fellow workers care for them and are interested in their welfare, but every Christian in the Caesarean church has the same attitude as well. They, too, want their greetings passed along.

But within this church there is a special group, one especially interested in the Christians at Philippi. These may have been soldiers, slaves or freedmen, who, because they have been involved in the service of the emperor in provincial matters for an extended period of time, had come to know many of the believers in the Roman city of Philippi. These wish to be remembered to them in a special way. This seemingly casual remark shows that the gospel was beginning to make its way into the imperial household.

The letter ends with a benedictory prayer calling down upon the church at Philippi the gracious, saving activity of God that comes to them solely through Jesus Christ whom they confess as Lord. With the concluding "amen" Paul affirms the truth of what he has said, and the congregation responds with its "yes" to the promises of God heard in the benediction.

Index of Ancient Authors

Index of Modern Authors

Index of Selected Subjects

Index of Biblical Texts
Old Testament

Apocrypha and Pseudepigrapha

New Testament

Index of Dead Sea Scrolls, Rabbinic and Mishnaic Writings

Index of Patristic Writings